The Economic Structure
of Corporate Law

The Economic Structure of Corporate Law

FRANK H. EASTERBROOK
DANIEL R. FISCHEL

HARVARD UNIVERSITY PRESS
Cambridge, Massachusetts
London, England

This book has been digitally reprinted. The content
remains identical to that of previous printings.

First Harvard University Press paperback edition, 1996

Library of Congress Cataloging in Publication Data

Easterbrook, Frank H., 1948–
    The economic structure of corporate law / Frank H. Easterbrook and
Daniel R. Fischel.
        p.   cm.
·   Includes index.
    ISBN 0-674-23538-X (cloth)
    ISBN 0-674-23539-8 (pbk.)
    1. Corporation law—Economic aspects—United States.
    2. Managerial economics—United States.   I. Fischel, Daniel R.   II. Title.
KF1416.E27   1991
246.73'066—dc20   91-6795
[347.30666]   CIP

For our parents
and for R. H. Coase

Preface

We seek to understand the logic of corporate law. Why are managers free to decide what the firm will produce, whether it will pay dividends, and how much to pay themselves as salaries and bonuses? Why are almost all of the important decisions the firm will make committed to private actors' discretion, while statutes prescribe such trivia as the maximum duration of voting trusts? Why do the same judges who aggressively review the design of aircraft (in product-liability cases) and the decisions of disinterested administrative agencies react in horror at the prospect of deciding whether a manager was negligent when introducing a new product after test-marketing in only two cities? Why are the principal legal constraints directed to the relation between managers and shareholders, leaving employees, bondholders, and other claimants to fend for themselves by contract? Why are there no punitive damages in securities cases, even though punitive damages are staples in other litigation?

These and other distinctive features of corporate law are not random. The same patterns emerge in state after state, firm after firm, decade after decade. They are patterns, adaptations with substantial value in the evolutionary struggle for corporate survival. These patterns are almost impossible to understand if "fairness" or paternalism are the objectives of corporate law, yet simple to understand from an economic perspective. We conclude that corporate law has an economic structure, that it increases the wealth of all by supplying the rules that investors would select if it were easy to contract more fully.

This book joins the legal and economic disciplines. Most of it is an exercise in positive economics—that is, we take the world and its laws as given and try to understand why they are as they are. Some of it is openly normative—we take a few economic principles and preach to legislatures and judges about what the law ought to be if it is to promote social welfare. Ours is on both fronts an exploratory treatment, a survey. A more complete assessment would examine additional doctrines in detail and offer an explanation not only for the dominant features of the law but also for the departures. Explaining the structure of corporate law, and the engine that drives it, is enough of a task for one book.

For more than a decade we have been bringing economic principles to bear on corporate law. Several of our articles form the core of chapters in this book; others make appearances only in footnotes; still other sections have been written from scratch, and all portions of the book (including those based on articles) have been substantially revised and updated. The abbreviation necessary to produce a tractable study puts us at risk of ignoring our intellectual debts, of which there are many. Although these cannot be repaid, they are acknowledged at the end of this book. In particular, we like all other contemporary scholars in corporate organization owe a great debt to R. H. Coase, who first pointed out the similarity (and differences) between corporations and markets. Although Coase had retired from the faculty of the University of Chicago by the time we joined it, his intellectual legacy enlivens the school and the profession. Without him the economic study of corporate law might lie ahead; to him we have dedicated this book. We dedicate it as well to our parents, also necessary conditions of its existence.

F. H. E.
D. R. F.

Contents

The Economic Structure
of Corporate Law

1

The Corporate Contract

For a long time public and academic discussion of corporations has started from the premise that managers have "control" and use this to exploit investors, customers, or both. The usual prescription is some form of intervention by the government. This may mean prescription of the firm's output, wages, and prices. It may be regulation of the securities markets. It may take the form of corporate law, which establishes minimum voting rules and restricts how managers can treat the firm and the investors.

The argument is simple. In most substantial corporations—firms with investment instruments that are freely traded, which we call "public corporations"—each investor has a small stake compared with the size of the venture. The investor is therefore "powerless." The managers, by contrast, know how the business is running and can conceal from investors information about the firm and their own activities. Armed with private knowledge and able to keep investors in the dark, the managers can divert income to themselves, stealing and mismanaging at the same time. Diversion and sloth may not be obvious, but they exist. Even when they do not, the potential for misconduct remains. Only some form of regulation can protect investors. And the limit on regulation is to be found not in principles of free contracting—for the corporate charter is at best a contract of adhesion by which the managers call all the shots—but in a concern that regulation not go "too far." Thus in the debate about whether public corporations should be permitted to issue nonvoting stock, most people assume that nonvoting stock is bad because it insulates the managers further from investors' control, and the only question is whether an outright ban (as opposed to severe regulation) would restrict "too much" the ability of firms to raise capital.

Although the language of regulation is everywhere, corporate law has developed along a different path. The corporate code in almost every state is an "enabling" statute. An enabling statute allows managers and investors to write their own tickets, to establish systems of governance without substantive scrutiny from a regulator. The handiwork of managers is final in all but exceptional or trivial instances. Courts apply the "business judgment rule," a hands-off approach that judges would not dream of applying to the decisions of administrative agencies. Yet administrative officials do not stand to profit from their decisions—and therefore, one might think, are not subject to the pressures that cause managers' goals to diverge from those of investors. So courts ride herd on disinterested administrators while leaving self-interested managers alone. What can be going on?

Consider the domain of managers' choice. The founders and managers of a firm choose whether to organize as a corporation, trust, partnership, mutual, or cooperative (a form of ownership by customers). They choose what the firm will make or do and whether it will operate for profit, not for profit, or hold a middle ground, pursuing profit but not to the exclusion of some other objective (as publishers of newspapers do). They choose whether to allow the public to invest or whether, instead, the firm will be closely held. They choose what kinds of claims (debt, equity, warrants) to issue, in what ratios, for what price, with what entitlements: not only the right to receive payments (how often, in what amounts) but also whether these investments allow their holders to vote—and if to vote, how many votes, and on what subjects. They choose where to incorporate (states have different legal rules). They choose how the firm will be organized (as a pyramidal hierarchy or a loose, multidivisional collective), whether central leadership will be strong or weak, and whether the firm will grow (internally or by merger) or shrink (by selling existing assets or spinning off divisions). Investors select the members of the board of directors, who may be "inside" (part of the management team) or "outside" (often associated with investors, suppliers, or customers), and the board decides who exercises which powers on the firm's behalf. As a practical matter boards are self-perpetuating until investors become dissatisfied and a majority decides to redo everything to a new taste. With trivial exceptions all business decisions—including the managers' pay, bonuses, stock options, pensions, and perquisites—are taken by or under the supervision of this board, with no substantial inquiry by anyone else. Anyone who asks a court to inquire will be brushed off with a reference to the business judgment rule.

Some things are off-limits. States almost uniformly forbid perpetual directorships (persons who cannot be displaced by holders of a majority of the voting power). They set quorum rules (on critical decisions, a third of the board and sometimes half of the investors must participate) and require "major" transactions to be presented to the board (occasionally shareholders too) rather than stand approved by managers or a committee. States also forbid the sale of votes divorced from the investment interest and the accumulation of votes in a corporate treasury (that is, boards cannot perpetuate themselves by voting "treasury shares" or by cross-holding shares of related corporations). They require managers to serve equity investors' interests loyally. Federal law requires firms to reveal certain things when they issue securities, and public firms must make annual disclosures.

Determined investors and managers can get 'round many of these rules, but the mechanisms for doing so are sidelights. Any theory of corporate law must account for the mandatory as well as the enabling features, and must account for the pattern of regulation—one that leaves managers effectively free to set their own salaries yet forbids them to delegate certain questions to subcommittees, that gives shareholders no entitlement to dividends or distributions of any kind but specifies a quorum of one-third of the board for certain decisions. We attend to that task throughout this book. For now it is enough to know that what is open to free choice is far more important to the daily operation of the firm, and to investors' welfare, than what the law prescribes. Restraints on contracts are common (for example, occupational safety laws limit the risks employees may agree to accept), but few of these concern corporate organization.

Why does corporate law allow managers to set the terms under which they will administer corporate assets? Why do courts grant more discretion to self-interested managers than to disinterested regulators? Why do investors entrust such stupendous sums to managers whose acts are essentially unconstrained by legal rules?

We offer answers to these questions, explanations of the economic structure of corporate law.

The Dynamic Shaping of the Corporate Form

The view you take of corporations and corporate law is apt to depend on your assumptions about how investors, employees, and other players come to be associated in a venture. You are likely to be driven to a regulatory view of corporations if you assume that corporations are born with a complement of managers, employees, and investors, in which managers have complete control of the corporation and investors are powerless. But corporations do not arise by spontaneous generation. Managers assume their roles with knowledge of the consequences. Investors part with their money willingly, putting dollars in equities instead of bonds or banks or land or gold because they believe the returns of equities more attractive. Managers obtain their positions after much trouble and toil, competing against others who wanted them. All interested persons participate. Firms begin small and grow. They must attract customers and investors by promising *and delivering* what those people value. Corporations that do not do so will not survive. When people observe that firms are very large in relation to single investors, they observe the product of success in satisfying investors and customers.

How is it that managers came to control such resources? It is no secret that scattered shareholders cannot control managers directly. If the investors know that the managers have lots of discretion, why did they fork over their money in the first place? If managers promise to return but a pittance, the investors will not put up very much capital. Investors simply pay less for the paper the firms issue. There is therefore a limit on managers' efforts to enrich themselves at investors' expense. Managers may do their best to take advantage of their investors, but they find that the dynamics of the market drive them to act as if they had investors' interests at heart. It is almost as if there were an invisible hand.

The corporation and its securities are products in financial markets to as great an extent as the sewing machines or other things the firm makes. Just as the founders of a firm have incentives to make the kinds of sewing machines people want to buy, they have incentives to create the kind of firm, governance structure, and securities the customers in capital markets want. The founders of the firm will find it profitable to establish the governance structure that is most beneficial to investors, net of the costs of maintaining the structure. People who seek resources to control will have to deliver more returns to investors. Those who promise the highest returns—and make the promises binding, hence believable—will obtain the largest investments.

The first question facing entrepreneurs is what promises to make, and the second is how to induce investors to believe them. Empty promises are worthless promises. Answering the first question depends on finding ways to reduce the effects of divergent interests; answering the second depends on finding legal and automatic enforcement devices. The more automatic the enforcement, the more investors will believe the promises.

What promises will the entrepreneurs make in order to induce investors to hand over more money? No set of promises is right for all firms at all times. No one thinks that the governance structure used for a neighborhood restaurant will work well for Exxon or Hydro Quebec. The best structure cannot be derived from theory; it must be developed by experience. We should be skeptical of claims that any one structure—or even a class of structures—is best. But we can see the sorts of promises that are likely to emerge in the competition for investments.

Some promises entail submitting to scrutiny in advance of action. Outside directors watch inside ones; inside directors watch other managers; the managers hire detectives to watch the employees or set up cross-check systems so that employees possess little ability to act independently. At other times, though, prior monitoring may be too costly in relation to its benefits, and the most desirable methods of control will rest on deterrence, on letting people act as they wish but penalizing mistakes and misdeeds. Fiduciary obligations and litigation are forms of subsequent settling-up included among these kinds of devices. Still other methods operate automatically. Managers enjoy hefty salaries and perquisites of office; the threat of losing these induces managers to act in investors' interest.

Managers in the United States must select the place of incorporation. The fifty states offer different menus of devices (from voting by shareholders to fiduciary rules to derivative litigation) for the protection of investors. The managers who pick the state of incorporation that is most desirable from the perspective of investors will attract the most money. The states that select the best combination of rules will attract the most corporate investment (and therefore increase their tax collections). So states compete to offer—and managers to use—beneficial sets of legal rules. These include not only rules about governance structures but also fiduciary rules and prohibitions of fraud.

Managers decide when to go public. Less experienced entrepreneurs start with venture capital, which comes with extensive strings. The venture capitalists control the operation of the firm with some care. Only after the managerial team and structure has matured will the firm issue public securities. Although the entrepreneurs commonly keep majority control on the initial public sale, they remain bound by contracts with venture capitalists that tie continuation of control to continuation of success. Eventually the entrepreneurs sell working control, and venture capitalists withdraw. The firm has become public in fact as well as in name.

Entrepreneurs make promises in the articles of incorporation and the securities they issue when they go public. The debt investors receive exceptionally detailed promises in indentures. These promises concern the riskiness of the firm's operations, the extent to which earnings may be paid out, and the domain of managerial discretion. These promises benefit equity investors as well as debt investors. The equity investors usually receive votes rather than explicit promises. Votes make it possible for the investors to replace the managers. (Those who believe that managers have unchecked control should ask themselves why the organizers of a firm issue equity claims that enable the investors to replace the managers.) The managers also promise, explicitly or otherwise, to abide by the standards of "fair dealing" embedded in the fiduciary rules of corporate law. Sometimes they make additional promises as well.

To sum up: self-interested entrepreneurs and managers, just like other investors, are driven to find the devices most likely to maximize net profits. If they do not, they pay for their mistakes because they receive lower prices for corporate paper. Any one firm may deviate from the optimal measures. Over tens of years and thousands of firms, though, tendencies emerge. The firms and managers that make the choices investors prefer will prosper relative to others. Because the choices do not impose costs on strangers to the contracts, what is optimal for the firms and investors is optimal for society. We can learn a great deal just by observing which devices are widely used and which are not.

It is important to distinguish between isolated transactions and governance structures. There are high costs of operating capital and managerial markets, just as there are high costs of other methods of dealing with the divergence of interest. It is inevitable that a substantial amount of undesirable slack or self-dealing will occur. The question is whether these costs can be cut by mechanisms that are not themselves more costly. Investors, like all of us in our daily lives, accept some unwelcome conduct because the costs of the remedy are even greater. We also use deterrence (say, the threat of punishment for fraud) rather than other forms of legal control when deterrence is the least costly method of handling a problem, which it generally is. The expensive legal system is not cranked up unless there is evidence of wrongdoing; if the anticipated penalty (the sanction multiplied by the probability of its application) is selected well, there will not be much wrongdoing, and the costs of the system will be correspondingly small. A regulatory system (one entailing scrutiny and approval in advance in each case) ensures that the costs of control will be high; they will be incurred even if the risk is small.

Markets that let particular episodes of wrongdoing slide by, or legal systems that use deterrence rather than regulatory supervision to handle the costs of management, are likely to be effective in making judgments about optimal governance structures. Governance structures are open and notorious, unlike the conduct they seek to control. Costs of knowing about a firm's governance are low. Firms and teams of managers can compete with each other over the decades to design governance structures and to build in penalties for malfeasance. There is no substantial impediment to the operation of the competitive process at the level of structure. The pressures that operate in the long run are exactly the forces that shape structure. Contractual promises and fiduciary rules arise as a result of these considerations.

Before tackling particular topics such as limited liability and takeovers, however, it is useful to step back and ask whether corporation-as-contract is a satisfying way of looking at things even in theory. No one portrays the relation between trustee and beneficiary as one of arm's-length contracting, and legal rules impose many restrictions that the trustee cannot avoid. Why think about corporations differently?

Markets, Firms, and Corporations

"Markets" are economic interactions among people dealing as strangers and seeking personal advantage. The extended conflict among selfish people produces prices that allocate resources to their best uses. This is an old story, and Adam Smith's *The Wealth of Nations* (1776) remains the best exposition. A series of short-term dealings in a market may be more useful for trading than for producing goods, however. The firm—an aggregation of people banded together for a longer period—permits greater use of specialization. People can organize as teams with the functions of each member identified, so that each member's specialization makes the team as a whole more productive than it would otherwise be.

Teams could be assembled every day, the way stevedore contractors hire longshore workers. The construction industry assembles teams by the project. More often, however, the value of a long-term relation among team members predominates, and to the extent it does recognizable firms grow. Yet as the size of a firm grows, there must be more and more transactions among members. A manufacturer of cars that makes its own paint must decide how much paint to use, and of what quality. Does it make sense to make the paint job a little less durable? This depends on the value of the paint the firm uses—and on whether someone else could provide the paint for less.

An integrated firm has difficulty assessing the value of the paint it makes for itself. It must take expensive steps to give the paint a value (called a "transfer price"), which at best duplicates information that markets produce and at worst may be quite inaccurate, leading the firm to make inefficient decisions. Managers may specify transfer prices that lead firms to produce paint they should have bought, or to use too much or too little paint in their products. Transacting for paint in markets has risks (will the seller deliver on time? will the quality be good?) that are costly to deal with. Letters of credit, the courts, organized exchanges and credit bureaus, and other institutions are among the costs of markets. The firm grows until the costs of organizing production internally exceed the costs of organizing through market transactions.

One cost of cooperative production inside the firm is the divergence of interest among the participants. It is sometimes useful to think of the atoms dealing in markets as individual people who reap the gains and bear the expenses of their own decisions. The organization of production in teams is not so simple. The firm may hire labor by the hour ("hourly employees") or the year ("salaried employees"); either arrangement hires a segment of time but not a specified effort. It is difficult to induce the employee to devote his best effort to the firm's fortunes. Why should he? His pay is the same no matter his performance. Although it may be possible to penalize sluggards by reducing their wages or firing them (a process sometimes called "*ex post* settling-up"), it is costly to monitor effort—and who monitors the monitors' efforts? On top of that, it is often very difficult to determine the quality of the work performed. A team of designers may put together an excellent airplane (the Lockheed L-1011 comes to mind) that fails in the market either for reasons beyond their control or because it was "too good" and so too costly. A system of monitoring that asked only whether the employees' work was profitable for the firm would lead to inaccurate rewards when there are risks beyond the control of the employees or knowledge beyond the reach of the monitors. Unless someone knows the quality of each person's work in relation to the demand, settling-up must be imperfect. Given that accounts may be settled well after the work has been performed, the time value of money sometimes will make a balancing of accounts impossible.

Another way around the difficulty of monitoring the work of the firm's employees is to give each the right to some profits from the firm's success. Each then will work hard and monitor the work of colleagues, lest their subpar performance reduce his rewards. But the allocation of the venture's profits to the employees—and by employees we mean managers, too—is another cost. It reduces the return to those who contribute the venture's capital. And it, too, is imperfect. Much production is performed in teams. Teams of employees sweep the floor, teams of engineers design new products, teams of managers decide whether and where to build new plants. So long as no monitor can determine what each member's marginal contribution to the team's output is, each member will be less than a perfectly faithful representative of the interests of the team as a whole. Unless one person receives all the rewards of success and penalties of failure, his incentives are not properly aligned with those of the venture as a whole. "Let George do it" is a predictable response, when any given employee gets some of the benefits of George's hard work and does not get all of the benefits of his own hard work.

Sometimes this division of interests will lead the employee to divert the firm's assets to himself. Theft is the dramatic way to do this; diversion of "corporate opportunities" may be another, and in general the discretion managers possess gives them an opportunity to favor themselves in dealing with the other actors. Sometimes this division of interests will lead to less diligent work. The employee may engage in goldbricking, and the upper manager may "slack off" by working seventy hours per week rather than the seventy-five he would work if he received more of the reward from his effort. Sometimes the division of interests dulls the willingness to take risks. The quiet life may be a perquisite of employment. All of these are costs. Monitoring by outsiders to reduce these costs also is costly.

Employees may reduce the amount of monitoring that is necessary by giving "bonds"—not physical certificates but automatic devices that impose penalties for a shortfall in performance. When managers hold the stock of their firm, they are "bonding" their performance (in part) by exposing their wealth to erosion if their performance, and hence the firm's profits, is substandard. Firms use different mixes of bonding devices, monitoring devices, and residual costs of the divergence of interest. The trick is to hold the total costs of these things as low as possible. It is foolish to spend $2 in monitoring to reduce by $1 the perquisites of employees. Throughout this book we refer to the combination of monitoring, bonding, and residual costs as "agency costs."

So far we have been describing the firm as an extra-market, team method of production with certain benefits and costs. Corporations are a subset of firms. The corporation is a financing device and is not otherwise distinctive. A corporation is characterized by a statement of capital contributions as formal claims against the firm's income that are distinct from participation in the firm's productive activities. The corporation issues "stock" in exchange for an investment; stock need not be held by the firm's employees. Investors bear the risk of failure (sometimes we call them "risk bearers") and receive the marginal rewards of success. Equity investors are paid last, after debt investors, employees, and other investors with (relatively) "fixed" claims. These equity investors have the "residual" claim in the sense that they get only what is left over—but they get all of what is left over.

The separation of risk bearing from employment is a form of the division of labor. Those who have wealth can employ it productively even if they are not good managers; those who can manage but lack wealth can hire capital in the market; and the existence of claims that can be traded separately from employment allows investors to diversify their investment interests. Diversification makes investment as a whole less risky and therefore makes investment both more attractive and more efficient. Investors bear most of the risk of business failure, in exchange for which they are promised most of the rewards of success. The penalty for this arrangement is that separation of management and risk bearing at least potentially increases agency costs by driving a broader wedge between employees' interests and those of the venture as a whole. Employees will receive less of the return; investors will be less effective monitors to the extent that holdings are widely scattered, for then no one investor has a good reason to monitor. (In other words, investors face their own agency costs that dissuade them from monitoring, which is why investors in public firms often are ignorant and passive.) The corporation will flourish when the gains from the division of labor exceed the augmentation of the agency costs.

Sometimes it is said that the distinctive features of the corporation are limited liability, legal identity, and perpetual existence, but these are misleading descriptions. "Limited liability" means only that those who contribute equity capital to a firm risk no more than their initial investments—it is an attribute of the investment rather than of "the corporation." This attribute of investors' risk is related to the benefits of widely held, liquid investment instruments. It often is altered by contract when these benefits are small. We discuss limited liability more fully in Chapter 2. Legal identity and perpetual existence mean only that the corporation lasts until dissolved and has a name in which it may transact and be sued. It is convenient to think of the firm as an "it." Many firms in addition to corporations, such as business trusts, are treated in the same way. It would be silly to attach a list of every one of Exxon's investors to an order for office furniture just to ensure that all investors share their percentage of the cost.

The "personhood" of a corporation is a matter of convenience rather than reality, however; we also treat the executor of an estate as a legal entity without submerging the fact that the executor is a stand-in for other people. It is meaningful to speak of the legislative branch of the U.S. Government, or Congress, or of the House, or of a committee of the Senate, or of members of Congress, depending on context, but it would be misleading to think of Congress—an entity with a name—only as an entity, or to believe that its status as an entity is the most significant thing about the institution. "Congress" is a collective noun for a group of independent political actors and their employees, and it acts as an entity only when certain forms have been followed (such as majority approval in each house). So too with corporations. There are many actors, from production employees to managers to equity investors to debt investors to holders of warranty and tort claims against the firm. The arrangements among these persons usually depend on contracts and on positive law, not on corporate law or the status of the corporation as an entity. More often than not a reference to the corporation as an entity will hide the essence of the transaction. So we often speak of the corporation as a "nexus of contracts" or a set of implicit and explicit contracts. This reference, too, is shorthand for the complex arrangements of many sorts that those who associate voluntarily in the corporation will work out among themselves. The form of reference is a reminder that the corporation is a voluntary adventure, and that we must always examine the terms on which real people have agreed to participate.

Agreements that have arisen are wonderfully diverse, matching the diversity of economic activity carried on within corporations. Managers sometimes hold a great deal of the firm's stock and are rewarded for success through appreciation of their investments prices; other employees may be paid on a piece-work basis; sometimes compensation is via salary and bonuses. Corporations sometimes are organized as hierarchies, with the higher parts of the pyramid issuing commands; sometimes they are organized as dictatorships; sometimes they are organized as divisional profit centers with loose or missing hierarchy. The choice of organization and compensation devices will depend on the size of the firm, the identity of the managers, and the industry (or spectrum of industries) in which the corporation participates. Organization and compensation in an investment bank is vastly different from organization and compensation in an industrial conglomerate, as industrial firms that acquired investment banks learned to their sorrow.

The organization of finance and control is equally variable. Small, close corporations may have only banks as outside investors, and these banks hold "debt" claims that carry residual rights to control the firm. Highly leveraged public firms may concentrate equity investments in managers while issuing tradable debt claims to the public; the public investors in these firms have no effective control, because debt conventionally does not carry voting rights. Public utilities and national banks may have more traded equity but still no effective shareholders' control, given both regulatory structures and the nature of the risks in the business. Many growing firms have almost no debt investment, and the equity investment pays no dividends; these firms are under the dictatorial control of the entrepreneur. Some firms go public under rules that stifle any attempt at control: Ford, for example, issued nonvoting stock, leaving the firm in family hands for a long time. Mature firms may be more bureaucratic, with boards of directors "independent" of managers and answerable to equity investors. Some managerial teams attempt to insulate themselves from investors' control in order to carry out programs that they view as more important than profits. Both the *New York Times* and the *Wall Street Journal* have established structures that give their managers substantial freedom to produce news at the (potential) expense of profit.

The way in which corporations run the business, control agency costs, raise money, and reward investors will change from business to business and from time to time within a firm. The structure suited to a dynamic, growing firm such as Xerox in 1965 is quite unsuited to Exxon in 1965 (or to Xerox in 1990). The participants in the venture need to be able to establish the arrangement most conducive to prosperity, and outsiders are unlikely to be able to prescribe a mold for corporations as a whole or even a firm through time. The history of corporations has been that firms failing to adapt their governance structures are ground under by competition.[1] The history of corporate law has been that states attempting to force all firms into a single mold are ground under as well.

1. Oliver E. Williamson, *The Economic Institutions of Capitalism* (1985); cf. Alfred D. Chandler, Jr., *The Visible Hand* (1977).

Corporations flee to find statutes that permit adaptations (as we discuss in Chapter 8). This is the reason for the drive toward enabling laws that control process but not structure.[2]

To say that a complex relation among many voluntary participants is adaptive is to say that it is contractual. Thus our reference to the corporation as a set of contracts. Voluntary arrangements are contracts. Some may be negotiated over a bargaining table. Some may be a set of terms that are dictated (by managers or investors) and accepted or not; only the price is negotiated. Some may be fixed and must be accepted at the "going price" (as when people buy investment instruments traded in the market). Some may be implied by courts or legislatures trying to supply the terms that would have been negotiated had people addressed the problem explicitly. Even terms that are invariant—such as the requirement that the board of directors act only by a majority of a quorum—are contractual to the extent that they produce offsetting voluntary arrangements. The result of all of these voluntary arrangements will be contractual.

Just as there is no right amount of paint in a car, there is no right relation among managers, investors, and other corporate participants. The relation must be worked out one firm at a time. A change in technology—whether the technology of applying paint or the technology of assembling blocs of shares to change control of a firm—will be reflected in changes in the operation or governance of corporations. To understand corporate law you must understand how the balance of advantage among devices for controlling agency costs differs across firms and shifts from time to time. The role of corporate law at any instant is to establish rights among participants in the venture. Who governs? For whose benefit? Without answering difficult questions about the effectiveness of different devices for controlling agency costs, one cannot determine the appropriate allocation of rights.

We use economic arguments about agency costs throughout this book to attempt to answer questions about background terms

---

2. The American Law Institute's *Corporate Governance Project,* under way for more than a decade, assumes that one size fits all. The few concessions to structural variations among firms are grudging and limited to unimportant matters. States have paid the project no heed, and any prescription for corporate law that tries to reduce governance options is doomed to similar failure.

(those applying in the absence of a different term incorporated in a particular corporate contract), mandatory terms, and changes in terms. The analogy to contract focuses attention on the voluntary and adaptive nature of any corporation. We treat corporate law as a standard-form contract, supplying terms most venturers would have chosen but yielding to explicit terms in all but a few instances. The normative thesis of the book is that corporate law should contain the terms people would have negotiated, were the costs of negotiating at arm's length for every contingency sufficiently low. The positive thesis is that corporate law almost always conforms to this model. It is enabling rather than directive. The standby terms grant great discretion to managers and facilitate actual contracts. They leave correction to the interplay of self-interested actors rather than to regulators. But many standby terms—for example, the presumption that equity shares have one vote apiece, that these votes can be used to oust the managers and govern the firm, and that debt investors have no voice in governance—have both important effects and solid economic rationales. We discuss many types of corporate rules in the substantive chapters of the book.

Real and Unreal Contracts

The rhetoric of contract is a staple of political and philosophical debate. Contract means voluntary and unanimous agreement among affected parties. It is therefore a powerful concept. It shows up in arguments about "social contracts" that justify political society. The founding of the United States was accompanied by much contractarian reasoning. Philosophers who resort to the "original position" to establish a definition of justice are using a contractarian argument. Yet arguments about social contracts are problematic. They are constructs rather than real contracts. And even if our forebears had entered into an actual contract, why would these rules bind later generations? Such doubts are also part of our political heritage; Jefferson accordingly suggested that the Constitution expire and be renewed whenever half of the population had been born since the last renegotiation. Perhaps the corporate contract, like the social contract, is no more than a rhetorical device. After all, investors do not sit down and haggle among themselves about the terms. Investors buy stock in the market and may know little more than its price. The terms were established by entrepreneurs, investment banks, and managers. Changes in the rules are accomplished by voting rather than unanimous consent. So why not view the corporation as a republican government rather than as a set of contracts?

The corporate venture has many real contracts. The terms present in the articles of incorporation at the time the firm is established or issues stock are real agreements. *Everything* to do with the relation between the firm and the suppliers of labor (employees), goods and services (suppliers and contractors) is contractual. If AT&T signs a contract allowing the next John Bardeen (the inventor of the transistor) to keep his inventions, this will be enforced; an allocation of rights to the firm also will be enforced. Although it is exceedingly hard to determine the value of things that have yet to be invented, neither the difficulty of attaching prices nor the substantial *ex post* variance among inventors' (and firms') wealth will matter. Just so with the rules in force when the firm raises money—whether by issuing debt, the terms of which often are negotiated at great length over a table, or by issuing equity, the terms of which affect the price of the issue. Many changes in the rules are approved by large investors after negotiation with management. And of course the rules that govern how rules change are also real contracts. The articles of incorporation typically allow changes to be made by bylaw or majority vote; they could as easily prevent changes, or call for supermajority vote, or allow change freely but require nonconsenting investors to be bought out. That the articles allow uncompensated changes through voting is a contractual choice. And many remaining terms of the corporate arrangement are contractual in the sense that they are "presets" of fallback terms specified by law and not varied by the corporation. These terms become part of the set of contracts just as provisions of the Uniform Commercial Code become part of commercial contracts when not addressed explicitly.

These contracts usually are negotiated by representatives. Indenture trustees negotiate on behalf of bondholders, unions on behalf of employees, and investment banks on behalf of equity investors. Sometimes terms are not negotiated directly but are simply promulgated, as auto rental companies promulgate the terms of their rental contracts. The entrepreneurs or managers may adopt a set of rules and say, "take them or leave them." This is contracting nonetheless. We enforce the terms in auto rental contracts, as we enforce the terms of a trust even though the beneficiaries had no say in their framing. The terms in rental contracts, warranties, and the like are real contracts because their value (or detriment) is reflected in price.

The corporation's choice of governance mechanisms does not create substantial third-party effects—that is, does not injure persons who are not voluntary participants in the venture. (We discuss below the few third-party effects that crop up.) Investors, employees, and others can participate or go elsewhere. Let us suppose that entrepreneurs simply pick terms out of a hat. They cannot force investors to pay more than the resulting investment instruments are worth; there are too many other places for the investors to put their money. Unless entrepreneurs can fool the investors, a choice of terms that reduces investors' expected returns will produce a corresponding reduction in price. So the people designing the terms under which the corporation will be run have the right incentives. Suppose they must decide whether to allow managers to take corporate opportunities or instead require them to be used by the firm (or sold to third parties unaffiliated with the firm). Managers' ability to appropriate opportunities poses obvious risks of diversion; it may also allow efficient use of opportunities and be a source of compensation for managers, which benefits investors. The net effects, for good or ill, will influence the price investors pay for stock. If the managers make the "wrong" decision—that is, choose the inferior term from the investors' point of view—they must pay for their mistake. To obtain an (inefficient) right to divert opportunities they must pay in advance. The same process applies to terms adopted later; undesirable terms reduce the price the stock fetches in the market, so that investors who buy thereafter will get no less than they pay for. All the terms in corporate governance are contractual in the sense that they are fully priced in transactions among the interested parties. They are thereafter tested for desirable properties; the firms that pick the wrong terms will fail in competition with other firms competing for capital. It is unimportant that they may not be "negotiated"; the pricing and testing mechanisms are all that matter, as long as there are no effects on third parties. This should come as no shock to anyone familiar with the Coase Theorem.[3]

Are terms priced? Provisions in articles of incorporation and

---

3. R. H. Coase, "The Problem of Social Cost," 3 *J. L. & Econ.* 1 (1960), reprinted in *The Firm, the Market, and the Law* 95–156 (1988).

bylaws often are picky and obscure. Many are not listed in the prospectus of the firm's stock. Buyers of the original issue and in the aftermarket alike may know nothing of the terms in use, let alone whether a staggered board of directors or the existence of cumulative voting will make them better off. They do not consult the *Journal of Financial Economics* before buying. Yet it is unimportant whether knowledge about the nature or effect of the terms is widespread, at least for public corporations. The mechanism by which stocks are valued ensures that the price reflects the terms of governance and operation, just as it reflects the identity of the managers and the products the firm produces.

The price of stocks traded in public markets is established by professional investors, not by amateurs.[4] These professionals—market makers, arbitrage departments of investment banks, managers of mutual funds and pension trusts, and others—handle huge sums that they are willing to use to purchase undervalued stocks. They study the firm's profits and prospects and bid or sell accordingly. People who do this poorly will find the funds at their disposal dwindling; people who do it well will command additional sums. At any given instant, the professional traders are those who have generally been successful at assessing the worth of stock.

If the price of a stock is not "right" in relation to the price it will have in the future, then professionals can make a lot of money. If the terms of corporate provisions and the details of corporate structure have any effect on investors' welfare, this will be reflected in the profits of the firm and hence the eventual price of the stock. Professionals trade among themselves in a way that brings the present value closer to the future value; if it is known that the stock will be worth $20 in a year, then people will bid that price (less the time value of money) now; no one has a good reason to wait, because if he does someone else will take the profit. The more astute the professional investors, and the more quickly they can

---

4. The process we describe below is reasonably well understood, and it has been so completely discussed elsewhere that we offer only a sketch. See Richard A. Brealey, *An Introduction to Risk and Return from Common Stocks* ch. 2 (2d ed. 1983); Ronald J. Gilson and Reinier Kraakman, "The Mechanisms of Market Efficiency," 70 *Va. L. Rev.* 549 (1984). Adjustment to information is exceptionally fast, usually within the day the professional investor learns the information. Douglas K. Pearce and V. Vance Roley, "Stock Prices and Economic News," 59 *J. Business* 49 (1985).

move funds into and out of particular holdings, the faster adjustment. The process eventually makes it difficult even for professional traders to make money, unless they are the first to obtain or act on a piece of information affecting future value. A great deal of data, including evidence that most professional investors are unable to "beat the market," supports the position that prices quickly and accurately reflect public information about firms. Amateur investors then trade at the same price the professionals obtain. These amateurs do not need to know anything about corporate governance and other provisions; the value of these mysterious things is wrapped up in the price established by the professionals. The price reflects the effects, good or bad, of corporate law and contracts, just as it reflects the effects of good and bad products. This is yet another example of the way in which markets transmit the value of information through price, which is more "informed" than any single participant in the market.[5]

To say that the price of a stock reflects the value of the firm's governance and related rules is not necessarily to say that the price does so perfectly. Research into the accuracy of prices suggests that prices often are "wrong," meaning that more information and more time yield improvements.[6] There may be surprises in store, for a firm or for all firms, that make estimates about the effects of governance provisions inaccurate. But these problems of information and assessment also affect any other way of evaluating the effects of governance devices. That is, if professional investors with their fortunes on the line are unable to anticipate the true effects of nonvoting stock or some other wrinkle, how are members of state legislatures or other alternative rule givers to do better? To put this differently, it does not matter if markets are not perfectly efficient, unless some other social institution does better at evaluating the likely effects of corporate governance devices. The prices will be more informative than the next best alternative, which is all anyone can demand of any device.

This means that we need not enter the debate about whether

---

5. See Thomas Sowell, *Knowledge and Decisions* (1982); Sanford J. Grossman and Joseph E. Stiglitz, "Information and Competitive Price Systems," 66 *Am. Econ. Rev.* 246 (1976); Robert E. Verrecchia, "Consensus Beliefs, Information Acquisition, and Market Information Efficiency," 70 *Am. Econ. Rev.* 874 (1980).

6. Stephen F. LeRoy, "Efficient Capital Markets and Martingales," 27 *J. Econ. Lit.* 1583 (1989), surveys the literature.

stocks are priced perfectly. Prices do not reflect very well information that is not available to the public. They reflect the value of
stock to public investors with scattered holdings rather than to
insiders or others with the ability to control the firm's destiny. For
any given firm, there will be an irreducible amount of error in the
pricing—after all, information that increases the accuracy of prices
is costly, and the "perfect price" may cost more to achieve than it
is worth. The more accurate the price becomes, the less private
gain is available to pros who study the stock and find bargains; thus
they do not find it profitable to pursue perfection. None of this
matters for our purposes, unless some better device is available.
Few believe that regulators are better at valuing terms of corporate
governance than are markets. Defects that undercut the performance of capital markets are an order of magnitude smaller than
the difficulties besetting regulators.

One might say that the effects of obscure terms in articles of
incorporation will be too small to affect price, but prices turn out to
be sensitive to changes in governance. As we proceed, we discuss
many studies showing how changes in the articles and other structural features have measurable, and predictable, effects on price. It
turns out to be hard to find any interesting item that does not have
an influence on price! No surprise. Markets price many things routinely. For example, insurance markets offer explicit prices for the
risk of theft (fidelity bonds and other insurance of the type is
common), so it is predictable that stock prices likewise reflect
events that change the risk of managerial delicts. The technology
for assessing repeated events (governance structures fall in that
category) is well developed.

The price effects generally support the thesis we have advanced.[7]

7. We mention many of these studies in the chapters addressing particular subjects in corporate governance. For a survey of evidence on most of the subjects in
this book, see Frank H. Easterbrook, "Managers' Discretion and Investors' Welfare: Theories and Evidence," 9 *Del. J. Corp. L.* 540 (1984). Empirical studies
pepper the economic literature, appearing too fast to keep track of, and review articles are out of date by the time they reach print. Symposium volumes, however,
offer useful surveys. See, for example, Symposium, The Structure and Governance
of Enterprise, 26 *J. Fin. Econ.* (1991); Symposium, The Distribution of Power
among Corporate Managers, Shareholders, and Directors, 20 *J. Fin. Econ.* 1–507
(1988); Symposium, Management Compensation and the Managerial Labor Market,
7 *J. Accounting & Econ.* 1–257 (1985); Conference, Corporations and Private Prop-

Even those who believe that markets are not particularly efficient concede that changes in prices reflect the marginal value, to investors outside the managerial group, of publicly disclosed information about the firm. Governance structures are known to anyone seeking the information, so the pricing mechanism will embody their effects for good or ill. It is easy to attach prices to risks of theft and incompetence, compared with attaching prices to, say, new products and other business prospects. Anyone who thinks markets even bearably good at pricing future profit from well-managed firms must think them better at pricing the effects of governance structures.

Let us now suppose, however, that markets do not price terms accurately. Unless prices are systematically wrong about the effects of features of governance, as opposed to being noisy and uninformative, managers still have appropriate incentives. The long run will arrive eventually, and terms that are not beneficial for investors will stand revealed; the firm will lose out in competition for investors' money. We therefore treat even hard-to-value terms as contractual. To disregard the terms that appear in corporate documents or to attempt to require corporations to employ governance devices that they have attempted to avoid would only induce the firms to make offsetting adjustments. For example, if corporate law should forbid managers to divert corporate opportunities to themselves, they might respond by drawing higher salaries or working less hard to open up new business opportunities. Similarly, a mandatory term that increased the length of a warranty supplied with a refrigerator would lead to an increase in the price. If the longer warranty was worth the price, the seller would have offered the term in the first place, charged the higher price, and made more money. One cannot tinker with one term in a contract confident that the change will make any party better off after other terms have been adjusted. Because so many terms are open to explicit contracting, it is almost always possible to make an end run around any effort to defeat a particular term.

If the terms chosen by firms are *both* unpriced and systematically perverse from investors' standpoints, then it might be possible to justify the prescription of a mandatory term by law. This makes

---

erty, 26 *J. L. & Econ.* 235–496 (1983); Symposium, The Market for Corporate Control: The Scientific Evidence, 11 *J. Fin. Econ.* 1–475 (1983).

sense, however, only when one is sure that the selected term will increase the joint wealth of the participants—that is, that it is the term that the parties would have selected with full information and costless contracting. But this, too, is a contractual way of looking at the corporation. This formula is the one courts use to fill the gaps in explicit contracts that inevitably arise because it is impossible to cover every contingency. Any system of law that recognizes explicit contracts must deal with gaps and ambiguities. The gap-filling rule will call on courts to duplicate the terms the parties would have selected, in their joint interest, if they had contracted explicitly. It promotes clear thought to understand that the silence or ambiguity in corporate documents is itself a problem of contract, one the parties could solve if they wished and if the costs of negotiating were worthwhile in light of the stakes. High information costs— which impede accurate reflection of governance features in the price of stock—also impede more complete transacting.

This is not to say that corporate documents are ideal. Perhaps there are third-party effects. Perhaps there are obstacles to reaching the appropriate agreements. Perhaps optimal terms, once reached, will be altered in ways that enable managers to escape the consequences of their acts; terms changed by voting may fit in this category. The next section discusses the limits of contracts, both actual and implied.

Trumping the Corporate Contract

Many parts of the law contain contract-defeating doctrines. Some of these may be applicable to corporate contracts. We look at the four principal ones.

PROTECTING CONTRACTING PARTIES

Think of the principal reasons why private agreements may not be honored. Contracts signed under threat of force displace voluntary arrangements and are unjust as well; force is therefore illegal. Some contractual choices are not enforced because unreliable: fraud vitiates a pact; infants and others who do not know their own interests cannot contract. Other parties to a contract may be lacking in perceptual powers: they may underestimate the chance that certain risks (floods, earthquakes, failures of the products they buy) will come to pass, so they may not choose rationally when confronted with choices about such risks; at other times they may think the probability greater than it is (nuclear calamity). When a person is confronted with a problem or risk for the first (or only) time in his life, the chance of error is greatest. Choices that are made repeatedly and tested against experience are more likely to be accurate—both because every person learns from experience, and because the population as a whole contains many astute searchers who identify "bargains" and so influence the terms on which all participants trade.

Some contracts are not honored because they have adverse effects on third parties. Contracts that yield pollution affect people who are not parties to the deal. Cartels (contracts among business rivals to raise price) affect customers. So we have laws to control pollution and monopolies, and much regulation (such as rate regulation of electrical utilities) is based on a belief that a dearth of competition produces monopoly prices. Legal rules that protect people in need of rescue (passengers on a sinking ship) from excessive prices charged by rescuers serve a similar function. Sometimes the argument for intervention by the state is reinforced by a claim that the person paying the price should be a beneficiary of an income transfer; for example, rent control and minimum wages sometimes are justified by reference to the relative wealth of landlord and tenant (or employer and employee).

None of these justifications for intervention applies to intra-corporate affairs. Investors are not candidates for transfers of wealth; this is not a branch of poverty law. Investors and other participants agree on the stakes: money. They therefore would agree unanimously to whatever rule maximizes the total value of the firm. Questions of distribution among investors are unimportant; allocating gains to one rather than another changes relative prices but not social wealth. There is no fraud; the rules of corporate governance are open for all to see. (There may be fraud in the operation of the firm, but concealed violations of any rules are wrongful; recall that our concern is with the selection of rules of governance.)

It might seem that the argument based on perceptual biases justifies intervention. Few investors know much about corporate governance; therefore most are likely to misunderstand the risks they take. Yet as we have explained, in corporate transactions risks are priced through the stock market, and these prices respond to the knowledge of professional investors. These prices protect ignorant investors automatically. The "game" of corporate governance is played repeatedly. People learn from experience. Each corporation has an extended life, so the effects of governance devices may be observed; and when scores of corporations use similar devices, it is possible to find out how they fare in comparison to one another. Investors as a whole (and therefore prices) will be informed and informative, even though most investors are baffled by the rules embedded in corporate contracts.

Participation in corporations is uniquely amenable to contracting because even the ignorant have an army of helpers. The stock market is one automatic helper. Employees work at terms negotiated by unions (and nonunion employees can observe the terms offered at other firms, which supply much information). Managers and corporations employ professional search firms (headhunters) to convey information and match person to job. Holders of bonds are protected by trustees, which negotiate terms and monitor compliance. Many people invest in corporations through their bank accounts; syndicates of banks (after conducting thorough reviews) pool the money of depositors for investment in corporations. Much pension money is under professional management; the funds hire expertise for the benefit of investors who need not even know what stocks they indirectly hold. Individual investors can hire professional advice directly (through brokerage houses) or indirectly (by investing in mutual funds). They can hedge their bets by buying diversified portfolios of investments, getting the return of the market as a whole (or some subset) rather than an individual firm.

In sum, knowledge about corporate transactions does not depend on the wisdom of individual investors. What is not understood through professional advice is priced, so that the investor gets what he pays for (in the absence of fraud). If we honor contracts for once-in-a-lifetime transactions, such as the construction of a house, the case for treating as binding contracts the terms under which corporations operate is ironclad. No contract used in our society is more likely to satisfy the conditions for enforcing voluntary agreements.

There is nonetheless a puzzle. Corporate law allows firms to strike almost any imaginable bargain with debt investors, with employees, with suppliers, and with local governments, which supply essential services from fire protection to the education of the next generation of workers. These will be enforced according to the law of contracts. All of these "constituencies" may make formidable investments in the firm (in the sense of irrevocable, specialized commitments of physical or human capital); all are left to protect themselves through contract. The scattered "mandatory" devices in corporate law operate with respect to the equity investors. The board of directors (which equity claimants alone choose) is subject to certain limits; managers (which the board, and hence equity investors, selects) may not contract out of the "duty of loyalty." We noted at the outset a few other mandatory terms. Yet the most powerful device for protecting participants in the venture—liquid markets with professional investors setting price—applies exclusively to investors, principally equity investors. Why is it that these well-protected participants are subject to mandatory terms, while others who gain less from markets must protect themselves, and devil take the hindmost? We suggest later on that the answer lies in part in the special nature of the claim held by equity investors—a claim to "what is left over" rather than to a definable return such as a wage or a payment of interest—and in part in one of the oddities of markets: that when shares are widely traded, no one has the right incentive to gather information and make optimal decisions. For now, though, the reader should keep this difference in mind as a puzzle.

THE INEFFICIENT TERM

The argument that contracts are optimal applies only if the contracting parties bear the full costs of their decisions and reap all the gains. It applies only if contracts are enforced after they have been reached. The argument also depends on the availability of the full set of possible contracts. If some types of agreements are foreclosed, then those actually reached may not be optimal. Some of these problems crop up in corporate law.

Third-Party Effects and Collective Decisions

One type of third-party effect is created by the peculiar nature of information and the difficulty of arranging reciprocal disclosure of information among firms. Securities laws impose a detailed set of rules. One possible reason is that firms would disclose too little information unless compelled. Managers seek to disclose all the information that is privately optimal to investors, because that will induce investors to part with more money for their shares. But some disclosures may be beneficial to other firms, too, and unless legal rules set up a requirement of reciprocal disclosure none of the firms may find it beneficial to disclose information that is valuable to investors. Some kinds of disclosure may be complex, and legal rules can establish a common language that will facilitate transmission of information.

To see another way in which one firm's acts may affect another's, consider tender offers—bids for the outstanding stock of a firm. A tender offer is a way of gathering up the equity interests to make some fundamental change in the firm that the existing managers oppose; it is an appeal over managers' heads to the equity investors. Usually a tender offer is made at a substantial premium over market price. Investors contracting at the time the firm goes public may wish to make tender offers easy to arrange. Bids are delightfully profitable events; moreover, putative bidders serve as possible monitors, holding down the agency costs of management whether or not a given firm is the object of a bid. So before a firm knows whether there will be a bid (that is, *ex ante*), all involved may find it useful to invite scrutiny and bids. But once potential bidders have become interested, or there is a bid on the table, it may be in the interest of the target's managers and investors alike to change plans and conduct an auction. This will raise the price, they realize. It may also discourage monitoring, but after the monitoring has occurred and the bidding has begun, the investors in the target no longer care about this benefit. The contract that is optimal *ex ante* may not be optimal *ex post*. The investors in the target may quickly change their own contracts, creating an auction. But if such change occurs, then it is not possible to enforce the contract that (by hypothesis) was optimal at the beginning.

Note that this presents a partial view of the available contracts. It assumes that only contracts among participants in targets are possible. Suppose, however, that investors in targets could make contracts with putative bidders. Perhaps they could sell options to purchase their shares at certain prices or under defined conditions. If it were possible to contract in advance with bidders, investors could restrain themselves from adopting new strategies when it looks like a bid is in prospect. Such options turn out to be both impractical (because they imply contracts with a world of potential bidders, at prohibitive transaction costs) and illegal (because the Williams Act forbids bidders to line up shares in advance of making a public announcement and also forbids the preferential purchases that such options imply). The impracticality and illegality of an important contractual device may mean that the contracts actually adopted are not optimal. This may mean that legal rules can improve on the corporate contracts.

The difficulty of enforcing contracts also may create other opportunities for beneficial intervention. The enforcement problem is simple to see. Suppose a contract to hold an auction is optimal, both *ex ante* and *ex post,* for investors in the putative target. They adopt such a contract explicitly. They also explicitly forbid the managers' "defending": that is, they want the firm sold at the highest possible price, not kept "independent." But can they get what they want? Any auctioneering strategy creates some risk of the bid falling through. If today's bids are not high enough, an auctioneer may take a painting off the market for a short time, until a higher-valuing bidder appears. The duration of an auction is flexible, and the highest bidder may not appear for a while. Yet any device that allows the managers to defeat all of the first few bids— such as a rule that no bid may be made without the managers' approval, a rule that poison pill stock approximates—also can be used to defeat any bid. How could anyone tell which strategy was being followed? Would the managers themselves know? They might set an unrealistic reservation price, subjectively believing that they were peddling the firm while objectively making the sale impossible. The difficulty of assuring compliance with the terms of the corporate contract makes particular kinds of contracts less useful.

As for observing contracts, consider this: A strategy of easy-to-acquire may be optimal *ex ante,* and a strategy of auctioneering may be optimal *ex post,* yet if an auctioneering strategy becomes known, bids may not materialize; therefore the best strategy for a given firm may be to look easily acquired at all times, but to follow an auctioneering strategy at all times. The strategy privately maximizing for the target, in other words, is to fool the bidders. This does not violate any rule of contracting; the strategy is beneficial to parties to the contract. Putative bidders have no entitlement to learn the target's true strategy, any more than owners of land have an entitlement to be told what use the buyer will make of the land. Holding information in confidence often is both privately and socially optimal; firms prospecting for ore would do less searching if they had to reveal to the world what they had found before acquiring the mineral-bearing lands. Yet if some putative targets adopt this hidden strategy, other firms with different strategies will be injured. Some firms may have adopted genuine easy-to-acquire policies. Putative bidders will have a hard time telling which firms will resist and which will not, and therefore they may reduce their monitoring and bidding activities even with respect to firms that would not conduct auctions. The uncertainty concerning the contractual strategy selected will interfere with the process of governance of other firms.

This introduces still another sort of problem: there may be a divergence between private and social optimality. We have assumed so far that investors and other corporate players design rules that are best for their firm. And so they do. Yet there is another perspective from which investors do not care about the performance of a given firm. They can invest in any or every firm. In the long run, therefore, they care about the performance of the economy, not a given firm in it. Some firms may do better, some worse, but an investor who does not know beforehand which firm will be which wants only to maximize the average performance. Investors who think themselves likely to hold interests in either bidders or targets are not interested in rules that try to engross a greater portion of gains for targets; they want instead to facilitate the process with the least possible cost devoted to attempting to allocate the gains among firms.

The idea underlying much of this section is that the investor wants to maximize the value of his holdings, not the value of a given stock. Whenever there is a question about the apportionment of gain, the investor prefers whatever rule maximizes the net gain to be had—which means increasing the probability of a gain-producing transaction and reducing the costs of realizing each gain. The rules for dealing with gain-creating opportunities will be established before any particular opportunity is in sight, and so each investor will prefer the set of rules that maximizes the total value (wealth) enjoyed by the investors, without regard to how the return is shared among corporations. Chapters 4 and 5 take up this subject in much greater detail. If investors want to maximize expected values, it follows that corporate rules which facilitate costly fighting over who gets the gains from some profitable transaction are not likely to survive in practice and that in filling gaps in existing contracts it is safe to disregard questions of allocation.

So in thinking about tender offers, an investor does not know whether his firm will be a bidder or a target, and we therefore should not expect him to worry much about creating rules that will transfer money to targets (if there is a bid), for that is likely to cost him if his firm turns out to be a bidder. There is one potential objection to this way of looking at optimal corporate contracts: risk aversion. We have assumed that an investor is indifferent between a 10 percent chance of receiving $1,000 and a certainty of receiving $100. Most investors are risk-averse, which implies that the division of gains may have a role in optimal contracts after all. Perhaps investors seek ways to cut down on risk even if that also cuts down on anticipated return. If they do, that has substantial implications for how to supply missing terms in corporate contracts—maybe even for when to override real contracts.

We shall nonetheless largely ignore risk aversion with respect to public corporations. Our rationale is simple: diversification. Investors who dislike risk can get rid of it. They may hold low-risk instruments (high-grade bonds and Treasury obligations). Investors hold equity if and only if the expected value of these investments beats the return available from other sources. Holding a basket of equities enables the investors to realize these expected returns, free from firm-specific risk (whether risk of the firm's business ventures or of managers' dishonesty). Those who hold equity instruments may do so through mutual funds or by selecting some other broad basket. A diversified portfolio will not eliminate risk that goes with the market. It will, however, essentially wipe out the risk that goes with conflicts among firms and scraps over the allocation of gains and losses. A person who holds a diversified portfolio has an investment in the economy as a whole and therefore wants whatever social or private governance rules maximize the value of all firms put together. He is not interested in maximizing one firm's value if that comes out of the hide of some other corporation. Diversification is cheap in the current economy. It costs less to buy and hold a diversified fund than to trade a small number of stocks.

This appears to overlook the fact that many people are not diversified. Some are undiversified by design. Corporate managers have much of their wealth tied up in the firms they manage, and this lack of diversification reduces the agency costs of management. These managers, as investors, will be risk-averse and interested in the allocation of gains and losses. This is not a reason to treat corporate law as if it ought to care about these allocations, however; managers' risk aversion is a regrettable cost of the corporate form, not a reason to select a rule other than the wealth-maximizing one. As for other undiversified investors, the "stock-pickers" who hold a few stocks or trade actively, these people are simply telling us that they are not risk-averse. Recall that the only reason to care about diversification is because if people are risk-averse they might want a rule maximizing the lower bound of returns rather than maximizing the expected return, and thus social wealth. If the people who do not like risk can look after themselves at low cost, then there is no remaining reason not to select whatever rule maximizes value. And for what it is worth, the vast majority of investments are held by people with diversified portfolios. The principal investors in most firms are institutions of one sort or another: mutual funds, trust departments of banks, pension funds, and other instrumentalities for diversifying holdings. It is a bad idea to reduce the wealth of the prudent many for the dubious benefit of gamblers.

Mistakes

Some people take particular aspects of corporate organization as proof that the provisions could not have been selected by any contractual process. Suppose the articles of Acme Widget Corporation provide that in deciding whether managers may take a corporate opportunity for their own benefit, interested directors are entitled to vote. Suppose the articles thrust on investors the burden of showing that a self-dealing transaction was unfair to the firm, whether or not the manager disclosed the transaction and obtained approval beforehand. Would not such provisions be so one-sided, so fraught with danger to investors, that their very existence shows managerial domination and overreaching? Would not that justify the imposition by law of terms more favorable to investors?

Two kinds of arguments might be at work here. One is that some third-party effect has caused the interests of a given corporation to diverge from the social optimum. The other is that the particular term in the corporate charter is a blunder, as its investors see things. Divergence between private and social interest is rare and does not appear to be at work in these examples. That leaves mistake. But whose mistake? The investors', for not seeing through the ruse and reducing the price paid for the securities? Or the critics', for believing that the terms disserve investors' interests? Unless the person challenging the portion of the corporate contract can make a convincing argument that the consequences of the term could not have been appreciated by investors and priced efficiently, there is no reason for intervening to correct a mistake. Any complexity that might prevent professional investors from recognizing the true effects of a given term probably has no less a baleful effect on the critics' ability to do so. So the presumptive hypothesis is that the mistake has been made by the critic, not by the firm and the investors.

Whenever the costs and benefits of a practice are knowable, they will be reflected in the prices at which the corporation's stock trades. The critic who says that some important term of corporate governance has escaped this mechanism is saying either that the costs and benefits are not knowable or that he alone knows the costs and benefits. Now of course he can reveal these; if people believe him, the market will respond without the need for governmental intervention. The more likely hypothesis, however, is that the people who are backing their beliefs with cash are correct; they have every reason to avoid mistakes, while critics (be they academics or regulators) are rewarded for novel rather than accurate beliefs. Market professionals who estimate these things wrongly suffer directly; academics and regulators who estimate wrongly do not pay a similar penalty. Persons who wager with their own money *may* be wrong, but they are less likely to be wrong than are academics and regulators, who are wagering with other peoples' money.

Corporate governance devices that have survived in many firms for extended periods are particularly unlikely candidates for challenge as mistakes. We have emphasized that the durability of a practice both enables people to gauge its effects and allows competition among firms to weed out the practices that do not assist investors. There is no similar process of weeding out among academic ideas or regulations. Quite the contrary, mandatory terms prescribed by law halt the process of natural selection and evaluation. Unless there is a strong reason to believe that regulation has a comparative advantage over competition in markets in evaluating the effects of corporate contracts—a reason that depends on the sort of features discussed in the preceding and following sections—there is no basis for displacing actual arrangements as "mistakes," "exploitation," and the like.

THE LATECOMER TERM

Much of the discussion so far has proceeded as if all parts of the corporate contract were established at the beginning. "The beginning" for any participant is when he enters the venture—when he becomes an employee, invests, and so on. This is the critical time for most purposes because the time of entry is when the costs and benefits of governance arrangements are priced. If a term is good (or bad) at the beginning, adjustments in the prices even everything up. But of course many things change after the beginning. The firm may reincorporate in Guam. It may adopt staggered terms for members of the board of directors or a "fair price amendment." It may abolish the executive committee of the board or get rid of all the independent directors (or create a board with a majority of independent directors). What are we to make of these changes?

Changes of this sort have some things in common: they are proposed by the existing managers (unless approved by the board of directors, no change in an ongoing firm's rules will be adopted), the proposals are accepted by voting among the equity investors, and the winning side in the vote does not compensate the losing side. If the changes are adverse to existing participants in the venture, there will be price adjustments—but these adjustments do not compensate the participants. If an amendment reduces the expected profitability of the firm by an amount worth $1 per share, the price will fall and existing investors will experience a capital loss of $1 per share. They can sell, but they can't avoid the loss. The buyers will get shares worth what they pay; the investors at the time of the change are out of luck. The mechanism by which entrepreneurs and managers bear the cost of unfavorable terms does not work—not in any direct way, anyway—for latecomer terms. It will work eventually. Latecomer terms that injure investors will reduce the firm's ability to raise money and compete in product markets. But these eventual reactions are not remedies; they explain why firms that choose inferior governance devices do not survive, and they show why widespread, enduring practices are likely to be beneficial, but they do nothing for participants in the ventures that are about to be ground under by the heel of history.

The process of voting controls adverse terms to a degree but not perfectly. Investors are rationally uninterested in votes, not only because no investor's vote will change the outcome of the election but also because the information necessary to cast an informed vote is not readily available. Shareholders' approval of changes is likely to be unreliable as an indicator of their interests, because scattered shareholders in public firms do not have the time, information, or incentives to review all proposed changes. Votes are not sold, at least not without the shares. The difference between governance provisions established at the beginning and provisions added later suggests some caution in treating the two categories alike. Some of the hardest questions in corporate law concern arrangements that are adopted or changed after the firm is under way and the capital has been raised. Thus doctrines of corporate law refusing to allow shareholders to ratify waste (except unanimously) are well-founded. Yet the rules for amending the rules are themselves part of the original articles, and it is (or should be) possible to draft limitations on amendment. These most commonly take the form of provisions designating some amendments as transactions from which investors may dissent and demand appraisal. Moreover, amendments to governance structures may spark proxy contests in which investors' attention is focused, and they also may call forth takeover bids. So voting, or at least the opportunity for review set in place by the voting mechanism, is a partial substitute for the pricing mechanism that applies at the beginning.

Law might overcome a problem in the contracting process by differentiating between terms according to the time of their adoption. Law could provide that terms in place at the beginning (at the time the firm is founded, goes public, or issues significant amounts of stock) are always to be honored unless there are demonstrable third-party effects, while terms adopted later that appear to increase the agency costs of management are valid only if adopted by supermajority vote at successive annual meetings or if dissenting investors are bought out. (The dual-meeting rule would allow an intervening proxy or takeover contest to prevent the change from going into effect.) Yet if such a constraint on amendments is beneficial to investors, why are supermajority and dual-meeting requirements so rare in corporate documents? Investors can and do appreciate the risk that latecomer terms will be damaging, yet perhaps rules that slow down the adoption of changes would be more damaging still on balance. It is not our purpose here to draft rules of law. It is important, however, to keep the latecomer term in mind as a potential problem in a contractual approach to corporate law.

WHY IS THERE CORPORATE LAW?

One natural question after all this business of corporation-as-contract is: why law? Why not just abolish corporate law and let people negotiate whatever contracts they please? The short but not entirely satisfactory answer is that corporate law is a set of terms available off-the-rack so that participants in corporate ventures can save the cost of contracting. There are lots of terms, such as rules for voting, establishing quorums, and so on, that almost everyone will want to adopt. Corporate codes and existing judicial decisions supply these terms "for free" to every corporation, enabling the venturers to concentrate on matters that are specific to their undertaking. Even when they work through all the issues they expect to arise, they are apt to miss something. All sorts of complexities will arise later. Corporate law—and in particular the fiduciary principle enforced by courts—fills in the blanks and oversights with the terms that people would have bargained for had they anticipated the problems and been able to transact costlessly in advance. On this view corporate law supplements but never displaces actual bargains, save in situations of third-party effects or latecomer terms.

There is a ready source of guidance for corporate codes and judicial decisions to draw on in filling in blanks (or establishing background terms): the deals people actually strike when they bargain over the subject. These actual bargains offer models for other firms as well. It is possible that firms that have come to actual bargains on a subject are different from firms that remain silent; the very difference is the reason for the bargain. Possible, but unlikely; differences in transaction costs or perspicacity are more plausible, unless there is some identifiable difference that calls for different rules of governance. Larger firms will find it worthwhile to specify things others leave open, because the gains from resolution increase with the size of the firm. As amateur investors benefit from the work of professionals, so smaller firms and courts can benefit from the work of professional negotiators who solve problems for larger firms.

The story is not complete, however, because it still does not answer the question: "why law?" Why don't law firms or corporate service bureaus or investment banks compile sets of terms on which corporations may be constructed? They can peddle these terms and recover the cost of working through all of the problems. Yet it is costly for the parties (or any private supplier of rules) to ponder unusual situations and dicker for the adoption of terms of any sort. Parties or their surrogates must identify problems and then transact in sufficient detail to solve them. This may all be wasted effort if the problem does not occur. Because change is the one constant of corporate life, waste is a certainty. Often the type of problem that the firm encounters does not occur to anyone until after the venture is under way. Court systems have a comparative advantage in supplying answers to questions that do not occur in time to be resolved *ex ante*. Common law systems need not answer questions unless they occur. This is an economizing device. The accumulation of cases dealing with unusual problems then supplies a level of detail that is costly to duplicate through private bargaining. To put it differently, "contractual" terms for many kinds of problems turn out to be public goods!

Even if law firms, investment banks, or other private suppliers of solutions could specify optimal solutions, they could not readily supply answers for all marginal cases. No one firm could capture all of the gains from working out all problems in advance, because other firms could copy the answers without paying the creator. If the value of new solutions is hard to appropriate, and if the gain from private bargaining is small, people will leave things to be worked out later. As we have emphasized repeatedly, what should be worked out and supplied by corporate law is the rule that, if uniformly applied, will maximize the value of corporate endeavor as a whole. The law completes open-ended contracts. There is no reason why it should be used to impose a term that defeats actual bargains or reduces the venturers' joint wealth.

Maximands

An approach that emphasizes the contractual nature of a corporation removes from the field of interesting questions one that has plagued many writers: what is the goal of the corporation? Is it profit, and for whom? Social welfare more broadly defined? Is there anything wrong with corporate charity? Should corporations try to maximize profit over the long run or the short run? Our response to such questions is: who cares? If the *New York Times* is formed to publish a newspaper first and make a profit second, no one should be allowed to object. Those who came in at the beginning consented, and those who came later bought stock the price of which reflected the corporation's tempered commitment to a profit objective. If a corporation is started with a promise to pay half of the profits to the employees rather than the equity investors, that too is simply a term of the contract. It will be an experiment. Professors might not expect the experiment to succeed, but such expectations by strangers to the bargain are no objection. Similarly, if a bank is formed with a declared purpose of giving priority to loans to minority-owned businesses or third-world nations, that is a matter for the venturers to settle among themselves. So too if a corporation, on building a plant, undertakes never to leave the community. Corporate ventures may select their preferred "constituencies."

The one thing on which a contractual framework focuses attention is surprises. If the venture at its formation is designed in the ordinary fashion—employees and debt investors holding rights to fixed payoffs and equity investors holding a residual claim to profits, which the other participants promise to maximize—that is a binding promise. If the firm suddenly acquires a newspaper and declares that it is no longer interested in profit, the equity investors have a legitimate complaint. It is a complaint for breach of contract, not for derogation from some ideal of corporate governance.

The role of corporate law here, as elsewhere, is to adopt a background term that prevails unless varied by contract. And the background term should be the one that is either picked by contract expressly or is the operational assumption of successful firms. For most firms the expectation is that the residual risk bearers have contracted for a promise to maximize long-run profits of the firm, which in turn maximizes the value of their stock. Other participants contract for fixed payouts—monthly interest, salaries, pensions, severance payments, and the like. We suggest later on that this allocation of rights among the holders of fixed and variable claims serves an economic function. Risk bearers get a residual claim to profit; those who do not bear risk on the margin get fixed terms of trade.

One thing that cannot survive is systematic efforts to fool participants. If investments are attracted on the promise of efforts to maximize profits, then that plan must be executed; otherwise new money cannot be raised and the firm will fail. If investors should come to doubt the worth of promises made to them, investment in the economy as a whole would fall. Similarly, if a firm building a new plant undertakes to operate it only so long as it is profitable and then to lay off the employees and move away, an effort to change the terms later on (if the feared condition materializes)—to lock the plant in place or compel severance payments—would be a breach of the agreement. Fear of such opportunistic conduct *ex post* would reduce the willingness of investors to put up new plants and hire new workers.

Notice that a contractual approach does not draw a sharp line between employees and contributors of capital. Employees may be investors in the sense that portions of their human capital are firm-specific—that is, are adapted to the corporation's business and are worth less in some other job. Holding firm-specific human capital is a way of investing in the firm. The question is not whether employees and other "constituencies" of the firm have entitlements or expectations—they do—but what those entitlements are. If employees negotiate for or accept a system of severance payments to protect their firm-specific human capital, they ought not grumble if they are held to their bargains when business goes bad. Each investor must live with the structure of risks built into the firm. Equity claimants lose out to debt claimants when times are bad and are not thereby entitled to some additional compensation. It is all a matter of enforcing the contracts. And for any employee or investor other than the residual claimant, that means the explicit, negotiated contract.

The choice of maximand is still important if political society wishes to change corporate behavior. Given wealth as a maximand, society may change corporate conduct by imposing monetary penalties. These reduce the venturers' wealth, so managers will attempt to avoid them. A pollution tax, for example, would induce the firm to emit less. It would behave as if it had the interests of others at heart. Society thus takes advantage of the wealth-maximizing incentives built into the firm in order to alter its behavior at least cost. Nothing in our approach asks whether political society should attempt to make firms behave as if they have the welfare of nonparticipants in mind. We do not address optimal ways to deal with pollution, bribery, plant closings, and other decisions that have effects on people who may not participate in the corporate contract. Society must choose whether to conscript the firm's strength (its tendency to maximize wealth) by changing the prices it confronts or by changing its structure so that it is less apt to maximize wealth. The latter choice will yield less of both good ends than the former.

One reason is obvious: a manager told to serve two masters (a little for the equity holders, a little for the community) has been freed of both and is answerable to neither. Faced with a demand from either group, the manager can appeal to the interests of the other. Agency costs rise and social wealth falls. Far better to alter incentives by establishing rules that attach prices to acts (such as pollution and layoffs) while leaving managers free to maximize the wealth of the residual claimants subject to the social constraints.

Another reason is no less important but more often missed: maximizing profits for equity investors assists the other "constituencies" automatically. The participants in the venture play complementary rather than antagonistic roles. In a market economy each party to a transaction is better off. A successful firm provides jobs for workers and goods and services for consumers. The more appealing the goods to consumers, the more profit (and jobs). Prosperity for stockholders, workers, and communities goes hand in glove with better products for consumers. Other objectives, too, come with profit. Wealthy firms provide better working conditions and clean up their outfalls; high profits produce social wealth that strengthens the demand for cleanliness. Environmental concerns are luxury goods; wealthy societies purchase much cleaner and healthier environments than do poorer nations—in part because well-to-do citizens want cleaner air and water, and in part because they can afford to pay for it. Soviet plants pollute more than American ones and produce less, *because* they give less attention to profit rather than *despite* the difference. Within this nation, goals competing with profits are most likely to be sacrificed as profits fall.

Frequently the harmony of interest between profit maximization and other objectives escapes attention. Firms that close plants in one area while relocating production elsewhere are accused of lacking a sense of responsibility to affected workers and communities. Yet such a statement ignores the greater benefits that workers and communities in the new locale enjoy. (They must be greater, or there would be no profit in the move.) Firms that cause dislocations by moving their plants are no less ethical than firms that cause dislocations by inventing new products that cause their rivals to go out of business, yielding unemployment at the failed firm. All competition produces dislocation—all progress produces dislocation (pity the makers of vacuum tubes and slide rules!)—and to try to stop the wrenching shifts of a capitalist economy is to try to stop economic growth.

We do not make the Panglossian claim that profit and social welfare are perfectly aligned. When costs fall on third parties—pollution is the common example—firms do injury because harm does not come back to them as private cost. Dumping offal may impose costs on downstream users exceeding the gains to the stockholders. But banning pollution is no panacea. Water is a resource, and if less of it can be used there will be fewer and more expensive products, and more of some substitute means of dealing with wastes, such as turning Staten Island into a garbage dump. Users of the stream impose costs on the firm (and its consumers) as fully as the firm imposes costs on the users of the stream. No rearrangement of corporate governance structures can change this. The task is to establish property rights so that the firm treats the social costs as private ones, and so that its reactions, as managers try to maximize profits given these new costs, duplicate what all of the parties (downstream users and customers alike) would have agreed to were bargaining among all possible without cost. To view pollution, or investment in South Africa, or other difficult moral and social questions as *governance* matters is to miss the point.

2

Limited Liability

Limited liability is a distinguishing feature of corporate law—perhaps *the* distinguishing feature. Although partners are personally liable for the debts of the partnership, shareholders are not liable for the debts of the corporation. We have emphasized the contractual nature of corporate law, yet limited liability seems to be the antithesis of contract, a privilege bestowed on investors. In exchange for this boon, many argue, corporations should be required to submit to regulation, or do favors for customers and workers and neighbors.

Not so fast. Limited liability may be depicted as anticontractual only if it is inaccurately described. *Corporations* do not have "limited liability"; they must pay all of their debts, just as anyone else must (unless, in either event, they receive absolution in bankruptcy). To say that liability is "limited" means that the investors in the corporation are not liable for more than the amount they chip in. A person who pays $100 for stock risks that $100, but no more. A person who buys a bond for $100 or sells goods to a firm for $100 on credit risks $100, but no more. Managers and other workers are not vicariously liable for a firm's deeds. No one risks more than he invests.

Limitation of liability to the amount invested is an attribute of most investment, not just of corporate law. Debt investors in sole proprietorships, general or limited partnerships, business trusts, and other ventures possess limited liability. Suppose a bank lends $100 to a partnership, and the partnership's liabilities later exceed its assets. The bank may lose the $100, but it will not be required to contribute any extra money. Its liability is limited to its investment, exactly as the shareholder's liability is limited in a corporation. Employees and other contributors of human capital enjoy limited liability no matter the organizational form. Equity investors

40

in publicly held corporations, limited partnerships, and business trusts need not contribute extra capital if the venture fails. The instances of "unlimited" liability are few. The general partners of a partnership may be required to contribute additional capital to satisfy the association's debts. Even here, though, a discharge in bankruptcy enables the partner to limit his liability to a portion of the assets he possesses at the time the partnership requires more capital. (Some assets are exempt from attachment even in bankruptcy.) Limitations on liability turn out to be pervasive.

The distinctive aspects of the publicly held corporation—delegation of management to a diverse group of agents and risk bearing by those who contribute capital—depend on an institution like limited liability. If limited liability were not the starting point in corporate law, firms would create it by contract—which is not hard to do. Lenders may advance "nonrecourse" credit, promising (in exchange for higher interest rates) not to sue the borrower for repayment. Nonrecourse lenders are limited to the assets securing the loan, just as lenders to corporations are limited to the corporate assets. A legal rule enables firms to obtain the benefits of limited liability at lower cost.

The Rationale of Limited Liability

We begin with a discussion of the relation between the theory of the firm and limited liability. We then analyze the effect of limited liability on firms' cost of capital.

LIMITED LIABILITY AND THE THEORY OF THE FIRM

Publicly held corporations dominate other organizational forms when the technology of production requires firms to combine both the specialized skills of multiple agents and large amounts of capital. Limited liability reduces the costs of this separation and specialization of functions in a number of respects.

First, limited liability decreases the need to monitor agents. To protect themselves, investors could monitor their agents more closely. The more risk they bear, the more they will monitor. But beyond a point extra monitoring is not worth the cost. Moreover, specialized risk bearing implies that many investors will have diversified holdings. Only a small portion of their wealth will be invested in one firm. These diversified investors have neither the expertise nor the incentive to monitor the actions of specialized agents. Limited liability makes diversification and passivity a more rational strategy and so potentially reduces the cost of operating the corporation.

Second, limited liability reduces the costs of monitoring other shareholders.[1] Under a rule exposing equity investors to unlimited liability, the greater the wealth of other shareholders, the lower the probability that any one shareholder's assets will be needed to pay a judgment. Thus existing shareholders would have incentives to engage in costly monitoring of other shareholders to ensure that they do not transfer assets to others or sell to others with less wealth. Limited liability makes the identity of other shareholders irrelevant and thus avoids these costs.

Third, by promoting free transfer of shares, limited liability gives managers incentives to act efficiently. Although individual shareholders lack the expertise and incentive to monitor the actions of specialized agents, the ability of investors to sell creates opportunities for investors as a group and constrains agents' actions. As long as shares are tied to votes, poorly run firms will attract new investors who can assemble large blocs at a discount and install new managerial teams. This potential for displacement gives existing managers incentives to operate efficiently in order to keep share prices high.

With limited liability, the value of shares is set by the present value of the income stream generated by a firm's assets. The identity and wealth of other investors is irrelevant. Shares are fungible; they trade at one price in liquid markets. Under a rule of unlimited liability, shares would not be fungible. Their value would be a function of the present value of future cash flows and of the wealth of shareholders. The lack of fungibility would impede their acquisition. A person who wanted to acquire a control bloc of shares might have to negotiate separately with each shareholder, paying different prices. Worse, the purchaser in corporate control transactions typically is much wealthier than the investors from which it acquires the shares. The anticipated cost of additional capital contributions

1. See Paul J. Halpern, Michael J. Trebilcock, and Stuart Turnbull, "An Economic Analysis of Limited Liability in Corporation Law," 30 *U. Toronto L. J.* 117 (1980).

would be higher to the new holder than the old ones. This may be quite important to a buyer considering the acquisition of a firm in financial trouble, for there would be a decent chance of being required to contribute to satisfy debts if the plan for revitalization of the firm should go awry. Limited liability allows a person to buy a large bloc without taking any risk of being surcharged, and thus it facilitates beneficial control transactions. A rule that facilitates transfers of control also induces managers to work more effectively to stave off such transfers, and so it reduces the costs of specialization whether or not a firm is acquired.

Fourth, limited liability makes it possible for market prices to reflect additional information about the value of firms. With unlimited liability, shares would not be homogeneous commodities and would no longer have one market price. Investors would be required to expend greater resources analyzing the prospects of the firm in order to know whether "the price is right." When all can trade on the same terms, though, investors trade until the price of shares reflects the available information about a firm's prospects. Most investors need not expend resources searching for additional information.

Fifth, as Henry Manne has emphasized, limited liability allows more efficient diversification.[2] Investors can cut risk by owning a diversified portfolio of assets. Firms can raise capital at lower costs because investors need not bear the special risk associated with nondiversified holdings. This applies only under a rule of limited liability or some good substitute. Diversification would increase rather than reduce risk under a rule of unlimited liability. If any one firm went bankrupt, an investor could lose his entire wealth. The rational strategy under unlimited liability, therefore, would be to minimize the number of securities held. As a result, investors would be forced to bear risk that could have been avoided by diversification, and the cost to firms of raising capital would be greater.

Sixth, limited liability facilitates optimal investment decisions. When investors hold diversified portfolios, managers maximize investors' welfare by investing in any project with a positive net present value. They can accept high-variance ventures (such as the

2. See Henry J. Manne, "Our Two Corporation Systems: Law and Economics," 53 *Va. L. Rev.* 259 (1967).

development of new products) without exposing the investors to ruin. Each investor can hedge against the failure of one project by holding stock in other firms. In a world of unlimited liability, managers would behave differently. They would reject as "too risky" some projects with positive net present values. Investors would want them to do this because it would be the best way to reduce risks. By definition this would be a social loss, because projects with a positive net present value are beneficial uses of capital.

Equity investors will do about as well under one rule of liability as another. Every investor must choose between risk-free securities such as T-bills and riskier investments. The more risk comes with an equity investment, the less the investor will pay. Investors bid down the price of equity until, at the margin, the risk-adjusted returns of stock and T-bills are the same. An inefficient rule would shrink the pool of funds available for investment in projects that put investments at risk. The increased availability of funds for projects with positive net values is the real benefit of limited liability.

Limited Liability and Firms' Cost of Capital

Limited liability does not eliminate ruin, and someone must bear losses when firms fail. Limited liability is an arrangement under which the loss is swallowed rather than shifted. Each investor has a cap on the loss he will bear. In a firm with debt, that guarantee is combined with a preference for the debt holder. The shareholder is wiped out first. To this extent risk is "shifted" from debt investor to equity investor. In a regime of unlimited liability still more risk would be shifted. Because someone must bear the whole cost of business failure under any rule, some have argued that the importance of limited liability has been exaggerated.[3]

The benefit to stockholders from limited liability, the argument runs, is exactly offset by the detriment to creditors. Stockholders are more secure and so demand a lower rate of return under limited liability, but creditors demand a higher rate; the opposite is true under unlimited liability. The firm's cost of capital, the argument

3. Robert B. Ekelund, Jr., and Robert D. Tollison, "Mercantilist Origins of the Corporation," 11 *Bell J. Econ.* 715 (1980); Roger E. Meiners, James S. Mofsky, and Robert D. Tollison, "Piercing the Veil of Limited Liability," 4 *Del. J. Corp. L.* 351 (1979).

continues, is the same under either rule. But this argument depends on an assumption that risk is borne equally well by creditors and stockholders, and several aspects of this assumption must be examined.

The extent of common interests. The argument that firms' cost of capital does not vary with the liability rule depends on the assumption that the benefit to stockholders from limited liability is exactly offset by the detriment to creditors. This assumption is false, for the reasons developed already.

Consider, for example, the relation between limited liability and monitoring by outsiders. The threat of takeovers (and other control transactions) induces managers to keep share prices up. Outside monitors' effects on creditors are less clear. Managers who pursue an overly conservative investment strategy that benefits creditors but does not maximize the value of the firm may be ousted by the board, in a proxy contest or a takeover. Some of these transitions thus must make creditors worse off *ex post*. But as long as takeovers increase the probability that the value of firms' assets will be maximized, shareholders and creditors, joint claimants to a bigger pie, will be better off. Thus a regime including involuntary changes of control benefits creditors as well as shareholders.

Relative monitoring costs. Under limited liability shareholders have less reason to incur costs in monitoring managers and other shareholders than they do under unlimited liability. The decreased incentive to monitor managers arguably is offset by the increased incentive of creditors to monitor managers' actions. But this will not happen because of the preference among the investors. Because equity investors lose their investments first, they have a greater interest in monitoring the firm. Indeed, this intra-investor preference is an important ingredient in a system of optimal monitoring. Concentrating the entire marginal gain and loss on one group of investors induces them to make the appropriate expenditures on monitoring (or to sell to someone who will), while enabling the more secure investors to avoid making redundant expenditures. The secured creditor has the safest claim of all and may elect to monitor only the state of its security rather than the state of the whole firm. Secured debt thus may be a way of reducing monitoring costs still further.

So debt claimants do not increase their monitoring of managers to offset shareholders' reductions exactly. Moreover, debt investors do not incur costs that offset the reduction of intra-shareholder monitoring under limited liability. The wealth of other creditors is irrelevant whether or not shareholders possess limited liability, because creditors possess limited liability under either rule. Monitoring costs are lower when both shareholders and creditors possess limited liability than when only creditors do.

Relative information and coordination costs. Another reason why shareholders pay creditors to assume more of the risk of business failure might be that the creditors possess a comparative advantage in monitoring particular managerial actions. Individual shareholders, as specialized suppliers of capital, do not actively monitor managers' actions. They rely on third parties (such as large institutional holders or prospective contestants for control) to do so and buy shares at appropriate moments. Although the debt investors do not have the residual claim, and thus do not have optimal incentives to monitor day-to-day activities, they may be especially well suited to watch certain kinds of conduct.

Banks and other institutional investors tend to have specialized knowledge about particular industries and may be good monitors of major decisions such as whether to build new plants. The lender may provide financing to several firms in an industry and thus augment this knowledge. These debt investors commonly negotiate detailed contracts giving them the right to disapprove managers' decisions that are important enough to create significant new risk for the firm, though perhaps not important enough to spark a contest for control.

Contractual powers are the least of creditors' tools, however. The greatest is the obligation to repay. Equity investors are in for the duration. Debt must be repaid, on schedule, or the creditors get control. Creditors may insist on short repayment schedules by charging higher interest rates for longer schedules. Firms obliged to repay their creditors must find new money to carry on their activities. Back in the credit market, they must submit to scrutiny of their business plans; they must pay the rate of interest appropriate to the risk they incur. Adjustments in the interest rate not only compensate creditors but also raise the firms' costs of capital if its operations are subpar. The mandatory-payout feature of debt facilitates this constant monitoring and repricing of the firm's ventures.

Differential coordination costs also account for some debt financing. Compare the situation of a sophisticated shareholder with that of a sophisticated creditor (or the indenture trustee for a group of creditors). Even if the sophisticated shareholder has the ability to monitor, he has little incentive to do so. He bears all the costs, but the benefits accrue to all other shareholders according to the size of their holdings. The creditor, by contrast, captures more of the benefits of his monitoring activity, because there are fewer other members of the same class of investor. When there are many creditors of the same class, and the debt is long-term, the indenture trustee is the response to the free-rider problem. When creditors have lower coordination and information costs than shareholders, limited liability has a clear advantage. Because creditors bear more of the risk of business failure under a rule of limited liability, they have more incentive to employ their knowledge.

Attitudes toward risk. Both equity and debt investors can diversify their holdings, minimizing the risk of investing in any one firm. Economy-wide (systematic) risk, however, cannot be eliminated by diversification. Where two parties are risk-averse, the optimal contractual arrangement is one in which each bears some risk. Limited liability is such a risk-sharing arrangement. Under limited liability, both shareholders and creditors risk the loss of their investments; under unlimited liability, shareholders would bear almost all risk.

INSURANCE AS AN ALTERNATIVE TO LIMITED LIABILITY

The advantages of limited liability suggest that, if it did not exist, firms would attempt to invent it. One close substitute is insurance. If firms could purchase "failure insurance" to cover their liabilities to debt investors, the firms' structure would be much the same as now. Shareholders' liability would be limited to the amount of their investment; creditors would receive a lower rate of return because of their greater security. Why do we see limited liability rather than insurance against bankruptcy?

For one thing, the transaction costs of shareholders' individually purchasing insurance are prohibitive. Each shareholder would have to negotiate with the insurer. The insurer would have to monitor the wealth of each insured and all other shareholders to assess the riskiness of its own position. There must be (and is) a cheaper way: the firm could buy insurance for investors as a group. Who sells insurance to the firm? Specialized insurers are only one option; the firm's creditors are another, and potentially cheaper, source of insurance.

Creditors might have a comparative advantage in assessing the riskiness of a transaction initially and superior ability to monitor the conduct of the firm for the duration of the agreement—particularly to prevent the increased risk taking that is an effect of all insurance. In other words, the firm would buy its insurance from the creditors. This is essentially what we observe. The creditors assume some risks of business failure, just as they would if they were "insurers" as well as creditors. The legal rule of limited liability is a shortcut to this position, avoiding the costs of separate transactions.

One advantage of purchasing insurance from separate insurers is that some of the free-rider problems that confront groups of creditors are avoided. Third-party insurers might have superior ability to monitor. Firms obtain insurance from the cheapest insurer regardless of the legal rule. Corporations commonly purchase insurance against fire, liability in tort, and other hazards despite the existence of limited liability. But if third-party insurers frequently had a comparative advantage in bearing risk, we would expect to see corporate "failure insurance" commonly used. The debt investors would pay the firm to secure such insurance, receiving lower risk in return. We do not see such transactions.

In light of the ability of firms to duplicate or at least approximate either limited or unlimited liability by contract, does the legal rule of limited liability matter? The answer is yes, but probably not much—not today, anyway. (We do not doubt that limited liability played a greater role in the growth of the publicly held corporation in the nineteenth century when insurance markets were less well developed.) Under the plausible assumption that creditors often are the most efficient risk bearers, a rule of limited liability economizes on transaction costs by eliminating the need for individual negotiations with every creditor. But limited liability will not cause a corresponding increase in the number of transactions with third-party insurers. Such transactions will occur whenever third parties are the cheapest insurers, no matter what the legal rule.

Limited liability also makes a difference if the firm would purchase inadequate insurance or if insurance would not be available in a competitive market. It is hard to imagine, for example, a market for insurance against all bankruptcy. Bankruptcies may be caused by economy-wide events against which the insurer cannot diversify. Moreover, complete bankruptcy insurance creates a moral hazard; it invites managers to take excessive risks. Both equity and debt investors would stop monitoring the managers, and insurers are not likely to provide optimal monitoring in the face of this moral hazard. Without complete bankruptcy insurance, some group must bear the risk of business failure. If shareholders bear all, the problems of unlimited liability reappear; if creditors share risk, the situation is identical to the rule of limited liability.

Bankruptcy raises a more general problem with insurance as an alternative to limited liability—who will insure the insurer? If insurers assume the risk of business failure, unpaid claims of the insured firms could exceed the capital of the insurer. This risk must be borne by someone. Shareholders of insurance companies might have unlimited liability, but this could inhibit the formation of large insurers, exacerbating the problem. Alternatively, both shareholders and creditors of the insured firm could bear the risk, and the same analysis would govern whether limited or unlimited liability is the superior arrangement.

In sum, the problem all along has been: is it better to allow losses to lie where they fall or to try to shift those losses to some other risk bearer? This is an empirical question. The market's answer is partial risk shifting. Equity investors bear more risk than debt investors, but debt investors continue to bear substantial risk, and the risk of all investors is limited to the amount they contribute at the outset. This arrangement has substantial survival value. If greater risk shifting were beneficial, we would have seen it evolve in the market. It is no answer to say that transaction costs are high, so the evidence from survival is ambiguous. It is easy to make contracts governing stockholders' liability. Lenders to close corporations commonly require personal guarantees by investors or other modifications of limited liability. We discuss later why they do so. For now the point is that if people frequently contract around limited liability for the smallest firms, it is impossible to attribute the failure to do likewise for larger firms to transaction costs. The survival of limited liability is indeed highly informative.

Limited Liability and the Externalization of Risk

Because limited liability increases the probability that there will be insufficient assets to pay creditors' claims, shareholders of a firm reap all of the benefits of risky activities but do not bear all of the costs. These are borne in part by creditors. Critics of limited liability have focused on this moral hazard—the incentive created by limited liability to transfer the cost of risky activities to creditors—as a justification for substantial modification of the doctrine.[4]

Externalization of risk imposes social costs and thus is undesirable. The implications of this point, however, are unclear, both because modifying limited liability has its costs and because moral hazard would exist without limited liability. The social loss from reducing investment in certain types of projects—a consequence of seriously modifying limited liability—might far exceed the gains from reducing moral hazard. Too, even the abolition of limited liability would not eliminate the moral hazard problem. The incentive to engage in overly risky activities exists whenever a person or firm has insufficient assets to cover its expected liabilities. Although the problem of moral hazard may be more severe under limited liability, it exists under any rule. The magnitude of these gains and losses is an empirical matter on which the dominance of limited liability—when it is simple to pass greater risks to equity investors by contract—speaks eloquently.

At all events, the magnitude of the externality under limited liability has been exaggerated. As Richard Posner has demonstrated, there is no externality with respect to voluntary creditors.[5] In addition, firms have incentives to insure for amounts greater than their existing capital. The insurance company becomes a contract creditor, reducing the externality.

LIMITED LIABILITY AND VOLUNTARY CREDITORS

Employees, consumers, trade creditors, and lenders are voluntary creditors. The compensation they demand will be a function of the risk they face. One risk is the possibility of nonpayment because of limited liability. Another is the prospect, common to all debtor-creditor relations, that after the terms of the transaction are set the debtor will take increased risk, to the detriment of the lender.

4. See, for example, Jonathan Landers, "A Unified Approach to Parent, Subsidiary, and Affiliate Questions in Bankruptcy," 42 *U. Chi. L. Rev.* 589 (1975); Christopher D. Stone, "The Place of Enterprise Liability in the Control of Corporate Conduct," 90 *Yale L. J.* 1, 65–76 (1980).

5. Richard A. Posner, "The Rights of Creditors of Affiliated Corporations," 43 *U. Chi. L. Rev.* 499 (1976).

As long as these risks are known, the firm pays for the freedom to engage in risky activities. Any creditor can get the risk-free rate by investing in T-bills or some low-risk substitute. The firm must offer a better risk-return combination to attract investment. If it cannot make credible promises to refrain from taking excessive risks, it must pay higher interest rates (or, when the creditors are employees and trade creditors, higher prices for the work or goods delivered on credit). Although managers may change the riskiness of the firm after borrowing, debt must be repaid; this drives the firm back to the credit market, where it must pay a rate of interest appropriate to the soundness and risk of its current projects. There is no "externality" except in the last period—that is, the time after which the firm no longer contemplates raising new money in capital markets. Then, and only then, may the firm take risk for which it has not paid. And even then, the firm has paid for the *privilege* of being in the position. Voluntary creditors receive compensation in advance for the chance that the firm will step up the risk of its projects and later be unable to meet its obligations.

Equity investors and managers have incentives to make arrangements that reduce risk and thus reduce the premium they must pay to debt claimants. Bond indentures, which commonly contain detailed provisions limiting the ability of the firm to engage in conduct to the detriment of creditors, are one method of reducing this premium.

If the compensation that must be paid to third parties for engaging in a particular activity exceeds the benefits to the firm, the activity will not be undertaken under a rule of either limited or unlimited liability. This is a simple application of the Coase Theorem. The optimal amount of risk is not zero, though. Managers will take steps to reduce risk only as long as the gains from risk reduction exceed the costs.

The incentive to take optimal precautions against increases in risk does not depend on all voluntary creditors having perfect information. In certain cases, the actions of informed actors will result in the appropriate risk premium being charged. For example, risks created by a firm's activities may be understood by an indenture trustee or a union even if not by individual bondholders or workers. If the risk premium is correctly set, it is irrelevant whether each voluntary creditor is informed. Each is protected by the market price. And so long as the firm must pay the correct risk premium, it has no incentive to engage in excessively risky conduct.

Sometimes, though, no voluntary creditor will have sufficient information or incentive to assess risk correctly or monitor the acquisition of debt. This might lead voluntary creditors to charge a risk premium that is prohibitively high, because they will equate their inability to monitor with a belief that firms will take too much risk. It is in precisely these situations, however, that firms have incentives to insure against hazards such as large tort judgments or the structural failure of their machinery. By contracting with a superior monitor (a more efficient insurer), the firm reduces the risk premium it must pay. The insurer, in turn, may use its superior monitoring ability to induce the firm to internalize the costs of its risky activities. Our point is not that limited liability never yields a socially excessive amount of risk taking. Rather, it is unlikely that any rule will lead to systematically excessive risk taking; indeed, it is unlikely that the legal rule will matter much at all.

Limited liability's greatest effect is on the probability that any given creditor will be paid *ex post*. Even if firms pay for engaging in risky activities, and thus take the right precautions, creditors of failed businesses are less likely to receive full compensation under a rule of limited liability. This is not an "argument" against limited liability, however, unless distributional concerns dominate. There is little role for distributional arguments when all of the parties are in privity, for they can strike their own bargains and are apt to contract around any unwelcome rule purportedly designed for their benefit. More to the point, they can choose to hold, under any rule, a different proportion of debt and equity, which alters the risk. At all events, first-party insurance makes distributional concerns much less serious than they might at first appear. The ability of potential victims to protect themselves against loss through insurance is a strong reason for disregarding distributional concerns in choosing among liability rules.

INVOLUNTARY CREDITORS AND CORPORATIONS' INCENTIVES TO INSURE

When corporations must pay for the right to engage in risky activities, they undertake projects only where social benefits equal social costs at the margin. Where high transactions costs prohibit those affected by risky activities from charging an appropriate risk premium, however, the probability that firms with limited liability will undertake projects with too much risk increases. Firms capture the benefits from such activities while bearing only some of the costs; other costs are shifted to involuntary creditors. This is a real cost of limited liability, but its magnitude is reduced by corporations' incentives to insure.

The common explanation for insurance is risk aversion. A risk-averse person may be willing to pay a known insurance premium to eliminate the possibility of a large, uncertain loss, even though the premium exceeds the expected value of the loss. By pooling unregulated risks, the insurer can diversify. A completely diversified insurer is risk-neutral. Insurance enables those who are risk-averse to pay risk-neutral parties to bear risk.

Corporate purchase of insurance seems inconsistent with this explanation. Investors can diversify, which is a cheap way to reduce risk. Limited liability facilitates this diversification. Thus investors should not be willing to pay insurers to reduce risk. Why buy something you already have for free?

But not all who enter into contracts with a firm have the same ability to minimize risk by diversification. Human capital, for example, is notoriously difficult to diversify. Managers who have firm-specific investments of human capital cannot diversify the risk of business failure. To the contrary, investors want managers' fortunes tied to the fate of the firms under their control, and so they induce managers to bear extra costs if these firms fail, and they offer disproportionate rewards for success. The possibility of bankruptcy also represents a real cost to those with firm-specific investments of human capital, and firms must compensate those who bear this risk. The purchase of insurance in amounts greater than the amount of the firm's capital is one method of reducing the amount that the firm must pay. A firm with insurance against tort claims is less likely to become bankrupt, and thus less likely to impose costs on managers and other employees. Insurance thus induces people to make firm-specific investments of human capital.

Whether the purchase of insurance in amounts greater than the size of the firm's capital will reduce the incentive to engage in overly risky activities is a complex question. Before purchasing insurance, the firm's investors have the full amount of their investment at risk. After the purchase, the investors have much less at risk—in the limit, none. The insurance company now bears the risk of business failure caused by tortious conduct. Insurance then might be thought to reduce the managers' incentives to take care, incentives already too low because of the existence of limited liability. The purchase of insurance has the effect, however, of creating a contract creditor where none may have existed before. The insured corporation must pay (through higher premiums) for engaging in risky activities. Because the firm now bears the costs of engaging in risky projects, it equates social benefits and costs when making investment decisions.

Our argument is not that firms' incentive to purchase insurance eliminates the possibility that firms will engage in excessively risky activities. There may well be situations where firms will decide not to insure even if insurance is available. If potential losses are extremely large, the premium paid to risk-averse managers with firm-specific investments of human capital to compensate them for bearing the risk of bankruptcy might be less than the premium that would have to be paid to the insurance company. In other words, the limited liability of the manager (particularly in a world where discharge in bankruptcy is available) coupled with the limited liability of the firm may cause firms faced with large expected liabilities to involuntary creditors to pay managers a premium and simultaneously decrease their capitalization. Moreover, there is no guarantee that insurance will be offered if risks are highly correlated. Even when offered, the insurance will exclude very large losses. Nevertheless, our discussion of firms' incentives to insure suggests that firms will insure in some situations where people and partnerships would not. A corporation with a fleet of trucks might insure for an amount in excess of its capital, for example, while an individual owner with few assets might insure for a small amount or not insure at all.

Piercing the Corporate Veil

Courts sometimes allow creditors to reach the assets of shareholders. The legal basis for this is obscure. State laws typically say that limited liability is absolute.[6] Moreover, the nominal tests used

6. See, for instance, 8 Del. Code §152 (stock is "fully paid and nonassessable" once paid for in cash); §162 (investor's liability on partially paid-for shares is limited to the balance of the agreed consideration); see also American Bar Association,

by courts—whether a corporation has a "separate mind of its own," whether it is a "mere instrumentality," and so forth—are singularly unhelpful.[7] Arbitrariness of these nominal tests implies lack of basis or function.

We conclude, however, that the doctrine of piercing the corporate veil, and the distinctions drawn by courts, makes more economic sense than at first appears. The cases may be understood, at least roughly, as attempts to balance the benefits of limited liability against its costs. Courts are more likely to allow creditors to reach the assets of shareholders where limited liability provides minimal gains from improved liquidity and diversification, while creating a high probability that a firm will engage in a socially excessive level of risk taking.

CLOSE VERSUS PUBLIC CORPORATIONS

Almost every case in which a court has allowed creditors to reach the assets of shareholders has involved a close corporation.[8] The distinction between close and public corporations is supported by economic logic. In close corporations (which we discuss at length in Chapter 9), there is much less separation between management and risk bearing. This has profound implications for the role of limited liability. Because those who supply capital in close corpora-

---

Model Business Corporation Act §6.22(b) (rev. 1984) ("Unless otherwise provided in the articles of incorporation, a shareholder is not personally liable for the acts or debts of the corporation except that he may become personally liable by reason of his own acts or conduct").

7. See generally Philip I. Blumberg, *The Law of Corporate Groups: Tort, Contract, and Other Common Law Problems in the Substantive Law of Parent and Subsidiary Corporations* §6.01 (1987); Secon Service System, Inc. v. St. Joseph Bank & Trust Co., 855 F.2d 406, 413–416 (7th Cir. 1988).

8. We say "almost every" only because we have not examined them all. The famous cases where piercing was an issue all involve close corporations. See Minton v. Cavaney, 56 Cal. 2d 576, 364 P.2d 473, 15 Cal. Rptr. 641 (1961); Walkovsky v. Carlton, 18 N.Y.2d 414, 223 N.E.2d 6, 276 N.Y.S.2d 585 (1966); Bartle v. Home Owners Cooperative, Inc., 309 N.Y. 103, 127 N.E.2d 832 (1955). Which is not to say that investors' liability is common even when the corporation and the manager are scarcely distinguishable. There is no reason to disregard a "shell" corporation in favor of a creditor that can negotiate for such protection as it desires. Courts routinely enforce limited liability in such cases: see Brunswick Corp. v. Waxman, 599 F.2d 34 (2d Cir. 1979).

tions typically are also involved in decision making, limited liability does not reduce monitoring costs. Other benefits of limited liability in public corporations—facilitating efficient risk bearing and monitoring by the capital market—also are absent in close corporations. Because those who contribute capital often manage, diversification is much less important in close corporations. Similarly, close corporations restrict the transfer of their shares to ensure that those who invest will be compatible with existing decision makers. Takeover bids are impossible; they are not needed because the management and risk-bearing functions are united.

Moreover, managers' incentive to undertake overly risky projects is greater in close corporations. Whatever the liability rule, managers of publicly held corporations do not bear all of the costs of their actions. There are many managers, and each owns but a small fraction of the firm's shares. This is not necessarily true in close corporations. Under a rule of unlimited liability, investor-managers bear all of the costs of their actions. Under a rule of absolutely limited liability, by contrast, investor-managers can limit their risk to the amount of capital in the corporate treasury and transfer more of the risk to third parties. Piercing the veil—especially in favor of trade and tort creditors who cannot negotiate with the firm—reduces the extent to which third parties bear these costs.

CORPORATE VERSUS PERSONAL SHAREHOLDERS

The other major category of piercing cases involves parent-subsidiary combinations, where creditors of the subsidiary attempt to reach assets of the parent.[9] Courts' greater willingness to allow creditors to reach the assets of corporate as opposed to personal shareholders is again consistent with economic principles.

Allowing creditors to reach the assets of parent corporations does not create unlimited liability for any investor. Thus the benefits of diversification, liquidity, and monitoring by the capital market are unaffected. Moreover, the moral-hazard problem is

9. See William P. Hackney and Tracey G. Bensen, "Shareholder Liability for Inadequate Capital," 43 *U. Pitt. L. Rev.* 837, 873 (1982) (citing cases for the proposition that courts are more willing to disregard the entity of a subsidiary corporation than one owned by one or more individuals); see also Robert W. Hamilton, "The Corporate Entity," 49 *Tex. L. Rev.* 979, 992 (1971).

probably greater in parent-subsidiary situations because subsidiaries have less incentive to insure. In publicly held corporations, the inability of managers to diversify their firm-specific investments in human capital creates incentives to insure. The same is not true for managers of subsidiaries if, as often will be the case, they are also managers of the parent. Bankruptcy of the subsidiary will not cause them to lose their positions in the parent or suffer any other loss of firm-specific human capital (though they might suffer a reputational loss). If limited liability is absolute, a parent can form a subsidiary with minimal capitalization for the purpose of engaging in risky activities. If things go well, the parent captures the benefits. If things go poorly, the subsidiary declares bankruptcy, and the parent creates another with the same managers to engage in the same activities. This asymmetry between the benefits and costs, if limited liability were absolute, would create incentives to engage in a socially excessive amount of risky activities.

It does not follow that parent and affiliate corporations routinely should be liable for the debts of those in which they hold stock. Far from it. Such general liability would give small or unaffiliated firms a competitive advantage.[10] Think of the taxicab business. Taxi firms may incorporate each cab or put just a few cabs in a firm. If courts routinely disregarded this arrangement and put the assets of the full venture at risk for the accidents of each cab, then "true" single-cab firms would have lower costs of operation because they alone could cut off liability. That would create a perverse incentive because, as we have emphasized, larger firms are apt to carry more insurance. Potential victims of torts would not gain from a legal rule that promoted corporate disintegration. Moreover, requiring a corporation to satisfy claims against its affiliate would induce creditors of each firm to monitor the others, squandering the benefits of creditors as specialized monitors of assets or projects. (This is parallel to the effect unlimited liability would have in inducing shareholders to monitor one another's wealth.) As a result, courts properly disregard the corporate form rarely: only when the corporate arrangement has increased risks over what they would be if firms generally were organized as separate ventures.

10. A proposition demonstrated formally by Jack L. Carr and G. Frank Mathewson, "Unlimited Liability as a Barrier to Entry," 96 *J. Pol. Econ.* 766 (1988), whose model incorporates effects of unlimited liability on monitoring of managers as well as size of firm.

CONTRACTS VERSUS TORTS, AND THE FRAUD OR MISREPRESENTATION EXCEPTION

Courts are more willing to disregard the corporate veil in tort than in contract cases.[11] The rationale for this distinction follows directly from the economics of moral hazard—where corporations must pay for the risk faced by creditors as a result of limited liability, they are less likely to engage in activities with social costs that exceed their social benefits. Contract creditors, in other words, are compensated *ex ante* for the increased risk of default *ex post*. Tort creditors, by contrast, are not compensated except to the extent that the prices of the firms' products adjust.

This distinction between contract and tort creditors breaks down when the debtor engages in fraud or misrepresentation. For the costs of excessive risk taking to be fully internalized, creditors must be able to assess the risk of default accurately. If the creditor is misled into believing that the risk of default is lower than it actually is, the creditor will not demand adequate compensation. This will lead to an excessive amount of risk taking by firms, because some of the costs will be shifted to creditors.

Courts respond to this problem by allowing creditors to go beyond the assets of the corporation in cases of fraud or misrepresentation.[12] The problem can arise in a variety of ways. The most obvious occurs when a corporation misrepresents the nature of its activities, its ability to perform, or its financial condition. Less obvious situations crop up when a firm misleads a creditor into believing that it would have recourse to the assets of other corporations in the event of nonperformance. This could occur if managers make express statements that a parent corporation will stand behind the debts of a subsidiary or if the parent and the subsidiary have confusingly similar names, so that the creditor believes it is dealing with the parent. In all these situations, creditors are unable

11. The difference in judicial treatment of contract and tort cases was noticed at least as early as William O. Douglas and Carrol M. Shanks, "Insulation from Liability through Subsidiary Corporations," 39 *Yale L. J.* 193, 210–211 (1929). Blumberg, supra note 7, supplies a contemporary exposition. For a recent case emphasizing the distinctions, see Edwards v. Monogram Indus., 730 F.2d 977, 980–984 (5th Cir. 1984) (in banc).

12. See Cathy S. Krendl and James R. Krendl, "Piercing the Corporate Veil: Focusing the Inquiry," 55 *Den. L. J.* 1, 31–34 (1978), and Blumberg, supra note 7, both of which compile cases.

to assess the risk of default accurately, and thus the probability that the firm will engage in excessively risky activities is increased.

UNDERCAPITALIZATION

A final factor commonly emphasized by courts in deciding whether to allow creditors to go beyond the corporation's assets is the extent of the firm's capitalization. Again the reason is clear: the lower the amount of the firm's capital, the greater the incentive to engage in excessively risky activities.

The extent of a firm's capitalization is most important in situations involving involuntary creditors, where high transactions costs preclude negotiation. But undercapitalization can also be relevant in situations involving voluntary creditors. Many credit transactions are too small to warrant a full investigation of the debtor's finances by the creditor. Someone who sells the firm a chair on thirty days' credit is not going to engage in detailed negotiations about risk and security. In these situations, it is desirable that creditors be able to assume that the debtor is adequately capitalized. The firm should have a duty to notify the creditor of any unusual capitalization. It is cheaper for the firm (which has the best information about its capital structure) to notify creditors in the unusual case than for creditors to investigate in all cases. (By "adequately" capitalized we mean an amount of equity that is within the ordinary range for the business in question. Both the absolute level of equity investment and the debt-equity ratio will depend on the kind of business on which the firm is embarked.)

Allowing creditors to look beyond the assets of the undercapitalized corporate debtor provides the debtor with the incentive to disclose its situation at the time of the transaction. The creditor then can decide not to transact or charge increased compensation for the increased risk. Alternatively, the creditor could ask for prepayment, personal guarantees, or other security. Under any of these alternatives, the debtor will have to pay for engaging in risky activities and thus will have better incentives to balance social benefits and costs.[13]

___

13. Though our discussion is addressed to "piercing," the same considerations apply to equitable subordination, a doctrine under which insiders' debt paper may be subordinated to the debt claims of trade creditors and others who did not have actual knowledge of the nature of the insiders' claims. A thinly capitalized firm ex-

Alternative Methods for Reducing Moral Hazard

Piercing the corporate veil is one of several methods for decreasing the incentive created by limited liability to engage in overly risky activities. We briefly look at the costs and benefits of four other methods of decreasing this risk: minimum-capital requirements, mandatory insurance, managerial liability, and regulation of inputs. Our discussion is general and descriptive. A normative analysis would require data, not currently available, on the size of the externality created by limited liability and the net effects of regulatory attempts to reduce it.

The lower a firm's capitalization, the higher the probability that it will engage in excessively risky activities. Legislatively imposed minimum-capitalization requirements are one method of internalizing the costs of risk taking. But such regulations have problems of their own. One is the obvious administrative cost associated with determining what amount of capital firms should raise. Another is the cost of error. If capital requirements are set too high, this will impede new entry and permit the existing firms to charge monopoly prices. Still another is the question of how firms must satisfy their capitalization requirements. For such requirements to be effective, the corporation must post a bond equal to its highest expected liability or hold sufficient funds in the corporate treasury and invest them in risk-free assets. The total held in this way will far exceed the expected risk created by firms as a group (because not all firms go bankrupt or incur the maximum possible loss). Under either alternative, the rate of return on equity investments will decrease. Thus at the margin people will shift capital away from equity investment in risky industries. This too represents a social cost.

Mandatory-insurance requirements are similar in some respects

---

poses trade creditors to unsuspected risks, and the doctrine of equitable subordination induces the insiders to make unusual patterns of equity and debt claims known. See Costello v. Fazio, 256 F.2d 903 (9th Cir. 1958); Robert Charles Clark, "The Duties of the Corporate Debtor to Its Creditors," 90 *Harv. L. Rev.* 505 (1977). Subordination should be handled as an implied term in the debt contract, not as a special rule of bankruptcy. See Thomas H. Jackson, "Translating Assets and Liabilities to the Bankruptcy Forum," 14 *J. Legal Stud.* 73, 86–87 (1985); cf. Taylor v. Standard Gas & Elec. Co., 306 U.S. 307 (1939) (holding that bankruptcy statute compelled subordination of parent company's claims against subsidiary, but suggesting that such a result would also follow from broader equitable principles).

to minimum-capitalization requirements. Both involve administrative costs and may act as barriers to entry. Whether mandatory insurance poses a greater barrier to entry is difficult to determine. New firms, with less experience than existing ones, have higher risks, from an insurer's standpoint, and must therefore pay higher premiums. These may be less than the cost of self-insurance, in which case mandatory insurance facilitates entry. Yet some firms, particularly new ones, might find it difficult to obtain insurance at all. The effect of mandatory insurance on new firms, therefore, might be greater than minimum-capitalization requirements.

One important difference between the two regimes is the effect each has on firms' incentives to engage in excessively risky activities. Minimum-capitalization requirements decrease this incentive. Mandatory-insurance requirements, by contrast, may increase or decrease the level of risky activities, depending on insurers' ability to monitor. Where the insurer is unable to monitor, the level of risky activities will increase because of the moral hazard that accompanies insurance. This is a problem, for example, in the market for automobile insurance. State laws frequently require insurance companies to issue insurance to poor drivers (the assigned risk pool) and forbid the setting of rates that would price these drivers out of the market. Mandatory insurance of other activities may have the same sorts of problems.

One method of minimizing the incentive to engage in overly risky activities while avoiding the administrative costs of minimum-capitalization requirements or mandatory insurance is to impose liability on managers as well as enterprises. Managerial liability is an additional risk for which firms must compensate the managers. From the firm's perspective, however, there are problems with paying managers for bearing risk. Because of their inability to diversify their human capital, managers are inefficient risk bearers. Thus firms have incentives to undo managerial liability by providing managers with indemnification or insurance.

This risk shifting does not, however, defeat the purpose of managerial liability. If only the firm may be held liable, the value-maximizing strategy for a firm with few firm-specific investments of human capital may well be to maintain assets less than expected liabilities. If managers may also be held liable, they have incentives to monitor the firm's capitalization and insurance, because they bear the cost of incomplete risk shifting. Thus the value-maximizing strategy under managerial liability is for firms to self-insure by increasing their capitalization or purchase insurance, whichever is cheaper. In either case, the incentive to engage in overly risky activities goes down.

The problem with managerial liability is that risk shifting may not work perfectly. It is unlikely, for example, that managers who are liable for mass torts, with mammoth but uncertain expected liabilities, could shift all of this risk. Because of the huge amounts involved and the difficulty of monitoring, insurers are unwilling to assume the highest possible expected liability. To the extent that risk is not completely shifted, a legal rule of managerial liability creates risk for a group with a comparative disadvantage in bearing that risk. This inefficiency leads to both an increase in the competitive wage for managers and a shift away from risky activities. And there is no guarantee that the social costs of this shift away from risky activities will not exceed the social costs of the excessively risky activities in the absence of managerial liability.

A final method of reducing the incentive to engage in overly risky activities created by limited liability is the regulation of inputs. The regulation of nuclear power plants, for example, could be justified as a response to the perverse incentives created by limited liability. Again, however, there are costs associated with direct regulation of risk taking. Regulators have no better incentives than market participants to balance the social costs and benefits of engaging in certain activities. Indeed the economic theory of regulation suggests that many regulatory schemes arise in order to create, rather than eliminate, "defects" in markets. Thus the regulation of nuclear power plants may have the purpose and effect of shielding other types of energy producers from competition rather than eliminating perverse incentives created by limited liability. Whether the social costs of regulation exceed the social costs of excessively risky activities is an empirical question. The desirability of regulation cannot be established simply by identifying the potential incentive to engage in overly risky activities created by limited liability.

3

Voting

If limited liability is the most distinctive feature of corporate law, voting is second. Shareholders elect a board, which chooses managers; shareholders can recall the directors and fundamentally alter the way the corporation runs. Creditors have no similar powers. Votes may not look much like contracts, but the *structure* of voting—who votes, using what institutions—is contractual, and efficient too.

Why Do Shareholders Vote?

"Why do shareholders vote?" is three questions in one. First, why do any investors have voting rights? Second, why do shareholders alone have voting rights? Third, why do shareholders exercise their voting rights? Our concern in this chapter is with publicly held corporations. We discuss voting in closely held corporations in Chapter 9.

RULES AND PRACTICES

Most states allow firms to establish almost any voting practices they please. For example, Delaware permits firms to give shares any number of votes (including none) and to give votes to bondholders in addition to (or instead of) shareholders.[1] The votes may cumulate or not, at the option of the firm. (Cumulative voting permits shareholders to cast multiple votes for a single candidate, so that a candidate may be elected by less than a majority of the shares.)[2] Investors may vote in person or by proxy. They may

1. 8 Del. Code §§151(a), 221.
2. 8 Del. Code §§102(b)(3), 214.

choose managers directly or through the mediation of a board of directors.[3] They may permit directors (or managers) to serve full terms or may oust them for any or no reason in midterm.[4] The necessary quorum may be set at less than half of the votes, and the firm may require supermajority approval on selected questions.[5] Any of these rules may be set or altered at any time by those with power to vote. The situation is much the same in other states.[6] Although different states create different presumptive rules (for example, votes may be cumulative unless provided otherwise), this does not detract from the status of the enactments as enabling statutes.

There are nonetheless recognizable patterns in corporate choice under these states. Almost all shares have one vote, and only shares possess votes. Preferred stock or bonds may acquire votes when the firm is in financial difficulty. Cumulative voting is rare in publicly held corporations, as is nonvoting stock or stock with seriously limited voting rights.[7] Shareholders rarely select managers; they instead select boards of directors, which in turn choose managers. There are no special elections between the scheduled

3. 8 Del. Code §§102(b)(1), 109(b), 141(a) & (f), 228(a).

4. 8 Del. Code §141(k). The only exception concerns directors elected by a minority of shares with cumulative voting. These directors may be fired only for good reasons or by a majority large enough to have prevented their election initially.

5. 8 Del. Code §216.

6. See American Bar Association, *Model Business Corporation Act* ch. 7 (rev. 1984), which a majority of states follow.

7. A few firms have multiple classes of common stock with different voting rights. For an analysis of this voting structure, see Daniel R. Fischel, "Organized Exchanges and the Regulation of Dual Class Common Stock," 54 *U. Chi. L. Rev.* 119 (1987). See also Gregg A. Jarrell and Annette B. Poulson, "Dual-Class Recapitalizations as Antitakeover Mechanisms: The Recent Evidence," 20 *J. Fin. Econ.* 129 (1988); Richard S. Ruback, "Coercive Dual-Class Exchange Offers," ibid. at 153; Kenneth Lehn, Jeffry Netter, and Annette Poulson, "Consolidating Corporate Control: The Choice between Dual-Class Recapitalizations and Leveraged Buyouts," 26 *J. Fin. Econ.* (1991). The volume of legal literature on stock with different voting rights outstrips the significance of the phenomenon. See Ronald J. Gilson, "Evaluating Dual Class Common Stock: The Relevance of Substitutes," 73 *Va. L. Rev.* 807 (1987); Jeffrey N. Gordon, "Ties That Bond: Dual Class Common Stock and the Problem of Shareholder Choice," 76 *Cal. L. Rev.* 1 (1988); Joel Seligman, "Equal Protection in Shareholder Voting Rights: The One Common Share, One Vote Controversy," 54 *Geo. Wash. L. Rev.* 687 (1986); George W. Dent, Jr., "Dual Class Capitalization: A Reply to Professor Seligman," ibid. at 725.

yearly ones; directors are not recalled from office. Shareholders vote by proxy, not in person, and elect the slate of candidates proposed by the incumbents. The quorum is half of the available votes, and issues are decided by a majority of the votes cast. Exceptions to these practices are infrequent.

A number of statutory rules limit the ability of firms to create the voting structures they prefer. For example, although investors may transfer their votes by selling the instruments to which votes are attached, they may not sell the vote independent of the instrument.[8] Statutes control evasion of the no-sale rule by limiting the ability of shareholders to grant irrevocable proxies. A proxy—that is, the voter's grant of authority to someone else to cast his votes— is revocable by the grant of a new proxy to someone else; even a proxy purporting to be irrevocable is binding only if coupled with an "interest" in the stock, such as a pledge to secure a loan.[9] The voting trust—a form of irrevocable proxy in which several shareholders convey their shares and the attached votes to a trustee who must vote them as a bloc in accordance with instructions—was unlawful at common law. When it was authorized by statute, the authorization was accompanied by rules setting time limits and requiring periodic renewals of the trustee's powers.[10] The statutory voting trust is employed only in close corporations.

Statutes in every state require votes to be taken on certain "fundamental" transactions, such as mergers and sales of substantially all the assets of the firm.[11] Statutes also require the board of directors to submit other proposals to voters when, for example, a sufficient number of voters or directors request such a submission.[12] There are a few more restrictions, of substantially less importance.

8. Some states ban sales of votes by statute (N.Y. Bus. Corp Law 609[e]), and other states do so by judicial decision (Macht v. Merchants Mortgage & Credit Co., 22 Del. Ch. 74, 194 A. 19 [1937]). See Schreiber v. Carney, 447 A.2d 17 (Del. Ch. 1982) (discussing the situations in which vote selling is prohibited).

9. For example, 8 Del. Code §212.

10. For example, 8 Del. Code §218 (ten years' duration).

11. For example, 8 Del. Code §251(c) (requiring vote of a majority of all stock, not just of a quorum, to approve a merger).

12. For instance, 8 Del. Code §109(a) (although the board of directors may be given the power to amend the bylaws, this "shall not divest the shareholders or members of the power" to adopt, alter, or repeal bylaws; §211(b), (d) (meetings and

VOTING AS AN ASPECT OF CONTRACTING

The combination of explicit contracts, the structural rules of corporate law, and the fiduciary principle (see Chapter 4) still leave much to discretion. The items left unspecified—who is to do which tasks and work with whom, what products to make, how to sell them, and so on—often will be more important than the items capable of specification. Something must fill in the details.

Voting serves that function. The right to vote is the right to make all decisions not otherwise provided by contract—whether the contract is express or supplied by legal rule. The right to make the decisions includes the right to delegate them. Thus voters may elect directors and give them discretionary powers over things voters otherwise could control.

Because voting is expensive, the participants in the venture will arrange to conserve on its use. It could be employed from time to time to select managers and set the ground rules for their performance and not used again unless the managers' performance was seriously inadequate. Indeed, the collective choice problems that attend voting in corporations with large numbers of contracting parties suggest that voting rarely serves any function except *in extremis*. When many are entitled to vote, none expects his votes to decide the contest. Consequently none of the voters has the appropriate incentive to study the firm's affairs and vote intelligently.[13] If, for example, a given election could result in each voter gaining or losing $1,000, and if each is sure that the election will come out the same way whether or not he participates, then the voter's optimal investment in information is zero. And even if a voter thinks his vote will be dispositive, so that an investment up to $1,000 is warranted, that may be insufficient. If there are 1,000 voters, the effect on them as a group will be $1 million. A thousand dollars' worth of information may be quite insufficient to make a $1 million decision; worse still, 1,000 people investing $1,000 each

---

special meetings to be held as provided in bylaws); §228 (voters may act without meeting by obtaining signatures of a majority). See also SEC v. Transamerica Corp., 163 F.2d 511 (3d Cir. 1947) (construing Delaware law as requiring directors to submit shareholders' proposals to a vote at a meeting).

13. See Anthony Downs, *An Economic Theory of Democracy* (1957); Mancur Olson, *The Logic of Collective Action* (1965).

may mean that all of them are acting on inadequate information, even though a single investment in $10,000 worth of knowledge might be adequate. Those who have more shares, such as investment companies, pension trusts, and some insiders, do not face the collective action problem to the same extent. Nonetheless no shareholder, no matter how large his stake, has the right incentives unless that stake is 100 percent.

Collective action problems may be overcome by aggregating the shares (and the attached votes) through acquisitions, such as mergers and tender offers. Voting serves its principal role in permitting those who have gathered up equity claims to exercise control. Short of aggregating, however, some sort of collective information-generating agency is necessary. In a firm, the managers serve this function, and consequently it is unlikely that voters would think themselves able to decide with greater insight than the managers do. No wonder voters delegate extensively to managers and almost always endorse their decisions. But this acquiescence should not obscure the fact that managers exercise authority at the sufferance of investors.

VOTING AS PART OF RISK BEARING

Voting exists in corporations because someone must have the residual power to act (or delegate) when contracts are not complete. Votes could be held by shareholders, bondholders, managers, or other employees in any combination. Given the collective choice problem, one might expect voting rights to be held by a small group with good access to information—the managers. Yet voting rights are universally held by shareholders, to the exclusion of creditors, managers, and other employees. When a firm's founders take the firm public, they almost always find it advantageous to sell claims that include votes, and thus ultimately the right to remove the insiders. Why do the insiders sell such claims? Why do investors pay extra for them? (They must pay something, or the insiders would not expose themselves to the risk of removal.)

The reason is that shareholders are the residual claimants to the firm's income. Creditors have fixed claims, and employees generally negotiate compensation schedules in advance of performance. The gains and losses from abnormally good or bad performance are the lot of the shareholders, whose claims stand last in line.

As the residual claimants, shareholders have the appropriate incentives (collective choice problems notwithstanding) to make discretionary decisions. The firm should invest in new products, plants, and so forth, until the gains and costs are identical at the margin. Yet all of the actors, except the shareholders, lack the appropriate incentives. Those with fixed claims on the income stream may receive only a tiny benefit (in increased security) from the undertaking of a new project. The shareholders receive most of the marginal gains and incur most of the marginal costs. They therefore have the right incentives to exercise discretion. And although the collective choice problem prevents dispersed shareholders from making the decisions day by day, managers' knowledge that they are being monitored by those who have the right incentives, and the further knowledge that the claims could be aggregated and votes exercised at any time, leads managers to act in shareholders' interest in order to advance their own careers and to avoid being ousted.

This is not, or course, a complete explanation. The interests of shareholders may conflict with the interests of creditors. Shareholders have an incentive to adopt various strategies with the effect of transferring wealth to themselves, such as choosing risky investment projects and withdrawing assets from the firm. Creditors seek to control this conduct in two ways. One is exquisitely detailed contracts.[14] Creditors become residual claimants when equity holders' conduct exposes to them to unanticipated risk. Thus we expect to, and do, observe creditors who possess rights to approve especially risky transactions, such as substantial construction projects, mergers, and the like. Approval rights of this sort are built into bond indentures and major bank loans, and the lending instruments also contain conditions that define certain risk-creating conditions as defaults and thus confer other approval powers on lenders. The other device is implicit in the nature of debt: what is borrowed must be repaid. The need to pay cash forces the firm into financial markets for fresh money, to an even greater extent than

14. See Clifford W. Smith, Jr., and Jerold B. Warner, "On Financial Contracting: An Analysis of Bond Covenants," 7 *J. Fin. Econ.* 117 (1979), for a discussion of some of the costs of writing detailed contracts. See also Laurentius Marais, Katherine Schipper, and Abbie Smith, "Wealth Effects of Going Private for Senior Securities," 23 *J. Fin. Econ.* 155 (1989).

dividends compel managers to return to equity markets. As we observed in Chapter 2, firms that continually must raise money are subject to continual monitoring. If they choose projects that create excessive risk or have low expected returns, they must pay more for capital. As long as they are being paid, and consent to participate at negotiated interest, creditors obtain both compensation and control without votes.

The right to vote (that is, the right to exercise discretion) follows the residual claim. When the firm is in distress, the shareholders' residual claim goes under water, and they lose the appropriate incentives to maximize on the margin. Other groups, such as preferred stockholders or creditors, then receive the benefits of new decisions and projects until their claims are satisfied. There is little reason for shareholders, or managers answerable to them, to invest the money and energy necessary to make improvements when someone else reaps the gain. Thus shareholders lose the controlling votes when their shares are under water, whether by contract or through the operation of bankruptcy laws; managers become answerable to other investors. They may choose to leave the managers in office through "workout" agreements, but this does not obscure the fact that the discretionary power has passed. Because managers try to enhance their own reputations, we would expect them to be as faithful in the pursuit of creditors' interests as they once were in pursuit of shareholders' interests.

The fact that voting rights flow to whichever group holds the residual claim at the moment strongly supports our analysis of the function of voting rights. It also suggests why, ordinarily, only one group holds voting rights at a time. The inclusion of multiple groups (say employees in addition to shareholders) would be a source of agency costs. People who did not receive the marginal gains would be influencing corporate discretion, and the influence would not maximize the wealth of the participants as a group. Thus the joint participation of different classes of participants in voting is rarely seen unless compelled—as, for example, "codetermination" (the participation of employees) in Germany and "good faith bargaining" with unions in the United States. There is another reason why only one class of participants in the venture commonly holds dispositive voting rights at one time. The voters, and the directors they elect, must determine both the objectives of the firm and the general methods of achieving them. It is well known, however, that when voters hold dissimilar preferences it is not possible to aggregate their preferences into a consistent system of choices.[15] If a firm makes inconsistent choices, it is likely to self-destruct. Consistency is possible, however, when voters commonly hold the same ranking of choices (or when the rankings are at least single-peaked).

The preferences of one class of participants are likely to be similar if not identical. This is true of shareholders especially, for people buy and sell in the market so that the shareholders of a given firm at a given time are a reasonably homogeneous group with respect to their desires for the firm. So firms with single classes of voters are likely to be firms with single objectives, and single-objective firms are likely to prosper relative to others. This suggests not only why only one class holds the controlling votes at a time but also why the law makes no effort to require firms to adhere to any objective other than profit maximization (as constrained by particular legal rules).

One final point on the relation between voting and residual claims. Shareholders do not always have equal power. Sometimes stable coalitions (a group of insider shareholders and some institutional allies) may hold effective control for long periods. This is beneficial, for reasons we have explained, because it alleviates the collective action problem. It is not troublesome if the gains from corporate action are divided proportionally among all shareholders. Even when gains are not proportionally divided, the aggregation of "voting power" is not significant if coalitions can change. As long as each share has an equal chance of participating in a winning coalition, the gains from monitoring will be apportioned so as to preserve appropriate incentives at the margin.

DOES VOTING MATTER?

Whether voting serves the functions we have assigned it is necessarily an empirical question. There are no conclusive answers, but several considerations are suggestive. One is simply the survival of voting. If it is not worth the costs of running elections, firms that eliminated voting would have prospered relative to others. That has not happened, and one may infer that voting is beneficial.

Second, voting facilitates takeovers. A tender offer for stock

15. Kenneth J. Arrow, *Social Choice and Collective Values* (2d ed. 1963); Duncan Black, *The Theory of Committees and Elections* (1958).

enables the buyer to assume control of the target by exercising the votes attached to the acquired shares. Such acquisitions are associated with substantial price premiums, and tactics that make takeovers more difficult are associated with price reductions.[16] (We return to this topic in Chapter 7.) Third, voting contests produce price increases—presumably reflecting real increases in the value of the firm—whether or not they lead to changes in control.[17] The price increase takes place when the market learns of the contest, and it persists even if the insurgents are defeated. This sequence is explicable only if voting and the prospect of future monitoring produces pressure on managers to act in the interest of investors.

Fourth, because the collective choice problem is the principal limit on the ability of the residual claimants to influence decisions by voting, one would expect that if votes are valuable then a reduction in the costs of collective action—as, for example, by the assembly of a large bloc of shares—would be associated with an increase in the price of all shares. The available data suggest that bloc assembly is associated with price increases for shares outside the bloc. Tender offers assemble the largest blocs and produce the largest increases, but smaller blocs produce price increases too. Fifth, in the rare cases in which firms have outstanding issues of stock with identical rights to share in the profits but significantly different voting rights, the stock with the stronger voting rights trades at a premium of 2–4 percent relative to the other series of stock. Similarly, in proxy contests, the price of all stock falls on the record date, after which stock generally is sold without the buyer acquiring a right to vote in the impending election.[18] This premium for voting rights probably represents the anticipated (and fully di-

16. See Jarrell and Poulson, supra note 7; Ruback, supra note 7. See also Sanford J. Grossman and Oliver D. Hart, "One Share–One Vote and the Market for Corporate Control," 20 *J. Fin. Econ.* 175 (1988).

17. Peter Dodd and Jerold B. Warner, "On Corporate Governance: A Study of Proxy Contests," 11 *J. Fin. Econ.* 401 (1983); Harry DeAngelo and Linda DeAngelo, "Proxy Contests and the Governance of Publicly Held Corporations," 23 *J. Fin. Econ.* 29 (1989) (tracing the gains to subsequent control transactions of the kind discussed in Chapters 5 and 7). See also John Pound, "Proxy Contests and the Efficiency of Shareholder Oversight," 20 *J. Fin. Econ.* 237 (1989).

18. Ronald C. Lease, John J. McConnell, and Wayne H. Mikkelson, "The Market Value of Control in Publicly-Traded Corporations," 11 *J. Fin. Econ.* 439 (1983); Dodd and Warner, supra note 17. See also Haim Levy, "Economic Evaluation of Voting Power of Common Stock," 38 *J. Finance* 79 (1983) (voting premium averaging 45 percent in Israel).

luted) value attributable to the opportunity of those votes to improve the performance of the corporation. It is not possible to attribute the premium to the privilege of those with votes to "divert" profits to themselves, because such diversions accrue (if at all) to insiders, while public investors who could not expect to get such diversions are willing to pay the premium.

Finally, there is some evidence about the performance of firms in which there are no residual claimants or in which the residual claimants do not vote. Firms without shareholders do poorly compared with other firms, and firms whose structure prevents the formation of a control bloc of shares also do relatively poorly.[19] Thus the evidence strongly suggests that votes are important despite the collective action problem, and that the voting process enables firms to operate more efficiently.

State Rules Concerning Elections

THE PRESUMPTION OF ONE SHARE, ONE VOTE

The most basic statutory rule of voting is the same in every state. It is this: all common shares vote, all votes have the same weight, and no other participant in the venture votes, unless there is some express agreement to the contrary.

Such agreements are rare.[20] Although there are hundreds of different voting arrangements, such as classified boards to which different shares vote for different posts, and preferred stock with contingent voting rights, almost all publicly traded shares in substantial firms have one vote each, and that vote may be cast for positions on an unclassified board. There have been persistent ar-

19. See, for example, Maureen O'Hara, "Property Rights and the Financial Firm," 24 *J. L & Econ.* 317 (1981) (mutual banks, in which voting power depends on depositions rather than transferable shares, do poorly relative to banks with transferable shares); Eric Rasmusen, "Mutual Banks and Stock Banks," 31 *J. L. & Econ.* 395 (1988); David G. Davies, "The Efficiency of Public versus Private Firms: The Case of Australia's Two Airlines," 14 *J. L. & Econ.* 149 (1971) (firms with identifiable residual claimants prospers relative to firms without them). Note that we limit this comparison to firms operating for profit.

20. See Lease, McConnell, and Mikkelson, supra note 18 (finding only thirty issues of nonvoting or unequally weighted voting common stock traded on any exchange or over the counter at any time between 1940 and 1978). On why they exist at all, see Fischel, supra note 7.

guments that this is not "democratic" because some people (those with more shares) have more votes than others.

The presumptively equal voting right attached to shares is, however, a logical consequence of the function of voting we have discussed above. Votes follow the residual interest in the firm, and unless each element of the residual interest carries an equal voting right, there will be a needless agency cost of management. Those with disproportionate voting power will not receive shares of the residual gains or losses from new endeavors and arrangements commensurate with their control; as a result, they will not make optimal decisions. Nonvoting bonds and nonvoting employees are not troublesome, however, because neither group has a residual claim.

This also explains why cumulative voting is rare in publicly traded firms and why most state statutes contain a presumption against cumulative voting. Cumulative voting gives disproportionate weight to certain "minority" shares, and the lack of proportion once more creates an agency cost of management. It makes realignments of control blocs difficult by distributing a form of holdup power widely; although every share has the same holdup potential, the aggregate holdup value exceeds the value of the firm and thus makes negotiation very difficult.

Cumulative voting (or any other method of requiring supermajority consent to corporate actions) has the additional property of impeding changes of control and thus supporting the position of managers *vis-à-vis* residual claimants. Cumulative voting thus produces the same costs as any other stratagem by which managers seek to insulate themselves from the displeasure of shareholders. Because cumulative voting permits representation of "minority" interests in the firm's governance, moreover, it increases the chance that there will be multipeaked preferences among the members of the board. Cumulative voting and other minority representation schemes thus expose the firm to an uncompensated risk of making inconsistent or illogical decisions.

These considerations also underlie the statutory limits on the establishment and duration of voting trusts and the fact that in practice such trusts are used only in closely held firms. Voting trusts are designed to inhibit transfers of control. In closely held firms they stop family feuds and promote monitoring; in public firms they would increase agency costs by separating the right of control from the residual claim. "Control share" statutes, which prevent holders of large blocs from voting unless other investors allow them to, similarly divorce control from the residual claim, and we predict that they reduce the value of the firm. (Chapters 7 and 8 discuss antitakeover laws in detail and present data about control share statutes and related developments.) No matter the source, the separation of control from the residual interest introduces a substantial, and in public firms unnecessary, agency cost.

THE PROHIBITION OF VOTE BUYING

It is not possible to separate the voting right from the equity interest. Someone who wants to buy a vote must buy the stock too. The restriction on irrevocable proxies, which are possible only when coupled with a pledge of the stock, also ensures that votes go with the equity interest.

These rules are, at first glance, curious limits on the ability of investors to make their own arrangements. Yet they are understandable on much the same basis as the equal-weighting rule. Attaching the vote firmly to the residual equity interest ensures that an unnecessary agency cost will not occur. Separation of shares from votes introduces a disproportion between expenditure and reward.

For example, if the owner of 20 percent of the residual claims acquires all of the votes, his incentive to take steps to improve the firm (or just to make discretionary decisions) is only one-fifth of the value of those decisions. The holder of the votes will invest too little. And he will also have an incentive to consume excessive leisure and perquisites and to engage in other behavior that does not maximize profits because much of the cost would be borne by the other residual claimants.[21] The risk of such shirking would reduce the value of investments in general, and the risk can be eliminated by tying votes to shares.

21. We therefore disagree with Dean Clark's argument that vote buying should be permitted, if the purchaser has a substantial equity interest and hopes to profit solely by appreciation in the value of that interest. Robert Charles Clark, "Vote Buying and Corporate Law," 29 *Case West. L. Rev.* 776 (1979). Clark does not discuss the agency cost problems associated with such vote buying, and he does not try to explain why vote buying is universally condemned.

One possible response is that the agency costs created would be eliminated if the owner of 20 percent of the residual claims could obtain returns disproportionate to his equity interest. As long as there is a market in votes that parallels the market in shares, competition among vote buyers could be sufficient to compensate equity investors for the value of the dilution of their interests.

This is intriguing but, we think, unsatisfactory. Transactions in votes would present difficult problems of valuation and create other costs without conferring any apparent benefit compared with transactions in votes tied to shares.[22] Moreover, the collective choice problem would exert a strong influence over the market price of votes. Because no voter expects to influence the outcome of the election, he would sell the vote (which to him is unimportant) for less than the expected dilution of his equity interest. He would reason that if he did not sell, others would; he would then lose on the equity side but get nothing for the vote. Thus any positive price would persuade him to sell.

Competition among those bidding for votes might drive the price up but not, ordinarily, all the way up to the value of the expected equity dilution. Each person bidding for votes would be concerned that he would end up with less than a majority, and unless he obtained a majority he would have nothing at all. Thus he would offer less than the prospective value of the equity dilution. This concern obviously does not apply to one who buys shares the day before the election, votes them, and sells the day after the election—and so "buys" votes in common parlance. Such a person bears the gains or losses attributable to the election, and his conduct is not unlawful in any state as vote buying.

One cannot exclude the possibility that competition among buyers of votes would fully compensate the sellers. In that event, however, the bidders would see no difference between buying votes and buying shares, which, after the votes had been cast, could be held or resold to their former owners. If state or federal law restricts the transfer of shares, then the sale of votes in a competitive

---

22. In vote-selling games there is no core solution when gains are not equally apportioned, and there may be no core solution even when they are equally apportioned. See Lester G. Telser, "Voting and Paying for Public Goods: An Application of the Theory of the Core," 227 *J. Econ. Theory* 376 (1982), for a related discussion.

market is an attractive second-best solution.[23] Chapters 7 and 8 discuss laws (and corporate practices) restricting trading in shares during contests for corporate control. The only other situation in which buying the votes without the shares is advantageous is when the buyer is planning to dilute the interests of the other equity owners. As we discuss in Chapter 5, investors would agree to prohibit such dilutions in order to ensure that all control changes increase value. Thus the legal rules tying votes to shares increase the efficiency of corporate organization, with the potential exception of control contests in which the shares themselves cannot be sold.

THE ABSENCE OF TENURE OF OFFICE

Although members of boards of directors typically are elected for specific terms, they do not have tenure of office. Voters may call elections on short notice and oust the directors for any reason or none. Delaware, the dominant corporate jurisdiction, has the least secure tenure of all.[24]

These rules denying tenure to the board put the voters firmly in control—should they choose to exercise it—at any time and ensure that the residual claimants have the final say. Managers may be given a quick boot if agency costs become unacceptable. It is true that in public corporations directors are rarely evicted in midterm, but the possibility of ouster may be sufficient to ensure that directors act as faithful agents of the residual claimants. The ability to change directors at once would be most important in contested takeovers, in which a bidder that had acquired a majority of the stock wanted to install its own team.

It is interesting to compare the political system's treatment of tenure. Most elected officeholders have tenure for defined periods.

23. See Thomas J. André, Jr., "A Preliminary Inquiry into the Utility of Vote Buying in the Market for Corporate Control," 63 *S. Cal. L. Rev.* 533 (1990).

24. See note 5, supra, and, for example, Campbell v. Loew's, Inc., 36 Del. Ch. 563, 134 A.2d 852 (1957). Compare Schnell v. Chris-Craft Industries, Inc., 285 A.2d 437 (Del. 1971) (board may not change the date of meeting so as to disadvantage the opposition). Provisions in bylaws purporting to furnish tenure of office through supermajority vote requirements for ouster sometimes are sustained, but they are of questionable effectiveness in many states. See Texas Partners v. Conrock Co., 685 F.2d 1116 (9th Cir. 1982) (Delaware law).

Even states that allow recall of officeholders in theory do not recall them in practice. Why do political officeholders have more secure (if more limited) tenure? One possible explanation is that managers do not need tenure to motivate them to act in investors' interests. Because the consequences of their acts are reflected in stock prices and in their own future salaries, they strive to maximize firms' discounted future returns even if they have insecure tenure. There is no similar monitoring and reward system for political office-holders, who therefore tend to discount the future more steeply than their constituents. Tenure of office may be a partial antidote to this discounting problem.

THE COMMON LAW RULES FOR THE CONDUCT OF ELECTIONS

Unlike federal law, which we discuss in the next section, state law usually imposes no restrictions on the conduct of elections apart from requiring the incumbents to furnish lists of shareholders to prospective challengers at the challengers' expense.[25] Managers may campaign against shareholders' proposals, and for their own reelection, at corporate expense; the firm may reimburse insurgents' expenses if they win, and incumbents may reimburse insurgents even if they lose (although this is rare).[26] It is sometimes said that incumbents may use the firm's resources to defend their positions only if the dispute concerns corporate "policy" rather than "personal" matters. But it would be a poor director indeed who could not find some element of policy in the dispute. People do not wage proxy campaigns to eject directors just because they wear gaudy clothes; they object to how the incumbents run the firm. Thus the distinction between policy and personal issues stated in the cases turns out to be no limit at all.

All of these rules (or, rather, the lack of rules in all of these instances) are consistent with the analysis we have proposed. Because proxy fights may be waged by parties who lack significant

25. Delaware has an elaborate set of rules concerning the circumstances under which shareholders' lists must be furnished. See 8 Del. Code §220.

26. For example, Hall v. Trans-Lux Daylight Screen Picture Corp., 20 Del. Ch. 78, 171 A. 226 (1934); Rosenfield v. Fairchild Engine & Airplane Corp. 309 N.Y. 168, 128 N.E.2d 291 (1955).

ownership of shares, a successful contest could put in office insurgents inferior to the incumbents in managerial skill (but superior in ability to siphon wealth). These insurgents gain more in perquisites and side payments than they lose in diminution of the value of their stock. All residual claimants benefit if such insurgents are defeated. Incumbents' use of corporate funds to campaign for reelection or for the election of their nominees spreads the costs of the election across all of the residual claimants. Like the other principles we have discussed, this reduces the agency costs that would arise if particular directors incurred expenses disproportionate to their shareholdings. The gains and losses of the directors' decisions accrue to all residual claimants; if the costs are not similarly spread, the directors will not equate costs and benefits to the firm at the margin. The same consideration explains why insurgents may reimburse themselves if they prevail and why incumbents may reimburse unsuccessful insurgents.

It may seem odd, however, that challengers are not reimbursed by the firm as a matter of course. There are substantial free-riding problems in mounting a campaign. The collective choice problem that inhibits voters from learning about the firm in order to cast intelligent ballots applies in spades to waging a fight. The full costs are borne by the challengers in every case, yet they obtain reimbursement only if they prevail, and they obtain the gains (if any) from changes in management only in proportion to their equity interests. The divergence between cost and benefit makes proxy contests rare and drives challengers to the more costly alternative of the tender offer. Because the firm appears to gain whether or not the insurgents prevail, it could be argued that the firm should pick up the expenses of those who seek election to at least the same extent as it picks up the incumbents' expenses.

There is nonetheless a substantial problem with allowing challenges at the firm's expense. The firm's offer to pay for the contest may become an attractive nuisance. There are always publicity seekers willing to stand for office on someone else's money. An offer to pay for the contest is worthwhile only if, in its absence, significant numbers of otherwise beneficial contests will be stifled, and even then only if there is a good way to distinguish plausible challengers from frivolous ones.

We may put the difficulty of weeding out frivolous candidates to one side. Almost all proxy contests are waged by owners of substantial blocks or by former officeholders, and it is precisely such people who do not need the lure of automatic compensation by the firm in order to make the contest worthwhile.

Issue Voting

Shareholders' voting is not limited to the election of directors. State law typically requires that certain actions such as fundamental corporate changes (mergers, liquidations, sales of assets) and charter amendments be approved by a specified percentage of outstanding shares.[27] Moreover, a variety of other actions are commonly submitted for shareholders' votes even though not required by statute. We consider these aspects of issue voting below.

Fundamental Corporate Changes

The corporate law of every state provides that the business of the corporation shall be managed by, or under the direction of, the board of directors. Shareholders typically do not vote on matters of ordinary business judgment. All statutes provide, however, that in situations of "extraordinary" action—fundamental corporate changes—the issue must be submitted to shareholders. This rule, too, helps reduce agency costs.

Shareholders, as residual claimants, have the most to lose (or to gain) as a result of fundamental corporate changes. Moreover, the possibility of large gain or loss in these transactions because of their size is sufficient to overcome the collective action problems, particularly for institutional investors, that would make voting on ordinary business decisions meaningless. The vote on the merger can be viewed as a midterm election of directors, a vote of confidence on a major decision. The statute requires the midterm election as a partial response to the collective action problems that make it difficult for shareholders to organize to oust directors between elections. The right to vote is simply an additional monitoring device possessed by the residual claimants when the stakes

27. 8 Del. Code §242 (shareholders' approval required for amendments to the certificate of incorporation); §251 (shareholders' approval required for mergers); §271 (shareholders' approval required for sales of assets); §275 (shareholders' approval required for dissolutions).

are high enough. Although shareholders approve almost all mergers, this may be attributable to advance consent by institutional investors, consent that would not be necessary if there were no right to vote.

CHARTER AMENDMENTS

The other area in which shareholders' approval is commonly required is charter amendments. Of particular interest in this regard are amendments designed to deter potential bidders from making a tender offer. Because these amendments reduce the probability that the firms' shareholders will be the beneficiaries of a tender offer at a significant premium over market price, they reduce shareholders' wealth on average. (Chapter 7 summarizes the data; see also note 7 in this chapter.) If shareholders' voting serves as a monitoring device on self-interested behavior by management, shareholders should vote against these amendments. The evidence is consistent with this hypothesis. Many institutional investors depart from their customary adherence to the Wall Street Rule (vote with management or sell your shares) and vote against "shark-repellent" amendments.[28] The more shares held by institutions, the less likely an antitakeover amendment's adoption—and the less damaging the amendments that are adopted.

SHAREHOLDERS' VOTING WHEN IT IS NOT REQUIRED

Our analysis thus far has focused on voting that is required by law. But managers routinely submit a wide range of issues to shareholders including stock option plans, the selection of an independent auditor, and mergers where vote is not required. What explains this pattern?

Managers submit issues for approval because legal rules encourage them to do so. Shareholders' approval of a transaction decreases the probability of a successful attack in court. Transac-

28. See Office of the Chief Economist, Securities and Exchange Commission, "Shark Repellants and Stock Prices: The Effects of Antitakeover Amendments Since 1980" (1985); James A. Brickley, Ronald C. Lease, and Clifford W. Smith, Jr., "Ownership Structure and Voting on Antitakeover Amendments," 20 *J. Fin. Econ.* 267 (1988); Paul H. Malatesta and Ralph A. Walkling, "Poison Pill Securities: Stockholder Wealth, Profitability, and Ownership Structure," 20 *J. Fin. Econ.* 347 (1988).

tions between a director or officer and a corporation will not be void or voidable, despite the conflict of interest, if the transaction is approved by a vote of the shareholders.[29] Similarly, a merger will more likely survive a judicial challenge if it is approved by a majority of the shares not held by the acquirer.

The effect of these rules is unclear. Legal rules encouraging managers to submit issues to a vote where the need for monitoring is high—such as in situations involving self-interested transactions—may increase shareholders' welfare. But the collective action problem yields ratification as a matter of course. The risk that wealth-reducing transactions will be permitted because of shareholders' ratification is minimized, however, by the common law rule that shareholders cannot ratify fraud[30] and the tendency of courts to scrutinize whether self-interested transactions are beneficial to firms. Again, the survivorship principle suggests that there is a net benefit of legal rules encouraging shareholders' approval of certain transactions (although the rules here are less well entrenched and consistent than in the case of fundamental corporate changes).

Federal Regulation of the Proxy Machinery

Firms have incentives to locate in states that enable them to adopt voting procedures that promote the wealth of investors (see Chapter 8). Firms use their leeway under state law to design rules that assign votes to the optimal holders and help them overcome the collective action problem (principally by facilitating cheap transfers of shares), while at the same time ensuring that the voters share common objectives (overcoming the difficulty of aggregating preferences in democracies). They develop practices concerning the types of issues resolved by voting (that is, by direct rather than representative decisions) and the amount of disclosure before voting. Enduring practices are the best evidence of what constitutes the optimal allocation of resources on voting procedures.

Many others writing in the Berle and Means tradition[31] have not

29. 8 Del. Code §144(a)(2).

30. For example, Kerbs v. California Eastern Airways, 33 Del. Ch. 474, 184 A.2d 602 (1962); Continental Securities Co. v. Belmont, 206 N.Y. 7, 99 N.E. 138 (1912).

31. See Adolph A. Berle and Gardiner C. Means, *The Modern Corporation and Private Property* (1933). See generally Symposium, Corporations and Private Property, 26 *J. L. & Econ.* 235–496 (1983), assessing the significance of this book.

viewed the corporate world this way. The modern corporation, according to Berle and Means, is characterized by omnipotent managers who, through control over the proxy machinery, keep themselves in office. Section 14 of the Securities Exchange Act of 1934 was believed to rectify this perceived imbalance by guaranteeing shareholders a right to more say in the management of their property.[32]

The proxy rules have four principal components: (1) general disclosure provisions designed to keep shareholders informed even if there is no contested election; (2) provisions requiring disclosure by rival groups in the event of a proxy fight to ensure that shareholders will be adequately informed and able to vote intelligently; (3) a general antifraud provision prohibiting the use of false or misleading statements in cases where proxies are solicited; and (4) a provision allowing shareholders, subject to certain exceptions, to communicate with other shareholders by placing a proposal in the proxy materials.

The proxy rules displace private arrangements with respect to both the issues on which shareholders are entitled to vote and the information they are entitled to have. Regulation is not entitled to the same presumption of efficiency as long-standing voluntary arrangements.

The Behavioral Assumptions of the Proxy Rules

The proxy rules depend on two principal assumptions: that shareholders demand more information about corporate matters than managers provide voluntarily and desire to be more involved in setting corporate policy than state law allows. A corollary assumption is that shareholders are easily misled and will vote contrary to

32. 15 U.S.C. §78n. The implementing rules appear in 17 C.F.R. §240.14a. The design of §14 was expressed in the House Report: "Managements of properties owned by the investing public should not be permitted to perpetuate themselves by the misuse of corporate proxies. Insiders having little or no substantial interest in the properties they manage have often retained their control without an adequate disclosure of their interest and without an adequate explanation of the management policies they intend to pursue. Insiders have at times solicited proxies without fairly informing the stockholders of the purposes for which the proxies are to be used and have used such proxies to take from the stockholders for their own selfish advantage valuable property rights." H.R. Rep. No. 1383, 73d Cong., 2d Sess. 13–14 (1934).

their interests (their "true" wishes) unless the type and accuracy of information provided to them is carefully specified.

These assumptions are not supported by evidence. Indeed, both casual empiricism and economic theory contradict the behavioral assumptions that underlie the federal proxy rules. Shareholders' involvement in the voting process has not increased with the adoption of the proxy rules. Managers still are rarely displaced by voters; managers' recommendations on fundamental corporate changes, amendments of bylaws, or other matters are routinely followed; shareholders' proposals do well if they receive 5 percent of the vote. In those rare situations where a proxy fight for control develops, the insurgent's chance for success is determined by the number of shares he owns rather than by the force of his arguments.

Proponents of the need for greater shareholders' involvement through the proxy machinery do not so much dispute the fact of shareholders' apathy as argue that this indifference is attributable to lack of a meaningful opportunity to participate. Thus if more information were disclosed, if shareholders were given a more "meaningful" opportunity to participate, the argument runs, they would assume their proper role as decision makers and owners of the corporation.

The more plausible explanation for the disparity between the rhetoric of shareholders' democracy and the conduct of shareholders themselves is that the behavioral assumptions underlying the proxy system do not hold. As we have emphasized, there is no reason why those who supply capital to the firm should have interest or expertise in managing the firm's affairs. Given the combination of a collective action problem and easy exit through the stock market, the rational strategy for most dissatisfied shareholders is to sell rather than incur costs in attempting to bring about change through votes.[33] There are, however, good reasons why investors would choose to limit both the scope of voting and the information supplied: rational ignorance implies delegation implies less voting; and the costs of information imply limits on disclosure to investors who won't act on information even if they possess it.

It is interesting to compare the regulation of proxy voting with

33. The greater the availability of the sale or exit option, the less desirable is the voting or voice option. See Albert O. Hirschman, *Exit, Voice, and Loyalty* (1970). It is difficult to imagine a more effective exit option than the market in shares.

the regulation of union elections in labor law. The National Labor Relations Board has long regulated parties' statements in union elections, acting on the belief that employees are attentive to election campaigns and that the exercise of their free choice is easily affected by campaign propaganda. Research strongly suggests, however, that employees do not pay careful attention to election campaigns and are not easily misled by rhetoric.[34] If words do not mislead employees—if, indeed, they do not even pay attention to campaigns that strongly affect their future—how much less is the concern for sophisticated investors in stocks, investors for whom, because of the exit option, voting is much less important than for the employees?

This is not at odds with our analysis about the role of voting in monitoring managers. There is an optimal amount of monitoring, which firms facilitate in their own interest. As we pointed out, voting is used only for large events (mergers and the like), when the gains exceed the substantial costs of information and aggregation of blocs. The existence of these gains is no warrant for inferring, as the Securities and Exchange Commission (SEC) has done, that if some voting is good, more disclosure and more voting must be better still. Because it is so easy to sell one's shares, and because managers must set attractive terms for new securities (including terms for voting) if they are to maximize their returns, there is no good reason to think that the voting rules designed by the firms themselves will be inferior to those the SEC prescribes.[35]

IMPLICATIONS OF THE ASSUMPTIONS UNDERLYING THE PROXY SYSTEM

Many specific legal rules and doctrines are based on the behavioral assumption of the interested and attentive shareholder. In this sec-

34. Julius G. Getman, Stephen B. Goldberg, and Jeanne B. Herman, *Union Representation Elections: Law and Reality* (1976). Compare the articles questioning the methodology in 28 *Stan. L. Rev.* 1161–1207 (1976) with the authors' defense, Stephen B. Goldberg, Julius G. Getman, and Jeanne M. Brett, "Union Representation Elections: Law and Reality: The Authors Respond to the Critics," 79 *Mich. L. Rev.* 564 (1981).

35. See also John Pound, "Proxy Voting and the SEC: The Case for Deregulation," 26 *J. Fin. Econ.* (1991), concluding along our lines that the proxy rules disserve investors' interests.

tion we discuss some of these rules and doctrines and also analyze them under more reasonable assumptions of shareholders' behavior.

Under the accepted definition, a misrepresentation or withheld piece of information is material if there is "a substantial likelihood that a reasonable shareholder would consider it important in deciding how to vote."[36] The difficulty with this definition is that it provides no guidance on what the "reasonable shareholder" considers important when voting. One possibility would be not to regulate the content of speech and rely instead on the marketplace of ideas and the incentives of parties to disclose the optimal amount of information. Corporate elections then would approach political elections, where the value of the vote is greater given the lesser availability of the exit option, yet speech is unregulated.

The behavioral assumptions underlying federal proxy regulation are most clearly evident in the shareholders' proposal rule. Rule 14a-8 of the federal proxy rules provides that a publicly held corporation must include any shareholder proposal that does not fit within one of the exceptions to the rule. What could be more democratic than allowing each interested and attentive shareholder to submit proposals to be carefully considered by other interested and attentive shareholders?

The reality is that the shareholders' proposal rule is an antidemocratic device. Because most shareholders are passive, the vast majority show no interest in others' proposals, which are routinely defeated by huge margins. Yet the majority must subsidize the activities of the minority who are allowed to make proposals without incurring the costs.

Supporters of the rule are unfazed by costs or lack of success of shareholders' proposals. They argue that the rule is beneficial because it has a "healthy indirect impact" on corporate behavior.[37] What this presumably means is that the proposal, because of the publicity generated or otherwise, causes the firm to abandon a profit-maximizing strategy in favor of one that some find more "moral" or "socially responsible." But this argument stands the

36. TSC Industries, Inc. v. Northway, Inc., 426 U.S. 438, 449 (1976).
37. Donald Schwartz and Elliot L. Weiss, "An Assessment of the Shareholder Proposal Rule Proposal," 65 *Geo. L. J.* 635 (1977); David Vogel, *Lobbying the Corporation* (1978).

rationale for shareholders' voting—and federal proxy regulation—on its head. If the purpose of the federal proxy rules is to enable shareholders to influence corporate policy, it is difficult to find merit in a device that forces the majority of shareholders to subsidize conduct of a minority that is contrary to their presumptive goal of profit maximization.

Among contemporary proposals, fewer ask firms to abandon profitable but hazardous activities and more ask firms to abandon devices that protect the managers, such as poison pills. For reasons developed in Chapter 7, we are sympathetic to the merits of such proposals. Still, whatever costs takeover defenses create have not altered the cost-benefit ratio for the shareholders' proposal mechanism. If ready access to the ballot (for issues of investors' choosing) were beneficial on balance, it would be adopted by the firms themselves or by state law.

PROPOSED REFORMS OF THE PROXY SYSTEM

Because proponents of federal regulation ignore the economic realities of shareholders' voting and instead assume that shareholders demand more involvement in the corporate decision-making process, they also assume that the shareholders enduring indifference to voting is attributable to defects in the regulatory process. A variety of reforms have been proposed, including increased disclosure, greater access to the proxy machinery, and increased regulation of institutional investors. Each would reduce shareholders' welfare.

Increased Disclosure

One explanation for the low level of shareholders' involvement is that investors lack the information necessary to vote intelligently. Thus it has been argued that the firm should be required to disclose more information about its activities and the background and qualifications of its management. As we have emphasized, there is no evidence that shareholders have any interest in this information. Since disclosure is costly, and these costs must be borne by the firms' existing investors, increased mandatory disclosure of this type makes shareholders worse off. Shareholders' welfare may be reduced in another, and perhaps more fundamental, respect. Mandatory disclosure of the kind commonly proposed may have the effect, and perhaps the intended effect, of deterring profit-maximizing behavior. Requiring firms to disclose their policy with respect to compliance with the environmental laws, violations of regulatory statutes, or questionable foreign or domestic payments all may affect the willingness of the firm to undertake the conduct at issue. Due to a fear of litigation, adverse publicity, or regulatory intervention, managers may simply decide that the costs of disclosure may exceed the expected benefits from the activity.

Greater Access to the Proxy Machinery

Another common explanation for shareholders' apparent lack of interest in corporate decision making is that they lack the ability to participate meaningfully in the electoral process. Under the current system, the incumbent board nominates directors who are then routinely elected by shareholders. This system of self-perpetuating management is anathema to those who believe that shareholders should have the right to control the nomination and election process. To remedy this perceived defect, a number of reforms have been proposed, ranging from granting shareholders the right to have their nominees for directors included in the proxy materials to requiring that all corporations have nominating committees composed entirely of independent directors who would select nominees after consideration of proposals by shareholders.

The only defect in the current system that proponents of greater shareholders' access to the proxy machinery have identified, however, is that it is inconsistent with the behavioral assumption of the interested and informed shareholder. If this assumption is incorrect, there is no basis for concluding that shareholders should have control over the nomination process. On the contrary, a fundamental premise of the economics of shareholders' voting is that shareholders, because of the collective action problem, lack the expertise and incentive in most cases to identify and evaluate different potential candidates for the purpose of deciding how to vote.

Moreover, adoption of these proposed reforms may impose substantial costs. Apart from increased administrative costs generated by complicating the proxy machinery and creating a new bureaucratic layer, agency costs would increase. Unless they have no effect whatsoever (other than increasing administrative costs), the proposed reforms increase the ability of small investors, or even those with no financial stake in the firm, to place their nominees on the board at the expense of large investors. This violation of the principle of one share, one vote would increase agency costs for the reasons that we have discussed. The result is lower share prices to the detriment of all shareholders.

Increased Involvement by Institutional Investors

The largest shareholders of many corporations are financial institutions that invest and manage funds for the benefit of smaller investors. These institutions typically possess sole or shared authority for the voting of shares. In this capacity, institutional investors have been criticized for investing insufficient resources in deciding how to vote. The staff of the SEC, for example, has "urged" institutions to "discontinue the practice of categorizing an uncontested election of directors as a routine matter warranting an automatic vote for the entire slate of nominees, bearing in mind that more exacting judgments with respect to the elections of directors may improve corporate accountability and long-term profitability."[38] To achieve this objective, proposals have been made to require institutions to establish voting criteria and disclose their voting policies to beneficiaries or to pass the vote through to beneficiaries who could then vote themselves.[39]

The impression one gets from this rather dismal literature is that institutional investors are disserving their beneficiaries by not taking their voting responsibilities more seriously. But this is implausible. Professional money managers operate in a competitive industry where the liquidity of assets makes it easy to assess managers' performance and shift from one investment to another. Money managers who do not make sound decisions regarding the costs of establishing more elaborate voting procedures in relation to the benefit of such procedures would not be able to attract investment dollars. Institutional investors thus have every incentive to

38. SEC Staff Report on Corporate Accountability, Committee Print, Senate Committee on Banking, 96th Cong., 2d Sess. 422 (1980).

39. Myron P. Curzan and Mark L. Pelesh, "Revitalizing Corporate Democracy: Control of Investment Managers' Voting on Social Responsibility Proxy Issues," 93 *Harv. L. Rev.* 670, 694 (1980).

expend the optimal amount on voting procedures. Indeed, the practice of institutional investors' voting against antitakeover amendments suggests that such investors vote against managements when it is in their interest to do so. Their perceived unwillingness to make "more exacting judgments" is no doubt rational behavior in light of the economics of shareholders' voting discussed above. The problem lies in the behavioral assumptions of the regulators and reformers, not in the voting practices of institutional investors.

Pass-through voting raises additional problems. The cost of locating and transmitting information to widely scattered beneficiaries would be substantial, and there is no reason to believe that the beneficiaries value the right to vote enough to justify these costs because individual shareholders have less incentive to monitor management than does one large institutional investor. Thus the effect of pass-through voting is to aggravate the collective decision problem by breaking up voting blocs. Like greater shareholders' access to the proxy machinery, pass-through voting will lead to higher agency costs and lower share prices, to the detriment of investors. Economic analysis vindicates the current state of the law.

4

The Fiduciary Principle, the Business
Judgment Rule, and the Derivative Suit

We arrive at the relation between shareholders and managers,
which holds center stage in the rest of this book. We focus in this
chapter on the meaning and function of fiduciary duties and the
business judgment rule. We also discuss the derivative suit, the
usual method by which fiduciary duties are enforced.

The Functions of Fiduciary Duties

Corporate directors and other managers are said to be fiduciaries
who must behave in upright ways toward the beneficiaries of
fiduciary duties. Yet as Justice Frankfurter put it, "to say that a
man is a fiduciary only begins analysis; it gives direction to further
inquiry. To whom is he a fiduciary? What obligations does he owe
as a fiduciary?"[1] The answers depend on why we should want to
call a corporate manager a "fiduciary" in the first place.

Fiduciary principles are uncommon in contractual relations. Parties dealing at arm's length may bargain hard and enforce their
deals to the letter, no matter how severe the consequences for the
other side. We treat corporations as complex sets of contracts, so
the reader is entitled to ask: how do fiduciary duties sneak into
these contracts? Our answer, sketched in Chapter 1 and developed
further in Chapter 3 (investors' voting rights), starts from the proposition that people cannot see the future well enough to resolve all
contingencies ahead of time. Corporations are enduring (relational)
contracts. Some persons' rights may be specified. Those of suppliers, laborers, and debt investors fall in this category. If contracts
can be written in enough detail, there is no need for "fiduciary"
duties as well. This point is well understood. Workers and bond-

1. SEC v. Chenery Corp., 318 U.S. 80, 85–86 (1943).

holders alike must look to their contractual rights rather than invoke fiduciary claims.[2] The corporate contract locates the uncertainties in the holders of the residual claims—conventionally the equity investors. They receive few explicit promises. Instead they get the right to vote and the protection of fiduciary principles: the duty of loyalty and the duty of care. As we explained in Chapter 3, these attach to the residual claim because the holders of these claims bear the marginal risks of the firm and so have the best incentives to make the optimal investment and management decisions—not perfect incentives, just best. The only promise that makes sense in such an open-ended relation is to work hard and honestly. In other words, the corporate contract makes managers the agents of the equity investors but does not specify the agents' duties. To make such an arrangement palatable to investors, managers must pledge their careful and honest services.

When one person exercises authority that affects another's wealth, interests may diverge. The smaller the managers' share in the enterprise, the more the managers' interests diverge from the interests of those who contributed capital. This phenomenon exists in any agency relation. For example, a real estate agent on a 5 percent commission will not undertake even $10 worth of effort to improve the realized price by $100, because the agent reaps only $5 of this sum. The $10 effort, however, would be highly advantageous to the principal.

Divergence of interests may be controlled in several ways. There is the employment market: an unfaithful or indolent manager may be penalized by a lower salary, and a diligent one rewarded by a bonus for good performance. In addition, the threat of sales of corporate control induces managers to perform well in order to keep their positions. Finally, competition in product markets helps to control agents' conduct, because a poorly managed firm cannot survive in competition with a well-managed firm (other things being equal). These mechanisms reduce but do not eliminate the divergence of interests. They require extensive, costly monitoring so

2. For example, Broad v. Rockwell Int'l Corp., 642 F.2d 929, 955–960 (5th Cir. 1981) (in banc) (managers must abide by contractual bargains with debt investors and disregard considerations of fairness). On the extent to which firms contract explicitly with debt investors, see Clifford W. Smith, Jr., and Jerold B. Warner, "On Financial Contracting: An Analysis of Bond Covenants," 7 *J. Fin. Econ.* 117 (1979).

that investors and others know how well the managers perform. And the mechanisms may be inadequate to deal with one-time defalcations, when the manager concludes that the opportunities of the moment exceed any subsequent penalties in the employment market.

Investors might try to deal with these problems by combining ever more elaborate contractual strictures with full-time monitors to look over the shoulders of managers. More contractual detail is an implausible solution; recall that the need for managerial discretion comes precisely from the high costs of anticipating all problems, contracting about them, and enforcing these contracts through the courts. As for monitors, who monitors the monitors? Full-time monitors are managers in all but name, and part-time monitors lack both the incentive to watch carefully and the information to determine how well others are performing their tasks.

The fiduciary principle is an alternative to elaborate promises and extra monitoring. It replaces prior supervision with deterrence, much as criminal law uses penalties for bank robbery rather than pat-down searches of everyone entering banks. Socially optimal fiduciary rules approximate the bargain that investors and managers would have reached if they could have bargained (and enforced their agreements) at no cost. Such rules preserve the gains resulting from the separation of management from risk bearing while limiting the ability of managers to give priority to their own interests over those of investors.

Fiduciary principles contain antitheft directives, constraints on conflict of interest, and other restrictions on the ability of managers to line their own pockets at the expense of investors. But these principles have limits that reflect the distinction between managerial practices that harm investors' interests and practices that simultaneously benefit managers and investors. For example, managers of a corporation are free to funnel business to another corporation in which they have an interest if the transaction is approved by disinterested directors or is "fair" (advantageous) to the firm. The fiduciary duty of a corporate director diverges sharply from the fiduciary duty of a trustee in this respect precisely because the interests of the principals are different.

Because the fiduciary principle is a rule for completing incomplete bargains in a contractual structure, it makes little sense to say that "fiduciary duties" trump *actual* contracts. Similarly it misses the point to say that managers may sacrifice the interests of investors to other ends, so long as investors are not hurt "too much." Presumably "too much" in this context means "by so much that investors start contracting around the rule." Because the reason for having a fiduciary principle in the first place is the high cost of specifying things by (express) contract, the suggested constraint denies the only function of the rule. Detailed contracting, costly enough at the outset of a venture, is almost impossible once a firm has been established. After the firm has raised necessary capital, investors have no practical way of revising the articles on their own to overcome intervening legal surprises. To use the fiduciary principle for any purpose other than maximizing the welfare of investors subverts its function by turning the high costs of direct monitoring—the reasons fiduciary principles are needed—into a shield that prevents investors from controlling managers' conduct.

Business Judgment and the Limits of Liability Rules

The fiduciary principle suggests that courts should routinely conduct wide-ranging inquiries to determine the bargain that managers and investors would have reached if transactions costs were zero. This sounds like the inquiry in tort law: the court would ask whether the costs of making a decision (taking a precaution) are less than the gains to be had (harms to be avoided), discounted by the probability of the gain (harm) occurring. Hearing tort cases, judges routinely make such calculations and impose stiff penalties on all who flunk felicific calculus. Yet judges invoke the "business judgment rule," a doctrine absolving managers of liability even though their conduct is negligent. Statements of the rule vary; its terms are far less important than the fact that there is a specially deferential approach.

Why both demand that managers maximize investors' wealth and then refuse to carry through with the demand by hitting managers in their wallets (a particularly appropriate place)? Behind the business judgment rule lies recognition that investors' wealth would be lower if managers' decisions were routinely subjected to strict judicial review.

Precisely why investors' wealth would not be maximized by close judicial scrutiny is less clear. The standard justifications are that judges lack competence in making business decisions and that the fear of personal liability will cause corporate managers to be more cautious and also result in fewer talented people being willing to serve as directors. These are helpful but not sufficient. They do not explain why the same judges who decide whether engineers have designed the compressors on jet engines properly, whether the farmer delivered pomegranates conforming to the industry's specifications, and whether the prison system adversely affects the mental states of prisoners cannot decide whether a manager negligently failed to sack a subordinate who made improvident loans. Nor do the standard explanations tell us why leading corporate managers to exercise caution is not beneficial in the same manner that threatening automobile drivers with liability (thus encouraging them to be more careful) is beneficial.

The business judgment rule must rest on something more. It reflects limits on the use of liability rules to assure contractual performance. We discuss below why liability rules have only limited usefulness as a governance mechanism in the publicly held corporation.[3]

SELF-ENFORCING CONTRACTS

Many torts and breaches of contract are one-shot deals. Unless the legal system requires the parties to bear the costs they create, there will be too much negligence and too many broken contracts. Long-

---

3. Our discussion is in the spirit of much recent work showing how markets best courts in enforcing contracts between parties that have enduring relations. See Charles Goetz and Robert E. Scott, "Principles of Relational Contracts," 67 *Va. L. Rev.* 1089 (1981); Benjamin Klein and Keith B. Leffler, "The Role of Market Forces in Assuring Contractual Performance," 89 *J. Pol. Econ.* 615 (1981); Benjamin Klein and Kevin M. Murphy, "Vertical Restraints as Contract Enforcement Mechanisms," 31 *J. L. & Econ.* 265 (1988); Charles R. Knoeber, "An Alternative Mechanism to Assure Contractual Reliability," 12 *J. Legal Stud.* 333 (1983); Anthony T. Kronman, "Contract Law and the State of Nature," 1 *J. L. Econ. & Org.* 5 (1985); Lester G. Telser, "A Theory of Self-Enforcing Agreements," 53 *J. Bus.* 27 (1980); Oliver E. Williamson, "Credible Commitments: Using Hostages to Support Exchange," 73 *Am. Econ. Rev.* 519 (1983); Williamson, "Transaction-Cost Economics: The Governance of Contractual Relations," 22 *J. L. & Econ.* 233 (1979).

term relations of the sort that corporations create also provide opportunities to return costs to their creators without the aid of the legal system.

Repeat Transactions

Poor performance is rational, as managers see things, when current gains exceed the present value of future costs. The relation between gains and future costs depends in large part on the likelihood of repeat transactions. The higher the probability of repeat transactions, the greater the incentive to perform well. Consider itinerant vendors. They have no brand name to protect and seldom engage in multiple transactions with the same buyer, so they have strong incentives to misrepresent the quality of their wares in order to obtain a higher price; the present value of future costs of such conduct is likely to be small. The opposite case, a long-term relation in which each party gains from doing business with the other in the future, creates the opposite incentive. Losing the other's repeat business may be a penalty vastly exceeding the gains of misrepresenting performance today.

Managers of public corporations are repeat players in several respects. Firms need to raise money continually (debt must be rolled over even when the firm does not plan to sell new stock). Firms—meaning managers—repeatedly stand for scrutiny and pay a high price in capital markets for subpar performance. Managers also face scrutiny in labor markets. If sacked today, they may have trouble matching their income elsewhere. In the limit this "*ex post* settling up" in labor markets is alone sufficient to create proper incentives.[4] Even if managers need not regularly tap capital markets to raise funds, their wealth is tied to the value of the firm's securities and so reflects some of the value of their performance. As the present value of forgone compensation in future periods

4. Gary S. Becker and George J. Stigler, "Law Enforcement, Malfeasance, and Compensation of Enforcers," 3 *J. Legal Studies* 1 (1974); Eugene F. Fama, "Agency Problems and the Theory of the Firm," 88 *J. Pol. Econ.* 288, 295–306 (1980). Which is not to say that the method works perfectly. If inferior management is not discovered for some time after the event, it may be impossible to achieve a satisfactory *ex post* settling up given the time value of money.

increases relative to the current gains from poor performance, liability rules become less important.

The Efficiency of Information Markets

Markets in information are one way to induce people to act as if they are in a relation with repeat transactions, even when they are not. *Consumer Reports* supplies information to customers who have never dealt with the vendor. One who knows that the transaction with the first customer influences the second will treat the first better. Other markets are less powerful in reflecting news. For example, poor performance by a physician may cause a patient to go elsewhere, unless the patient equates the bad result with bad luck. Although the chance of losing business gives doctors some incentive to perform well, it is not much because the disease and treatment will not be perfectly replicated. Disappointed patients cannot look up a physician in *Consumer Reports* or sell shares in a physician short to communicate information to the market.

Managers of public corporations face a potent information market. Few markets are as efficient as capital markets. Poor performance leads the markets to respond in ways that bring the costs home to the managers. First, investors (both informed and uninformed) will pay less for shares. The more investors believe that their dollars will be used by those in control of firms in ways inconsistent with maximizing the value of the firm, the less they will pay for shares. To minimize this rational fear, those in control have incentives to adopt governance mechanisms that limit their discretion to benefit at investors' expense.

Second, accurate price signals in capital markets contribute to the efficiency of labor markets. Share price information provides a relatively low-cost method of evaluating the performance of corporate managers. Such information can be used (imperfectly) to set managers' compensation within the firm as well as to measure their opportunity wage in external labor markets.

Finally, capital markets facilitate the operation of the market for corporate control (on which see Chapter 7). Managers must perform well to keep share prices high; if they do not, they can expect to be replaced. The efficient operation of the capital, labor, and takeover markets all raise the future costs of poor performance, thereby helping to assure contractual performance.

Firm-Specific Investments of Human Capital

Gains from exchange often do not depend on the identity of the other party to the contract. If *A* purchases wheat from *B*, who refuses to perform, *A* probably can purchase wheat of identical quality from *C* without difficulty. Neither *A* nor *B* has an investment specific to the transaction, and the gains from exchange thus do not depend on the continued presence of either party.

Not all contracts are of this type. Assume *A* contracts with *B* for the construction of a nuclear power plant. At the time the contract was entered into *B* was one of many contractors with the necessary expertise. Over time, however, it is likely that *B* will acquire certain skills and expertise specialized to this transaction. Other contractors who were once close substitutes for *B* now are decidedly inferior because they have not made the same transaction-specific investment.

Now assume that *B* breaches some term of the agreement. *A* is in a bind. If *A* fires *B* or causes *B* to walk off the job by suing *B*, the cost and expense of the plant might go up substantially because some other contractor will need to acquire the transaction-specific skills of *B*. *A* might well conclude that it is better off by continuing to deal with *B*, the breaching party, and avoiding these costs. Indeed, one of the striking findings of those who have studied contracts where transaction-specific investments are common is how rarely litigation is actually used to enforce contractual obligations.

Contracts involving labor have great potential for firm- or transaction-specific investments. Corporate managers frequently possess expertise and skills specialized to a firm. Changing managers is costly because the replacements lack equivalent firm-specific expertise—costly to the managers, too, for they must acquire specific capital to be useful elsewhere. Both sides try to avoid these costs, the threat of which induces both to perform well in the first place. Even if managers perform poorly in the short term, the incentive remains. Discharge (voluntary or induced by litigation) may be much less effective if it forces the costs to be incurred.

Gains from Breach

The larger the potential gains from misconduct or inattention, the more important are liability rules. A specter of civil liability (plus criminal penalties) is probably useful to deter large one-shot frauds. So the business judgment rule does not protect fraudulent conduct. In the main, however, managers' personal gains from negligent conduct are small, making the costs they bear without regard to the legal system quite sufficient.

COSTLY AND INACCURATE LITIGATION

Although markets bring home to managers most of the costs of their suboptimal performance, they are imperfect. If the legal system offered a better (cheaper) way, courts should use their comparative advantage. Unfortunately, courts are less well suited to detecting and rectifying shortcomings in the boardroom than they are to detecting and rectifying shortcomings in product design—and they aren't very good at the latter.

Breach or Mischance?

Recall from the first portion of this chapter why there are fiduciary duties: because it is too costly to contract for every contingency. Courts experience the same costs as the contracting parties. True, courts view the subject after the events, so the range of questions is narrowed. But judges encounter most of the nagging questions of information and estimation that make it hard to agree *ex ante*. How can the court know whether a poor outcome of a business decision is attributable to poor management (inputs) or to the many other things that affect firms?

A decision is good to the extent it has a high *expected* value, although it may also have a high variance. To observe that things turned out poorly *ex post,* perhaps because of competitors' reactions, or regulations, or changes in interest rates, or consumers' fickleness, is not to know that the decision was wrong *ex ante*. Only after learning all of the possible outcomes, and the probability attached to each, could the court determine the wisdom of the decision at the time it was made. Occasionally the decision will be a howler, making inquiry easy. More often it will be hard to reconstruct possible outcomes. Businesses rarely encounter "sure things." Often managers must act now and learn later; delay for more study may be the *worst* decision; the market will decide whether the decision was good. Competition pares away the unsuccessful choices. Only in retrospect, observing which decisions were fruitful and which were not, can we say which was best. Yet because failure does not show that the decision was inferior when made, a court lacks the information to decide.

Costs of decision *ex post* will be highest precisely when it was also most difficult to contract *ex ante*. So when claims are made on the basis of the fiduciary principle—as opposed to a specific contract—courts are likely to lack essential tools of decision. This means that *ex post* settling up in markets has a comparative advantage over courts at enforcing the fiduciary principle *except* in the case of startling gaffes and large, one-shot, self-interested transactions. It should be no surprise, then, to learn that the business judgment rule confines courts to exactly these rare cases.

Because managers work in teams, and outcomes are strongly influenced by events external to the firm, a court is forced to examine inputs rather than outputs. Yet how is this to be done? Monitoring the effort or output of any individual manager is very costly; reconstructing it by testimony years later is both costly and inaccurate. It is difficult even to imagine using liability rules as a remedy for poor effort by managers, although lack of gumption is the single largest source of agency costs.

The problem of error costs is similar. Courts have as much difficulty as other outsiders in measuring managers' efforts or output. The court's difficulties are complicated by selection bias. Most lawsuits follow poor outcomes, and judges naturally assume that such outcomes are a product of bad actions. This bias can be a source of substantial error costs.

Relative Attitudes toward Risk

Because information is costly, a poor outcome may be equated with poor performance. Agents who are penalized for poor outcomes as well as poor performance tend to undertake projects with lower variance. Managers especially want to avoid risk because they cannot diversify the value of their human capital. Shareholders, however, readily diversify risk through capital markets. They want managers to take the projects with the highest mean returns, which may entail high risk. (No pain, no gain.) Exposure to liability causes managers' incentives to diverge from the path of wealth maximization.

Even liability for loony decisions has costs. Damages hurt risk-averse managers more than they help risk-neutral investors. This difference creates opportunities for gains from trade. Investors may agree to release managers from liability in order to reduce risk and thus to reduce the amount that must be paid in compensation and insurance. Investors would contract to accept lower damages in exchange for lower salaries. They do this explicitly through absolution clauses and implicitly through insurance; the business judgment rule acts as an implicit contract with similar effects.

Natural Selection in Courts and Markets

We have stressed the role of incentive-compatible contracts—that is, arrangements that reward managers automatically for good performance and penalize them for bad. All this attention to managers' incentives slights another, equally interesting question: what are judges' incentives? However much judges want to decide cases "correctly," they do not receive extra pay for extra work or more astute estimates of market conditions. Inferior managers eventually are "selected out" by competitive process. Investors likewise are selected out, and markets therefore tend to value decisions accurately. Judges are neither chosen for business acumen nor fired or subject to reductions in salary if they err in assessing business situations. Judges also are accustomed to deciding cases on full records and may be too quick to blame managers who act—as often they should—in haste or on incomplete information. It is better to insulate all honest decisions from review than to expose managers and directors to review by judges and juries who do not face market pressures. The business judgment rule does this.

DERIVATIVE LITIGATION

Any comparison of markets' and courts' enforcement of the fiduciary principle must take into account how the judicial process works. The mechanism is the derivative suit. When the board of directors decides to bring (or not bring) an action against an officer or director, this is a business judgment like any other. Derivative litigation attacks the propriety of this nonenforcement decision. Incentive-compatible devices attach weights to outcomes. Small benefits yield small rewards, large losses large penalties, and so on. So too with votes, which are tied directly to stakes and so improve incentives (see Chapter 3). A dominating characteristic of the derivative action is the lack of any link between stake and reward—not only on the judge's part but also on the plaintiff's.

Shareholders with tiny holdings can bring derivative actions. Holders of small stakes have little incentive to consider the effect of the action on other shareholders, the supposed beneficiaries, who ultimately bear the costs. If the action appears to be a positive net value project because of the possible recovery of attorneys' fees, an attorney will pursue it regardless of its effect on the value of the firm. (This suggests that the method of compensating attorneys and assessing costs will have a large influence on the costs and benefits of derivative litigation. For current purposes it is enough to know that no system of awarding attorneys' fees or assessing costs is perfect. However attorneys may be compensated, the value of managers' time cannot be recouped, no matter how frivolous the action.)

Sometimes the combination of uninterested nominal plaintiffs and interested attorneys produces striking effects. The spate of derivative suits in the 1970s challenging payment of baksheesh abroad, notwithstanding the profitability of the practice, shows how the lure of fees (or ideology) may lead to litigation inconsistent with investors' interests. Other conflicts are less apparent. Statutes typically require a majority, or at most two-thirds, of votes to approve mergers. Unanimous consent is not required because a demand for unanimity would create incentives for shareholders to behave strategically. Any shareholder, even if convinced the merger was beneficial and the terms fair, could refuse consent and hope to be bought off. A shareholder would reason that the cost imposed on all other shareholders (the premium forgone) would force the corporation to "buy" the shareholder's approval with some type of side payment. Such behavior is privately rational but wealth reducing. Derivative litigation can create some holdup power.

All problems of incentives to one side, there is the problem of access to information and expertise. Outsiders do not have access to (or means to evaluate) knowledge within the firm. What looks like a hasty decision by corporate managers may simply reflect experience or an effort to avoid the expense of hiring outside experts. For instance, a seemingly self-interested decision to accelerate the exercise of a stock option may well be the most efficient method of awarding an increase in compensation. Paucity of information frequently makes it difficult for either plaintiffs or judges to determine which actions promote maximum value for the firm. In the end, then, derivative litigation is bound to fall short of any ideal conception of the role of the legal system.[5]

Applications

THE DECLINE OF THE *ULTRA VIRES* DOCTRINE

In the nineteenth century, judges often treated corporate actions such as charitable contributions and expenditures on behalf of employees as beyond the power of the corporation, or *ultra vires*. Under modern corporate law, however, such actions are routinely upheld. The decline of the *ultra vires* doctrine is consistent with the principles that we have discussed.

Payment to a widow of a deceased employee, for example, may create goodwill among other employees and increase productivity. Similarly, charitable contributions may create favorable publicity for the firm and thus be an effective form of advertising. They may depict the firm as a "good citizen" and stave off regulation, and so on. Maybe not; maybe the manager causes the firm to give money to the opera so that it can afford to hire a singer the manager wants to hear. Contributions then are like perquisites, which courts also decline to investigate. You cannot tell in advance that a category of expenses always is antithetical to investors' interests. So courts

---

5. Data showing that derivative suits do not have significant effects on the price of stock strongly support this proposition. Daniel R. Fischel and Michael C. Bradley, "The Role of Liability Rules and the Derivative Suit in Corporate Law: A Theoretical and Empirical Analysis," 71 *Cornell L. Rev.* 261 (1986). Data on the effect of changes in laws concerning derivative suits are mixed. Compare Elliott J. Weiss and Lawrence J. White, "Of Econometrics and Indeterminacy: A Study of Investors' Reactions to 'Changes' in Corporate Law," 75 *Calif. L. Rev.* 551 (1987), with Michael C. Bradley and Cindy A. Schipani, "The Relevance of the Duty of Care Standard in Corporate Governance," 75 *Iowa L. Rev.* 1 (1989). Note 4 in Chapter 8 discusses some of these studies.

now leave such questions to markets, again demonstrating confor-
mity of law and economics.

THE DISTINCTION BETWEEN THE DUTY OF CARE AND THE DUTY OF LOYALTY

It is conventional to draw a sharp distinction between the duty of
care (to act as a prudent person does in the management of his own
affairs of equal gravity) and the duty of loyalty (to maximize the
investors' wealth rather than one's own). Judges scrutinize alleged
violations of the duty of loyalty more closely than alleged violations
of the duty of care. The usual explanation for this dichotomous
treatment is that the decisions tainted by a conflict of interest are
entitled to less judicial deference than those that are not. Some
have argued that the differences between the duty of care and the
duty of loyalty are so fundamental that the latter should be
strengthened and the former abolished.[6]

Ultimately, though, there is no sharp line between the duty of
care and the duty of loyalty. What is the difference between
working less hard than promised at a given level of compensation
(a breach of the duty of care) and being compensated more than
promised at a given level of work (a breach of the duty of loyalty)?
Both are agency costs, conflicts of interest in an economic sense,
that reduce shareholders' wealth. The existence of a conflict of
interest, therefore, cannot explain the distinction between the duties of care and loyalty.

A satisfactory explanation for the distinction may be found in the
differential payoffs from breach and policing. Duty-of-loyalty problems often involve spectacular, one-shot appropriations, of the
"take the money and run" sort, in which subsequent penalties
through markets are inadequate. Liability rules are most helpful
when other mechanisms fail. A manager on the verge of retirement
is not likely to be deterred from wrongdoing by the decline in his
future wage. The duty of loyalty supplements market penalties for
breach in those situations where the market penalties themselves
might be insufficient. It is also easier for courts to detect appropriations than to detect negligence, so the costs of inquiry and error
are lower.

6. See Kenneth E. Scott, "Corporation Law and the American Law Institute
Corporate Governance Project," 35 *Stan. L. Rev.* 927 (1983).

PROCEDURAL BUT NOT SUBSTANTIVE REVIEW OF CONFLICT-OF-INTEREST TRANSACTIONS

Managers must prefer investors' interests to their own in the event of conflict. That is the core of the duty of loyalty. Ordinarily courts require managers to prove that any conflict-of-interest transaction is "fair" to the firm—that is, that the firm receives a deal at least as good as it could have obtained in an arm's-length transaction with a stranger. That is a market test, again consistent with the contractual view of the firm.

Even this inquiry into market conditions is forgone when the transactions have been approved by independent monitors. Disinterested directors, for example, are proxies for investors and can be cheap substitutes for liability rules in assuring contractual performance. After all, the disinterested monitors have reputational interests of their own and face *ex post* settling up in labor and capital markets. Because they gain little from approving an insider's transaction, even a modest penalty in other markets makes them effective monitors. (Notice that we say "little" rather than "nothing." "Disinterested" directors are quite interested in maintaining the managers' esteem and places on the board, which are worth something.)

Corporate law has recognized this by allowing such directors to validate transactions that would otherwise be tainted by conflict of interest. Thus, a decision to resist a tender offer, dismiss a derivative suit, enter into a transaction with an interested director, or negotiate a merger with a related entity may be subject to a lower standard of judicial review if it is made by disinterested directors. These decisions allow firms to opt out of stricter standards of judicial review by adopting alternative governance mechanisms. Shareholder approval of a transaction can also lead judges to be more deferential in reviewing a transaction.[7]

Neither independent directors nor a shareholder vote necessarily *ensures* that a particular transaction will increase shareholders' wealth. Independent directors may be too uninformed to make intelligent decisions. Or maybe friendship in conjunction with directors' fees and a belief that the market won't notice "just this

7. See, for instance, Rosenblatt v. Getty Oil Co., 493 A.2d 929, 937 (Del. 1985); Weinberger v. UOP, Inc., 457 A.2d 701, 703 (Del. 1983).

one time" lead them to play dead. Similarly, collective action problems may cause rational shareholders to vote in favor of a particular transaction even if it is wealth-reducing (see Chapter 3). For these reasons, courts have been unwilling to abdicate in favor of independent directors or shareholders. To say that approval by disinterested parties leaves *some* costs and risks is not to say that they are large; as we know that the costs and error rate of the legal system are large, the judicial role is correspondingly small.

INDEMNIFICATION AND INSURANCE

Corporate law provides firms with flexibility in deciding whether to provide indemnification or insurance to managers for expenses incurred in litigation.[8] Firms commonly indemnify or insure corporate officers against litigation expenses and certain types of judgments. This contractual response, which many have criticized,[9] can be explained along the lines we have suggested. Indemnification and insurance allow firms to contract around liability rules when markets are cheaper than courts. These are *real* contracts and accordingly are enforced almost without exception.

RESTRICTIONS ON DERIVATIVE LITIGATION

Our discussion of the poor incentive of small shareholders and their attorneys to maximize the value of the firm implies that legal rules should place restrictions on the ability to bring derivative suits. The demand requirement, the contemporaneous ownership rule, stat-

---

8. See 8 Del. Code §145(f) ("The indemnification provided by this section shall not be deemed exclusive of any other rights to which those seeking indemnification may be entitled under any bylaw, agreement, vote of stockholders or disinterested directors or otherwise"). Corporations also may purchase insurance for directors even where indemnification is prohibited. Ibid. at §145(g). Other states follow the same pattern. American Law Institute, *Principles of Corporate Governance: Analysis and Recommendations* 199–214 (Tent. Draft No. 10, 1990) (collecting statutes, decisions, and practices).

9. See Joseph Bishop, *The Law of Corporate Officers and Directors: Indemnification and Insurance* (1981). Bishop and others have argued that indemnification and insurance erode the deterrent effect of liability rules. As Charles Goetz points out, and as we contended in Chapter 2, insurers often may be the best monitors of managerial misconduct. "A Verdict on Corporate Liability Rules and the Derivative Suit: Not Proven," 71 *Cornell L. Rev.* 344, 349 (1986).

utes requiring plaintiffs to give security for expenses, and, perhaps most important, the ability of directors to terminate derivative suits by making ordinary business judgments about the costs and benefits of further litigation, all have this effect.[10]

Undoubtedly directors named as defendants in derivative suits do not exercise impartial judgment in deciding whether to sue themselves. Similarly, special litigation committees appointed by the managers will not be impartial. It is *also* true that there are real, and substantial, costs associated with the derivative suit, given the plaintiffs' incentives to behave strategically, the shortfall of information available to judges, and the opportunity costs of the managers' time devoted to defense. One cannot look at the costs of dismissal in isolation. Hence "structural bias" of the board—the reluctance of managers who are named as wrongdoers or special litigation committees appointed by such managers to take "enough" action—hardly demonstrates the need for more vigorous enforcement of derivative suits. That is only the half of it. Courts (and markets) regularly accept the decisions of interested managers—about salary, about the identity of the auditors, and so on. We must avoid the Nirvana fallacy, the comparison of imperfect markets against a mythical perfect judicial or regulatory scheme. Perfection dominates this choice, but it is not a real one.

The tough question is, which of two very imperfect classes of decision makers—managers allegedly involved in wrongdoing or the persons they seat on special litigation committees on the one hand; shareholders with a small economic stake in the venture represented by plaintiffs' attorneys and judges on the other hand—is more likely to make decisions that increase the value of the firm? There is no ready answer. Not surprisingly, different judges have reached different conclusions about when directors charged with wrongdoing can dismiss derivative suits.[11]

10. For descriptions of all of these rules and extensive discussion of the cases, see Deborah A. DeMott, *Shareholder Derivative Actions* (1987 & Supp. 1989). See also Starrels v. First National Bank of Chicago, 870 F.2d 1168, 1172–76 (7th Cir. 1989) (concurring opinion); Kamen v. Kemper Financial Services, Inc., 908 F.2d 1338 (7th Cir. 1990) certiorari granted, 111 S. Ct. (1990).

11. Compare Auerbach v. Bennett, 47 N.Y.2d 619, 393 N.E.2d 994, 419 N.Y.S.2d 920 (1979) (decision by independent members of special litigation committee to terminate derivative suit subjected to scrutiny under business judgment rule), with Miller v. Register & Tribune Syndicate, 336 N.W.2d 709 (Iowa 1983)

The Anomalous Duty to Be Informed

In *Smith v. Van Gorkom*[12] the Supreme Court of Delaware held that
the business judgment rule applies only to decisions that are "informed." The court further held that managers who accepted a
merger proposal at a large premium over the market price in an
arm's-length transaction but who did not study the proposal or
consult any outside experts breached their fiduciary duty to make
an informed decision. It may be that this case is a specialty of
tender offer law, which we will visit in Chapter 7.[13] Perhaps it
establishes a special rule for last-period problems (the firm was to
be acquired in the transaction). If *Van Gorkom* is a more traditional
business judgment case, it is an outlier. In either event, it led to a
big change in Delaware law: a provision in the corporate code,
added in 1986, authorizing firms to eliminate damages liability in
duty-of-care cases.[14] Here we find one of the most explicit ac-
knowledgments of the role of contract in corporate law.[15]

It is not hard to see why the case produced such a swift and
sweeping reaction. Judicial inquiry into the amount of information
managers should acquire before deciding creates the precise
difficulties that the business judgment rule is designed to avoid.
Information is necessary for corporate managers to maximize the

---

(directors named as defendants cannot create special litigation committee to study
whether derivative suit should be dismissed), Zapata Corp. v. Maldonado, 430 A.2d
779 (Del. 1981) (intermediate standard), with Alford v. Shaw, 358 S.E.2d 323 (N.C.
1987) (firm may dismiss action when its pursuit would injure the corporation, even
though a majority of the board is "interested," but court must review the decision to
do this), and Joy v. North, 692 F.2d 880 (2d Cir. 1982) (similar).

12. 488 A.2d 858 (Del. 1985).

13. Jonathan Macey and Geoffrey Miller, "Trans Union Reconsidered," 98 *Yale
L. J.* 127 (1988), treat it this way. Daniel R. Fischel, "The Business Judgment Rule
and the Trans-Union Case," 40 *Bus. Law.* 1437 (1985), treats it as an ordinary business judgment case.

14. 8 Del. Code §102(b)(7). Other states have followed suit. Deborah A. DeMott,
"Limiting Directors' Liability," 66 *Wash. U. L. Q.* 295 (1988), collects the permuta-
tions. See also American Law Institute, *Principles of Corporate Governance: Analysis and Recommendations* §7.17 (Tent. Draft No. 9, 1989) (recommending, in one
of its few concessions to contract, that corporations be allowed to limit damages in
duty-of-care cases to the manager's or director's income for the year of the delict).

15. Though not one without problems—the "latecomer term" difficulty, to which
we return at the end of Chapter 6 when discussing the appraisal remedy.

value of the firm. But there is a limit to how much managers should know before making a decision. It would make no sense, for example, for a manager who has to decide whether to give his or her secretary a $10-a-week raise to commission a $100,000 study of secretarial compensation in the United States. Information is costly, and investors want managers to spend on knowledge only to the point where an additional dollar generates that much in better decisions. Exactly how much information to gather depends on such factors as how much the managers already know, the costs of obtaining additional information, the likely benefit of such information, and the variance of possible outcomes. Perhaps the Supreme Court of Delaware has changed course again, for in 1985 it remarked that "informed decision to delegate a task is as much an exercise of business judgment as any other."[16] Managers can delegate tasks to the market as easily as to investment bankers—and markets are cheaper.

The ultimate issue is who should decide how much information to acquire in advance of a business decision. Allowing shareholders to challenge business decisions that they say were not "informed" has the effect of substituting the business judgment of some shareholders, their attorneys, and a court for that of the managers. Because the managers have the best incentives (particularly when, in a case like *Van Gorkom,* they hold large blocs of the firm's stock), the legal process is distinctly inferior.

16. Rosenblatt v. Getty Oil Co., 493 A.2d 929, 943 (Del. 1985).

5

Corporate Control Transactions

The preceding chapters implicitly take "the firm" as a constant. Yet the only constant feature of corporate organization is change. Firms are in motion. They build new plants and enter or retreat from markets. They also change their own structure—setting up new divisions, entering or leaving markets, buying or selling plants, acquiring or being acquired, increasing and decreasing leverage, going public or private, selling stock or buying it back (generally or from particular investors). We call these changes "corporate control transactions."

Control transactions may make some investors rich while they leave others unaffected or poorer. For example, owners of controlling blocs may sell at a substantial premium, without any obligation to share the bounty with other shareholders. Firms may make "targeted" repurchases of shares, paying a premium to some investors while not offering the opportunity to others. Managers may arrange to take a corporate opportunity for themselves, with the consent of the directors, or may allocate an opportunity for a family of connected corporations to the firm that can make the most profitable use of it. Mergers set up in arm's-length bargaining may distribute the lion's share of the gain to one party, even though both parties to the merger are controlled by the same people.

Firms may alter internal structure and the structure of ownership as they please—or refuse to do so—subject only to the fiduciary standard. Managers who live up to the all-purpose duties of care and loyalty face few, if any, additional constraints. These doctrines, and the exceedingly limited judicial role they entail, have run into withering criticism from scholars demanding two kinds of change: an obligation to "share" the gains from corporate control transactions, and a prohibition against certain kinds of transactions. (Different critics put different transactions under the bans.)

109

Criticism has had little visible effect on the law. Well it should not, for rules requiring the sharing of gains may prevent their creation, and the transactions most vociferously attacked serve important functions (hence the profits). Courts' laissez-faire approach to corporate control transactions is economically sound, another example of the economic structure of corporate law. Many of the arguments pro and con on this topic refer to "fiduciary duties." Everyone believes that fiduciary duties, "properly understood," favor his approach. Chapter 4 defined fiduciary duties as implicit contractual terms—obligations to act in shareholders' interests, when explicit contracts are silent, in the fashion the parties would have provided by contract had they been able to negotiate without transactions costs. We apply that understanding to corporate control transactions.

Equal Treatment, Fiduciary Duty, and Shareholders' Welfare

Many scholars, though few courts, conclude that one aspect of fiduciary duty is the equal treatment of investors. Their argument takes the following form: fiduciary principles require fair conduct; equal treatment is fair conduct; hence, fiduciary principles require equal treatment. The conclusion does not follow. The argument depends on an equivalence between *equal* and *fair* treatment. To say that fiduciary principles require equal treatment is to beg the question whether investors would contract for equal or even equivalent treatment.

Proper analysis of this question employs a distinction between rules that maximize value *ex ante* and actions that maximize the returns of certain investors *ex post*. A simple example illustrates the point. A corporation may choose to invest its capital in one of two ventures. Venture 1 will pay $100, and the returns can be divided equally among the firm's investors. Thus if there are ten investors in the firm, the expected value to each investor is $10. Venture 2 will pay $150, but only if the extra returns are given wholly to five of the ten investors. Five "lucky" investors will receive $20 apiece, and the unlucky ones $10. Because each investor has a 50 percent chance of being chosen, each would think

Venture 2 worth $15. The directors of the firm should choose Venture 2 over Venture 1 because it has the higher value and because none of the investors is worse off under Venture 2.

Now consider Venture 3, in which $200 in gains are to be divided among only five of the ten investors with nothing for the rest. If investors are risk-neutral, fiduciaries should choose Venture 3 over Venture 2 (despite the fact that some investors end up worse off under Venture 3), because the expected value to each investor is $20 under Venture 3 and only $15 under Venture 2.

If the terms under which the directors obtain control of the firm call for them to maximize the wealth of the investors, they select the highest-paying venture and abide by its rules of distribution. If unequal distribution is necessary to make the stakes higher, then duty requires inequality. The firm's managers could not easily justify a choice of Venture 2 or 3, followed by a "surprise" equal distribution of the proceeds among the ten investors. In the example we posed, the firm obtained the higher returns only by agreeing to unequal distribution. It might get away with a breach of these conditions once, but Ventures 2 and 3 or their equivalent soon would become unavailable. Besides, if the firm promises to pay some investors unequally when it undertakes the venture, the managers could not be "fair" to the unlucky investors without being unfair to the lucky ones. The *ex post* inequality under Ventures 2 and 3 is no more "unfair" than the *ex post* inequality of a lottery, in which all players invest a certain amount but only a few collect. The equal treatment of the investors going into Ventures 2 and 3, and the gains they receive from taking chances, make the *ex post* inequality both fair and desirable.

Our analysis of Ventures 2 and 3 should be uncontroversial. If corporate control transactions sufficiently resemble Ventures 2 and 3, this analysis supplies a guide for analyzing the fiduciary duties of corporate managers. A class of control transactions resembles Ventures 2 and 3 if: (1) control changes and financial restructurings produce gains for investors to enjoy; (2) the existence or amount of the gain depends on unequal distribution; and (3) shareholders prefer the unequal distribution to a more equal distribution of smaller gains from an alternative transaction (or no transaction). We take up these conditions in turn.

POTENTIAL GAINS FROM CONTROL TRANSACTIONS

Managers do not always maximize the wealth of investors. We have already discussed the costs of principal-agent relationships. Because managers have only a small stake in the fortunes of the firm, these costs may be quite high. Managers may not work as hard as they would if they could claim a higher share of the proceeds—they may consume excessive perquisites, and they may select inferior projects for the firm without bearing the consequences of their action. Corporate control transactions can reduce agency costs if better managers obtain control of the firm's assets or if they alter the incentive structure facing existing managers. This means, in turn, greater wealth for all. The gains from control transactions may be exceedingly great. Going private, sales of plants, tender offers, these and more yield gains as great as doubling the market value of the firm.[1] The number of going-private transactions and spinoffs into private hands of divisions of public corporations is large and growing (see Table 1).

Why? Control transactions reflect substantial gains. Sale of a control bloc of stock, for example, allows the buyer to install his own management team, producing any gains available from the new structure. Because such a buyer believes he can manage the assets of a firm more profitably, he is willing to pay a premium over the market price to acquire control. The premium will be some percentage of the anticipated increase in value once the transfer of control is effectuated. If there were no anticipated increase in value, it would be irrational for the buyer to pay the premium.

1. See Symposium, The Structure and Governance of Enterprise, *J. Fin. Econ.* (forthcoming 1990) (containing many empirical studies of the subject); Harry DeAngelo, Linda DeAngelo, and Edward M. Rice, "Going Private: Minority Freezeouts and Stockholder Wealth," 23 *J. L. & Econ.* 367 (1984); Clifford G. Holderness and Dennis Sheehan, "The Role of Majority Shareholders in Publicly Held Corporations: An Exploratory Analysis," 20 *J. Fin.* 317 (1988); Gregg A. Jarrell, James A. Brickley, and Jeffrey M. Netter, "The Market for Corporate Control: The Empirical Evidence Since 1980," 2 *J. Econ. Perspectives* 49 (Winter 1988) (survey article); Steven Kaplan, "The Effects of Management Buyouts on Operating Performance and Value," 24 *J. Fin. Econ.* 217 (1989); Laurentius Marais, Katherine Schipper, and Abbie Smith, "Wealth Effects of Going Private for Senior Securities," 23 *J. Fin. Econ.* 155 (1989). Chapter 7 presents in detail the evidence concerning tender offers, one type of corporate control transaction.

Table 1

| Year | Public-firm buyouts | | Divisional buyouts | | Total value of buyouts (billion 1989$) |
	Number	Average value (million 1989$)	Number	Average value (million 1989$)	
1979	16	64.9	59	5.4	1.4
1980	13	74.4	47	24.2	2.1
1981	17	137.6	83	16.1	3.7
1982	31	91.5	115	33.2	6.7
1983	36	198.5	139	49.0	14.0
1984	57	415.6	122	91.3	34.8
1985	76	317.6	132	100.1	37.4
1986	76	281.0	144	167.4	45.5
1987	47	469.3	90	138.5	34.5
1988	125	487.4	89	181.3	77.0
1989	80	231.4	91	106.6	28.2

Source: Michael C. Jensen, "Eclipse of the Public Corporation," 89 *Harv. Bus. Rev.* 61, 65 (Sept.–Oct. 1989), compiled from several other sources through 1988; revalued by the authors and updated to include 1989 transactions.

Self-interest thus assures us that changes of corporate control, like other voluntary exchanges, move assets to higher valued uses.

Other transactions present similar opportunities for gain. The elimination of minority shareholders in a subsidiary produces gains if the combined entity can achieve economies of scale, centralized management and corporate planning, or economies of information. A parent may withhold projects from a subsidiary, for example, if the parent's investors must guarantee loans to finance them. Under these circumstances, the parent's investors bear a proportionally greater risk of loss than the minority shareholders in the subsidiary, but they do not receive a proportionally greater share of any gains. Eliminating the minority shareholders can increase the likelihood that profitable new ventures will be undertaken.

Other control transactions attack agency costs directly. When firms go private they eliminate—or substantially reduce—the separation of ownership and control that creates the clash of interest between principal and agent.[2] The effect is real when a single investor ends up with much of the equity, as in a leveraged buyout (LBO), and especially great when the managers end up owning a substantial chunk of the firm, as in a management buyout (MBO). Other things being equal, the lower agency costs mean higher returns to investors. LBOs, MBOs, and related transactions greatly increase the debt-equity ratio, which has further effects. Firms with additional debt are obliged by contract to pay out most of their profits. This compels managers to return to capital markets if they seek additional funds; lenders monitor the managers' conduct and increase the interest rate to protect themselves if things are amiss. Higher interest rates come out of shareholders' profits (and managers' income), alerting all to the problem and penalizing managers automatically. The compulsory payment obligation also puts the fear (and prospect) of bankruptcy into managers' minds, and the desire to avoid failure may be a powerful spur to success.[3] If success is not forthcoming, the debt associated with going-private transactions precipitates bankruptcy quickly, stopping the deterioration more quickly than in firms that are capitalized principally with equity.

Extra debt introduces to the firm the specialized monitoring services of secured debtors; certain structures with assets dedicated to particular purposes may be more efficiently monitored by specialized lenders than by residual claimants. Then there are tax advantages (when the marginal rate of taxation on income falls, as it has over the last ten years, debt becomes more attractive because it is deductible at the corporate level and bears less of a penalty, compared with capital gains, at the investor's level). Finally, going-pri-

2. Frank H. Easterbrook, "High-Yield Debt as an Incentive Device," *International J. L. & Econ.* (forthcoming 1991), describes in much greater detail both the theory and data concerning the effects on agency costs of going-private transactions.

3. On the ways payment obligations may affect agency costs and monitoring, see Frank H. Easterbrook, "Two Agency-Cost Explanations of Dividends," 74 *Am. Econ. Rev.* 650 (1984); Michael C. Jensen, "Agency Costs of Free Cash Flow, Corporate Finance, and Takeovers," 76 *Am. Econ. Rev. Papers & Proceedings* 323 (1986); Sanford J. Grossman and Oliver D. Hart, "Corporate Financial Structure and Managerial Incentives," in *The Economics of Information and Uncertainty* (J. J. McCall ed. 1982). See generally the contributions to *Leveraged Management Buyouts: Causes and Consequences* (Yakov Amihud ed. 1989).

vate transactions may eliminate costs attributable to public ownership, which include substantial expenditures for legal and auditing fees, stockholder relations, and compliance with the SEC's and the stock exchanges' disclosure requirements. A private firm can reduce these costs, along with the risk of liability that disclosure obligations create.[4]

Allocation of a "corporate opportunity" to a corporate insider may allow that opportunity to be exploited more effectively or at lower cost. The firm incurs substantial agency costs in the exploitation of the opportunity because managers, who cannot capture the gains, lack the appropriate incentives. Managers who assign opportunities to themselves can appropriate a greater portion of the marginal gains from their efforts, and thus they have a greater incentive to produce such gains. The manager can compensate the firm by taking a lower salary and bonus, and the reduction in agency costs may be mutually beneficial.

Doubtless control transactions do not always produce gains. Some, although designed to achieve gains, fail. Organizational changes come with no more guarantees than do new plants and products. Any innovation may flop. Some changes in control may be attributable to self-aggrandizement rather than to gains in the use of the acquired firms' assets. If one firm wants to squander its money by paying too much for control, managers have no duty to turn the money away; an auctioneer does not stop the auction at the "right" price in order to protect bidders from paying too much. The market penalizes buyers who pay too much money for a deal, and those losses serve as signals to future buyers. The corporate law ignores overpayments, for they are self-deterring.

Some corporate control transactions that do not produce gains, however, are not self-deterring. Looting may explain certain transfers of control. Some going-private transactions may be motivated by a desire to exploit inside information rather than to reduce

4. The costs of disclosure include not only payments to underwriters, auditors, lawyers, and printers, but also the opportunity costs of managers' time (they must provide information to the market) and the costs entailed in revealing either products or corporate strategies to market too soon. See Flamm v. Eberstadt, 814 F.2d 1169, 1174–78 (7th Cir. 1987). Expected liability costs increased when the Supreme Court declined to adopt a bright-line rule governing disclosure of impending corporate control transactions. Basic, Inc. v. Levinson, 485 U.S. 224, 232–236 (1988).

agency costs. And sometimes a manager may appropriate control of a corporate opportunity even though the firm would have been able to exploit the opportunity more profitably.

At least for publicly traded firms, the market offers information that distinguishes value-increasing control transactions from others in which looting or mismanagement may be in store. The information is contained in the price of a firm's shares. If the control change is associated with an increase in price, the investors apparently do not fear looting or other harm to the firm. If a syndicate acquires a control bloc of shares, and the price of the remaining shares rises, relative to the market as a whole, then the shareholders are betting on the basis of available information that the new controller will be better for their interests than the old. Precisely the same reasoning can be used when analyzing whether a manager has appropriated a corporate opportunity that could have been used more profitably by the firm. If the firm's share prices do not fall after the taking of the corporate opportunity, investors do not believe that they have been injured.

Fewer price signals are available in going-private transactions, because such a transaction frequently eliminates public trading of the firm's shares. Even these transactions, however, leave some traces. If the price paid to frozen-out shareholders is higher than the price that the shares commanded before the transaction, the buyer anticipates that the transaction will produce gains. There is little percentage in paying $15 for shares selling at $10. If the only purpose of the transaction is to eliminate minority shareholders, it is irrational for the controlling shareholder to pay a premium over the market price. By using corporate assets to pay minority shareholders more than their shares are worth, the controlling shareholder will have decreased the value of his own holdings and therefore be worse off as a result.

All of these observations follow from the proposition that investors have no desire to give away their money. If they pay more for shares after a transaction than before, their dollar votes are a signal of gain and loss. One can obtain reliable information from the direction of price changes without believing that the prevailing price perfectly embodies the available knowledge. And price data speak clearly. Prices paid for shares acquired in control transactions exceed the market price by substantial amounts, in the range of 30 to 70 percent. The prices of the shares that are *not* acquired also rise smartly, although not by so much (the range of 10 to 20 percent is more common). Other investors, such as holders of unsecured debt, do not share in these gains—but they also do not lose. (See note 1 above for studies demonstrating these effects.)

Gains May Depend on Unequal Division

In many cases the apportionment of the gain makes little difference to the success of the transaction. If the gain from taking over a corporation exceeds the cost incurred by the acquirer, it does not matter who receives the premium that is necessary to obtain control. But the fact that apportionment may be irrelevant to the acquirer does not mean that apportionment of gains is always immaterial—sometimes apportionment is the decisive factor. Suppose a prospective acquirer of control concludes that, by expending $10, it can create a 50 percent chance of producing $30 in gains. If the prospective acquirer is risk-neutral, the transaction will go forward because the expected gains of $15 exceed the $10 cost of the transaction. If the fiduciary principle is interpreted to require the prospective acquirer to share the $20 gain in the event it is realized, however, and absorb the entire loss if the gain is not realized, the deal may become unprofitable because the costs exceed the expected gains.

In theory the law could require sharing of the $5 expected gain, but courts could not calculate this amount because they could not observe the *ex ante* risk of failure. Moreover, a large part of the cost to the acquirer is an opportunity cost—the money the acquirer could have made by devoting its talents to other projects. Another cost is the premium required to compensate risk-averse acquirers for risk bearing. Because it is difficult if not impossible to compute opportunity costs and risk premiums in litigation, it would be difficult or impossible to implement a sensible sharing rule. Even if opportunity costs could be approximated, judicial errors would arise, and beneficial control changes would be stifled.

A sharing requirement also may make an otherwise profitable transaction unattractive to the prospective seller of control. Suppose the owner of a control bloc of shares finds that his perquisites or the other amenities of his position are worth $10. A prospective acquirer of control concludes that, by eliminating these perquisites and other amenities, it could produce a gain of $15. The shareholders in the company benefit if the acquirer pays a premium of $11 to the owner of the controlling bloc, ousts the current managers, and makes the improvements. The net gains of $4 inure to each investor according to his holdings, and although the acquirer obtains the largest portion because it holds the largest bloc, no one is left out. If the owner of the control bloc must share the $11 premium with all of the existing shareholders, however, the deal collapses. The owner will not part with his bloc for less than a $10 premium. A sharing requirement would make the deal unprofitable to him, and the other investors would lose the prospective gain from the installation of better managers.

Other value-increasing transactions also would be deterred by a sharing requirement. First, as we have pointed out, sometimes a purchase of control is profitable to the purchaser only if it can prevent minority shareholders from sharing in the gains. Freezeouts after a transfer of control perform this function. Second, if the controlling shareholder in a going-private transaction or merger of a subsidiary into a parent corporation must underwrite the costs of future value-increasing transactions and thereby incur a proportionally greater risk of loss than the minority shareholders in the event expectations are not realized, then the deal may become unprofitable to the controlling shareholder if it must share the gains with minority shareholders if all goes well. Thus, a sharing principle in these transactions leads to a reduction in total wealth as shareholders desist from entering into otherwise profitable transactions.

There are other ways in which the gains from corporate control transactions may depend on unequal distribution. Because investors in the firm must cooperate to transfer control, sharing creates incentives to take a free ride. In a tender offer, for example, shareholders must tender rather than hold their shares if the bid is to succeed; in a merger (other than a short-form merger), they must vote favorably rather than abstain. If gains must be shared equally, however, each shareholder may find it worthwhile not to cooperate in the transaction. Suppose that all of the gains from a tender offer must be shared equally among the investors in the target corporation and that, if there is a follow-up merger, nontendering shareholders cannot be eliminated for less than the tender offer price. When a prospective acquirer makes a bid, the investors recognize that the acquirer can profit only to the extent it causes the value of shares to rise. If the bidder is offering $50 per share, the reasoning runs, it cannot profit unless value eventually rises above $50. Under the legal rules assumed above, it may be rational for every shareholder to spurn the $50 offer and hope that enough other shareholders tender to make the offer succeed. If there is a follow-up merger, the "fair" price cannot be less than $50 for the untendered shares. If there is no follow-up merger, the shareholder expects the price to exceed $50. Each shareholder, in other words, may attempt to take a free ride on the efforts of the bidder and other shareholders. To the extent free riding prevails, it reduces the chance that the beneficial transaction will go forward.

A final reason why the gains from beneficial transactions may depend on unequal division is that sharing rules may lead to costly attempts to appropriate greater parts of the profit. The appropriation problem arises because most gain-sharing rules do not produce determinate results: it is difficult to determine the "fair" price. If all investors are entitled to a "fair" share of the bounty, each will find it advantageous to fight for as much as possible and will spend as much as a dollar, on the margin, to claim another dollar of the benefits. It is possible for a substantial part of the gain to be frittered away, therefore, as claimants attempt to make the argument that they are entitled to more. Fear of this eventuality may cause otherwise beneficial control transactions to fall through; in any event resources will be wasted in litigation or other skirmishes.

INVESTORS PREFER THE PRINCIPLE THAT MAXIMIZES AGGREGATE GAINS

Do investors prefer a legal rule creating a larger pie even if not everyone may have a larger slice? They do, for two reasons. First, their expected wealth is greatest under this interpretation of the fiduciary principle. Second, they may deal with any risk by holding diversified portfolios of investments.

If control transactions produce gains, and if the gains depend on unequal allocation, then the expected wealth of the shareholders in the aggregate is maximized by a rule allowing unequal allocation. All share prices *ex ante* will be highest when the probability of a value-increasing transaction in the future is the greatest. Shareholders can realize this value at any time by selling their shares, or they can hold the shares and take the chance of gaining still more as a result of the unequal allocation of gains *ex post*.

This argument seems to disregard the fact that many investors are risk-averse; they prefer a sure $10, say, to a one in ten chance of receiving $100. On the surface, therefore, it seems that investors might benefit from equal or fair division of gains notwithstanding the loss of some gains as a result. As long as the market contains investors who are (or act as if they are) risk-neutral, however, the risk aversion of some investors is irrelevant. They can sell their (risky) stocks to the risk-neutral investors and invest in T-bills and other instruments that do not come with the possibility of unequal gain allocation. Grant the possibility of realizing the gains by sale, and every investor prefers the value-maximizing rule.

Well, not quite. We have smuggled some assumptions into this discussion. We have assumed that there are "enough" risk-neutral investors—a reasonable assumption in a world in which most stocks are in the hands of mutual funds, pension funds, insurance companies, university endowments, and other financial intermediaries that are the next best thing to the economist's hypothetical risk-neutral person. We have also assumed competitive capital markets. It is possible to show rigorously that competitive capital markets plus enough investors who are indifferent to risk leads all investors to prefer the wealth-maximizing rule.[5] Roughly speaking, capital markets are competitive when any one firm's production and financing decisions have negligible effects on both the price of any given investment (that is, any given bundle of risk and return from one firm or many) and the menu of risk-return combinations that investors can obtain by holding portfolios of instruments issued by different firms. When there is competition, investors agree that the corporation should have the objective of maximizing wealth because greater wealth gives them the ability to consume or rejuggle their portfolios to yield greater returns—in either event, investors exercise greater command over resources. Given the depth and richness of the world's capital markets, and the incessant creation of new financial instruments to fill any gaps in the available

5. The formal conditions for unanimous assent are set out in Harry DeAngelo, "Competition and Unanimity," 71 *Am. Econ. Rev.* 18 (1981). See also Louis Makowski, "Competition and Unanimity Revisited," 73 *Am. Econ. Rev.* 329 (1983); Makowski and Lynne Pepall, "Easy Proofs of Unanimity and Optimality without Spanning: A Pedagogical Note," 40 *J. Finance* 1245 (1985).

sets of risk and return, the conditions for investors' unanimity are satisfied in practice.

Let us suppose, however, that there is either too much risk aversion or too little competition to produce unanimous assent to a wealth-maximization rule. Does it follow that the risk-averse investor will want a compulsory gain-sharing rule as a means of reducing his exposure? No. *Compulsory* gain sharing as a result of legal rules reduces the number of options available to investors and their firms. Even risk-averse investors may prefer the wealth-maximizing result for some of their investments, while providing by contract for sharing in others. Corporations (especially close corporations, the subject of Chapter 9) contain many gain-spreading devices; legal rules giving investors the option of targeting gains allow them to tailor the degree of spreading to their taste. Risk-averse investors may wish to allow substantial inequality in distribution if these contractual remedies are cheap (they are), and if they can protect themselves by self-help the rest of the time. As it turns out, there is a ready self-help remedy: diversification.

There are two kinds of risk: systematic risk, which is common to all investments in the portfolio (for example, risk that a change in the interest rate will affect the value of all equity interests), and unsystematic or diversifiable risk. Risk is diversifiable to the extent that an investor, by investing in a portfolio containing many separate securities, can insulate himself from the risk. Suppose, for example, that ten firms bid for a single license to operate a television station. After the Federal Communications Commission makes the award, the stock of one firm will be worth $100 per share, and the stock of the other nine firms will be worthless. Each investment, standing alone, is very risky. But a shareholder can purchase one share in each of the ten firms, and this portfolio of investments will be worth $100 with certainty.

It is difficult to find firms whose fortunes are so closely intertwined. Nonetheless, diversification is highly useful in reducing risk because even an imperfectly negative correlation between the risks of different firms will dampen the volatility of the portfolio as a whole. An investor holding a diversified portfolio of New York Stock Exchange firms would barely notice the wreck of the Penn Central Railroad—not only because Penn Central stock would be a small part of the portfolio but also because bad news for the Penn Central is good news for the Chesapeake and Ohio.

Risks involved in corporate control transactions are diversifiable. Corporate control transactions are pervasive. There are mergers, takeovers, freezeouts, tender offers, going-private transactions and related events in abundance. Indeed, there is a strongly negative correlation among the risks. An investor with a reasonably diversified portfolio would be on the winning side of some transactions and the losing side of others. For example, if shareholders of one corporation obtain little of the gain from a given merger, the shareholders of the other corporation obtain more. An investor holding a diversified portfolio with stock in both corporations is concerned with the total gain from the transaction, not with how the gain is allocated. Indeed, the investor with shares of both would see any expense in allocating the gain as pure loss. To the extent an unequal allocation raises the number and amount of gain transactions, therefore, investors with diversified portfolios prefer to allow the unequal allocation to continue.

Diversification is available at remarkably low cost. In fact, it is less expensive to hold a diversified portfolio of investments than to hold an undiversified one, because diversification allows investors to avoid the expenses of investigating, picking, and trading stocks. Investors with little personal wealth can diversify by purchasing shares of mutual funds, which hold representative samples of stocks, mortgages, and many other investment vehicles. Most persons are much better diversified than they realize, because they hold wealth through their own human capital, their homes, and insurance and pension funds that are well diversified.[6]

The existence of diversification—not its employment—supports allowing the gains from corporate control transactions to be apportioned unequally even when investors are risk-averse and markets are not competitive. The availability of diversified investment portfolios means that investors who seek shelter from risk can find it. Others may elect to take greater risks in pursuit of larger gains, just as they may elect to hold only one risky stock. Perhaps they will become fabulously wealthy, but if they do not they will have little claim that they were treated inequitably. Any attempt to set fair

6. How much diversification is "enough" is a tough question, but gains taper off rapidly after ten stocks, and most investors are better diversified than that. Meir Statman, "How Many Stocks Make a Diversified Portfolio?" 22 *J. Fin. & Quant. Anal.* 353 (1987).

prices for corporate control transactions, in the name of protecting investors who choose not to diversify, penalizes other investors who eliminate risk through diversification, and in the process it reduces the number of value-increasing control transactions.

We have shown that the *ex post* inequality under Ventures 2 and 3, like the *ex post* inequality in a lottery, is not "unfair" if, *ex ante*, all investors have an equal chance to win and can eliminate risk through diversification. Now consider a potential objection to this reasoning. One might argue that this *ex ante* equality is absent in corporate control transactions because insiders systematically benefit at the expense of outsiders. Small shareholders, the argument runs, consistently will be frozen out, deprived of control premiums, and otherwise disadvantaged by insiders. Too, some investors are not diversified—shouldn't be diversified. Think of managers' human capital, tied up in a single firm, or the investors who, by controlling large blocs of stock, provide the monitoring services that redound to the gain of others.[7]

Our argument does not depend, though, on perfect or costless diversification. Recall how we got here: first we established that risk-neutral investors in competitive capital markets prefer the wealth-maximizing rule, then we drew out limits on that preference, and finally we introduced diversification to show that the limits are not serious, given possibilities for self-protection. Of course some investors will not be diversified, but by and large they are telling us that they are not the risk-averse ones. All that matters to our argument is that "enough" of the risk-averse investors be able to protect their interests—through diversification *or* holding low-risk instruments such as T-bills *or* through contractual gain-sharing provisions (as in close corporations)—that they would throw in their lot with the cause of wealth maximization as the *legal* norm when contracts are silent.

7. See William J. Carney, "The Theory of the Firm: Investor Coordination Costs, Control Premiums, and Capital Structure," 65 *Washington U. L. Q.* 1, 11–23 (1987); Jeffrey N. Gordon and Lewis A. Kornhauser, "Efficient Markets, Costly Information, and Securities Research," 60 *N.Y.U. L. Rev.* 761, 830–833 (1985). Although these articles take different approaches, each offers a thoughtful challenge to the ideas we have been presenting. Alan Schwartz, "Search Theory and the Tender Offer Auction," 2 *J. L. Econ. & Org.* 229, 244–249 (1986), presents support of, and extensions to, the argument in the text that investors choose maximum rather than fairly distributed gains.

For what it is worth—although this is not necessary to the argument—we think that even the "little" investor does well with simple diversification and is unlikely to opt for contractual sharing rules. One need not be wealthy to be on the "winning side" of a control transaction, and neither wealth nor status as an insider ensures being a winner. If corporation A purchases from corporation B a control block of shares in corporation C, a small (or outside) shareholder might participate in the gains by holding shares in any of the three firms. Similarly, if corporation D merges with corporation E (its long-held subsidiary) and freezes out the minority shareholders of corporation E, these shareholders may participate in the gains by holding shares of corporation D. Small shareholders also may participate in the gains resulting from tender offers, going-private transactions, allocation of a corporate opportunity to a parent rather than a subsidiary, and other types of corporate control transactions by holding shares in the firm that produces the gains. There is no need for the small shareholder to identify these situations in advance. By holding a diversified portfolio containing the securities of many firms, the small shareholder can ensure that he will participate in the gains produced. All shareholders therefore have a chance of receiving gains produced by corporate control transactions—not an equal chance, because some bidders will be close corporations, but enough of a chance to allow substantial diversification. If the chance is not "enough" given risk aversion, then large investors who invite minority participation must pay a premium, and again the risk-averse investor comes out well.

MARKET VALUE AS A BENCHMARK UNDER THE FIDUCIARY PRINCIPLE

In the circumstances we have discussed, shareholders unanimously prefer legal rules under which the amount of gains is maximized, regardless of how the gains are distributed. The ideal transaction is one like Venture 2 above, in which the gains are unequally distributed but all shareholders are at least as well off as they were before the transaction. Shareholders may also benefit from transactions in which the distribution of gains leave some shareholders worse off than before the transaction—as in Venture 3—but there are probably few such transactions. We cannot imagine why gains would depend on making some investors worse off, and we have not encountered any example of such a transaction. In a world of costly information, investors will view Venture 2 transactions very differently from Venture 3 transactions, which would raise all but insuperable difficulties in determining whether the transaction produced gain. One can imagine instances, of which looting is a good example, in which the person acquiring control pays a premium to some investor(s) in order to obtain control and obliterate the remaining claims, recouping the premium without putting resources to a more productive use. A requirement that all investors receive at least the market value of their positions prior to the transactions would be a useful rule of thumb for separating beneficial deals from potentially harmful ones. If every investor receives at least what he had before, and some receive a premium, the transaction must produce gains.

The requirement that everyone receive at least the value of his investment under existing conditions serves much the same function as the rule against theft. A thief might be able to put stolen resources to a better use than his victim, but if so then he can pay for those resources. Requiring payment increases the likelihood that transactions are value-increasing. Moreover, the proscription of theft also reduces the incentive of property owners to take elaborate precautions against theft. For example, investors might resort to costly monitoring devices to reduce the chance of confiscation of their shares. When all transactions are consensual, these precautions become unnecessary. By prohibiting confiscation, therefore, the fiduciary principle reduces wasteful expenditures while simultaneously reducing the number of socially inefficient corporate control transactions.

A rule against confiscation would be created by contract even if it were not part of the law. Whoever controlled a corporation would find it advantageous to insert an anticonfiscation provision in the articles of incorporation. If he did not, the firm could not expect to receive much for its shares. New shareholders would fear confiscation and take (expensive) steps to protect their interest. Because no firm has monopoly power over investment opportunities, the expected costs of these precautions would reduce by an equal amount the price that purchasers would be willing to pay. Thus the sums that the controlling party receives would reflect the costs created by the risk of confiscation (as Chapter 1 explained in greater detail.)

The Fiduciary Principle in Operation

A legal rule that permits unequal division of gains from corporate control changes, subject to the constraint that no investor be made worse off by the transaction, maximizes investors' wealth. This is really nothing more than an application of the Pareto principle of welfare economics. Turning to the law, we show that the cases and statutes by and large mirror these economic principles.

SALES OF CONTROL BLOCS

Sales of controlling blocs of shares provide a good example of transactions in which the movement of control is beneficial. The sale of control may lead to new offers, new plans, and new working arrangements with other firms that reduce agency costs and create gains from new business relationships. The premium price received by the seller of the control bloc amounts to an unequal distribution of the gains. Sales at a premium are lawful, and the controlling shareholder generally has no duty to spread the bounty.[8] For the reasons we have discussed, this unequal distribution may cut the costs to purchasers of control, increasing the number of beneficial control transfers by the incentive for inefficient controllers to relinquish their positions.

8. Treadway Co. v. Care Corp., 638 F.2d 357 (2d Cir. 1981); Zetlin v. Hanson Holdings, 48 N.Y.2d 684, 397 N.E.2d 387 (1979); Tryon v. Smith, 191 Ore. 172, 229 P.2d 251 (1951). See Robert W. Hamilton, "Private Sale of Control Transactions: Where We Stand Today," 36 *Case W. Res. L. Rev.* 248 (1985). To cut down on footnotes we recap some related doctrines. Firms may repurchase shares from particular investors at a premium or make a general offer but exclude one or more named investors. Unocal Corp. v. Mesa Petroleum Co., 493 A.2d 946 (Del. 1985). See generally Jonathan R. Macey and Fred S. McChesney, "A Theoretical Analysis of Corporate Greenmail," 95 *Yale L. J.* 13 (1985); Andrei Schleifer and Robert W. Vishny, "Greenmail, White Knights, and Shareholders' Interest," 17 *Rand J. Econ.* 293 (1986). Getty Oil Co. v. Skelly Oil Co., 267 A.2d 883 (Del. 1970), is among the many cases allowing firms to allocate corporate opportunities to privileged insiders. E. I. Du Pont de Nemours & Co. v. Collins, 432 U.S. 46 (1977), and Weinberger v. UOP, Inc., 457 A.2d 701 (Del. 1983), allow unequal division of the gains from mergers. See also Fins v. Pearlman, 424 A.2d 305 (Del. 1980).

Numerous commentators, however, argue for compulsory sharing. Adolph Berle argued that control is a "corporate asset" so that premiums must go into the corporate treasury.[9] A related proposal is the "equal opportunity" rule advocated by Professors Jennings and Andrews.[10] They would entitle minority shareholders to sell their shares on the same terms as the controlling shareholder. There are many similar proposals, reflecting persistent academic dismay with the state of the law.

Sharing the control premium would stifle transfers rather than enrich minority investors. If the premium must be paid into the corporate treasury, those who hold the controlling bloc may refuse to sell; if minority shareholders may sell on the same terms as the controlling shareholder, bidders may have to purchase more shares than necessary, possibly causing the transaction to become unprofitable (or leading to a uniform but lower price, again tempting refusal to sell). Minority shareholders would suffer under either rule, as the probability of improvements in the quality of management declined. Although the mountain of academic commentary calling for some type of sharing requirement has been uninfluential, now and again a supporting voice may be heard among the chorus of judges. We look at one such case, the famous *Perlman v. Feldmann.*[11]

Feldmann, president and chairman of the board of Newport (a producer of steel sheets), sold his controlling bloc of shares for $20 per share at a time when the market price was less than $12. The purchasers, a syndicate called Wilport, were end-users of steel from across the country, who were interested in a secure supply during the Korean War. During the war, price controls blocked steel producers from raising prices. The "Feldmann Plan," adopted by Newport and some other steel producers, effectively raised the price of steel to the (high) market-clearing level available during the shortage. Aspiring purchasers provided Newport with interest-free

9. Adolph A. Berle and Gardiner C. Means, *The Modern Corporation and Private Property* (1932); Berle, "The Price of Power: Sale of Corporate Control," 50 *Cornell L. Q.* 628 (1965); Berle, "'Control' in Corporate Law," 58 *Colum. L. Rev.* 1212 (1958).

10. William D. Andrews, "The Stockholders' Right to Equal Opportunity in the Sale of Shares," 78 *Harv. L. Rev.* 505 (1965); Richard W. Jennings, "Trading in Corporate Control," 44 *Calif. L. Rev.* 1 (1956).

11. 219 F.2d 173 (2d Cir. 1955).

advances in exchange for commitments for future production. Newport used those advances to replace equipment in order to expand and compete more effectively.

The Second Circuit held that the seller of the control bloc had a duty to share the control premium with other shareholders. The court's holding that Feldmann could not accept the premium was based on a belief that the shortage allowed Newport to finance needed expansion via the "plan," and that the premium represented an attempt by Wilport to divert a corporate opportunity—to secure for itself the benefits resulting from the shortage. The court stated that "[o]nly if defendants had been able to negate completely any possibility of gain by Newport could they have prevailed."[12]

This assumes that the gain resulting from the plan was not reflected in the price of Newport's stock. Yet the stock was widely traded, and the existence of the plan was known to investors. The price of shares prior to the transaction therefore reflected the value to Newport of advances under the plan. The Wilport syndicate paid two-thirds more than the going price and thus could not profit from the deal unless (a) the sale of control resulted in an increase in the value of Newport, or (b) Wilport's control of Newport denuded it of a business advantage (the advances), the equivalent of looting.

Consider the following simplified representation of the transaction, on the assumption that Wilport "took" something of value to Newport. Newport has 100 shares, and Wilport pays $20 for each of 37 shares. The market price of shares is $12, and hence the premium over the market price is $8 \times 37 = $296. Wilport must get more than $296 from Newport in order to profit; this comes at the expense of the other 63 shares, which must drop approximately $4.75 each, to $7.25. So if Wilport extracted a corporate asset, we will be able to see the effects in the market. Unless the price of Newport's outstanding shares plummeted, the Wilport syndicate could not be extracting enough to profit. In fact, however, the value of Newport's shares rose substantially after the transaction. Part of this increase may have been attributable to the rising market for steel companies at the time, but even holding this factor constant, Newport's shares appreciated.[13] The data refute the court's propo-

12. Ibid. at 177.

13. Charles Cope computed changes in the price of Newport's shares using the capital asset pricing model, under which the rate of return on a firm's shares is a function of the market rate of return, the volatility of the firm's price in the past, a

sition that Wilport appropriated a corporate opportunity of Newport. They support an inference that Wilport installed a better
group of managers and, in addition, furnished Newport with a more
stable market for its products. These contributions must have exceeded any loss from abolition of the Feldmann Plan.

LOOTING

Doubtless not all investors have the same good fortune as those
who held Newport. A specter of "looting" haunts opinions about
corporate control transactions. Cases imply (and occasionally hold)
that managers may, even must, nose out and rebuff raptors.[14] This
all-weather bogeyman of corporate law provides an argument for
every occasion, whether managers seek to preserve their own control ("Sorry, investors, we can't take that bid at 50 percent over
market because the buyer might denude your company"),[15] or commentators peddle their critique of prevailing doctrines ("Profits
should be shared fairly because then looting won't be profitable").
We interrupt our tour of corporate control transactions to say a few
things about looting, a concern applicable to all flavors of control
transaction.

Looting—more neutrally, removing from corporate solution assets exceeding in value the consideration to the firm—may be

---

constant, and a residual component that represents the consequences of unanticipated events. Increases in this residual reflect good news for the firm. (We explain this model in detail in Chapter 7.) Cope found a significant positive residual for
Newport in the month of the sale to Wilport. The raw price data are no less telling.
The $12 price to which the court referred was the highest price at which shares
changed hands before the sale of control. The average monthly bid prices for Newport stock during 1950 were: July, $6^3/4$; August, $8^1/2$; September, $10^7/8$; October,
$12^1/2$; November, $12^3/8$; December, 12. The sale to the Wilport syndicate took place
on August 31, 1950. This pattern of prices certainly does not suggest that the 63
percent interest excluded from the premium perceived injury to Newport.

14. For example, Insuranshares Corp. v. Northern Financial Corp., 35 F.
Supp. 22 (E.D. Pa. 1941), and Gerdes v. Reynolds, 28 N.Y.S. 2d 622 (1941), hold a
controlling investor liable on account of failure to investigate a purchaser.

15. See Cheff v. Mathes, 199 A.2d 548 (1964), in which the family controlling
Holland Furnace Co. refused to sell to Maremont, arguing that Maremont had an
unsavory reputation. Holland repurchased Maremont's shares at a premium price,
to the dismay of most of Holland's shareholders. After fending off Maremont, Holland slid downhill. Its woes are spelled out in William L. Cary and Melvin Aron
Eisenberg, *Corporations* 677–678 (5th ed. 1980).

profitable under some circumstances. Theft sometimes pays. Existing holders of control, no less than prospective purchasers, however, have an incentive to put their hands in the till, and a proposal to ban one or another corporate control transaction as an antidote to looting is like a proposal to ban investments in common stocks as an antidote to bankruptcy.

If it were feasible to detect looters in advance—if they all wore yellow carnations and pinkie rings, and smelled of sulfur—it might make sense to forbid the sellers of control to allow shares to pass to scoundrels (or even to the honest but inept). Certainly the sellers of control can detect knavery at a lower cost than the public shareholders who are not parties to the transaction. Yet it is difficult if not impossible to detect looters early on. Looting is by nature a one-time transaction. Once looters have plundered one firm, their reputation (or their residence in jail) prevents them from doing so again. But when they first obtain control, they may appear innocuous. Any rule that blocks sales in advance is equivalent to a program of preventive detention for people who have never robbed banks but have acquisitive personalities.

Although sellers could spend substantial sums investigating buyers and investors and still more in litigating over the quality of investigation, almost all of these efforts would be wasted. If investigations blocked transfers, most of these refusals would be false positives. That is, they would be refusals that reduced the gains available from transferring control. Sometimes the best way to manage a firm is to break it up—to sell off some operations and reorganize the rest. Spinoffs and splitups are no more suspect than mergers and the construction of new plants; both are efforts to obtain the optimal allocation of assets among management teams. Some managers are especially skilled in reorganizing or liquidating ailing firms. Yet the suspicion of looting falls most heavily on such people, for it is hard to say in advance whether a radical restructuring of a firm is good or bad for investors. A legal rule that has its bite when a firm is approached by a buyer with a proposal for radical (and potentially highly beneficial) surgery is unlikely to increase the value of investments.

We do not suggest that the legal system should disregard looting, but the best remedies are based on deterrence rather than prior scrutiny. Looters, when caught, may be fined or imprisoned. Penalties could be made high enough to be effective, making the transaction unprofitable *ex ante*. The costs of deterrence are less than the costs of dealing with looting through a system of prior scrutiny that would scotch many valuable control shifts as a by-product.

CHANGES IN CONTROL STRUCTURE

Many practices may affect the way in which investments are pooled to obtain or hold control. Voting trusts, holding companies, and other devices allocate control as effectively as sales. These control transactions have the same sort of potential benefits and accordingly they should be evaluated the same way. By and large, corporate law does so. Shareholders may form voting trusts and holding companies without any obligation to share the gains; the only significant limitation, usually imposed by statute, is that voting trusts lapse unless periodically renewed.

One prominent case charts a different course. In *Jones v. H.F. Ahmanson & Co.*[16] the owners of 85 percent of the stock of United Savings and Loan Association, a closely held corporation, organized a Delaware holding company. In exchange for shares of the holding company, they transferred all of their shares in the savings and loan along with several other businesses. The holding company went public, issuing stock and debentures. The original controlling shareholders of the savings and loan ended up with stock in a leveraged holding company; the position of the minority shareholders of United was unaffected. In the next few years, the profits of the savings and loan went up, while the prices of the shares of the holding company went up even faster. *After* the rise in the holding company's price, the minority shareholders demanded admission. When offered only $2,400 per share (the United shares placed in the holding company at the outset had risen to the equivalent of $8,800), they sued.

The Supreme Court of California, citing *Perlman* and referring to the gain-sharing proposals of Berle and Jennings, held that "the controlling shareholders may not use their power to control the corporation for the purpose of promising a marketing scheme that benefits themselves alone to the detriment of the minority." It insisted that "the minority shareholders be placed in a position at least as favorable as that the majority created for themselves." The

16. 1 Cal. 3d 93, 460 P.2d 464, 81 Cal. Rptr. 592 (1969). The quotations in the next paragraph appear at 1 Cal. 3d at 115, 118, 460 P.2d at 476, 478, 81 Cal. Rptr. at 604, 606.

court permitted minority shareholders to elect between the appraised value of their shares at the time of the exchange and the price of the holding company stock that they would have had at the time of the action.

At first blush the case presents a classic usurpation of a corporate opportunity (the ability to go public) by the controlling shareholders. Because the majority could have included the minority without jeopardizing the transaction, there was no need to exclude the minority. But this interpretation won't wash. The controlling shareholders wished to consolidate their 85 percent stock ownership of the savings and loan together with several other businesses into one corporation. Such a consolidation could produce efficiencies, from sources such as centralized management. Participation by the minority in the holding company would decrease the incentive of the controlling shareholders to create the gains by incurring the costs of consolidating the related businesses. The court failed to perceive this difficulty with a sharing requirement.

More fundamentally, the court did not grasp the significance of the minority shareholders' delay in bringing suit. The costs and risks of creating the holding company were borne by the controlling shareholders, and their expected reward was the premium resulting from the increased value of the transformed asset. The minority shareholders bore none of the costs, and allowing them to take a free ride on the benefits would reduce the number of value-increasing transactions in the future. Moreover, a substantial part of the increase in the price of the holding company's shares was attributable to its leverage. The minority shareholders waited to see whether United's earnings rose before demanding to participate; if United's earnings had fallen, the minority doubtless would have held onto their United shares while those who participated in the holding company were wiped out in favor of the debenture holders. If generally accepted, the court's *ex post* view of fairness, giving the minority a right to participate in the gains without taking the risk of loss, would go a long way toward discouraging beneficial control transactions. But *Ahmanson* has not been generally accepted.

SALE OF OFFICE

Managers could transfer control by selling their offices. A sale of office is unlawful in every state, however, in the absence of contractual permission.[17] This application of the fiduciary principle is usually explained as resting on the belief that "[a] fiduciary endeavoring to influence the selection of a successor must do so with an eye single to the best interests of the beneficiaries. Experience has taught that, no matter how high-minded a particular fiduciary may be, the only certain way to insure full compliance with that duty is to eliminate any possibility of personal gain."[18] Doubtless the only "certain" way to prevent defalcations is to remove "any possibility of personal gain," as the only "certain" way to prevent drunk driving is to scrap every automobile in the world. No legal rule demands that there be zero possibility of evil befalling us—and corporate law does not try to answer any such demand. A principle that personal gains may not influence the transfer of control would proscribe any sale of control blocs of shares even though the law allows these sales.

It is more accurate to say that the fiduciary principle bans the sale of office, while allowing the sale of control, because control sales have built-in guarantees of the buyer's good intentions but office sales do not. One who buys a controlling bloc of shares cannot hurt the corporation without hurting himself too. Substantial investment acts as a bond for honest conduct. One who buys an office may obtain control too cheaply. The argument is fundamentally the same one we presented in Chapter 3 to show why votes may not be sold without the equity interest. Offices would sell for their value to the incumbent, including any value attributable to the incumbent's ability to extract profits and perquisites. It is possible to argue that because the incumbent would insist on full payment for value, only a buyer who could put the firm's assets to better use would be able to meet the incumbent's demands. On this view there would be no reason to prohibit the sale of office. But this would be an accurate assessment only if managers now could fully extract the value of their positions. As we have emphasized repeatedly, they cannot: markets for control and managerial services constrain them.

The law is consistent with this rationale for the ban on selling offices. Managers may agree, as part of the sale of a controlling

17. In general, an agent may not sell his position of authority. See *Restatement (Second) of Agency* 18 (1958) (restriction on ability of agent to delegate his authority).

18. Rosenfeld v. Black, 445 F.2d 1337, 1342 (2d Cir. 1971) (Friendly, J.).

block of shares, to turn over their offices. In such cases part of the premium reflects the value of the office. Managers also may accept payment for recommending that the shareholders approve a merger, when the payment is disclosed and the managers simultaneously sell their own shares.[19] The sale of office violates the fiduciary principle only when the office is sold by itself.

Freezeouts, Squeezeouts, LBOs, and MBOs

Transactions eliminating public or minority shareholders (which we call "freezeouts," although they go by many other names) serve a variety of purposes. The freezeout of minority shareholders soon after a transfer in control allows the bidder to capture a disproportionate share of the gains from the acquisition; the elimination of minority shareholders in a subsidiary corporation may facilitate various economies of operation and eliminate conflict of interest problems; going private directly reduces agency costs and the costs attributable to public ownership. We discussed earlier in this chapter some of the sources of these gains.

It used to be very difficult to force a shareholder to disinvest involuntarily, because courts viewed shares as vested rights that could not be taken without consent. Because this rule of unanimity created intolerable holdout problems and frustrated many efficient corporate transactions, it was jettisoned in favor of a rule that allowed the majority to freeze out minority shareholders.[20] Under the modern view, the shareholders' only entitlement is to demand an appraisal of their shares, a remedy that does not give dissenting shareholders any element of value attributable to the transaction from which they dissent.

Within the last few years, however, freezeout transactions have come under greater scrutiny by courts and increasing attack by scholars. It has been suggested that freezeouts are unfair to the shareholders and lack a business purpose. They go on all the time,

19. Essex Universal Corp. v. Yates, 305 F.2d 572 (2d Cir. 1962) (office plus control shares); Nelson v. Gammon, 647 F.2d 710 (6th Cir. 1981) (office plus merger).

20. See William J. Carney, "Fundamental Corporate Changes, Minority Shareholders, and Business Purposes," 1980 *Am. Bar Found. Res. J.* 69, 77–97; Elliott J. Weiss, "The Law of Take Out Mergers: A Historical Perspective," 56 *N.Y.U. L. Rev.* 624 (1981).

however, subject only to the constraints of the customary duties of care and loyalty.

Our outlier is *Singer v. Magnavox Co.*[21] A company called Development Corp. made a tender offer for the common stock of Magnavox. The price was $9 per share, and 84.1 percent of the stock was tendered. Development merged Magnavox with T.M.C. Development, its wholly owned subsidiary, paying $9 for every outstanding share. The result of this two-step process was that every original shareholder of Magnavox received $9, and Development got all of the common stock. Development told the non-tendering shareholders that they had the right to appraisal under Delaware law. Some shareholders, however, spurned the appraisal and sought an injunction, contending that the merger was unfair and did not serve a valid business purpose because it allowed Development to keep "a disproportionate amount of the gain [Development] anticipated would be recognized from consummation of the merger."

Development argued that the shareholders' only right was to the value of the existing investment, protected by the appraisal remedy (see Chapter 6). The court replied that shareholders have a protected right in the form of their investment as well as in its value. Thus the court set the case for trial to determine whether there was a business purpose for the merger and whether $9 was a fair price. Because the directors of Magnavox, the nominees of Development, owed fiduciary duties to the shareholders, the price paid in the freezeout had to satisfy "entire fairness" as well as the appraisal standard.

Invocation of the fiduciary principle does not answer the question whether shareholders would contract for (and fiduciaries thus must provide) some sharing of gains, and the court begged this question in *Singer*. Perhaps the price had to exceed $9 to be entirely fair, but the court did not say so; indeed, it did not foreclose the possibility that $8 or even $5 would have been entirely fair. It left these matters to the chancellor. Courts in other states have been hesitant to embrace *Singer's* holding, and the case is defunct in Delaware. Delaware has held that a merger may be approved when all of the gain accrues to one firm; that the appraisal standard continues to exclude elements of value attributable to the transac-

21. 380 A.2d 969 (Del. 1977). The following quotations are from pages 978, 980.

tion that provokes the dissent; and that managers may exercise ordinary business judgment in structuring control transactions.[22] *Singer* has been consigned to oblivion—so insignificant that the latest edition of the leading casebook omits it.

What has lingered in Delaware law is a belief that the market price of a firm's stock is not (necessarily) its "real" or "intrinsic" value, a proposition that can cause much grief from time to time. This sometimes comes together with a belief that a transaction conducted at two different prices must reflect "coercion" to accept the high price (we should all be so unlucky) or that the low tier lies below the "intrinsic value" of the firm. Neither of these themes has significantly affected the ability of firms to restructure themselves as they please—provided they spend a few hundred thousand dollars to get an investment banker's "fairness opinion" that a price higher than market is indeed at the "intrinsic" value of the stock—although both of them have been important in *contests* for corporate control, as we discuss in Chapter 7 in connection with tender offers. Here, we limit further comments to arguments about transactions that are initiated by the firm being restructured.

William Carney has argued that compensation of the minority at market value is inadequate because the minority may value its shares more highly than either the majority or the market.[23] If the minority values its shares at $30 even though the market price is $10, the argument runs, they may lose more than the majority gains, and the transaction may decrease value. This argument is flawed, however, because if different shareholders place different values on the same investment, those who had the higher valuation would purchase the shares held by the remaining investors. In-

22. Examples outside Delaware include Yanow v. Teal Indus., 178 Conn. 262, 422 A.2d 311 (1979) (rejecting *Singer*); Deutsch v. Blue Chip Stamps, 116 Cal. App. 3d 97, 172 Cal. Rptr. 21 (2d Dist. 1981) (apparently rejecting *Singer*); Gabhart v. Gabhart, 370 N.E.2d 345 (Ind. 1977) (adopting modified version of *Singer;* holding that courts must inquire into business purpose but may not inquire into entire fairness). Within Delaware see Weinberger v. UOP, Inc., 457 A.2d 701 (Del. 1983) (discarding *Singer*); Tanzer v. International Gen. Indus., 379 A.2d 1121 (Del. 1977) (one firm may keep all of the gain); Bell v. Kirby Lumber Corp., 413 A.2d 137 (Del. 1980) (pure going-private transaction lawful, and dissenting investors are not entitled to any gain produced by the transaction from which they dissent). See also Coleman v. Taub, 638 F.2d 628 (3d Cir. 1981) (applying Delaware law); Dower v. Mosser Industries, 648 F.2d 183, 189 (3d Cir. 1981) (applying Pennsylvania law but decided on assumption that Delaware law was useful guide).

23. Carney, supra note 20, at 112–118.

vestors can make mutually beneficial trades until those holding any given firm's stock have reasonably homogeneous expectations about its performance, and there is little risk that the pessimistic investors in a firm can use freezeout transactions to exploit optimists.

Victor Brudney and Marvin Chirelstein maintain that "fairness" requires any gains from the merger of a parent corporation and a subsidiary to be calculated and shared among all investors according to the premerger ratio of the equity investments in the two firms.[24] For the reasons we have covered above, this would deter value-increasing transactions. Moreover, the suggestion that sharing promotes "fairness" is dubious. How does the controlling shareholder know what the gains will be in order to apportion them fairly? How can "synergy gains"—the subject of the Brudney and Chirelstein sharing proposals—be separated from the ordinary return on the time, effort, and resources that the controlling firm put into accomplishing the merger, or from the opportunity costs of the controlling shareholder? What if the merger results in a loss rather than a gain? Why does fairness require sharing in proportion to equity value rather than in proportion to total asset value or some other standard? There is no accepted standard of fairness, one more reason why the cases and the fiduciary principle do not require sharing.

An argument occasionally heard from the press, though rarely from scholars, is that the freezeout price is unfair (even though above market) when it is below the price at which the shares were sold to the public. The assumption must be that insiders somehow bilked the public into paying too much—or perhaps have confused the market so that the current price is too low—and should not be permitted to profit by their chicanery. Those who make that argument both underestimate the efficiency of the stock market and misconceive the importance of yesterday's stock prices. In an efficient capital market, the informational value of prior prices is incorporated into today's price, and the fact that the firm's price was once high does not indicate that it will rise again. A freezeout price above the current market price is no less beneficial to shareholders because the price was once higher, and the person paying

24. Victor Brudney and Marvin A. Chirelstein, "A Restatement of Corporate Freezeouts," 87 *Yale L. J.* 1354 (1978). See also Brudney and Chirelstein, "Fair Shares in Corporate Mergers," 88 *Harv. L. Rev.* 297 (1974).

the above-market price cannot hope to profit unless the transaction is value-increasing.

A related, and more plausible, argument has it that the insiders in freezeouts know more than the outsiders and use this knowledge either to depress the price of the stock just before the transaction, so that the "premium" is illusory, or to take out the public investors with knowledge that the firm's prospects are better than outsiders believe, thus scooping up gains that the public would have enjoyed but for the freezeout. If a firm makes a valuable mineral discovery, for example, and this information is not yet reflected in the price of the firm's shares, a controlling shareholder might be able to reap a considerable gain by freezing out the minority, even though the value of the firm is not increased. Such concerns have been expressed especially loudly concerning MBOs. But this possibility has not led to a ban on going-private transactions, for several good reasons.

First, its likelihood has been exaggerated.[25] Second, the possibility of insiders' profiting is a well-known risk for which investors can demand compensation. Third, tricking the market about current value is hard. Freezeouts usually take some time to accomplish and almost always require the shareholders to vote. During the delay the truth may come out—generally the insiders must reveal the news when they seek the needed votes—or an auction develop. If insiders attempt to go private at a price less than the firm's future prospects indicate, the firm in all likelihood will be the subject of a higher bid.[26] Auctions in response to proposed MBOs are common.

For what it is worth, data do not support a belief that insiders are

25. In the famous Zahn v. Transamerica Corp., 162 F.2d 36 (3d Cir. 1947), for example, minority shareholders alleged that the controlling shareholder unlawfully attempted a freezeout without disclosing that the value of tobacco, the firm's principal asset, had tripled. The court held that the planned transaction was a breach of fiduciary duty. Yet it is very unlikely that an increase in the price of tobacco, a commodity with a readily ascertainable price, was inside information not reflected in the firm's stock price. *Zahn* makes sense only if the shareholders were unaware of the quantity or kind of tobacco held by the firm, which would be known to insiders, and then only if the ignorance affected their decision concerning conversion between classes of shares. Perhaps they were ignorant, but the court did not discuss the problem.

26. The American Law Institute's *Principles of Corporate Governance: Analysis and Recommendations* 5.15 (Tent. Draft No. 10, 1990), comes to this same conclusion when allowing restructurings subject only to disclosure and a market test. The reporters of this provision treat it as a restatement of current law.

trying to scoop up the shares before the market wises up. LBOs and MBOs commonly carry premiums of 30 to 50 percent over existing prices. If, on the one hand, these are based on temporary distortions (or knowledge of a brighter tomorrow), we should expect to see prices soon rise higher still when the transaction is called off; if, on the other hand, the premium is attributable to real changes made possible by the transaction, it will disappear if the transaction is called off. Harry DeAngelo, Linda DeAngelo, and Edward Rice looked at successful and unsuccessful LBOs and MBOs and discovered that when the transaction collapses, so does the price. Clifford Holderness and Dennis Sheehan found that shares not acquired in these transactions appreciate in value. Several scholars, most recently Laurentius Marais, Katherine Schipper, and Abbie Smith, have found that debt investors whose interests remain outstanding do not lose as a result of LBOs and MBOs. These conclusions (see note 1) collectively supply powerful evidence in favor of the efficiency hypothesis for corporate control transactions.

The Appraisal Remedy

Statutes and cases routinely require certain minimum payments to the investors that are affected by a corporate control transaction. These minimum payments, codified in most states by the appraisal statute, require that shareholders receive the equivalent of what they give up but do not require sharing of the gain from the change in control. The Delaware statute is most explicit, providing that the court "shall appraise the shares, determining their fair value exclusive of any element of value arising from the accomplishment or expectation" of the event giving rise to appraisal rights.[27]

The appraisal standard reflects the economic principles we have discussed. Gains need not be shared, and every investor receives at least what he had before. As a rule, the fiduciary principle is satisfied if some investors receive a premium over the market price of their shares, and other investors do not suffer a loss. Appraisal puts that floor under all investors. We return in Chapter 6 to a detailed treatment of how the appraisal procedure does so, and whether there is room for improvement in its operation.

27. 8 Del. Code 262(h).

CORPORATE OPPORTUNITIES

Corporate opportunities are business ventures of some sort, and the allocation of an opportunity within a family of affiliated corporations, or between a corporation and an officer, is a control transaction as we have used that term. Given the survey of the law to this point, it is not surprising that there is no sharing principle in the law of corporate opportunities. A parent corporation may allocate a business opportunity to itself, for example, even though public shareholders in a subsidiary believe that this is unfair.[28] A corporation also may allocate an opportunity to one of its managers. The "corporate opportunity doctrine," far from forbidding such allocations, simply requires that the opportunity be presented to and passed on by the firm's directors or other officers. The firm is free to decline to pursue the opportunity, releasing it to a director or officer. Such releases are common when an employee of the firm has an invention or an idea for a new product that he holds in higher esteem than does the firm. The classic corporate opportunity doctrine cases deal with undisclosed conversions of opportunities; they are to corporate control transactions as theft is to salary.

A number of scholars have decried the state of the law, proposing that current rules be replaced with doctrine of equitable sharing or even absolute bans on the allocation of opportunities to parent corporations or corporate managers. Victor Brudney and Robert Clark contend, for example, that the prospect of overreaching by managers is so great that nothing save prohibition could protect the interests of shareholders.[29]

One response to these proposals is that they will deter the undertaking of some value-increasing ventures or cause them to be undertaken inefficiently. Moreover, in most cases there is no agency cost problem requiring attention. When managers decide whether to allocate an opportunity to a parent or a subsidiary, the allocation decision will reflect the managers' best judgment about which firm can best develop the opportunity because the same people effectively control both firms. The managers' interests in allocation coin-

28. Getty Oil Co. v. Skelly Oil Co., 267 A.2d 883 (Del. 1970); Myerson v. El Paso Natural Gas Co., 246 A.2d 789 (Del. Ch. 1967).
29. Victor Brudney and Robert Charles Clark, "A New Look at Corporate Opportunities," 94 *Harv. L. Rev.* 997 (1981).

cide with shareholders' interests—each wants the venture to be exploited by the corporate structure that can do so best, because that result will generate the greatest profits, and thus the highest share prices for investors and the highest salaries for managers.

Much of the existing literature assumes that a parent corporation will allocate corporate opportunities to itself to avoid sharing of the gains with minority shareholders of the subsidiary corporation. Brudney and Clark, for example, argue that this danger is so great that corporate opportunities should presumptively be awarded to the subsidiary corporation. The argument is defective because it ignores the possibility of side payments. Assume that a corporate opportunity is worth $100 to a 70 percent owned subsidiary but only $80 to the parent. It might appear that the parent would allocate the opportunity to itself even though it could use the opportunity less profitably, because the $80 gain is greater than the $70 (70 percent of $100) gained if the opportunity is allocated to the subsidiary. But the parent corporation could gain more than $80 by allocating the opportunity to the subsidiary and charging it some amount between $11 and $30. The charge could be explicit or implicit. That is, the parent's other dealings with the subsidiary could be adjusted to compensate it for the release of the opportunity—transfer pricing between parents and subsidiaries is extremely flexible. Thus the opportunity would be allocated to the firm that could use it more efficiently, and all parties, including the minority shareholders of the subsidiary, would benefit as a result.

The same is true when managers take opportunities for themselves. Assigning the opportunity to the manager may reduce agency costs by enabling the manager to receive a greater part of the marginal gains produced by his efforts. The manager would view the business opportunity as just another form of compensation similar to (but more risky than) salary, bonuses, and stock options. Managers properly take opportunities for themselves when they can exploit them more profitably than the firm. The increase in the value of the opportunity creates the possibility of a mutually beneficial transaction between manager and firm: the manager takes the venture, and the firm reduces the manager's other compensation.

Such a transaction is the equivalent of a decision to hire the manager only part-time, leaving him free to pursue other things during the rest of his time. Part-time employment is common in labor markets. Sometimes firms want to hire only 1 or 2 percent of a person's time, and they obtain such labor inputs from independent contractors (among them law firms and architects). Sometimes firms want 100 percent of the agent's time. But figures in between are sensible, too. Law schools typically hire approximately 50 percent of professors' time, giving them four months in the summer and some time off during the year to do as they please (consulting, travel, teaching elsewhere, even writing). Part-time employment arises when, at the margin, a person's time is more valuable to some other employer or to the agent himself (pursuing other projects or simply taking life at leisure) than to the firm. The part-time employee compensates the firm through a reduced salary.

This might appear misleading, because executives who take opportunities typically do not reduce their salaries on the spot or explicitly accept part-time employment. But managers' time commitments are flexible; taking an opportunity may coincide with a reduction from sixty to fifty hours spent on the firm's business each week. The salary reduction may be part of a settling up with the firm as the employee receives a lower bonus or a lower salary for the future. The adjustment also may come *ex ante* because employees will accept a lower salary from a firm that allows its officials to exploit business opportunities on the side. Either way, the executive will pay for what he takes.

It will not do to say that executives have "bargaining power" that they use to avoid this settling up. Although managers doubtless can exploit their positions to a degree, they are constrained by labor markets, product markets, and the market for corporate control. No matter how much bargaining power the managers have, they are better off if they do what shareholders prefer and assign the opportunity to the corporation or person that can put it to best use. Such behavior creates a bigger pie, which managers may slice in favor of both investors and themselves. A ban on the assignment of opportunities to managers would not reduce their bargaining power or facilitate monitoring.

Perhaps it is generally beneficial for managers to abjure opportunities. If so, then they can benefit by promising to allocate all new ventures to the firm. Although it should be relatively easy to reach such contracts, they appear to be rare, which suggests that shareholders' interests coincide with the existing legal rules.

Fiduciary Duty in Related Contexts

We have shown that a legal rule allowing unequal division of the gains from corporate control transactions furthers the shareholders' interests, provided that no shareholder be made worse off. We have also shown that existing legal rules, for the most part, are consistent with our analysis. We conclude by mentioning and distinguishing several situations where equal division of gains is the norm.

A familiar rule of partnership law is that, unless the partners otherwise agree, profits must be shared equally and no partner is entitled to a salary. The rationale for this rule is clear—because the number of partners is typically small, it is relatively easy for partners to reach contractual agreements relating to particular contributions. If unequal division is necessary to provide an incentive to create gains, the partners can accomplish this by private agreement. Moreover, because partners generally invest much of their human capital in the partnership, they are unable to diversify this part of their investment "portfolio." Partners who are risk-averse therefore benefit from a rule of equal division.

Another rule of law is that dividends must be distributed pro rata to each shareholder of the same class in a corporation. There is no tension between this rule and the fiduciary principle in corporate control transactions. Firms may and do create different classes of stock with different entitlements, just as they may agree to unequal division of other elements of value. Unequal division of the gains resulting from corporate control transactions increases shareholders' welfare by creating an incentive to produce such gains and thereby to add to the value of the firm. The same is not true with respect to dividends. The payment of a dividend is simply a transfer of assets from a firm to its shareholders. No gains are created in the process. Thus a legal rule allowing unequal distribution of dividends might increase the frequency of dividend payments, but this would not increase the value of the firm. On the contrary, a rule allowing unequal division of dividends would make shareholders worse off because they would have an incentive to incur wasteful expenditures by monitoring the withdrawal of assets from the firm. Thus the rule prohibiting unequal payment of dividends, like the fiduciary principle allowing unequal division of gains resulting from corporate transactions, is perfectly consistent with the goal of maximizing shareholders' wealth.

In general, the likelihood of a sharing rule turns on two things: the probability that unequal divisions would produce gains, and the number of participants in the venture. As either quantum rises, a sharing rule becomes less useful in maximizing the wealth of investors. Chapter 9, on close corporations, provides further evidence of this.

6

The Appraisal Remedy

The preceding chapter treated appraisal as a presumptive contractual term setting the minimum price at which the firm may be sold in situations where those in control are tempted to appropriate wealth. This price floor implements the Pareto principle of welfare economics: it ensures that corporate control transactions increase value by seeing to it that the transaction makes no one worse off. This chapter extends our treatment of appraisal.

Functions of Appraisal

The conventional view of appraisal focuses on its role in protecting minority shareholders from certain types of control transactions. Exclusive attention to a perceived need for protection of minority shareholders once a transaction has been announced ignores the role of the remedy in affecting the probability of the transaction taking place, the terms of any transaction, and the agency costs of management in the event no transaction occurs. Appraisal's principal effects occur *ex ante* and increase the welfare of all shareholders, not just those who happen to be in a minority *ex post*. It puts under a firm's price a floor ensuring that corporate control transactions increase value. Appraisal gives investors the worth their shares had before the transaction in question, excluding elements created or destroyed by the deal.[1] In other words, the ap-

1. 8 Del. Code. §262(h), providing that the court "shall appraise the shares, determining their fair value exclusive of any element of value arising from the accomplishment or expectation" of the event giving rise to appraisal rights. The American Bar Association's *Model Business Corporation Act* (rev. 1984), which supplies the model for a majority of the states, is quite similar. The model statute provides that dissenters receive "fair value" for their shares and defines this term in §13.01(3) as

praisal remedy disdains "sharing," and in so doing increases total wealth.

Contrary voices invite us to consider a hypothetical. A sole owner of a firm wants to sell a 49 percent share of the residual cash flows while maintaining 51 percent. Assume that state law requires 51 percent of the shareholders of both corporations to approve the merger before it can go through. The controlling shareholder retains the ability to eliminate the minority shareholders on unilateral terms. A controlling shareholder who can sell the share initially at a high price and then eliminate the minority shareholders at a low price may make large profits. This shows, critics maintain, that appraisal allows exploitation.

Yet the possibility of a freezeout at a low price affects the price that the minority pays for shares at the time of issuance. The greater the probability that the shares will be acquired by the majority, the less the minority will pay. So the majority, not the minority, bears the cost *ex ante* of the potential exploitation of the minority *ex post*. Dominant investors want to constrain their later conduct in order to realize the best price at the outset. Appraisal, reducing the probability that the minority's shares will be acquired at a price unilaterally set by the majority, increases the price the minority will pay for the shares to the benefit of both the majority and the minority. Exactly the same is true with parent-subsidiary transactions and recapitalizations affecting the rights of preferred stockholders.

To this the critic replies that reliance on pretransaction value is inadequate because that value depends on the rules for corporate control transactions. If the fiduciary principle permits a freezeout at a low price, the argument goes, then shares will sell for a low price in the market, and a requirement that shareholders be paid that low price is not of much use. The point is useful but misleading. The argument is based on the erroneous premise that rules for corporate control transactions allow investors to be frozen out at an artificially low price. Values in appraisal proceedings typically are determined by reference to a weighted percentage of assets, earnings, and market price values (which creates a different set of problems, to which we return). This method greatly reduces the

---

"the value of the shares immediately before the effectuation of the corporate action to which the dissenter objects, excluding any appreciation or depreciation in anticipation of the corporate action unless exclusion would be inequitable."

chance that shareholders will receive less than the pretransaction value of their investment, and there is no evidence that shareholders are undercompensated in appraisals. Moreover, even if the rules for corporate control transactions allowed shareholders to be cashed out at an artificially low price, this prospect again would lead purchasers to pay less in the market; again the insiders would pay in advance for the right to scoop up shares later. Purchasers still would obtain the ordinary rate of return on their investments. If they were then squeezed out at more than the current price of their shares—even if that price is "depressed"—they would obtain more than an ordinary rate of return on their money.

Suppose, however, that a firm's shares trade at "depressed" prices not because of the prospect of a cash-out but because the shareholder in control of the firm uses that control to prevent other investors from receiving the benefits of the enterprise. Perhaps he siphons all profits to himself in exorbitant salaries and perquisites, leaving nothing for other investors. This siphoning may be open to attack on the usual grounds, just as theft by managers is open to attack. If the diversion of profits is sufficiently subtle that it escapes effective challenge, the controlling shareholder may be able to depress the value of others' investments perpetually. Does it then follow that pretransaction market value is the wrong standard to use in corporate control transactions?

We think not. If the controlling party can depress prices forever, the helpless investors will be delighted to receive an extra penny for their shares. They would not assert a claim for more, if such a claim would prevent the change of control. Moreover, the shareholders suffer their loss when the wastrel takes control, because the lower profit expectation is reflected in lower share prices. People who buy shares after the existing control group becomes entrenched will receive an ordinary return on their investment. If a control change in the future is accompanied by a premium payment to these owners, they will receive a windfall, and the other shareholders who sold in the interim will receive nothing. We can think of no argument for such windfalls when part of the cost is the suppression of at least some otherwise beneficial transactions.

Does Appraisal Matter?

Bayless Manning has argued that appraisal serves no economic purpose, fails to protect minority shareholders, and so drains the corporation's treasury for no good reason.[2] Manning's powerful essay points out much of the mythology that characterized the development of the appraisal remedy in the nineteenth century and the difficulties of the remedy from the perspective of the firm and its shareholders. Although packed with interesting points, Manning's treatment ultimately asks the wrong question.

Manning focuses on the risk of loss faced by groups that deal with the corporation. Such risk exists, Manning claims, as a result of what he describes as external events, such as a change in the value of the dollar against the yen, and internal events to which appraisal does not apply, such as mass resignations by management, bankruptcy, a demand for higher wages or a strike, a change in product line, a change in dividend policy, or a decision to list or delist on the New York Stock Exchange. Risk of loss, moreover, is not confined to shareholders but is shared in greater or lesser degree by employees, creditors, the community, and so forth. Manning concludes that the distinction between triggering transactions that create an appraisal remedy for shareholders and other events that impose comparable or greater risks cannot be defended on economic grounds.

The relevant question, however, is not whether triggering transactions create a unique risk of loss *ex post* but rather in what situations a floor under the value of stock maximizes the worth of the firm *ex ante*. Providing an appraisal remedy for balance-of-payments deficits would not provide incentives to increase the value of the firm. In other situations, an appraisal remedy would create perverse incentives. Consider a rule that gave shareholders the ability to demand appraisal any time the value of their holdings was decreased as a result of a particular business decision such as introduction of a new product. Managers then would have an incentive to reject projects with high net present value yet create high variance, lest the corporate treasury vanish if the decision did not turn out well. Since managers have strong incentives to maximize the value of the firm, shareholders are better off by leaving most decisions to managers without incurring the costs, both direct and of opportunity loss, of the appraisal remedy.

Indeed, it is only where the value-increasing strategy is not likely

2. Bayless Manning, "The Shareholder's Appraisal Remedy: An Essay for Frank Coker," 72 *Yale L. J.* 233 (1962).

to be followed, either because of coordination or conflict of interest problems, that the appraisal remedy is worth the costs. The pattern of appraisal statutes can be explained, roughly at least, on this basis.[3] Manning did not appreciate the distinction between triggering and nontriggering transactions because he focused on the risk of loss *ex post* rather than on the role of the appraisal remedy in creating incentives to maximize the value of the firm and thus increase the value of investments *ex ante*.

The Stock Market Exception

The most dramatic restriction on appraisal is the stock market exception. Twenty-three states, including Delaware, deny appraisal rights to shareholders whose stock is listed on a stock exchange or is so widely held that a substantial trading market exists, and who receive in exchange for their holdings stock in some other firm.[4] The theory of this restriction on appraisal rights is that a judicially created "appraisal market" for dissenting shareholders is unnecessary where a substantial trading market already exists.

Critics have argued that the stock market exception provides insufficient protection to dissenting shareholders because it incorporates the assumption that dissenters can receive "fair value" for their shares by selling in the market. For example, this comment accompanied the elimination of the stock market exception in the 1978 revision of the Model Business Corporation Act: "The former exception for shares listed on stock exchanges has been eliminated in the light of facts which have become more visible since the stock

3. The two major anomalies are statutes that provide appraisal rights for shareholders in mergers negotiated at arms' length and those that provide rights for shareholders of acquiring firms. Almost all statutes provide for appraisal rights in negotiated mergers. The requirement that shareholders of acquiring firms have appraisal rights is often tempered by a restriction that the right to dissent is available only if a vote is required. See, for instance, ABA, *Model Business Corporation Act* §13.02(1)(i). There are also a few other ways to avoid appraisal rights for shareholders of acquiring firms. See Alan Schenk and Steven H. Schulman, "Shareholders' Voting and Appraisal Rights in Corporate Acquisition Transactions," 38 *Bus. Law.* 1529 (1983). In practice, most appraisal cases involve shareholders frozen out on terms set by controlling shareholders. See Elmer J. Schaefer, "The Fallacy of Weighting Asset Value and Earnings Value in the Appraisal of Corporate Stock," 55 *S. Cal. L. Rev.* 1031, 1032 & n.6 (1982) (citing cases).

4. 3 *Model Business Corporation Act Annotated* 1372 (3d ed. 1989).

market exception was added to the Model Act in 1969. The 1970s have demonstrated again the possibility of a demoralized market in which fair prices are not available, and in which many companies publicly offer to buy their own shares because the market grossly undervalues them. Under these circumstances, access to market value is not a reasonable alternative for a dissenting shareholder."[5] This is an assertion that capital markets are not efficient—that they do not reflect publicly available information about the value of a firm's securities. Chapters 1, 7, and 11 discuss why markets, for all their flaws, do better at estimating "value" than other institutions, such as courts. Depressed stock prices no more indicate that shareholders who must sell in the market are treated "unfairly" than high prices indicate they are receiving a windfall. In both situations, the market price reflects publicly available information about the value of the firm.

The real problem is that the stock market exception is inconsistent with the function of appraisal—establishing a reservation price. Recall the example of the owner of a firm who sells 49 percent control to outside shareholders in a public offering. Withdrawing the appraisal rights of the shareholders of the 49 percent bloc if their shares are publicly traded or if the owners receive shares that are publicly traded will not solve the problem of the majority being able to appropriate wealth from the minority *ex post,* causing the minority to be willing to pay only a low price for the shares *ex ante.* The stock market exception ensures that shareholders who are denied appraisal rights will have low costs in disposing of their shares, but it does nothing for the appropriation problem. Appraisal statutes to this extent diverge from the ideal description of them we gave in Chapter 5. (But then we have never contended that state laws are perfectly designed to promote investors' wealth, only that the structure of corporate law is well designed.)

This appropriation problem is less significant when, as the Delaware statute provides, appraisal rights are available if a shareholder must exchange his shares, even though publicly traded, for cash or debt.[6] If the theory of the stock market exception is that appraisal is unnecessary when there is a public market, the clearest case for

5. Ibid. at 1368–69.
6. 8 Del. Code §262(k)(1).

denying appraisal rights would be where the consideration received was cash, the most liquid form of investment. But elimination of minority shareholders is one of the frequent purposes of certain types of freezeout mergers. This goal cannot be achieved if minority shareholders receive shares of the surviving firm and thus retain a continuing equity investment. (Of course, equity participation does not eliminate the possibility of appropriation. Minority investors who receive $50 worth of new paper for every $100 of old paper have been stripped of $50, whether the new paper is stock or specie. Our point is that the risk of confiscation is greatest in 100 percent cash-outs.) The availability of appraisal rights where the consideration is cash represents a recognition, therefore, that appraisal should be available when the danger of appropriation is the greatest. Even so, we predict that states recognizing a market-out will deny that the appraisal remedy is exclusive—that is, they will find ways to ensure that the price received in the market reflects the value of the shares. As we shall see, Delaware has done just that.

Hideki Kanda and Saul Levmore believe that the market exemption is more readily understandable if appraisal serves a function we have so far slighted: compensating investors who place on stock a value different from the market's.[7] The absence of liquid markets for shares of closely held corporations means that different investors may attach different values to their shares, differences that would disappear with active trading but that persist with stasis. Even when shares are widely traded, differences may endure. If Jones values the expected profits of Apple Computer at $30 per share and the market price is $22, Jones will buy—but only to a point, beyond which the costs (in reduced diversification) of holding extra Apple stock in the portfolio exceed the difference between the private valuation and the market price. The vast public market ensures that the Joneses of the world find lots of other opportunities, and prices will close in on marginal private valuation. Thinly traded stocks may not experience this convergence between price and value. Hence, Kanda and Levmore argue, the structure of the exception: appraisal is unavailable when the stock to be acquired is widely traded (so that private and marker value converge) and is available otherwise.

7. Hideki Kanda and Saul Levmore, "The Appraisal Remedy and the Goals of Corporate Law," 32 *U.C.L.A. L. Rev.* 429, 438–441, 446–451 (1985).

Although the Kanda-Levmore assessment is thoughtful, we are not persuaded. Kanda and Levmore concentrate on what the investors give up; the market exception determines only what they receive. Their explanation would work if the statutes provided that when the stock is widely traded investors get the market price (in cash) as it was before the market learned of the proposed transaction (the standard of "fair value" we discuss below). Then the availability of appraisal for closely held firms could be explained as an accommodation to different private values. This is not, however, what the statutes do. The market-out in the twenty-three states applies when the investors of public firms are *paid* in stock. The conversion rate between old and new investments is the central variable in a control transaction. The market-out means that this conversion rate is not limited by law, that there is no floor.

What Is "Fair Value"?

The efficacy of the appraisal remedy depends in large part on how the statutes are drafted and interpreted. One of the most important issues is the measure of compensation that dissenters receive. The usual answer—"fair value"—could mean anything from *ex ante* value to anything the majority realizes with the assets, the ultimate in *ex post* approaches. Most appraisal statutes provide that value is fixed *ex ante*, exclusive of any gains or losses caused by the transaction dissented from (see note 1 above). The pretransaction value standard is best for investors for reasons we developed in Chapter 5.

In 1983 the Supreme Court of Delaware hinted in *Weinberger v. UOP, Inc.*[8] that the controlling investor had to disclose and pay the highest value that it (or any other known person) placed on the minority's shares. Later cases reiterated the *ex ante* approach.[9] Although the "third-party value" standard—that is, a rule that the minority must receive the price any person would pay in an auction in which all changes in the firm would be taken into account—has

8. 457 A.2d 701 (Del. 1983).
9. Rosenblatt v. Getty Oil Co., 493 A.2d 929, 939–940 (Del. 1985); Cede & Co. v. Technicolor, Inc., 542 A.2d 1182, 1187 (Del. 1988); Cavalier Oil Corp. v. Harnett, 564 A.2d 1137, 1144, 1146 (Del. 1989). See also the extensive discussion in 3 *Model Business Corporation Act Annotated* 1430–35 (collecting cases from many states).

a siren's attraction to some judges and scholars, we pretermit further discussion here. Chapter 5 develops the basic approach, and Chapter 7 contains an extended discussion of the "auctioneering" approach to valuation.

One further comment on Kanda and Levmore is appropriate. To the extent they treat appraisal in the main as a remedy for the inframarginal investor of a public corporation who values stock more than the market price, they come up short on two accounts. First, the "fair value" paid in an appraisal is the same for all investors. No state tries to find and compensate for idiosyncratic value. Single-price assessments of value conform well, however, with our understanding of the function of appraisal. Second, data show that the supply schedules of actively traded shares are shallow, implying that at the margin the bulk of holders attach the market value to them.[10] There is no inframarginal value to find, except in closely held firms.

Problems of Valuation

Appraisal requires valuation. The most common technique has been the Delaware block method—estimating value by constructing a weighted average of market, net asset, and earnings value.[11]

10. Determining the slope of demand and supply schedules for individual stocks presents substantial difficulty. Both data and interpretations are mixed. See Lynn A. Stout, "Are Takeover Premiums Really Premiums? Market Price, Fair Value, and Corporate Law," 99 *Yale L. J.* 1235, 1252–58 (1990) (collecting studies). Students of the subject regularly find that the sale of large blocs depresses the price and that the purchase of large blocs increases it. See Myron S. Scholes, "The Market for Securities: Substitution versus Price Pressure and the Effects of Information on Share Prices," 45 *J. Bus.* 179 (1972). The critical question is whether this occurs because the sales transmit information to the market or because there is a downward-sloping supply schedule. Bloc sales may show that insiders have learned unfavorable news; bloc acquisitions may telegraph a takeover bid or changes in management. In either case, the price moves without implying downward-sloping demand. The most sophisticated efforts to disentangle information from quantity effects conclude that large bloc sales that transmit no new information do not significantly affect the price of the stock, implying a shallow if not flat supply schedule and homogeneous expectations.

11. See Bell v. Kirby Lumber Corp., 413 A.2d 137 (Del. 1980); Universal City Studios v. Francis I. duPont & Co., 334 A.2d 216 (Del. 1975); In re Delaware Racing Ass'n, 213 A.2d 203 (Del. 1965). The block method is widely used in other states. See Florsheim v. Twenty Five Thirty Two Broadway Corp., 432 S.W.2d 245

Weinberger abandoned that method and held that "all generally accepted techniques of valuation used in the financial community" should be considered.[12] We analyze the problems with these approaches and suggest an alternative method.

THE DELAWARE BLOCK METHOD

Under the Delaware block method, the appraiser computes separate values for market, earnings, and net assets, gives a weight to each, and then adds them together. This approach is fraught with difficulties. The market price of a security at any given time represents the present value of the firm's net cash flows divided by the number of shares. If a market price can be observed that is uninfluenced by the transaction being dissented from, this market price is the best evidence of the value of the dissenter's shares. Separate inquiry into earnings or net asset values is redundant. As long as securities markets are efficient, these values are impounded in market prices. The more liquid the market, the more justified is reliance on the market price. A liquid market should not, however, be a prerequisite for using the market price. Isolated trades, if at arm's length, are an unbiased indicator of value and can obviate the need for other inquiries.

The principal difficulty with relying on market price is the one that concerned us in dealing with the market-out to appraisal: the price may have been influenced by the transaction being dissented from. The minority-held shares of a subsidiary, for example, will not trade for a higher price than the expected acquisition price discounted by the probability of occurrence unless some greater amount will be available in an appraisal. But if the prevailing

---

(Mo. 1968); Brown v. Hendahl's-Q-B & R, Inc., 185 N.W.2d 249 (N.D. 1971); Fogleson v. Thurston Nat. Life Ins. Co., 555 P.2d 606 (Okla. 1976). Some states, led by New York, rely more heavily on market price. See In re Marcus, 273 App. Div. 725, 79 N.Y.S.2d 76 (1948); Application of Behrens, 61 N.Y.S.2d 179 (Sup. Ct. 1946), affirmed, 271 App. Div. 1007, 69 N.Y.S.3d 910 (1947). But see Endicott Johnson Corp. v. Bade, 37 N.Y.2d 585, 376 N.Y.S.2d 103, 338 N.E.2d 614 (1975) (deemphasizing the importance of market price).

12. Cede & Co. v. Technicolor, Inc., 542 A.2d 1182, 1186–87 (Del. 1988), following Weinberger v. UOP, Inc., 457 A.2d 701, 712–713 (Del. 1983). See also Cavalier Oil Corp. v. Harnett, 564 A.2d 1137, 1142–45 (Del. 1989).

market price is the standard for appraisal, the prospect of appraisal will not affect the market price. Appraisal will then be meaningless and its value in facilitating efficient actions is lost.

If market price cannot be observed or reconstructed, the logical alternative is earnings value.[13] Earnings value can be measured by estimating the firm's net cash flows in future periods and discounting them to present value by choosing an appropriate capitalization rate or rates. This process is notoriously uncertain—both the estimation of positive and negative future cash flows and the determination of the capitalization rate reflecting the riskiness of these cash flows are subject to a wide range of disagreement. This means that almost any value may be propounded with a straight face, as the Supreme Court of Delaware recently acknowledged.[14] The uncertainty of this process underscores the superiority of the market price when it is available. The collective judgment of thousands of self-interested investors, voting their wallets, is more likely to be accurate than a guess by a single appraiser hired to serve a party's cause.

The standards for calculating earnings value established by the Delaware court illustrate the randomness in estimating value rather than looking it up in the *Wall Street Journal*. The earnings-per-share figure is derived from an average of past earnings per share for a five-year period as opposed to current or estimated future earnings. Since only future earnings are relevant for calculating present value, however, the focus on past earnings is arbitrary. Once the earnings figure is determined, a capitalization rate is chosen by analyzing the price-earnings ratios of other comparable firms. This is tricky, however, because the price-earnings ratio reflects not only the riskiness of cash flows but also expected future earnings. Thus a high price-earnings ratio can indicate an expected increase in future earnings rather than low risk. Moreover, price-earnings ratios are affected by capital structure. The greater the

13. "Reconstruction" is a process of interpolation using market prices and subsequent movements, along the lines discussed in Chapters 7 and 11. Daniel R. Fischel, "The Appraisal Remedy in Corporate Law," 1983 *Am. Bar Found. Res. J.* 875, 893–894, has spelled out the method with particular reference to appraisal.

14. Mills Acquisition Co. v. Macmillan, Inc., 559 A.2d 1261 (Del. 1989). See also Lucian Arye Bebchuk and Marcel Kahan, "Fairness Opinions: How Fair Are They and What Can Be Done about It?" 1989 *Duke L. J.* 27; Metlyn Realty Corp. v. Esmark, Inc., 763 F.2d 826, 834–837 (7th Cir. 1985).

amount of debt, the higher the earnings per share and the higher the risk. Thus firms with more debt will sell at lower price-earnings ratios than firms with less debt if the firms are otherwise identical. Serious distortions can occur, therefore, if a capitalization rate is inferred from the price-earnings ratios of other firms unless their capital structures are identical. Finally, the assumption that one capitalization rate is appropriate may also lead to distortions. It is far more likely that the riskiness of cash flows will vary across years and across projects. Some of these distortions may cancel each other out if the firms chosen are sufficiently comparable in terms of their past, current, and future cash flows, riskiness of cash flows, and capital structure, but any earnings value arrived at in this manner will be subject to a large amount of uncertainty.

Asset value is even more problematic as a base. If a market price can be observed or reconstructed, asset value is taken into account automatically. If market price cannot be used, asset value generally adds nothing to earnings value—the value of an asset can be expressed at the present value of the future stream of earnings generated by that asset. Courts often treat assets as elements of value independent of earnings where liquidation value is alleged to be greater than going-concern value. The assertion that liquidation value exceeds going-concern value is common in cases involving natural resources such as oil and gas or timber.[15] The premise of this claim is that market prices do not fully reflect the "intrinsic value" of natural resources, and therefore reliance on asset values is required. No evidence supports this premise, though. Market prices are as likely to reflect the value of natural resources as any other type of asset.

Market value is harder to use when the dissenting investor maintains that the firm's assets will have a higher value in liquidation than as a going concern. Delaware, in common with other states, responds to this by saying that *only* going-concern value counts.[16] This conclusion conforms with the framework established in

15. See Lynch v. Vickers Energy Corp., 429 A.2d 497, 505 (Del. 1981) (asset value important because "oil was [and is] a limited and much needed energy source which significantly affected its value as a corporate asset"); Bell v. Kirby Lumber Corp., 413 A.2d 137 (Del. 1980).

16. For example, Rosenblatt v. Getty Oil Co., 493 A.2d 929, 942 (Del. 1985); Tri-Continental Corp. v. Battye, 74 A.2d 71, 72 (Del. 1950); Sporborg v. City Specialty Stores, 123 A.2d 121, 126 (Del. Ch. 1956).

Chapter 5. Gains that could be had by restructuring the firm—including liquidating it—should be excluded in order to reward those who bear the costs and risk of undertaking these changes.

VALUATION IN DELAWARE AFTER *WEINBERGER*

Weinberger tossed out the Delaware block method, and for the reasons we have given this is all to the good. Yet what does a court do in its stead? The techniques "generally used in the financial community" include the market price. They also include a bucket full of methods to discount projected future profits to present value—methods that either duplicate the Delaware block or are less reliable. Since *Weinberger* the court has allowed investors to recover elements of value attributable to pursuing a corporate-opportunity claim against insiders,[17] a value *ex ante* the control transaction and therefore appropriate from an economic perspective. The court also has rebuffed efforts to obtain for existing investors elements of value created by the reorganization (see note 9 above). Appraisal cases are sufficiently rare that much else remains to be settled. Perhaps the best that can be said is that if rules had gone seriously wrong in this corner of the law, we would see much more litigation than we do.

The Exclusivity of the Appraisal Remedy

The relation between appraisal and other remedies such as injunctions and damages has long been a subject of considerable controversy and litigation. For many years, appraisal was regarded as the exclusive remedy of dissenting shareholders except in cases of fraud or illegality.[18] In *Singer v. Magnavox*[19] Delaware held that a minority shareholder could have a merger enjoined if he could show that it lacked a "proper business purpose" or was not "entirely fair." And in *Lynch v. Vickers Energy*,[20] that court held that a minority shareholder could obtain rescissory damages against an

17. Cavalier Oil Corp. v. Harnett, 564 A.2d 1137, 1142–45 (Del. 1989).
18. Which is what the statutes, including Delaware's, say. Stauffer v. Standard Brands, 187 A.2d 78 (Del. 1962); David J. Greene & Co. v. Schenley Industries, 281 A.2d 30 (Del. Ch. 1971).
19. 380 A.2d 969 (Del. 1977).
20. 429 A.2d 497 (Del. 1981).

acquiring firm for misrepresentations or other breach of fiduciary duty in connection with tender offer. *Weinberger* discarded the business purpose requirement of *Singer* and made appraisal exclusive except in the event of fraud or misrepresentation. The court also overruled *Lynch* to the extent it allowed rescissory damages in all cases of fraud or misrepresentation but stated that such damages can be awarded in appraisal proceedings if they can be proven. Then *Rabkin v. Philip A. Hunt Chemical Corp.*[21] added that a court may enjoin a merger to prevent the firm from forcing appraisal to get around a contractual payment obligation, and *Cede & Co. v. Technicolor*[22] held that the court may enjoin a merger if fraud bilked the investor into demanding an appraisal (and an injunction is otherwise appropriate). As a practical matter, then, appraisal is far from "exclusive."

INJUNCTIONS AND DAMAGES

Whether appraisal should be the exclusive remedy depends in part on whether the price offered in an appraisal proceeding accurately reflects pretransaction value. The less accurate the appraisal price, the more useful other remedies. We have suggested two respects in which appraisal proceedings fall short of the mark: the market-out rule, which may leave investors without a floor even though the insiders have depressed the price, and the variegated and inconsistent methods for arriving at "fair value."

Does it follow that courts should enjoin detrimental transactions instead of trying to attach prices to shares? Legal rules that control fraud force insiders to contract for what they want. A rule that gives each investor the ability to obtain an injunction forces people to bargain and so may improve the operation of the market in corporate control.

Which is not to say that we can be confident that hunting for fraud will improve things even in a world of imperfect appraisal pricing. After all, the search for fraud is itself costly and prone to error. Injunctions create holdup value. Only by purchasing the plaintiff's right to seek an injunction can the firm proceed with the transaction. With a damages rule, by contrast, no transactions are necessary. If transactions costs are zero, the choice between a

21. 498 A.2d 1099 (Del. 1985).
22. 542 F.2d 1182 (Del. 1988).

property rule (injunctions) and a liability rule (damages) is irrelevant. The defendant will be able to pay damages or purchase the investor's right to seek an injunction where the gains exceed the losses to the investor. If the losses exceed the gains to the defendant, the defendant will be unwilling to purchase the plaintiff's right to seek an injunction or pay damages—but then the transaction should not proceed anyway.

Under the realistic assumption that transactions costs are high when there are many investors, the choice between property and liability rules frequently is determinative. If there are many shareholders, it will be extremely difficult for a defendant to negotiate with each to purchase the right to seek an injunction. In addition, each shareholder wants to hold out for a high price in order to capture as much of the gains for himself as possible. This type of strategic behavior could lead to the threat of an injunction even though both the plaintiff individually and the shareholders as a class actually benefit from the challenged transaction. Large numbers of parties, holdout problems, or conflicts of interest among plaintiffs can frustrate the ability of the parties to reach the optimal outcome by bargaining. Injunctions thus ought to be available only when the appraisal remedy is plainly deficient or the fraud quite clear (so that the costs of error are low).

THE FRAUD EXCEPTION

Weinberger reaffirmed the traditional rule that injunctive relief is available only in cases involving fraud.[23] "Fraud" is a plastic term, and some language in *Weinberger* implied that courts could find fraud whenever persuaded that the firm offered its investors too little money or failed to help them hold out for a slice of the value to be created by the transaction. Such an approach would create stupendous holdout value, and Delaware quickly retreated. Two recent cases say that a price properly derived is not "fraudulent" even though low relative to investors' expectations, and that the persons proposing control transactions need not reveal their best

23. Weinberger v. UOP, Inc., 457 A.2d 701 (Del. 1983). See, for example, *Model Business Corporation Act* §13.02(b) (appraisal remedy exclusive unless the action taken is "unlawful or fraudulent with respect to the shareholder or the corporation"); N.Y. Bus. Corp. Law §623(h) (appraisal remedy not exclusive where corporate action is unlawful or fraudulent as to complaining shareholder).

price (or estimates of other potential bidders' offers).[24] This approach largely confines injunctions to cases in which deceit makes the appraisal remedy less accurate.

Do not confuse us with Dr. Pangloss. In practice it will be exceptionally difficult for a court to identify fraud coupled with inadequacy of the appraisal process, not only because data are scarce and judgments hard but also because plaintiffs acting strategically have an incentive to characterize the most beneficial transactions as "fraudulent" precisely because there are large gains in which they seek to participate. Any search for fraud creates a risk of courts mistakenly enjoining value-increasing transactions.

Appraisal would be a more attractive candidate for a truly exclusive remedy if the procedural problems with the appraisal remedy could be eliminated. More accurate valuation based on market prices,[25] coupled with the inclusion of interest as an element of recovery and a shift to the firm of the costs (including legal fees) of the proceeding itself, would improve the utility of the appraisal proceeding and make other remedies less appropriate. The American Bar Association's 1984 revision of the Model Business Corporation Act takes large steps in this direction, requiring the firm to initiate (and bear the costs of) the appraisal process—expediting the disposition and consolidating all claims in a single forum.[26]

The Scope of the Appraisal Remedy

When appraisal appeared in the middle of the nineteenth century, it applied to very few transactions and was essentially limited to the

24. Bershad v. Curtiss-Wright Corp., 535 A.2d 840 (Del. 1987); Rosenblatt v. Getty Oil Co., 493 A.2d 929, 944–945 (Del. 1985). See also 3 *Model Business Corporation Act Annotated* 1430–35 (citing cases from other states).

25. To say that accurately determined damages are preferable to injunctions is most certainly not to say that all damages remedies are preferable. This is so not only for reasons we have already emphasized but also because dissenters' favorite candidate for damages—rescissory remedies—is inferior to injunctions from the perspective of wealth maximization. Rescissory damages compensate plaintiffs for increases in market value having nothing to do with the transaction and any fraud that occurs. They provide plaintiffs with a costless option on increases in market value long after the existence and effect of the alleged fraud are known. Rescissory damages deter value-increasing transactions and are thus inconsistent with the contract that investors and managers would negotiate were costs low enough.

26. See §§13.30 and 13.31.

investors in firms that were being dissolved.[27] The list of covered transactions increased throughout this century. Today investors in acquiring as well as acquired firms are entitled to dissent and appraisal, provided the transaction is sufficiently important to trigger a vote among the acquiring firm's investors. More interesting, investors are entitled to appraisal on account of a growing list of changes in the articles of incorporation. The 1984 version of the Model Business Corporation Act grants appraisal if changes in the articles affect preferences or voting rights of shares, preemptive rights, or cumulative voting, and it allows the articles and bylaws to add other transactions to the list of triggering events.[28]

If, on the one hand, appraisal is some sort of substitute for markets, then the expansion of the remedy is inexplicable. Securities markets are much more widespread and efficient now than one hundred years ago. If, on the other hand, appraisal establishes a reservation price, then the increase in the portion of wealth held through anonymous public markets makes appraisal all the more important. Chapter 1 suggested that appraisal may be an appropriate solution to the "latecomer term"—unanticipated changes in the articles, bylaws, and structure of securities that change the risk or expected return of investment. We expect continuing expansion in the scope of appraisal as firms and their lawyers become increasingly creative in altering the risk-return attributes of investment through methods that do not require the managers to raise new capital and submit to the judgment of the market.

27. See William J. Carney, "Fundamental Corporate Changes, Minority Shareholders, and Business Purposes," 1980 *Am. Bar Found. Research J.* 69, 77–94; Melvin Aron Eisenberg, *The Structure of the Corporation* 69–84 (1976); Elliott L. Weiss, "The Law of Take Out Mergers: A Historical Perspective," 56 *N.Y.U. L. Rev.* 624 (1981).

28. §13.02(a)(4) and (5).

7

Tender Offers

Cash tender offers are a species of corporate control transaction. One firm solicits "tenders" of another's stock. The offer runs to the shareholders, not the managers. If the bidder obtains enough stock, it takes control through one of the standard devices: it uses the shares to vote out the existing board and install its own, or it merges the acquired firm into itself or a subsidiary. Because the tender offer is a voluntary transaction between the bidder and the target's investors, it has a built-in market test. Investors won't tender unless the offer is higher than the one prevailing in the market (which reflects the price of potentially competitive bids); bidders won't make such offers unless they believe they can use the target's assets well enough to make the premium payment profitable, which implies increased productivity.

Tender offers differ from the transactions we have studied so far, however, because of the presence of the hostile outside party. Managers of the target perceive bids as reflecting poorly on their service, since the bidders commonly propose to change the way the target is run. Within three years of an acquisition, half of all managers at targets are out of work. So they may try to resist—whether crassly to save their jobs or because they genuinely believe that their program for the firm is superior to the bidder's. Deficient managers are no less likely to *believe* that they are doing the best for the firm than are superior managers; inability to tell what is best for the firm may be what makes a managerial team deficient. And craven managers, like the rest of us, reduce cognitive dissonance by believing that what's best for them is also best for their firms. Tender offers are involuntary from managers' perspective. Resistance is the phenomenon of interest.

We concentrate on resistance conscious that many persons focus instead on the question: "What is the source of the large premium

162

in tender offers?" Is it synergy, tax, managerial changes, financial flimflam? Other explanations are possible, and we shall address sources of gains briefly. But the gains (if any) come from the subsequent changes in the corporate structure and operations. What distinguishes the tender offer from the vanilla merger or the board's selection of a new CEO is its hostile quality. Bidders and shareholders go over the heads of managers. If there are gains to be had from synergistic combinations, we expect managers to achieve these without the need for force, just as they design new products and open new plants without guns held to their temples. Involuntary control transactions must mean either (a) the current managerial team has missed an opportunity to increase value, or (b) the bidder has found a way to make itself better off at the target's expense. In either event, the thing to be explained is why force has to be used.

The Contract Paradigm

Tender offers, no less than other control transactions, could be approached through the contractual paradigm. Indeed contracts dominate. Most firms are "born" takeover-proof. Closely held corporations lack public markets for their stock, which often is tied up with buy-sell agreements or other devices that give managers or shareholders the right to veto or preempt any investor's attempt to sell to a stranger. Many firms have no tradable equity claims. Think of cooperatives, mutual insurance companies, universities and other nonprofit enterprises. Other firms, although publicly held, have established structures that make tender offers difficult. When Ford Motor Company first issued stock to the public, it sold nonvoting shares. The family retained the voting stock. Acquisition of the public shares by tender offer could not have accomplished a change of control. All of these contractual devices, and more, are consistent with our economic framework and lawful, too. The difficult questions arise when firms take steps after going public that alter investors' ability to change control via tender offer.

State and Federal Rules

Delaware allows firms to adopt in advance of a bid almost any device that will affect the likelihood of a tender offer, subject only to the customary (and highly deferential) standards of the business judgment rule.[1] Firms may stagger the terms of members of the board of directors, which may defer the bidder's effective control of the target; they may issue stock with lesser voting rights (or rights that collapse if held in blocs), again interfering with an acquirer's ability to use the shares to control the target. Firms may adopt supermajority requirements (the acquirer needs more than half of the stock to carry out a merger) or "fair price rules" that require the bidder to acquire the remaining shares at a price fixed by reference to that paid in the offer. A common form of fair-price amendment provides that the price in a squeezeout merger must be at least as high as the price paid in the tender offer, and that the merger must be approved by a majority of the shares other than those owned by the bidder. Firms also may issue "poison pill" stock—rights that mature once any person owns more than a specified bloc (commonly 20 percent) and entitle their owners (except the bloc holder) to purchase additional shares at a discount. The "flip-in" feature of poison pill stock dilutes the bloc owner's interest, making each share worth less (and requiring the bidder to buy more to get control)—a combination fatal when swallowed (hence "poison pill"). Sometimes the flip-in cancels automatically if the bidder obtains a large portion of the stock (80 to 90 percent). A "flip-over" feature of pills may have similar dilution effects for the bidder's own stock after a merger, inducing the target's shareholders not to tender (if they keep the target's stock, they can buy the bidder's stock at a discount if the deal goes through) and inducing the bidder's shareholders to oppose the transaction (to avoid having their interests diluted).

Once a bid is on the table, Delaware requires the target's managers to take additional care and to demonstrate that their acts may well benefit the firm. Although this casts the burden on the managers, courts have been quite tolerant in accepting justifications

1. Delaware has by far the most developed body of case law on tender offers. The principal cases are: Paramount Communications, Inc. v. Time Inc., 571 A.2d 1140 (Del. 1990); Revlon, Inc. v. MacAndrews & Forbes Holdings, Inc., 506 A.2d 173 (Del. 1986); Moran v. Household International, Inc., 500 A.2d 1346 (Del. 1985); Unocal Corp. v. Mesa Petroleum Co., 493 A.2d 946 (Del. 1985); Grand Metropolitan PLC v. Pillsbury Co., 558 A.2d 1049 (Del. Ch. 1988); City Capital Associates v. Interco Inc., 551 A.2d 787 (Del. Ch. 1988). See generally Ronald J. Gilson and Reinier Kraakman, "Delaware's Intermediate Standard for Defensive Tactics: Is There Substance to Proportionality Review?" 44 *Bus. Law.* 247 (1989).

offered for carrying on with existing plans (such as merger with a third party) that are mutually exclusive with the bid, targeted repurchases from bloc holders ("greenmail"), purchases at a premium from everyone *except* the bloc holder, purchasing the bidder's stock, issuing a bloc of stock to a firm that promises to support management, litigating to stop the offer on antitrust or securities grounds, and failing to redeem poison pill stock before the "trigger" has been activated.

Delaware has clamped down on targets' strategies only once the management itself decides to put the firm on the block. If an auction develops, the management may be required to redeem poison pill stock and to avoid "lock-up" options (options to sell corporate assets at a discount, with the same kind of dilution effect for a bidder as poison pill stock). Such auctions must give bidders equal opportunity, so that the highest bid prevails.

To this case law we must add both the federal Williams Act[2] and the control share statutes adopted by approximately forty states. Anyone acquiring more than 5 percent of the stock of a publicly traded firm must file a report disclosing his position and intentions. Bidders must file more elaborate reports concerning their financing and plans, and tender offers must remain open for about a month. Bidders may not buy stock in the market during their offers and must purchase shares in oversubscribed offers pro rata, at the highest price offered to anyone. These rules eliminate any advantage to making early tenders. The Williams Act gives targets both time to maneuver (whether to block the bid or seek competing offers) and legal grounds for objecting, while depriving bidders of strategies that would facilitate acquisitions.

State control share laws fall into two groups. One stripe of law sterilizes the acquirer's shares until the remaining investors vote to give the bidder control. This majority-of-the-minority approach has effects similar to those of fair-price amendments. The other variety blocks the bidder from merging with the target for some period (often three years) after the tender offer, unless the target's management consents in advance. Most states with this kind of statute allow firms to opt out by amending their articles of incorporation and provide that if the bidder acquires enough shares (in Delaware, 85 percent of the stock not held by management) the restriction is lifted. Statutes that melt away if the bidder acquires enough stock

2. 15 U.S.C. §§78m(d), (e), 78n(d)-(f).

again operate like fair-price amendments, requiring bidders to seek all of the stock at a price generally attractive. Statutes without such an option prevent nonconsensual bids whenever a merger is an ingredient of the changes that justify the premium price. Whether managers must give their consent is a question no state court has addressed. In principle this is the same as the question whether managers must redeem poison pill stock to allow a bid to proceed.

THE ARGUMENT FOR CONTRACT

Because firms may (and do) adopt structures, and issue securities that make them takeover-proof or takeover-prone, this subject appears to be another illustration of our proposition that corporate law is just contract law on a large scale. Taken to its limits, the contract approach implies that anything goes—that managers should be allowed to exploit any available devices to respond to offers, while being bound to respect any contractual limits on their powers. Courts' only role would be to enforce the contracts.[3] Needless to say we find this an attractive starting point.

It is not hard to imagine the uses of contract. Some firms will leave themselves open to offers. Others will be immune (as most closely held firms are today). Investors may choose among strategies, and the set of rules that maximizes value will endure. Some firms may be managed best if guaranteed "independence"—not only from bidders but also from meddling by their own investors. Perhaps tenure for managers promotes long-run planning at some firms. Perhaps the ability to keep a firm independent will assist managers in negotiating the best terms for any given acquisition. Other firms will make themselves readily acquired, or readily digested if the bidder takes all the shares but not otherwise (the fair-price regimen). The very diversity of firms and contractual arrangements ensures that no one approach will maximize the value of all firms. No legal or economic institution other than contract permits the useful matching of structure to need; no other institution permits such potent sorting of useful from counterproductive adaptations.

3. David D. Haddock, Jonathan R. Macey, and Fred S. McChesney, "Property Rights in Assets and Resistance to Tender Offers," 73 *Va. L. Rev.* 701 (1987), is the best presentation of this position.

Firms offer a dazzling number of investment instruments (bonds, preferred stock, convertible subordinated debentures, common stock with different sorts of rights, warrants, and so on) to attract investors' money. They compete in the products they offer. They compete in the kinds of internal governance they use, including all sorts of differences in management structure and voting. These differences evolve according to the vicissitudes of the market and the value investors place on them. Promoting or deterring tender offers is just one of the dimensions in which firms compete. Left alone, corporations could offer investors as many different regimens of tender offer bidding and defense as they now offer different investment instruments and governance structures. The more beneficial a structure for investors, the more likely it is to survive.

If antitakeover provisions are not beneficial to investors, they will depress the price of the stocks affected by them. At lower prices, these stocks will be more attractive as takeover targets. The market thus has an automatic compensation device for undesired opposition. Firms that excessively insulate their managers from (or expose them to) the pressure of takeover will falter in their product markets, their stocks will decline in value, and they will change course, or fail, or be acquired. In the long run, useful provisions will dominate.

THE LIMITS OF CONTRACT

Despite the attractions of the purely contractual approach to tender offers—not least among them consistency with the analysis in the rest of this book!—it has shortcomings that illustrate the limits to writing and enforcing the corporate contract. For contracting to work optimally, the markets must be completely free. That is, all possible contracts must be lawful. They must be stable and enforceable at low cost; breach must be detectable and remediable. Finally, the contracts concerning one firm's operation must have no effect on other firms. Each of these steps is problematic.

Regulatory Interference with Contract

Contracting depends on a full menu of choices. Investors have contracts with their own firm, but this is only half of the equation. Investors also would like to strike bargains about when, and at what price, they could sell. Perhaps investors would benefit from contractual "puts"—rights to sell stock back to the firm or to a third party in specified circumstances. Perhaps they could benefit from selling "calls"—giving would-be acquirers the right to take up their stock at a fixed price in the future. Bidders would exercise these rights if the target's stock traded at less than the call price and the bidder thought the value greater. Potential purchasers, too, need freedom of contract if the contractual regimen is to succeed. The full menu of contractual devices is enormous, and in an unhindered contractual equilibrium putative bidders could go shopping in the market for call options on firms they fancied as targets.

Many of these potential contracts are illegal in addition to being impractical. The securities laws do not permit potential bidders to line up extensive portfolios of call options, so that they could acquire a firm on a moment's notice. Quite the contrary, the Williams Act bans some devices that bidders commonly used and bestows weapons on the targets' managers. Whatever the optimal regime may be in a world of completely free contracting, we do not live in that world.

Relational Contracts and the Fiduciary Principle

Even if all possible contracts were lawful, they might not be practical. Holders of fixed claims (bondholders, employees) may have rights and obligations fixed by contract in excruciating detail. Chapters 4 and 5 show that equity investors, the holders of the residual claims, get the benefit of the fiduciary principle rather than detailed contracts because fully specifying terms is too costly. As firms evolve, the appropriate relation between residual risk bearers and the managers evolves too. Even if it were possible in principle to specify everything in advance, the terms would have to be changed from time to time.

Agency relations (as between managers and equity investors) exist precisely because full contractual specification is unbearably costly. Some combination of the fiduciary principle with a mechanism to replace the managers makes extensive discretion work the rest of the time. This makes it correspondingly difficult to call on the contractual paradigm to explain why managers could have a right to resist their own removal.

Last-Period and Ex Post Problems

If every detail could be negotiated *ex ante*, it could not be enforced *ex post*. Imagine, for example, a contract providing that in the event of an offer the managers must conduct an auction and sell the firm for the highest available price but may not seek to preserve independence. Most steps useful in running an auction also have the potential to prevent the sale. Think of the reservation price common in auctions: if the bid doesn't beat the price, the auctioneer takes the item off the block. Extending the time can be valuable. How much time is right? The owner of a Miró painting could wait years for the right price; how could we tell whether managers are running an extended auction or simply extending their tenure? Distinguishing these is especially difficult once we recognize that time must be *purchased* in a tender offer auction. Firms must take steps that delay the first bidder; yet anything potent enough to delay the bidder (such as a poison pill that delays the auction until the managers redeem the rights) also could be used to squelch the contest.[4]

There is a further problem: terms optimal when adopted may not be optimal given a bid. Firms that have made themselves easy to take over, so as to maximize the probability of a bid, find that once a bid appears it is profitable to provoke an auction. Perhaps it will issue a friendly bloc of stock or a lock-up auction. This puts the first bidder at a disadvantage, deterring first bids as surely as any express provision in the articles. Preventing such opportunistic switches is next to impossible.

So too is dealing with the last-period problem. Managers commonly protect investors' interests in order to promote their own—whether it be advancement in the labor market or the ability to raise new capital. Comes the "last period," however, when managers no longer contemplate returning to the labor market or raising capital, their incentives change and they may dig in their heels. Courts are not nearly as good as markets at enforcing long-term contracts, yet when last-period problems crop up only the cumbersome (expensive, imprecise) methods of litigation are available.

4. See Michael Rosenzweig, "Target Litigation," 85 *Mich. L. Rev.* 110 (1986). See also William J. Carney, "Controlling Management Opportunism in the Market for Corporate Control: An Agency Cost Model," 1988 *Wis. L. Rev.* 385.

Contractual arguments become especially difficult once we recognize that many of the provisions in question are latecomer terms, not "priced" when adopted. Recall from Chapter 1 that the contractual model draws much of its power because managers and entrepreneurs must "pay" for any inefficient terms by accepting lower prices for the securities they sell. Terms adopted after securities have been sold are not subject to an equivalent market test.

Enforcing terms present when the firm is created or raises substantial capital is not problematic. Many a firm goes public with terms that make it easy to acquire—board serving a short term, majority rule among the shareholders, no fair-price rules or poison pills, and so on. Provisions designed to make a firm indigestible may be added later on. Poison pills and several other devices may be added without so much as a vote among investors. New provisions approved by voting encounter the problem of rational ignorance (which we discussed in Chapter 3). Holders of large blocs will protect themselves; managers test the waters before making proposals, and when the holders of large blocs say no, managers turn to devices such as poison pills that do not require voting. Data we present later shows that antitakeover amendments are most common in firms without large bloc holders. At all events, voting works best when the shares may be gathered up and voted as a bloc in the event of a value-reducing proposal—but this presupposes free transfer to make the voting mechanism reliable. Latecomer terms adopted by voting (or with voting but without the possibility of reconcentrating the votes in the market) carry no assurance of progress. Indeed, latecomer terms pose a substantial threat of making at least some investors worse off, defeating the market-value floor that (we argued in Chapter 5) is the guarantee that corporate control transactions will be value-increasing.

Third-Party Effects

Contracts maximize private value. Whether they also maximize social welfare depends on whether the contracting parties bear the costs of their deals at the same time as they reap the benefits. Throughout this book we have treated the corporate contract as one without third-party effects. All of the actors, we said, take part in the contract. This is so for equity and debt investors, managers and other workers, suppliers and customers.

Tender offers put third parties in the picture for the first time. Contracts dealing with defensive tactics affect investors in bidders and in bystanders (firms that are neither bidders nor targets). Before saying that a regimen of contract does (or does not) maximize social wealth, we shall have to take these third-party effects into account. We develop the third-party effects in the next section, together with our own perspective on tender offers.

Agency Costs and Tender Offers

GOING OVER MANAGERS' HEADS

Takeovers are a device for limiting the costs of contracting—in particular, for holding down the costs of monitoring and replacing managers. In other words, tender offers control the agency costs of management. Their existence makes contractarianism on other subjects practical.

Market price reflects the value of assets as deployed by the incumbent managers. That the bid occurs at a premium over the market price indicates that revamping the target's structure or management would generate private and, in all likelihood, social gains. Successful resistance frustrates the achievement of these gains. Consequently managers should remain passive and let investors decide whether to tender.

Business consolidations may yield benefits from greater integration of production, more effective use of information, "synergy," changes in management (personnel or structure), and other sources. The benefits usually are achieved by mergers, which are less costly than hostile tender offers and can be set up to avoid recognition of taxable gains. Hostile tender offers are responses to the failures of the target's managers, who might be missing business opportunities, including profitable opportunities to merge. A tender offer gives the shareholders a chance to go over the head of managers when agency costs become too high.

Shareholders might be able to reap substantial gains from cutting down on agency costs, which we have explored in earlier chapters. But improvement is difficult to achieve, leading to the role for outside bidders. Agency costs typically go undetected by individual investors, who are diversified and passive. No shareholder can collect all of the gains available from monitoring. The benefits would be dispersed according to their investments, not according to their monitoring efforts. Because other shareholders take a free ride on anyone's monitoring, small shareholders find it in their self-interest to be passive. Holders of large blocs will do more monitoring. A surprisingly large portion of public firms have blocs of 20 percent or more.[5] In such firms monitoring by the blocs' owners may suffice. When the firm has no large bloc, or when 20 percent of the gains from monitoring is not enough to spark attentive supervision, some other device to concentrate the gains is essential.

The free-rider problems are aggravated by the difficulty shareholders face in doing anything about the firm's managers once they discover the existence of excessive agency costs. The shareholder who makes the discovery has no authority to compel the firm to change its ways. He must either persuade the managers or induce his fellow shareholders to act. Neither is likely in a world of atomistic holdings with the consequent rational ignorance and passivity (see Chapter 3).

To make matters worse, even when outsiders have good incentives to monitor, they have trouble separating bad luck from poor work and isolating contributors to any problem. Because managers typically work in teams, it is hard to determine the contribution of each. The output of one group of managers depends on the quality of information and options supplied by another group, and so on. Determining the marginal contribution of each manager is bound to be difficult and costly. Worse, the attempt to meter the contributions of each manager, and to dispense rewards accordingly, encounters the free-rider problem we have discussed. Because no manager can obtain all of the benefits of monitoring his colleagues, each one will be less than fully dedicated to the task. Even the most dedicated manager will find it difficult to fire or discipline an old friend when the benefit of ruthlessness accrues to distant and unknown shareholders. Metering and monitoring within a firm are likely to work better when the management team as a whole is subject to supervision.

Those making the tender offer can profit by scrutinizing management teams. Prospective bidders monitor the performance of teams by comparing a corporation's potential value with its value (as

---

5. Harold Demsetz and Kenneth Lehn, "The Structure of Corporate Ownership: Causes and Consequences," 93 *J. Pol. Econ.* 1155 (1985).

reflected by share prices) under current management. When the difference becomes too great, an outsider can profit by buying the firm and making changes. The outsider, after acquiring a majority of the shares, has superior incentives at the margin. All parties benefit in this process. The target's shareholders gain because they receive a premium over the market price. The bidder obtains the difference between the new value of the firm and the payment to the old shareholders. Nontendering shareholders receive part of the appreciation in the price of the shares.

Investors benefit even if their corporation never becomes the subject of a tender offer. The reality and prospect of monitoring by outsiders poses a threat of takeover if performance lags. Managers must attempt to improve the firm's performance, which leads to higher prices for shares and so reduces the chance of takeover.

High stock prices are the beneficial way to ward off takeovers, but not the easiest way. Managers have other resources to deploy. They may seek approval of antitakeover devices such as super-majority rules, or use those (poison pills, lock-up options, litigation) that do not require assent. If takeovers are beneficial to both shareholders and society, any strategy designed to prevent tender offers reduces welfare. We except devices in place at the time the firm was established or raised substantial capital, for these passed the market test explained in Chapter 1. Even these truly consensual devices have their costs, however, because there is a gap between private and social optimality.

When a target resists a tender offer or extracts a higher price through an auction, this influences the future conduct of bidders and thus the wealth of investors in other firms. Whether resistance drives up the price or reduces the probability of an acquisition, it makes the process of monitoring and bidding less profitable. When the price of anything goes up, the quantity demanded falls. Changes in the incentives of bidders affect the utility of monitoring by outsiders, and that affects the size of agency costs and in turn the preoffer price of all firms' stock.

In order to explore the nature of these effects, consider the effects of two polar rules. Under the first rule, management is passive in the face of tender offers. If there are no competing bidders, the first to make an offer prevails at the lowest premium that induces investors to surrender their shares. Under the second rule, management uses all available means to resist the offer. This resistance creates an auction, so that no bidder can acquire the target without paying a price almost as high as the shares would be worth under the best practicable management. For example, shares of firm X are trading for $40. Outsiders could manage the firm better so that the shares would be valued at $90 each. A bid of $50 would induce a substantial majority of X's shareholders to tender their shares. Under managerial acquiescence the bid of $50 ensures success. With resistance a tender offerer could not acquire X for much less than $90 per share.

Which of these rules maximizes wealth? If the question is asked *ex post,* after a tender offer has been made, investors in targets would prefer the bidding war. The *ex ante* answer may be different. If the target's shareholders obtain *all* the gains from the transaction, no one has an incentive to monitor and make offers. Stock prices of all firms will fall to reflect this. If managers pursue a path of "independence" the effect is the same: no profit in being an outside monitor, hence all firms' stock price falls *ex ante.* Agency costs increase (and prices fall) to the point where further changes precipitate a change of control. Because investors prefer the wealth-maximizing rule for reasons Chapters 4 and 5 develop, the optimal legal rule prevents resistance unless expressly authorized by contract *ex ante.* Investors are willing to allow acquisitions for "bargain" prices (that is, without demanding the "sharing" of profits) to promote outside monitoring.[6] *Given* a bid, however, an attempt to engross the profits by defense or auctioneering—privately rational for the target or its managers—leads to too little future monitoring. Conclusion: Managers should leave to shareholders and rival bidders the task of "responding" to offers. Managerial passivity is best, *ex ante,* but privately and socially.

OTHER PERSPECTIVES

Our agency cost model of tender offers is only one among many rivalrous approaches. We lay out some other ways of under-

6. See Sanford J. Grossman and Oliver D. Hart, "The Allocational Role of Takeover Bids in Situations of Asymmetric Information," 36 *J. Fin.* 253 (1981); Grossman and Hart, "Disclosure Laws and Takeover Bids," 35 *J. Fin.* 323 (1980); Grossman and Hart, "Takeover Bids, the Free Rider Problem, and the Theory of the Corporation," 11 *Bell J. Econ.* 42 (1980). This work, like our own, is an outgrowth of Henry Manne, "Mergers and the Market for Corporate Control," 73 *J. Pol. Econ.* 110 (1965).

standing bids and resistance and explain why we do not find them logically satisfying. Logical arguments are not dispositive, however, so the next section of this chapter tests each approach against data.

Market Failure Models

Markets do not always work well. Our approach emphasizes one problem with markets—agency costs. Perhaps some different problem is more important.

Wasted Capital

One common argument is that tender offers are themselves a species of market failure, that they "use up credit" and divert resources from productive investment.[7] This argument is based on a misunderstanding of how capital markets work. Money disbursed by bidders is received and reinvested by targets' shareholders. It returns to the banking system and is available for relending or is invested directly in some other firm's stock. Tender offers are no different from other capital transactions, such as the purchase of one to two hundred million shares on the New York Stock Exchange every business day. Money flows from one investment to another. Neither real resources nor credit are used up, and if changes of control enable the new owners to make better use of the assets than the old owners and managers, there are substantial benefits for the economy.

Related to this is the assertion that money borrowed to finance bids leaves society with "too much debt." Here the claim is not that tender offers "use up" credit but that they cause it to breed. This is first of all not an argument about tender offers; LBOs and other transactions increase leverage without a tender offer, and if the substitution of debt for equity serves some function it will proceed even if tender offers were banned. Anyway, what's wrong with debt? Even the least secure of "junk bonds" have more investor-security features than blue-chip common stock. If the issuer gets into trouble and does not pay, the bonds become common stock—either because they have a conversion feature on default or because un-

7. See Robert B. Reich, *The Next American Frontier* 140–172 (1983).

paid debt is the residual claim and acquires working control of the firm by virtue of votes (these instruments have super voting power when payments are in arrears).

One of the best-understood propositions in financial economics is that debt in the sense of leverage is irrelevant to the value of the firm. Debt matters only when it affects some other variable, such as taxes, or the probability of bankruptcy (with attendant costs of restructuring or fighting over spoils), or when it changes the incentives of investors to monitor the managers.[8] There are three principal differences between debt and equity: (1) interest payments are deductible to the firm; (2) debt holders get contractual rather than fiduciary protections; (3) debt means a mandatory payout. Each of these features may be beneficial for reasons given in Chapter 5 in the discussion of LBOs and MBOs.[9] Whether debt is superior may be a tough question, but it is a question for the particular firm, no different in principle from the question "should this firm build this plant?" or "should we have cumulative preferred stock rather than convertible subordinated debentures?"

Debt puts managers on a shorter leash; they must raise the money to meet the payment obligations. This leads debt to be used for established firms ("cash cows") rather than startup ventures (we do not see high debt at growing firms). Many say that debt forces managers to concentrate on short-term returns, at the expense of long-run value, to get cash to pay the creditors. Why should this be? If the firm chooses a project that has a lower net present value (though higher immediate cash payoffs) than some alternative, in the long run the debt investors won't be paid, and the managers' careers will be shattered. If the firm *really* has in hand a project with good long-term returns but a cash outflow in the near term, it will be able to raise from equity investors the money to finance it, while paying debt investors from existing projects. In reply one hears that the market is myopic and does not understand long-run

8. See Franco Modigliani and Merton H. Miller, "The Cost of Capital, Corporation Finance, and the Theory of Investment," 48 *Am. Econ. Rev.* 261 (1958). See also Merton H. Miller, "The Modigliani-Miller Propositions after Thirty Years," 2 *J. Econ. Perspectives* 99 (Fall 1988), followed by an exchange of views on the subject.

9. See also Frank H. Easterbrook, "High-Yield Debt as an Incentive Device," *Int'l Rev. L. & Econ.* (forthcoming 1991).

values. We doubt it (more on this below). But if the market is myopic, the firm won't be able to finance the project even if it is 100 percent equity! Nothing about the "debt burden" on any given day affects in the slightest the firm's ability or incentive to raise money for new projects.

The third and final "wasted capital" argument is that tender offers lead to "bust ups" of established firms, as segments of the business must be sold to pay the debt. This is a non sequitur; if the segment being sold will fetch money that can be paid out to reduce debt, it can be retained, and its profits used for debt service. At all events, lines of business do not vanish when sold. Often the gains from a tender offer lie in a better match of assets to managerial teams and corporate structures. There can be too much conglomeration as well as too little. Bust ups often follow the takeover of a conglomerate that has got its fingers in so many projects that it cannot manage any one of them very well. De-conglomeration may be the source of substantial improvements in productivity. (Why else, ask yourself, would the buyers of these divisions pay all that money?)

Exploiting Investors

Stock markets are reasonably efficient but not perfectly so. Suppose markets get the price right 90 percent of the time. The other 10 percent of the time someone can make a profit by scooping the market—finding a firm the price of which does not reflect its true value, purchasing its stock, and selling again once the price finally catches up to true value. Such a process diverts wealth from existing investors to the bidder. It may produce some benefits by aligning prices better with true values. That is, if stock prices are poor estimates of "true value," then perhaps we should welcome tender offers for their effect in moving prices *a lot,* and *fast,* making the capital-formation process work better. Let us suppose, however, that these are second-order effects and ask whether bids are likely to stem from inefficient prices.

Whether bids are largely a process for diverting wealth from existing investors to bidders is an empirical question, depending on the efficiency of stock markets and the power of competition among bidders in driving the acquisition price to the level reflecting the firm's true value. But there are logical grounds to doubt that scooping up bargains is much of a problem. The principal one is that if the market price does not fully reflect the firm's value, the managers, faced with a bid, can reveal the news on which the bidder is acting. Investors may evaluate it for themselves. They would tender only if they did not share the managers' optimism. Someone is making a mistake when managers say, "this stock is worth $40 per share," and it persists in trading for $20. By and large, managers are the mistaken parties—for they have their egos on the line, while professional investors are betting their wallets, and there are enormous profits to be made by buying bargains before other investors wise up. In the end, there must be few bargains.

Suppose investors discount managers' revelations, knowing their self-interest. In that event the price won't rise to true value. But investors also would discount the *new* managers' revelations after the takeover, for the self-interest is the same. Again price won't rise. If price does not rise, however, the bidders can't beat the market in the fashion this tale supposes. So investors must ultimately believe some set of managers. Why believe only the bidders? Initial managers may make their promises believable by repurchasing shares, obliging themselves to pay out the firm's profits (that is, issuing debt), and so on. Scooping the market implies that bidders expropriate wealth from the investors whose shares they acquire. Investors could defend themselves against this by believing the initial managers, causing price to follow value accurately. The scooping-the-market story therefore does not hang together.

Indeed, investors' rational reactions may defeat bids even when the target, as currently run, is worth less than the price offered in the bid. A stock's price depends in part on the prospect that the firm will be acquired at a premium. The existence of a bid causes investors to reevaluate their beliefs about the likelihood of a takeover. If they perceive the prospect of a higher bid—even one six months or more down the road—the price will rise to reflect its value. Many times the price quickly rises to exceed that of the bid on the table. At this point the bid is dead, defeated by the rational expectations of investors without any action on managers' part. Bids succeed only when the combination of expectations about value under current management and expectations about other potential bids comes to less than what has been offered.

Perhaps, however, the bidders expropriate the wealth of the investors whose shares they do *not* acquire. A firm may buy just enough shares to obtain control, then raid the target's treasury. (Equivalently, it may purchase the target's goods at a price below the market, or acquire the target's productive assets for too little.) Such a strategy adds nothing to social wealth but does transfer wealth to Bidder from the minority shareholders in Target. The transfer is the source of the premium for the shares Bidder acquires.

"Coercion" is a variant on the theme of looting. The looter offers an implicit two-tier price: something over market to those who sell, and something less (maybe much less) to those who hold out. The two-tier bid could be express. Assuming no theft later on, the first tier is well over market and the second tier less so: for example, if the stock is trading for $50, Bidder may offer $80 cash for 51 percent of the stock and $60 in debentures for the remaining 49 percent in a merger, a "blended" price of $70.20. If the true value of the firm is $75, everyone will tender to Bidder: $80 exceeds $75, and more important the front-end price exceeds the back-end of $60. But by hypothesis the investors are being took, because they are giving up stock worth $75 in exchange for a package worth $70. They were coerced to tender to the first tier.[10]

Notice that this argument supposes that the stock's price is "wrong"; it depends on a belief that true value exceeds the market price. It also depends on a belief that Target's shareholders "ought" to get the true value, a form of the gain-sharing proposal we considered and rejected in Chapter 5. Victor Brudney and Marvin Chirelstein made explicit the gain-sharing impetus for objecting to two-tier bids.[11] On our view, however, a two-price bid addresses a holdout problem with benefits for all investors. Collective action problems cut both ways here: the essential problem is not that

10. See Martin Lipton, "Corporate Governance in the Age of Finance Corporatism," 136 *U. Pa. L. Rev.* 1, 18–20 (1987). Lipton's screed against tender offers presents many of the objections we cover in the text.

11. Victor Brudney and Marvin A. Chirelstein, "A Restatement of Corporate Freezeouts," 87 *Yale L. J.* 1354, 1359–65 (1978). See also Brudney and Chirelstein, "Fair Shares in Corporate Mergers," 88 *Harv. L. Rev.* 297 (1974).

investors find it too hard to act collectively to hold out but that they find it too *easy* to hold out! If investors think that Bidder will improve the value of Target—something Bidder likely believes, for it can't make a profit without producing a value exceeding the price it offers—they will be inclined to sit on their shares and obtain that higher value. If enough investors do this, the offer fails. The two-tier bid induces them to tender and make the offer succeed. It overcomes the tendency of passive investors to take a free ride on Bidder's efforts, a tendency that if widespread causes beneficial offers to fail. Two-tier bids lead investors to tender rather than hold.

Those who protest two-tier bids assume that some shareholders value the stock more than the tender price and fear that, if they do not tender at once, they will fare even worse in a subsequent freezeout. The assertion that shareholders have multiple subjective values for stock, however, is unfounded. It is far more likely that those with high estimates of a firm's value will buy the stock of other investors than that the pessimists will bid for the stock held by optimists.

A two-tier offer cannot be used to reduce the value of the firm, for the back-end price must exceed the market price on any view. It is also hard to see how the two-tier bid could lead to success by anyone other than the firm placing the highest value on the target's assets. Some writers proceed as if no bidder other than the first may make the two-tier offer. Bidder 1, valuing the firm at $71 per share, makes the two tier offer of $80/60; Bidder 2, valuing Target at $76 per share, makes a flat bid of $75, which is worth more than Bidder 1's offer but which loses because all investors tender to the $80 offer. This treats everyone as short-sighted. Investors know that if they tender to Bidder 1 they will get $70.20, not $80. If everyone tenders, shares will be taken up pro rata with a blended reward of $70.20. So they tender to Bidder 2, whose pool has the highest expected value per share tendered. Bidder 2 could pursue its own strategy: matching Bidder 1's back-end price of $60 while beating the front-end price of $80.

Competition from outsiders is not the only way value-decreasing offers meet their demise. Investors as a whole lose from such offers; rather than throw their money away, they may arrange (more accurately, the managers may arrange) for an issuer tender offer. The firm offers to buy back its shares at their "real" value, using money borrowed from banks and others who recognize that value.

The need to borrow imposes a market test on beliefs about value. Because by hypothesis the value exceeds the bidder's price, investors sell back to the firm. The value-decreasing bid fails.[12] If the target does not act, arbitrageurs can assemble blocs and overcome the collective action problem. It is hard to see how any two-tier bid can beat a higher offer—including the higher offer implicit in sitting on one's shares if their value exceeds the price bid, hoping the bidder will go away but falling back on the appraisal remedy if it does not.

Just as the bidder might hope to make money by raiding the treasury at the expense of minority shares, the bidder might dip into the treasury for the benefit of all equity holders (perhaps paying a huge dividend) at the expense of debt investors. A new owner could embark on projects with extra risk, with big (potential) payoffs to the equity claimants and equally big risks of failure. Bondholders, exposed to the risk of failure without any entitlement to the gains of success, could see this as a substantial loss.

Exposure of creditors to exploitation by large payouts or excessively risky projects is old news, however. Debt investors negotiate for protections. These will be imperfect (for the ultimate security is not investing at all, and elaborate contractual rules may so tie managers' hands that they prevent value-increasing projects and make repayment less likely). Today's managers could pursue either the payout or the high-risk strategy at bondholders' expense; sometimes it is said that LBOs represent such a decision. In any case, the possibility of injury does not mean that it occurs; exploiting bondholders has some of the same costs as exploiting labor (discussed immediately below). We have an empirical question.

Exploiting Labor (and Other Constituencies)

Many firms purchase labor, as they hire capital, with contracts containing implicit as well as explicit terms. Although workers may be employees at will, firms may promise to treat them "fairly"—an important promise considering that many workers invest heavily in human capital that cannot be picked up and transferred elsewhere. In order to induce managers and other workers to develop this human capital, firms maintain reputations for honest treatment (in-

---

12. See Michael Bradley and Michael Rosenzweig, "Defensive Stock Repurchases," 99 *Harv. L. Rev.* 1377, 1393–99, 1412–17 (1986).

cluding gradual increases in salary to reflect increments in skills). Such contracts could be made explicit, but they would be very hard to write, and attempts to enforce them in court could be worse than no contracts at all. Hence the attraction of implicit promises—and the opportunity for exploitation. Managers could decide to squeeze other employees, cutting wages (knowing that the workers' specific capital is worthless at other firms), firing those that no longer justify their salaries (despite implicit promises to "carry" workers late in life in exchange for highly productive work earlier). They could abolish severance pay (a form of refunding to workers accumulated firm-specific capital) and cut pensions (another form of deferred payment for work). New investors could play the same trick on upper managers.

Although this is a logically possible method of exploitation, it also comes with a logical obstacle. Incumbent managers don't pull this trick on other workers because the firm's success depends on its reputation for honest and reliable dealing. You can confiscate capital in this way only once, and then only if the firm is shrinking—for it cuts off access to the labor market on equal terms with competitors. Exploiting suppliers of human capital makes sense only at the end of a firm's life cycle. Any given firm may be approaching that end. If so, opportunistic conduct toward workers may be in the offing. It makes no sense for an *acquiring* firm to pull off this stunt, however. Even if it can find a target at the end of its life cycle, the bidder must worry about its own reputation. Needing to attract its own labor force, it cannot squeeze the target's workers without paying a large price. In other words, opportunistic, last-period exploitation of labor makes *less* sense when done by a bidder than when done by incumbent managers—the bidder's costs of this strategy are much larger. A desire to squeeze workers therefore is not a plausible explanation of tender offers.

A related form of squeeze is more likely. Some workers may be receiving more than their market wage, perhaps because regulations prevented competition in the labor market. Firms will try to reduce these wages. Air travel is a common example of this, and one study established that the premium paid in the tender offer for Trans World Airlines was substantially less than the savings from reducing the costs of labor. This, however, is not logically an explanation for *hostile* takeovers. Why should managers neglect this source of savings, which (unlike the last-period opportunism discussed above) has no costs to the firm? In fact new entrants such as People Express and Midway, and established air carriers such as American facing no serious threat of acquisition, were the leaders in reducing labor costs. Only managers sluggish in realizing this source of savings face takeover pressure—as they should.[13]

Exploiting Tomorrow (Myopic Markets)

Tender offers are profitable for bidders only if today's market price is less than the value of the firm in the bidder's hands. Thus the best defense against a takeover is a high stock price. If a high price means high productivity, there shall be dancing in the streets. Suppose, however, that stock markets are myopic—that they value the near horizon "too highly." Then managers can boost the price of their firms' stock by goosing up their short-run profits at the expense of longer term values. (Away with R&D and costly new plants and products!) In such a world, tender offers and the pressures they produce would be calamities.

Are markets myopic? Why should they be? Stock is valued for the returns through the years. If a given investor puts too much value on the present and too little on the future, someone else can make a lot of money by taking the stock off his hands at a bargain price. The process should continue (because there continues to be profit in it) until the price of stock fully reflects its long-term value. We know that markets value accurately the long-run payments on bonds; why should the same investors turn myopic when investing in stock? Price-earnings multiples of firms vary widely; some sell for 100 times earnings while others go for 10 or 2. Investors must be drawing distinctions on the basis of future profits.

Perhaps myopia lies in the eye of the beholder. Managers commonly believe that *their* firms are undervalued because they have rosy estimates of future profits; investors who are more skeptical will think the stock worth less than the managers do without a tinge of myopia. Managers most likely to grumble about "undervalued" stock would be those least astute at understanding the firm's future in their hands—and therefore the most likely candidates for a take-

13. If there was, indeed, a source of savings to exploit. One iconoclastic student of the subject has concluded that the real earnings of airline employees declined only modestly from 1978 to 1988. David Card, "Deregulation and Labor Earnings in the Airline Industry," Princeton University working paper (Oct. 1989).

over. But whether markets undervalue the future is an empirical question, to which we shall return.

Exploiting Consumers (Monopoly and Taxes)

Tender offers could make all investors better off while making society worse off. Suppose tender offers create monopolies, which jack up price to consumers. Or suppose tender offers raid the Treasury by creating extra deductible debt and stepping up the basis of the target's assets, producing depreciation deductions. Although we are tempted to say, "So go fix the tax and antitrust laws," there is a further problem: like many of the other "explanations" we have mentioned, this has nothing to do with tender offers. Maybe monopoly explains *mergers;* it does not explain why managers don't set about picking consumers' pockets with less muss and fuss. We must look elsewhere for an explanation that distinguishes hostile tender offers from friendly corporate control transactions.

Exploiting Bidders' Investors (Hubris)

The mechanism by which a premium price for targets' shares implies social gains is that bidders must be able to put targets' assets to better use or they could not afford the premium. What if bidders' managers are mistaken—if they, and not targets' managers, are running hog wild under the shield of costly monitoring? Richard Roll offered this hubris hypothesis of takeovers.[14] It has a foundation in economic theory, too. Many takeover contests are auctions. Participants in auctions try to estimate the value of the item for sale, and their bids reflect that value less discounts for uncertainty, cost, and profit. Perhaps the winner of the auction won because it (alone) was mistaken in estimating the value of the asset. When

14. Richard Roll, "The Hubris Hypothesis of Corporate Takeovers," 59 *J. Business* 197 (1986); see also Bernard S. Black, "Bidder Overpayment in Takeovers," 41 *Stan. L. Rev.* 597 (1989). On the economics of mistaken bids see R. Preston McAfee and John McMillian, "Auctions and Bidding," 25 *J. Econ. Lit.* 699 (1987) (survey article including summary of the winner's curse literature); Paul Milgrom, "Auctions and Bidding: A Primer," 3 *J. Econ. Perspectives* 3 (Summer 1989); Jean-Jacques Laffont and Jean Tirole, "Repeated Auctions of Incentive Contracts, Investment, and Bidding Parity with an Application to Takeovers," 19 *Rand J. Econ.* 516 (1988).

mistakes lead to high bids, then winners in auctions systematically lose money—the winner's curse.

Bidders know about the winner's curse and discount accordingly, but maybe takeovers are so infrequent that bidders cannot properly compute the right discount or learn from mistakes. Maybe—we shall discuss illuminating data later. For now we confess unconcern. If bidders pay too much, this is just a transfer payment. Investors in targets get what investors in bidders squander. Social welfare doesn't go up, but it doesn't go down either. And markets contain automatic penalties for failure, as for bad decisions to build plants and make new products. We would not say that because some products are unprofitable (most, actually), there is something wrong with the process of innovation. No more so with tender offers. If bidders' managers err, the price of their stock will fall. Bad bidders may make good targets. Mistakenly acquired assets will be spun off again. So it goes.

The Single-Owner Standard

The market standard we outlined means that investors gain by selling stock at any price higher than market. A competing perspective, the single-owner approach, posits that investors should hold out for the highest available price (the offer of the second-highest bidder plus ε). The argument for the single-owner approach starts with a question: How would a rational person sell his Rembrandt? Surely not to the first bidder at any old price. The owner would try to increase the price by holding it off the market for a while, keeping the painting "in play" until the maximum had been realized. Why not a "single-owner" standard for takeovers as well? Corporations, like works of art, are unique assets best sold the way the market tells us single owners sell art. Yet investors are scattered, uncoordinated; they cannot act as a single owner would, and the pressure to tender (lest their shares be left behind, unacquired) leads to sell for too little. The task of law then becomes to help them coordinate, to act as if one person owned all the stock.[15] This

15. Lucian Arye Bebchuk's "Toward Undistorted Choice and Equal Treatment in Corporate Takeovers," 98 *Harv. L. Rev.* 1695 (1985), and "The Sole Owner Standard for Takeover Policy," 17 *J. Legal Studies* 197 (1988), are the most prominent examples of this argument. For an effective response along lines related to those in

means not only delay (to facilitate auctions) but also other devices to produce top dollar for the owner's unique assets.

Let us continue the analogy. Why does the owner of the painting "shop" the work so extensively? Largely because no liquid market provides a value. Owners of wheat behave differently. The owner of art may have an idiosyncratic value, perhaps esteeming the slant of the model's eyebrow exceedingly. Owners of stock are not emotionally attached to their assets but want to maximize their value. The stock market provides the valuation that is missing (and must be created at great cost) in the art market. A bid over market necessarily implies greater productivity of the assets. Alan Schwartz put it well:

> Actual single owners of assets attempt to sell them for the highest prices, but efficiency requires only that assets move to higher-valuing users. That society allows single owners to decide when to sell—that is, to charge what the traffic will bear—is a prudential response to the inability of external decision makers to know just what transfers would be value increasing. This inability is not a problem here because stocks are financial assets whose values largely are reflected in market prices. Therefore, *any* transfer of corporate assets at a nontrivial premium above the market price is efficient ex ante, in the same sense than any voluntary contract is efficient ex ante.[16]

Because, as Chapters 4 and 5 explain, investors want to maximize expected value rather than their "fair share," value-increasing transfers are unambiguously desirable.

You say the stock market gives the value only of the marginal share and not of the firm as an "entity"? Very well. Continue the analogy. The Rembrandt's owner hires an agent but usually sets his own reservation price. The auction house's incentive is a percentage commission, not a salary, already a big difference from the corporate world. (Hiring an auctioneer on salary would be madness.) If the owner sees the auction house take a false step, he can fire it and hire another. Monitoring is ongoing; competition to be an

---

the text, see Alan Schwartz, "The Fairness of Tender Offer Prices in Utilitarian Theory," 17 *J. Legal Studies* 165 (1988), and "The Sole Owner Standard Revisited," ibid. at 231.

16. Schwartz, "Fairness of Tender Offer Prices," supra note 15 at 170 (emphasis in original).

agent is ongoing. A corporate investor, owning a small fraction of the shares, has no incentive to monitor in the same way. But if he did and saw a manager set too high a reservation price ("excessive" defense)—or, worse, observed the manager make an *ex post* change in the method of compensation (the firm hired him at $500,000 per year with no security, but now he says he has life tenure)—the investor could do only one thing: arrange for the firm to be taken over and sack the manager (the equivalent of changing auctioneers for art). Yet this supposes a functioning market in corporate control, the very assumption in question. If an auction house could change the terms of engagement *ex post* and prevent its own discharge, the terms of trade would change dramatically!

When markets depart from the model of individual decision makers operating in atomistic competition, we observe adaptations. Investors cannot monitor and fire managers the same way they can monitor and fire auctioneers, so the institutions surrounding sales should differ in turn. A principal difference between the art and corporate markets is the diffusion of investments that makes any one person's monitoring impractical and discharge of the manager even harder. One adaptation is a device that makes it worthwhile to be a monitor and facilitates the discharge: a tender offer in which the bidder keeps the profit attributable to the monitoring. A single-owner standard disregards the differences in the markets and casts aside the adaptation they have produced. Tender offers arise out of the agency costs of management; we cannot understand bids by assuming away these costs and the institutions that control them.

The Auction Alternative

A single-owner standard could imply the propriety of defense (on the ground that the "best" price is the reservation price in current hands) or managerial activity to increase price by auctions. Defensive tactics injure investors because they make monitoring by outsiders less profitable and so less common. Let us focus on the auction alternative as a means of increasing prices. Auctions (whether conducted by managers or facilitated by delays built in through law) also make monitoring less profitable. The first bidder spends time and money discovering things about many possible targets; the bid concentrates attention on a single target and reveals much of the knowledge. Subsequent bidders can enter the fray at lower cost, leaving the initial bidder with unrecoverable sunk costs. When it is better to be a second bidder than the first, there will be less monitoring.

Lucian Bebchuk and Ronald Gilson maintain that auctions do not produce the baleful effects of defense, and they would encourage auctions while banning defense.[17] Bebchuk and Gilson pursue three significant lines. First, they insist, bidders' sunk costs are not all that large (or can be recovered without prevailing, as by holding blocs of stock that appreciate during an auction). Second, they believe that auctions will direct assets to the highest valuing users, a productivity improvement compared with putting the assets in the hands of whoever makes the first bid. The third argument is related; targets search for bidders, just as bidders search for targets. A no-auction rule assumes that only bidders' sunk costs matter; allowing targets to auction off information they have acquired may promote outside monitoring on balance even though it discourages

17. Lucian Arye Bebchuk, "The Case for Facilitating Competing Tender Offers," 95 *Harv. L. Rev.* 1028 (1982); Bebchuk, "The Case for Facilitating Competing Tender Offers: A Reply and Extension," 35 *Stan. L. Rev.* 23 (1982); Bebchuk, "The Case for Facilitating Competing Tender Offers: A Last (?) Reply," 2 *J. L. Econ. & Org.* 253 (1986); Ronald J. Gilson, "A Structural Approach to Corporations: The Case against Defensive Tactics in Tender Offers," 33 *Stan. L. Rev.* 819, 868–875 (1981); Gilson, "Seeking Competitive Bids versus Pure Passivity in Tender Offer Defense," 35 *Stan. L. Rev.* 51 (1982). See also John Coffee, "Regulating the Market for Corporate Control: A Critical Assessment of the Tender Offer's Role in Corporate Governance," 84 *Colum. L. Rev.* 1145 (1984) (generally concluding that auctions are desirable while defense is not); Elazar Berkovitch, Michael Bradley, and Naveen Khanna, "Tender Offer Auctions, Resistance Strategies, and Social Welfare," 5 *J. L. Econ. & Org.* 395 (1989) (support for auctions, provided targets compensate bidders for putting firms in play). But see Alan Schwartz, "Search Theory and the Tender Offer Auction," 2 *J. L. Econ. & Org.* 229 (1986), "Bebchuk on Minimum Offer Periods," ibid. at 271, and "Defensive Tactics and Optimal Search," 5 *J. L. Econ. & Org.* 413 (1989). Schwartz, like Moshe Burnovski, "Reverse Price Tender Offers," 56 *Geo. Wash. L. Rev.* 295 (1988), and Yakov Amihud, "A Priority Rule in Tender Offers," Israel Institute of Business Research, Tel Aviv University, working paper (1986) (with Burnovski), believes that auctions reduce monitoring by bidders without offering offsetting benefits, and the text presents some of Schwartz's arguments together with those we made in a 1982 exchange with Bebchuk and Gilson. See Easterbrook and Fischel, "Auctions and Sunk Costs in Tender Offers," 35 *Stan. L. Rev.* 1 (1982), presenting our views concerning auctions at greater length. See also David P. Barron, "Tender Offers and Management Resistance," 38 *J. Finance* 331 (1983), concluding that efforts to defeat tender offers injure investors.

bidders' taking the initiative. (Their fourth argument, that bidders anticipate price movements without improving targets' efficiency, so that expenditures on search are wasteful, is the same as the scooping-the-market point we have already discussed.)

Auctions make prospecting by bidders less profitable. Does this *ex ante* effect outweigh (from targets' perspective) the fact that auctions raise the price realized if a bidder materializes? No answer can be given at the level of theory; we shall present some data later on. Whether or not data reveal that the prospect of auctions is good for *targets'* wealth, it is important to recognize that any dispute about the price effect of auctions is a dispute about gain sharing. A proponent of auctions starts from the single-owner standard of value, which is logically defective for reasons just presented. Investors do not want shared gains at the expense of lower aggregate gains. Any reduction in the amount of outside monitoring and number of bids is a reduction in social wealth. Investors in targets (who are also investors in bidders) want the maximum value for stocks as a whole. Transferring cash from investors' right pockets (where they keep bidders' stock) to their left pockets (where they keep targets' stock) is wasteful shuffling, and damaging if it costs two cents or decreases by a trifle the value of bystanders' stock—which it will because it reduces the amount of monitoring.

Auctions are *socially* beneficial only if they move assets more quickly to their highest-valuing users. They might do so if a higher premium paid to targets' shareholders leads to additional investment by targets in finding bidders (that is, leads targets to facilitate outside monitoring and synergistic combinations). A rule of passivity given an offer would not block *ex ante* search but could reduce its returns, although only slightly, because targets could condition disclosures to would-be acquirers on a promise not to make a hostile offer. This is a common condition when "shopping a deal," just as the owner of information about the location of valuable minerals will initiate discussions only with those who agree not to trade on the sly in this information. So although we do not denigrate the logical force of the observation that an antiauction rule could discourage search by targets, contractual responses are adequate to make the cost small indeed.

Auctions expedite the movement of assets to more efficient uses whether or not they call forth extra information from the target. Given uncertainty about the value of the target after a change in control, it may be difficult to match targets with highest-valuing bidders. The initial bidder may not be able to put the target to a use as productive as some other firm. If managers must remain passive in the face of an offer, there may be a series of trades among firms until the target's assets end up with their highest-valuing users; perhaps, along the way, different parts of the target's assets and operations would be sold to different firms. Bebchuk and Gilson, by contrast, are skeptical of first buyers' willingness to resell; they fear that managers would not reduce the size of their empires or that high transactions costs would impede subsequent transfers. Yet managers who value size rather than profit (and therefore will not resell to another firm that can make better use of the assets) also would be the high bidders at an auction. If their preference for size over profit is not great enough to make them the high bidders, it will not be great enough to justify holding onto the target at the expense of the (same) profit on resale. Any set of motives and maximands that causes a buy-and-resell model to fail also causes an auction model to fail.

If the value of many targets is highest if different bundles of their assets are transferred to different firms, a drawn-out auction would not avoid the need for subsequent retransfers. Firms routinely sell parts of their operations to other firms, and these transfers increase the value of investments in the selling and buying of firms alike. There is little evidence to sustain a belief that managers systematically reject the opportunity to profit by selling plants and divisions. If bidders resell, *en bloc* or in blocs, the allocative benefits of auctions are slight. If auctions increase bidders' rewards to gathering information (as Gilson believes) or cut the costs of matching assets efficiently to managers, then bidders themselves will favor auctions. Some takeover specialists plainly do so; they buy blocs and put firms "in play." Auctions orchestrated by targets (or compelled by law) turn out to be unnecessary. Many bidders, though, seek to capitalize on private information. Their decision to do this implies that auctions would have net costs. Costs (in both discouraging search by bidders and enabling managers to disguise out-and-out defense as auctioneering) could be substantial.

Testing the Theories about Takeovers

Capital markets provide a wealth of information with which to test the competing assertions about tender offers. Changes in stock prices help us infer the consequences of legal rules and corporate governance structures.

THE CAPITAL ASSET PRICING MODEL

The chain of inference starts from the proposition that stock prices measure something real: investors' expectations about future distributions of cash (including those on liquidation, merger, or take-over), discounted to present value. A change in the price of stock therefore reflects a change in the value of the firm, not perfectly, but reasonably accurately.[18] Prices track value without necessarily duplicating it. So many things, poorly understood or conjectural, influence the future profits of any given firm that prices are probabilities (as weather forecasts are) rather than certainties. It is enough for our purposes to say that although market prices do not match true value, nothing comes closer. However short of information professional investors may be, however much they fall under the sway of trends and bubbles, everyone *else's* information and incentives are worse.

If the price of a stock at any given time is not "right" in relation to the price the stock will have once people wise up (or the firm liquidates and hands out its real value), then arbitrageurs and other professionals can make a lot of money by buying "undervalued" stocks, selling "overvalued" ones, spreading the news, and covering once the price arrives at the appropriate level. The more astute these investors, and the more quickly they can move capital into and out of particular holdings, the faster this occurs. The process eventually makes it difficult even for professional traders to make money, unless they are the first to obtain and act on information. A great deal of data, including evidence that most professional traders are unable to beat the market, supports the proposition that prices quickly and accurately reflect the public information about the firms—at least that prices are always under pressure and in transition toward accurate valuation.

18. See Richard A. Brealey, *An Introduction to Risk and Return from Common Stocks* 67–96 (2d ed. 1983); E. Elton and Martin J. Gruber, *Modern Portfolio Theory and Investment Analysis* ch. 15 (1984) (collecting 167 studies supporting this proposition); Stephen F. LeRoy, "Efficient Capital Markets and Martingales," 27 *J. Econ. Lit.* 1583 (1989) (survey of the literature, with an emphasis on the limitations of prices as predictors of value).

One simple way to use prices is to assume that every change in price reflects some firm-specific news: increases in sales or profits, a new product or plant, a merger, a new CEO, a new governance structure. Unfortunately, however, events in the economy as a whole (changes in interest rates, international trade agreements, and the like) or in the industry (a rival's new product) also have powerful effects on the price of any given firm's stock. It becomes necessary to "take out the market," breaking the change in the price of stock into two components. If we know the co-variance between the price of the firm's stock and the market (or an industry group), the transformation is possible.

The technology for isolating firm-specific changes from market (or industry) effects is well developed.[19] It is possible to measure the historic relation between changes in the price of a firm's stock and changes in some larger basket of stocks (whether the market as a whole, an industry group, or some weighted mix). This relation takes the form

$$r_i = \alpha_i + \beta R_m + \gamma R_x + \varepsilon$$

where r_i is the change in the price of a firm's stock, α_i is a firm-specific constant, βR_m is the market-firm relation (β) times the market's movement in the interval (R_m), γR_x is the industry-firm relation (γ) times the industry group's movement in the interval (R_x), and ε, the "residual," is the unexplained portion of the change in price. This portion we attribute to firm-specific information.

Knowing how the market or other reference group behaved during a particular interval, we may determine the expected change in price of the firm's stock if nothing peculiar to the firm took place. If the firm's stock does not conform to the prediction, we chalk up the difference to some firm-specific news. The shorter the interval

19. See John J. Binder, "Measuring the Effects of Regulation with Stock Price Data," 16 *Rand J. Econ.* 167 (1985); Stephen J. Brown and Jerold B. Warner, "Measuring Security Price Performance," 8 *J. Fin. Econ.* 205 (1980); Brown and Warner, "Using Daily Stock Returns: The Case of Event Studies," 14 *J. Fin. Econ.* 1 (1985); G. William Schwert, "Using Financial Data to Measure Effects of Regulation," 24 *J. L. & Econ.* 121 (1981). See also Douglas K. Pearce and V. Vance Roley, "Stock Prices and Economic News," 58 *J. Bus.* 49 (1985) (the price effect occurs within the day the news is released—important because speedy adjustment is an ingredient in the method for isolating the effects of firm-specific changes).

over which the calculation is performed, the greater the ability to match particular pieces of news with the effects attributable to them. The more firms with similar events we can study, the more accurate the conclusion. (Random, "noisy" events that may spoil the inference for a single firm will cancel each other out if the study includes many firms.)

This method obviously is not perfect. Confounding events may be hard to disentangle. Sometimes the event window (the period during which the information comes out) is uncomfortably large. The method works much better for actively traded securities than for thinly traded stocks; it does not work at all for stock in closely held firms. The method assumes a particular relation between the market and individual stocks that is necessarily an oversimplification. It leaves out some influences, and it will perform badly if there is a sudden change in β or γ, the coefficients relating this stock to others, during the interval in question. Despite all of these problems, however, when the samples are large enough, the data may be powerfully informative.

One sometimes hears the objection that this method assumes that the market is "efficient" in the sense that the price always accurately represents the real value of the security, while the person raising the objection knows that the price is not always right. The objection misses the point, because the method does not depend on a belief that the price is always right. It rests on three more modest beliefs: (1) that prices change quickly in response to new information; (2) that the quick change is "unbiased" (that is, does not systematically overshoot or undershoot the change that ultimately will be deemed merited on the basis of more leisurely contemplation of the change); and (3) that the degree to which the price reflects the underlying economic reality does not change substantially during short periods. The method works, for example, if prices always reflect 50 percent of a given firm's true value; any change in the price will give an accurate representation of the marginal value of the change, as long as this relation stays constant.

DATA

Precisely because tender offers leave visible trails in the market, they have become the most studied economic phenomena of the century. Economists, like the rest of us, tend to concentrate on what is knowable (as opposed to what is interesting), but in the case of tender offers the knowable and the interesting overlap. Studies appear at a dizzying rate. An appendix to this chapter lists many of them—including survey articles that collect still more. Rather than stupefy you with a catalog, we summarize the principal findings without attributing them to particular scholars. Authors examining different transactions commonly report differences of a few percentage points in the results, which are trivial under the circumstances.

Returns to Targets

Average gains. When offers are announced, all shares of targets appreciate approximately 30 percent. This 30 percent comes on top of the run-up in the month preceding the bid, attributable to news about a bloc being assembled and, to some extent, inside information.

These returns measure the size of tender offer premiums: the larger the premium, the larger the return. The returns at the time of the offer are not as large as the premiums offered, though, because (a) the bidder may not seek all of the stock, and (b) traders anticipate some risk that the offer will not be successful, and hence they do not bid up the market price to the offer price.

When the offer succeeds, bidders pay a premium averaging 50 percent for the shares they acquire. Unacquired shares do not return to the preoffer price. They continue to trade at approximately a 30 percent premium relative to the preoffer price. This premium reflects investors' belief that either (a) the acquiring firm will carry out a merger at a premium, or (b) the value of the acquired firm is greater, for whatever reason, under the new control than the old.

Auctions and defense. There is a difference in the size of the premium according to the degree of rivalry among bidders. Single-bidder offers do not produce premiums as high as multiple-bidder (auction) contests. Auctions bring targets' shareholders about 4 to 6 percent more on average. There are gains of about 17 percent when the auction succeeds in selling the firm, but losses when the auction ends with all bids withdrawn.

Note that this does not measure the effect of the prospect of auctions. Prospective bidders' decisions depend on their profits. Auctioneering may discourage bids (by making them less profitable), reduce the initial price offered (to maintain the profitability of bidding), or both.

Targets that litigate in response to a hostile tender offer but that are eventually acquired account for nearly all of the multiple-bidder contests. Litigation apparently adds time and bargaining chips to the Williams Act delay, thus producing auctions. But the auction strategy also produces disparate results. When the auction ends in an acquisition, these litigating targets gain relative to the initial bid. Targets that defeat all offers (about a fourth of the litigating targets) lose the entire premium.

Unsuccessful bids. When a tender offer is unsuccessful, the initially large returns that accompany the announcements dissipate. Traders anticipate that the initial defeat may be just a way station in an extended auction. Targets that receive other offers within two years retain some, but not all, of the initial gains. The retention rate is about two-thirds. Targets that do not receive such offers (those that demonstrate willingness and ability to remain independent) lose the entire gains. Investors in both categories of target (the later-acquired and the never-acquired) do worse than investors in targets acquired on the initial bid (single or auction).

Returns to Bidders

Average gains. Investors in targets always gain from offers; investors in bidders gain only part of the time. During the 1960s bidders' gains averaged 5 percent; during the 1970s, 2.2 percent; during the 1980s bidders' gains have hovered around zero, with some studies showing 0.5 to 1.0 percent negative returns and others showing small positive returns. Returns in the 1980s are not statistically significantly from zero.

The difference in the size of the gains may surprise, because both bidders and targets are essential ingredients of the gains. There are several explanations. One is competition. If many different firms are able to do whatever produces the gains in an acquisition, they compete (in searching for targets, learning what to do with them, and offering higher bids) until the returns are driven down to zero. The lion's share of the gains ends up with investors in targets. Another is that bidders are larger than targets. Many bidders are diversified firms, and a given acquisition is not a large part of the bidder's operation. We would expect a smaller percentage change than when the bid affects the whole business (as it does for the targets). One must use a statistical magnifying glass, converting bidders and acquirers into "same-size" firms. Using this method shows that at least through the 1970s bidders received one-third of the total gains from takeovers.

Acquisition programs. Diversified firms gain when they announce, or the market infers, that they plan to undertake a program of acquisitions. These gains appear to be about 10 percent of the value of the acquiring firms, realized without regard to the outcome of a particular bid. These gains imply that the market views acquisitions as beneficial for bidders, leading to value capitalized in stock price before a particular bid. This may be why gains are small (or even negative) when a particular bid is announced: the proposed acquisition was no better (or worse) than what had been expected.

Combined Returns

Investments as a whole (that is, the securities of bidder and target taken together) experience gains of 7 to 8 percent from acquisitions. Net gains persist even when the bidder's stock declines. For example, when DuPont took over Conoco, DuPont's stock fell by an amount worth $800 million. Conoco's investors received a premium amounting to $3.2 billion, for a total gain of $2.4 billion. Obviously, when the bidder's stock rises, there are net gains to investors because both sides win.

Effects of Regulation and Defense

Poison pills and other devices. Firms that adopt antitakeover devices (more neutrally, devices that give incumbent managers the authority to accept or reject bids) experience immediate reductions in the price of their stock. Fair-price rules depress price by approximately 0.73 percent, an amount not statistically significant. Supermajority approval amendments lead to a significant 3 percent drop. (Studies also show that firms adopt fair-price and supermajority rules when managers' holdings are high and institutions' holdings low.) In general, antitakeover amendments of all kinds where the managers control large blocs are associated with 3 percent losses.

Poison pill securities, the principal device that may be used without investors' assent, produce a loss averaging 0.34 percent. If we confine attention to firms about which there has been takeover speculation, the loss is 1.51 percent; if the speculation has been recent (or a contest is in progress), the loss is 2.3 percent. If we confine attention to Delaware firms (on the theory that Delaware courts have announced willingness to enforce pills, while other states' law is less certain), the loss is about 2.6 percent, for a total reduction in equity value of about $2 billion for the 133 Delaware firms that adopted pills between November 1985 (when the principal decision was rendered) through the end of 1986. Managers of firms adopting poison pills own little of its stock (3 percent on average), dramatically less than those choosing other devices. (Perhaps this explains employment of a device that does not require voting by investors.) Firms earn profits below the average for their industry the year they issue pills.

Firms that recapitalize with dual-class stock (one having inferior voting rights all the time, or if held in a bloc) lose 0.64 percent of their value. Antitakeover devices supplied or approved by state law also depress price. When the Supreme Court of Delaware held in *Unocal* (see note 1) that firms could repurchase their own stock while excluding shares held by bidders, the price of all Delaware corporations then involved in contests fell 3 percent. This does not imply, however, that targeted repurchases (greenmail) from the bidder (and to the bidder's profit) are injurious. Although prices fall at the time of the repurchase, the prospect of a premium repurchase makes prospecting and bidding more profitable, and the loss at the time of the repurchase is less than the gain at the time the bidder appears.

Some of these defensive measures require shareholder approval. When some investors try to mobilize their fellows in opposition, they defeat the proposals about 25 percent of the time. Defeat causes the price of the stock to rise 4 percent on average; an unsuccessful antidefense campaign causes the price of the stock to drop 6 percent, with a maximum of a 30 percent loss and a minimum of 3 percent down. This shows that only the most serious value-reducing proposals make organized opposition worthwhile, given the problem of rational passivity we discussed in Chapter 3. It also shows how feeble the voting mechanism is as a safeguard against value-reducing antitakeover measures.

State and federal laws. Laws delaying takeovers or giving managers the authority to veto them (or the follow-up mergers) raise the premium in the event an acquisition takes place but diminish the number of acquisitions. The net of these two effects is a reduction of about 0.5 percent in the value of all firms covered by a statute.

(Firms that already have antitakeover provisions, such as poison pills, are unaffected; firms without them experience the fall in price.) Some states' laws produce a greater loss. Firms incorporated in Ohio lost 3 percent when that statute, one of the most stringent, was enacted.

The frequency of targets' litigation rises as the time needed to obtain control rises. The frequency of auctions rises, dramatically, with the length of delay. The more extensive the regulation (the longer the waiting periods and the more hurdles), the higher the premium in the event of a bid. The mean return has doubled since the Williams Act was passed (from about 30 to more than 50 percent) and is higher in states with more stringent regulation. The more extensive the regulation, the lower the average positive return for bidders. The more extensive the regulation, the fewer bids made. The more extensive the regulation, the lower the price of prospective bidders. Firms engaged in acquisition programs had returns of -6 percent when the Williams Act was enacted and experienced further negative returns when regulations were added.

INTERPRETING THE DATA

Market Failure?

Wasted Capital

If tender offers squander capital, they injure investors. Yet stock prices rise, by 30 percent and more. Investors in targets realized $346 billion in the decade 1977–1986, and investors in purchasers realized additional gains in the billions. Because stock prices estimate future returns, these are real social gains. Moreover, to the extent tender offers serve monitoring roles or promote other corporate control transactions, investors in firms that are not acquired gain too. Tender offers are a small portion of all corporate control transactions (forty to fifty per year, as opposed to thousands of mergers) yet may motivate others.

Takeovers are concentrated among firms showing profits below the industry average, in industries themselves lagging the national average (with the industry effect the more pronounced). This suggests that outside intervention is more important when the industry as a whole is in trouble than when the firm is doing poorly relative to a benchmark closer to home (which the board could monitor).

Exploiting Investors

If bidders are scooping up bargains before markets reflect true values, this implies that when targets defeat offers the stock should soon trade for more than the bidder offered (that is, the true value should come out). It does not; all the gains disappear within two years if the firm is not acquired by some other bidder. The proposition that bidders finagle the target's investors out of "their" gains implies that bidders reap substantial unearned profits. They don't; lately they seem not to obtain any.

The hypothesis that bidders are "raiders" or "looters," exploiting the investors whose shares they do not acquire, implies that those shares fall relative to their prebid price. They do not; instead shares left outstanding after an acquisition rise, on the order of 30 percent.

If two-tier offers "coerce" investors to part with their stock in exchange for inferior bids, then the average blended premium paid in such offers should be lower. It is not. In 1981–1984 the average yield of any-or-all offers was 56.6 percent, and the blended premium of two-tier offers was 55.9 percent, a statistically insignificant difference. No two-tier offer has ever prevailed over an all-or-any offer with a higher total value. Falsifying the "coercion" hypothesis about two-tier offers leaves the conclusion that they serve to overcome free-riding problems and promote beneficial monitoring and acquisitions.

If the data ever show "coercion" they do so with respect to one-price offers for less than all of the shares, because (a) these offers are worth less than either all-or-any or two-tier offers (partial offers carry an average premium of about 23 percent), and (b) when partial offers succeed, the unacquired shares trade for less than the price paid for those taken. Every partial offer is therefore an implicit two-tier offer—and without the promise to exchange the non-tendered shares for cash or other liquid securities.

Real coercion is possible when the target makes an exclusionary self-tender offer, as Unocal did. Unocal's shares were trading for $46 when T. Boone Pickens offered $54 in cash for 50.4 percent of the stock and notes worth $54 for the remainder. Unocal made a self-tender offer of $72 in notes for the stock Pickens did not possess and barred Pickens from tendering. Unocal's was a two-tier bid in response to Pickens's single-price offer: $72 for the front end and the market price for the remaining shares—a market price that would be depressed by the lavish commitment to the tendering investors. That price turned out to be $34. So the front-end price was more than double the back-end price, which was well below the prior market price of $46. We showed in Chapter 5 that a requirement that no investor do worse than the prior market price is essential to ensure that corporate control transactions be value-increasing. As it turns out, Unocal's offer was value-reducing. The total market value of its notes and stock was $8.3 billion; Pickens's offer was worth a total of $9.4 billion.[20] Unocal's victory is the *only* recorded instance of a two-tier offer beating a single-price offer with a higher total value. It prevailed for three reasons: as the issuer, it could arrange a security interest in its assets and demote the priority of its rival's notes; under state law, it could refuse to repurchase the bidder's stock, diluting its interest; under the Williams Act and the SEC's rules, it could close its offer ahead of the bidder's. None of these happens when the bidder makes the two-tier offer. And Unocal's victory is a freak even for an issuer tender offer, because the SEC promptly amended its rules to prohibit the exclusion feature that was essential to the strategy.[21] Two-tier offers cannot today beat single-price offers with higher total value.

Tender offers do not transfer wealth from bondholders to shareholders. The target's bonds and debentures retain their value when bids succeed.[22]

20. Michael C. Jensen, "When Unocal Won over Pickens, Shareholders and Society Lost," *Financier* 50 (Nov. 1985); Bradley and Rosenzweig, supra note 12, 99 *Harv. L. Rev.* at 1422–29.

21. 15 C.F.R. §13e-4(f)(8)(i).

22. Laurentius Marais, Katherine Schipper, and Abbie Smith, "Wealth Effects of Going Private for Senior Securities," 23 *J. Fin. Econ.* 155 (1989); Debra K. Denis and John J. McConnell, "Corporate Mergers and Security Returns," 16 *J. Fin. Econ.* 143 (1986); Paul R. Asquith and E. Han Kim, "The Impact of Merger Bids on the Participating Firms' Security Holders," 37 *J. Finance* 1209 (1982). But see Asquith and Thierry A. Wizman, "Event Risk, Wealth Redistribution, and the Return to Existing Bondholders in Corporate Buyouts," 26 *J. Fin. Econ.* (1991), finding that creditors whose instruments lack conversion privileges lose about 3 percent in LBOs. Asquith and Wizman also find that in 17 of their 65 firms the creditors experience gains, and that the losses to bondholders in the remaining firms represent only 7 percent of the total gain received by other investors. So although locked-in

Exploiting Labor (and Other Constituencies)

Stock market data do not reveal whether tender offers produce the substantial gains for shareholders by exploiting managers and other workers. Studies of the labor market suggest, however, that acquired firms do not reduce wages or close plants at a rate any different from that of similar, but independent, firms.[23]

New owners undoubtedly make many changes in acquired firms, and some of these affect labor. If, for example, an air carrier is paying a wage exceeding the market price to its pilots, and managers do not do anything about it, an acquisition may lead to a change. This seems to have happened in the airline business, where the premiums paid in acquisitions are less than the value of reduced payments to labor. Yet there is no visible difference between the results of voluntary acquisitions in mergers and those accomplished by hostile tender offer. Changing wages are an outcome of deregulation, and airlines have cut labor costs whether or not facing a threat. (American, with its two-tier wage scale, is a good example.) Getting to the competitive wage faster means benefits for consumers (lower travel prices) and smaller costs of adjustment (TWA did not face the bankruptcy costs Eastern has incurred to make this transition). To the extent that reducing wages to the competitive level produces a transfer to investors, the payments do not directly reflect efficiency (the transfer exceeds the allocative efficiency gain); but they do not come from a reduction in efficiency either.

Exploiting Tomorrow (Myopic Markets)

If markets are myopic, valuing current profits rather than the net present value of long-term projects, this should leave a trail in the data. For example, firms that announce the construction of new

---

creditors may suffer losses as their instruments become more risky, one cannot understand the premiums in tender offers as transfers from creditors. See Easterbrook, supra note 9, at §§2.2.3, 3.2.3.

23. Charles Brown and James L. Medoff, "The Impact of Firm Acquisitions on Labor," in *Corporate Takeovers: Causes and Consequences* 9 (A. Auerbach ed. 1988); see also Roberta Romano, "The Future of Hostile Takeovers: Legislation and Public Opinion," 57 *U. Cin. L. Rev.* 457 (1988); C. Steven Bradford, "Protecting Shareholders from Themselves? A Policy and Constitutional Review of a State Takeover Statute," 67 *Neb. L. Rev.* 459, 529–534 (1988).

plants will depress the price of their stock, because construction means extended periods of outlays with no income (profits, if any, come much later). Similarly, stock prices will fall when firms increase their research and development budgets. A third prediction of the myopia hypothesis is that acquired firms will be above the industry average in R & D, because the value of these projects will not be reflected in stock prices (enabling bidders to acquire these firms on the cheap).

None of these predictions turns out to be true.[24] Firms that announce new plants rise in value. More R&D increases the price of a firm's stock even though it depresses current earnings. Acquired firms are below, rather than above, industry average in R&D. Firms *reduce* their R&D expenditures after adopting shark repellent provisions.[25] So stock markets do not value the "short run" unduly, and the threat of tender offers does not induce firms to cut back on R&D. Quite the contrary, managers desiring to raise the price of their stock, so as to ward off offers, should authorize more R&D, build more plants, and introduce new products.

Exploiting Consumers (Monopoly and Taxes)

Reduction in taxes surely accounts for some of the premium from offers, but no study suggests more than one-third. Moreover, these gains largely can be accomplished by LBOs, MBOs, and related devices without the need for a hostile bid, suggesting that managers who neglect opportunities to reduce taxes face pressure in the cap-

24. In addition to the survey articles cited in the appendix to this chapter, see George F. Baker and Karen H. Wruck, "Organizational Changes and Value Creation in Leveraged Buyouts: The Case of O.M. Scott & Sons Company," 25 *J. Fin. Econ.* 163 (1989); John J. McConnell and Chris J. Muscarella, "Capital Expenditure Decisions and Market Value of the Firm," 14 *J. Fin. Econ.* 523 (1985); Office of the Chief Economist, Securities and Exchange Commission, *Institutional Ownership, Tender Offers, and Long Term Investment* (1985); Abbie Smith, "Corporate Ownership Structure and Performance: The Case of Management Buyouts," 26 *J. Fin. Econ.* (1991). See also Larry H. P. Lang, René M. Stulz, and Ralph A. Walkling, "Managerial Performance, Tobin's *q*, and the Gains from Successful Tender Offers," 24 *J. Fin. Econ.* 137 (1989) (showing that gains from combinations are greatest when targets have low *q* ratios—that is, have been doing poorly relative to asset values).

25. Lisa K. Meulbroek, Mark L. Mitchell, J. Harold Muhlerin, Jeffrey N. Netter, and Annette B. Poulson, "Shark Repellants and Managerial Myopia," 98 *J. Pol. Econ.* 1108 (1990).

ital market (as they ought). Tender offers actually are tax-disadvan-taged relative to mergers. Cash paid in an offer is a realized gain, on which investors must pay taxes. Mergers may be arranged as tax-free exchanges, so that investors carry over the basis of their stock to the new firm. Because cash offers carry this tax penalty, tax considerations cannot account for tender offers no matter how important they are in explaining gains from mergers and LBOs.

Monopoly too is not behind *hostile* bids, even if it is behind mergers. Few cash tender offers occur in the same industry, and corporate control transactions as a whole to not promote concen-tration. Capital markets arrange divestitures as well as mergers. In 1986 divestitures worth $60 billion occurred, an amount greater than that of tender offer activity. Stock prices also suggest that the mergers allowed by the antitrust laws do not produce monopoly. If on the one hand mergers allow monopoly profits, then the stock prices of firms in the same industry should rise—when market price goes up, all firms can collect it. If on the other hand acquisitions promote efficient production, the stock prices of rivals will fall (the more efficient firm is a tougher competitor). On average, rivals' stock prices fall when firms merge.[26]

Exploiting Bidders' Investors (Hubris)

If premiums reflect only bidders' hubris or mismanagement, then the joint value of the bidder and target should remain the same (the bidders' investors lose what the targets' investors receive) or even fall (the targets' assets will be coming into the grasp of inferior managers). In fact, however, the securities of bidder and target taken together experience a gain of some 8 percent. Bernard Black hypothesizes (see note 14) that these net gains could reflect dimin-ished pessimism—investors in the bidders expected the managers to be even more stupid than they were and are pleasantly surprised that so little has been wasted—but this won't wash. Why should the market overestimate agency costs? Why should a bid lead to the correction in the estimate? And why, if the bid is too high, should

26. B. Espen Eckbo, "Mergers and the Market Concentration Doctrine: Evi-dence from the Capital Market," 58 *J. Business* 325 (1985); Robert Stillman, "Ex-amining Antitrust Policy towards Horizontal Mergers," 11 *J. Fin. Econ.* 225 (1983); Peggy Wier, "The Costs of Antimerger Lawsuits: Evidence from the Stock Market," 11 *J. Fin. Econ.* 207 (1983).

this be good news? After all, the bidder could have distributed cash to its own investors with better effect (if indeed it has paid too much). We conclude that the net appreciation in the stock of bidder and target taken together is unambiguous evidence of social gains.

None of this is to deny that some bidders overpay. There is a pattern: overpaying firms are diversifying into unrelated industries. Such acquisitions paid off during the 1970s but not during the 1980s; divestitures or functional realignments bring rewards in today's business environment. Firms that engage in excessive diversification may be acquired themselves, followed by divestiture—evidence that the capital market penalizes and corrects imperfections in itself.

The Single-Owner Standard and Auctions

The single-owner measure of value and its corollary, the preference for auctions, imply that devices that facilitate higher prices benefit both investors in targets and society as a whole. One kind of evidence favors this view: legal rules and private devices that facilitate auctioneering lead to higher premiums when offers occur. Moreover, once a bid appears, devices (such as litigation) that string out the bidding produce further increases on average.

Because these same devices also depress bidders' expected (and actual) profits, and therefore lead to fewer acquisitions, the question arises whether the frequency effect overcomes the wealth effect. It does. State and federal laws that draw out the duration of contests lead to lower prices for prospective targets. Shark repellent devices, whether approved by the shareholders (as with fair-price amendments and staggered boards) or created unilaterally by management (as with poison pill securities) uniformly depress prices. There do not turn out to be some good devices and some bad ones. *Every* device giving managers the power to delay or prevent an acquisition makes shareholders worse off. And although each of these effects looks small (they range from a fraction of a percent to 3 percent), these add up. A percent here, a percent there—that's a lot of money when the base is many trillions of dollars!

If investors value auctioneering in the event of an offer, devices to facilitate it should be included in the articles of incorporation or securities as firms go public. If valued, these devices would enable the entrepreneurs to get extra money for their venture. Yet they are not included. Instead firms go public in easy-to-acquire form: no poison pill securities, no supermajority rules or staggered boards. Defensive measures are added later, a sequence that reveals much.

Proponents of the single-owner standard and auctions are entitled to reply that these data do not really refute their position. They advocate rules to facilitate auctions (such as long bidding periods coupled with mandatory disclosures by bidders) coupled with prohibitions on defensive measures by managers. Auctions should be orchestrated, in their view, solely on the bidders' side, by the forces of competition, rather than by managers who might seek to ward off any change of control under the cover of selling the firm in a more leisurely way. This is a shortfall in the data; all the devices in use today facilitate defense at the same time that they elicit more competition among bidders.

Although we therefore cannot reject the single-owner and auctions approach with the same confidence we reject others, the absence of *any* existing device that increases targets' market value—and proof that *all* existing devices reduce bidders' value—leads us to doubt that auctions could be socially beneficial. It is easy to write the articles of incorporation (or poison pill securities) to facilitate auctions while tying managers' hands. For example, instead of writing a poison pill that may be redeemed if and only if the managers choose to do so, the firm could have a pill that cancels itself if an all-and-any offer is open for ninety days. According to the single-owner and auctions approach, such a security would be valuable. Yet *no* firm has adopted it—not on going public, not later. Although agency costs are high, many managerial teams are scrupulously dedicated to investors' interests. Why have these managers not employed such devices? By increasing the value of the firm, they would do themselves a favor (most managers' compensation is linked to the stock market, and they own stock too). Nonexistence of securities said to be beneficial to investors is telling.

Delaware's Intermediate Standard

Delaware, the principal corporate jurisdiction, follows neither our passivity proposal nor the single-owner and auctions approach nor the view that tender offers should be discouraged as inefficient. Managers of Delaware corporations may adopt devices such as poison pills that give them substantial control over whether premium bids can succeed—that decrease the chance of receiving a bid and may prevent success if it is made. If a bidder appears, however, managers may not stubbornly say no; they may foil the offer only if they show that they had good reasons to do so, and they bear the burden of establishing these reasons. (See the cases listed in note 1.) If the firm is put up for sale, managers must do their utmost to realize the maximum price for equity investors—but managers have discretion not to sell.

Muddling through in this fashion has the virtue of conserving judges' information costs. It also creates an odd set of incentives for managers. If they adopt shark repellent provisions and so scare away bidders, they face no risk of liability. If, however, they sell the firm, they may be mulcted in damages for getting "only" 50 percent over market rather than the higher price the court supposes they might have had.[27] If they commit themselves firmly (beyond the possibility of argument to a corporate plan), they may block bids that entail a change of plans; if they are flexible and seek out handsome opportunities for investors, they may be deemed to have put the firm on the block and will be compelled to raffle it off.[28] Even dedicated managers, faced with such choices, may be expected to adopt devices that save their skins at some expense to investors.

Delaware's intermediate approach rests on two articulated premises: (a) there is a difference between a firm's short-run value, reflected in market prices, and "intrinsic value"; because managers must maximize intrinsic value, the "inadequacy of the price offered"[29] justifies (nay, compels) resistance; and (b) directors have a duty to repel "threats" to the investors and the enterprise. Neither reason holds water.

INTRINSIC VALUE

That there is a difference between market and "intrinsic value" is an old theme in Delaware cases. The "Delaware bloc" method of appraisal (see Chapter 6) gave market prices only partial weight in determining the true value of a firm's stock. For reasons we have canvassed under the "scooping the market" and "market myopia"

27. Smith v. Van Gorkom, 488 A.2d 858 (1985).
28. Paramount Communications, Inc. v. Time Inc., 571 A.2d 1140 (Del. 1990).
29. Unocal Corp. v. Mesa Petroleum Co., 493 A.2d 946, 955 (Del. 1985).

headings, neither logic nor data supports the belief that there is a difference between the current price and intrinsic value. If a firm has a particular value, the market will reflect it; anything bidders can see, professional investors can see too. All of the predictions of the intrinsic value approach—that the price of firms defeating offers exceeds the bid, that announcements reducing short-run profits but adding long-run value depress stock prices, and so on— turn out to be false. Not a scrap of data supports the position taken in the Delaware cases. It is depressing to see "earth is flat" reasoning from our premier corporate court.

Intrinsic value is a prediction, a hope. *If* profits grow at such-and-such a rate, and *if* the rate of interest is so-and-so, *then* the stock will be worth a particular price. Capitalization analyses of this kind are notoriously sensitive to their assumptions; any competent investment banker can make the numbers vary by an order of magnitude, as the Supreme Court of Delaware has recognized.[30] Managers naturally are optimistic about the success of their business plans and therefore believe that the "true value" of the stock exceeds the market price. Optimistic *investors,* however, quickly lose their cash to realists. Prices reflect the consensus projections of hard-nosed players with their own dollars on the line.

Talk is cheap; anyone can project intrinsic value; when projections are backed by money the most accurate prevail. The gap is not between current and intrinsic value but between a market measure of value, embedded in price, and speculation. Takeovers tend to be concentrated on firms whose managers' projections are *least* realistic—which is why the bid must be hostile, why the bidder believes it can make money by doing things differently. In the best of faith the targets' managers will explain why they think their firms' value exceeds market price, but no one should listen unless managers reveal some new facts.

THREATS

To investors. If tender offers pose a "threat" to targets' investors, managers must intervene to protect them. Although the Supreme Court of Delaware often mentions "threats" from bids, the only two

---

30. Mills Acquisition Co. v. Macmillan, Inc., 559 A.2d 1261 (Del. 1989). See also Lucian Arye Bebchuk and Marcel Kahan, "Fairness Opinions: How Fair Are They and What Can Be Done about It?" 1989 *Duke L. J.* 27; Metlyn Realty Corp. v. Esmark, Inc., 763 F.2d 826, 834–837 (7th Cir. 1985).

it has identified are those posed by "coercive" two-tier offers and potential looters. Having dealt with looting in Chapter 5 and earlier in this chapter, we note here that two-tier bids cannot threaten shareholders' wealth, and there is no evidence that bidders make profits by looting targets. Defending against nonexistent threats makes everyone worse off.

To corporate plans. Judges sometimes say that managers may rebuff threats to corporate plans. Well and good, if corporate plans promise value for the investors exceeding the price offered in the bid. But elements of value created by existing plans are reflected in the price of the stock; premium bids therefore show the prospect that replacing the managers' preferred plans with new ones would create new value. (The response that the market price does not reflect the "true value" of the plans is the "intrinsic value" or "market myopia" refrain again.)

If the bidder will replace a "good" plan with a "bad" one, what of it? Existing investors can sell out; the loss will fall on the bidder (provided every existing investor is guaranteed the market price). Offerers do not plan to make money by destroying value, falling on their swords, but if this happens it is comforting to know that they pay for their own mistakes.

To other constituencies. Although some commentators maintain that firms should protect the interests of "other constituencies" at the expense of equity investors, Delaware does not share this view. Managers must display "the most scrupulous adherence to ordinary standards of fairness in the interest of promoting the highest values reasonably attainable for the stockholders' benefit."[31] Undoubtedly firms may consider the interests of workers, suppliers, communities, and others with stakes in the venture. The question has to do only with the role of contract versus fiduciary duties. For reasons we developed in Chapters 1, 3, and 5, only the residual claim holder has the right to faithful management. Other participants look to contract.

SOCIAL WEALTH IN A WORLD OF THREATS

"Put your money where your mouth is" should be the key adage of corporate control transactions, as of commerce in general. Prices

---

31. Mills Acquisition Co. v. Macmillan, Inc., 559 A.2d 1261, 1264 (Del. 1989). See also ibid. at 1285, 1288.

reflect hard-won information in which people trust enough to stake their wealth. Bids at more than the market price reflect increases in private wealth for targets and bidders alike, and therefore for society. Premium bids do not necessarily reflect the optimum use of the assets, but they reflect a superior use. Only risk-averse investors might object to a process that moves assets continually toward higher valued uses. Risk aversion is not a serious obstacle, for reasons we covered in Chapter 1.

Current law on takeovers reflects infatuation with gain sharing at the expense of wealth, and with target shareholders' wealth at the expense of bidder shareholders' wealth. It reflects a devotion to intrinsic value that has as much empirical support as the proposition that hurricanes are caused by witches. Even if there were an intrinsic value, courts could not identify it—could not, in other words, separate managers who are *right* that the price is too low from managers who just *believe* that the price is too low. Judicial inability to separate one from the other, to identify the "best" strategy to maximize investors' wealth, is a fundamental premise of the business judgment rule.

Judicial attitudes toward tender offers reflect, finally, a dualism in the approach to regulation. If a tactic by bidder ever can be harmful (for example, two-tier offers), then it is considered an abuse to be stamped out; if a tactic by target ever could be beneficial (for example, poison pills used to spark bidding), then it is fine and review is deferential. Such an approach might be justifiable if only the welfare of targets' investors mattered. But why should it? Courts shape the corporate contract, and legal rules influence the wealth of *investors* who may hold stock in bidders, targets, bystanders, or (most likely) all three groups. Robbing Peter to pay Paul is poor use of corporate law, especially when Peter is just Paul's nom de plume.

Appendix

Finance economists have devoted more effort in recent years to understanding tender offers than to any other subject. The papers, in addition to those appearing in the footnotes, underlying the empirical propositions in the text of this chapter include:

Bradley, Michael, Anand Desai, and E. Han Kim, "Synergistic Gains from Corporate Acquisitions and Their Division between the Stockholders of Target and Acquiring Firms," 21 *J. Fin. Econ.* 3 (1988).

Choi, Dosoung, Sreenivas Kamma, and Joseph Weintrop, "The Delaware Courts, Poison Pills, and Shareholder Wealth," 5 *J. L. Econ. & Org.* 375 (1989).

Comment, Robert, and Gregg A. Jarrell, "Two-Tier and Negotiated Tender Offers: The Imprisonment of the Free-riding Shareholder," 19 *J. Fin. Econ.* 283 (1987).

Hackl, Jo Watson, and Rosa Anna Testani, "Second Generation State Takeover Statutes and Shareholder Wealth: An Empirical Study," 97 *Yale L. J.* 1193 (1988).

Jarrell, Gregg A., and Annette B. Poulson, "Shark Repellents and Stock Prices: The Effects of Antitakeover Amendments Since 1980," 19 *J. Fin. Econ.* 127 (1987).

Jarrell, Gregg A., James A. Brickley, and Jeffrey M. Netter, "The Market for Corporate Control: The Empirical Evidence Since 1980," 2 *J. Econ. Perspectives* 49 (Winter 1988) (survey of other studies).

Jensen, Michael C. "Takeovers: Their Causes and Consequences," 2 *J. Econ. Perspectives* 21 (Winter 1988).

Jensen, Michael C., and Richard S. Ruback, "The Market for Corporate Control: The Scientific Evidence," 11 *J. Fin. Econ.* 5 (1983) (summarizing the findings of other papers in a symposium volume).

Jensen, Michael C., and Jerold B. Warner, "The Distribution of Power among Corporate Managers, Shareholders, and Directors," 20 *J. Fin. Econ.* 3 (1988) (summarizing the findings of other papers in a symposium volume).

Karpoff, Jonathan M., and Paul H. Malatesta, "The Wealth Effects of Second Generation State Takeover Legislation," 25 *J. Fin. Econ.* 291 (1989).

Mikkelson, Wayne H., and Richard S. Ruback, "An Empirical Analysis of the Interfirm Equity Investment Process," 14 *J. Fin. Econ.* 523 (1985).

Mitchell, Mark L., and Kenneth Lehn, "Do Bad Bidders Become Good Targets?" 98 *J. Pol. Econ.* 372 (1990).

Office of the Chief Economist, Securities and Exchange Commission, *The Economics of Any-or-All, Partial, and Two-Tier Tender Offers* (1985).

————*The Effects of Poison Pills on the Wealth of Target Shareholders* (1986).

————*Shareholder Wealth Effects of Ohio Legislation Affecting Takeovers* (1987).

Pound, John. "The Effects of Antitakeover Amendments on Takeover Activity: Some Direct Evidence," 30 *J. L. & Econ.* 353 (1987).

————"Shareholder Activism and Share Values: The Causes and Consequences of Countersolicitations against Management Antitakeover Proposals," 32 *J. L. & Econ.* 357 (1989).

Ryngaert, Michael. "The Effect of Poison Pill Securities on Shareholder Wealth," 20 *J. Fin. Econ.* 377 (1988).

Ryngaert, Michael, and Jeffrey M. Netter, "Shareholder Wealth Effects and the Ohio Anti-Takeover Law," 4 *J. L. Econ. & Org.* 373 (1988).

Schumann, Laurence. "State Regulation of Takeovers and Shareholder Wealth: The Case of New York's 1985 Takeover Statutes," 19 *Rand J. Econ.* 557 (1988).

All of the preceding studies use stock market data. A few scholars using accounting data have concluded that acquisitions do not produce observable productivity gains: Richard E. Caves, "Effects of Mergers and Acquisitions on the Economy: An Industrial Organization Perspective," in *The Merger Boom* 149 (Lynne E. Browne and Eric S. Rosengren eds. 1987); F. M. Scherer, "Corporate Takeovers: The Efficiency Arguments," 2 *J. Econ. Perspectives* 69 (Winter 1988). Accounting data do not always lead to this conclusion, though. Symposium, The Structure and Governance of Enterprise, 26 *J. Fin. Econ.* (1991), contains a number of papers, using methods other than market-model ones, concluding that control transactions increase efficiency. See also Frank R. Lichtenberg and Donald Siegel, "Productivity and Changes in Ownership of Manufacturing Plants," *Brookings Papers on Economic Activity* 643–673 (1987); Lichtenberg and Siegel, "The Effects of Ownership Changes on the Employment and Wages of Central-Office and Other Personnel," 33 *J. L. & Econ.* 383 (1990); John D. Paulus and Robert S. Gay, *Is America Helping Herself? Corporate Restructuring and Global Competitiveness* (Morgan Stanley & Co. 1987). See also John Pound, "The Information Effects of Takeover Bids and Resistance," 22 *J. Fin. Econ.* 207 (1988), finding that the profits of firms defeating offers fall by about 10 percent.

8

The Incorporation Debate and State
Antitakeover Statutes

At this point two of our themes run headlong into each other. We
have said repeatedly that corporate law works like a standard-form
contract in promoting the wealth of investors. Chapter 7 concludes
that the rules concerning takeovers have the opposite effect. Which
is it to be? Is corporate law efficient or not? Things look even
darker for the efficiency thesis because during the last twenty years
some forty states have enacted one or another form of antitakeover
legislation.

If these state laws injure investors, how about others? What
prevents managers from choosing to incorporate in states that maximize managers' discretion at investors' expense? In short, does
not the takeover experience establish that in state law there is a
"race for the bottom"? This chapter looks at the influences behind
state law and the choice of the place of incorporation. Then we
examine antitakeover statutes as a special (but important) case.

Is There a "Race for the Bottom"?

Managers may incorporate in any state, no matter where the firm's
assets, employees, and investors are located. States thus must
compete with each other to attract incorporations. Jurisdictions
successful in this competition obtain revenue from franchise fees
and taxes and create demand for the services of the local bar.

Delaware is by far the most successful in attracting firms. Notwithstanding its small size, Delaware is the state of incorporation
of roughly half of the Fortune 500 companies. Approximately 80
percent of firms that change their state of incorporation move to

Delaware.[1] Its success comes from its enabling statute, its large body of precedents and sophisticated corporate bar, and its credible commitment to be receptive to corporate needs because of the large percentage of its state revenues derived from franchise fees and taxes.

The Role of Markets

This much is uncontroversial. What is disputed is the effect this triumph of Delaware yields. The traditional view espoused by William Cary is that the competition for franchise taxes and other revenues resulting from incorporation leads to a "race for the bottom."[2] Since managers choose the state of incorporation, Cary thought that states have incentives to choose legal rules that allow managers to exploit investors. Delaware, the state that in Cary's view had the loosest enabling statute, which allowed managers to siphon the most from investors, was therefore the most successful in raising revenues from incorporations. Other states had to follow the leader.

Ralph Winter characterized the "race for the bottom thesis" as bilge.[3] How could states' competition to please managers be the only well-functioning market? Entrepreneurs must compete for capital. One dimension of this competition is the rules governing the firm, provided by the state of incorporation. To attract investment, therefore, entrepreneurs choosing a state of incorporation will search for legal rules that maximize investor's welfare. Managers cannot exploit investors they cannot attract. Thus states, to compete for the revenue produced by incorporations, must adopt rules that are in the interest of investors. To put the point differently, investors who possess ample investment substitutes—from land to T-bills to Japanese firms—have no incentive to place money

1. Data on the success of Delaware appear in Peter Dodd and Richard Leftwich, "The Market for Corporate Charters: 'Unhealthy Competition' versus Federal Regulation," 53 *J. Bus.* 59 (1980); Roberta Romano, "Law as a Product: Some Pieces of the Incorporation Puzzle," 1 *J. L. Econ. & Org.* 225, 273 (1985); Romano, "The State Competition Debate in Corporate Law," 8 *Cardozo L. Rev.* 709 (1987).

2. William L. Cary, "Federalism and Corporate Law: Reflections upon Delaware," 83 *Yale L. J.* 663 (1974).

3. Ralph K. Winter, Jr., "State Law, Shareholder Protection, and the Theory of the Corporation," 6 *J. Legal Studies* 251 (1977).

in firms incorporated in states with rules that operate to their detriment. So we, too, argue at the outset of Chapter 1.

The success of Delaware, Winter claimed, results from its having provided investors with a package of legal rules that operates to the benefit of managers and investors alike. For example, Winter demonstrated that the discretion given to corporate managers by Delaware's enabling statute and in court decisions criticized by Cary was simply a recognition of the specialization of functions in public corporations, a theme we have stressed. Winter's proposition that shareholders benefit from a legal regime that intrudes only minimally, and then largely to enforce contracts and stop theft, turned Cary's thesis on its head. Winter roused the corporate professoriat from comfortable lethargy, and things have never been the same.

As a matter of theory, the "race for the bottom" cannot exist. Empirical studies confirmed the force of competition. Share prices of firms reincorporating in Delaware increase both before the reincorporation and in response to the decision itself.[4] These

4. See Dodd and Leftwich, supra note 1; Romano, supra note 1, 1 *J. L. Econ. & Org.* at 273 (1985). See also Barry Baysinger and Henry N. Butler, "Race for the Bottom v. Climb to the Top: The ALI Project and Uniformity in Corporate Law," 10 *J. Corp. L.* 431 (1985). Professor Eisenberg, the Chief Reporter of the American Law Institute's Corporate Governance Project, has written that the empirical findings support Cary, because they show prices rising before the move and stable afterward. Melvin Aron Eisenberg, "The Structure of Corporate Law," 89 *Colum. L. Rev.* 1461, 1509 (1989). Professor Eisenberg misunderstands the significance of residuals in market studies. They are the *unanticipated* portion of stock price movements, net of market movements. So if the firm does something (say, moves to a state whose rules improve the wealth of investors by 10 percent), the *entire* value of the increase appears in residuals before the change, as information about it reaches the market and probabilities become certainties. Prices (net of market) would change thereafter only in response to further news. When a change is beneficial, residuals rise before the change and not after; when it is harmful, residuals fall before the change and not after. Professor Eisenberg also believes that a paper by Elliott J. Weiss and Lawrence J. White, "Of Econometrics and Indeterminacy: A Study of Investors' Reactions to 'Changes' in Corporate Law," 75 *Calif. L. Rev.* 551 (1987), undermines Winter by showing that stock prices do not change in response to changes in the law. Michael C. Bradley and Cindy A. Schipani, "The Economic Importance of the Business Judgment Rule: An Empirical Analysis of the Trans Union Decision and Subsequent Delaware Legislation," in *Corporate Governance, Restructuring, and the Market for Corporate Control* (A. Sametz and J. Bicksler eds. 1990), reaches a similar no-effect conclusion. Both Weiss-White

findings fatally undermine Cary's position that shareholders are victimized by a move to Delaware. This need not mean that all aspects of Delaware's corporate law are optimal. Indeed, we have criticized both some of its statutes and decisions of the Supreme Court of Delaware. Notwithstanding the imperfections inevitable in any institution so complex as a body of law, the evidence indicates that investors benefit when firms incorporate in Delaware. The direction of the competitive pressure is plain.

Still, Winter's emphasis on competition among states for revenues, and among managers for capital, does not fully explain the dynamics of the competition among states. Consider three puzzles. First, although Delaware has a disproportionate share of incorporations and reincorporations, many corporations incorporate elsewhere and never move to Delaware. California has many more incorporations than Delaware, even though Delaware has the lion's share of the largest firms. Second, why do state legislators compete for revenues in the way Winter suggests? What's in it for them? Where's the invisible hand? Third, what of opportunism by managers who do not anticipate returning to capital markets—whether because their firms have peaked or because the managers themselves are about to retire?

WHY DO SO FEW FIRMS INCORPORATE IN DELAWARE?

What leads so many firms to disdain Delaware, even though both Cary and Winter depict it as Nirvana? Richard Posner and Kenneth Scott have suggested that Delaware's enabling statute is particularly attractive for large firms where the benefits resulting from the

---

and Bradley-Schipani go astray by taking as the "events" the dates the statutes were enacted. See Ronald J. Gilson, "The Law and Finance of the Business Judgment Rule," in *Corporate Governance, Restructuring, and the Market for Corporate Control*. Laws are widely discussed before enactment, and it is necessary to track down whatever increases or reduces the probability of passage. Prices *are* sensitive to structural changes, a point the many studies collected in Chapter 7 demonstrate. No one can read the *Journal of Financial Economics* and come away with a sense that investors fail to adjust prices to the smallest change in corporate structure and legal rules. Nevertheless, there may be sound reasons why we should expect changes in the law affecting derivative suits to have slight effects. Chapter 4 discusses many of them.

specialization of function are the greatest.[5] Barry Baysinger and Henry Butler give a similar explanation, contending that greater statutory control is superior for smaller firms (those for which capital markets are less efficient), and that investors prefer smaller firms that seek states with greater constraints.[6] On this view, whether an enabling or strict corporate law is optimal for a particular firm depends on its capital structure.[7] Finally, in the most careful study of reincorporations, Roberta Romano demonstrated (see note 1) that firms typically move to Delaware in anticipation of a major corporate event such as a public offering, a merger and acquisition program, or maneuvering against a takeover. For these firms, Delaware's large body of legal precedents and sophisticated corporate bar lowers the cost of transacting and thus justifies the move.

None of these explanations detracts from the power of competition; all three are consistent with it. Yet the recognition that different bodies of law may be best for different firms (or the same firm at different times) implies limits to the competitive process. There are only fifty states, perhaps too few to offer the complete menu of terms needed for the thousands of different corporate ventures. Corporate laws have hundreds of provisions apiece, and each provision could take many forms; with only fifty jurisdictions, lots of (potentially desirable) combinations of these provisions will be missing, and the resulting laws cannot be perfect.

WHAT ARE LEGISLATORS' MOTIVES?

Winter (like Cary) focused on incorporations as a source of tax revenue. This is an oversimplification of the legislative process. From the perspective of individual state legislators, revenue from franchise taxes is a public good. No legislator can capture the benefits to the state of increased revenue (which means a lower tax rate for the populace and greater economic development because residents keep a larger fraction of their product). Thus the prospect

5. Richard A. Posner and Kenneth E. Scott, *Economics of Corporate Law and Securities Regulation* 111 (1980).

6. Baysinger and Butler, supra note 4.

7. For a critique of the classification scheme used by Baysinger and Butler and the role of capital structure in the incorporation decision, see Romano, supra note 1, 8 *Cardozo L. Rev.* at 714–717.

of increased revenues need not dominate the decisions of individual legislators even in Delaware, where corporate franchise fees are 19 percent of the budget. Legislators can capture the benefits from more direct payments such as campaign contributions and indirect inducements such as political support.[8] Such direct payment can motivate individual legislators to act even if the long-run economic vitality of the state is reduced. It is an old (and sad) story that concentrated interest groups can produce private-interest legislation at the expense of general welfare. Managers may be such a concentrated interest group, unless they are constrained in turn by capital markets (to which we attend below).

For judges, increased revenues at the state level are even more of a public good. They are less likely to be moved by campaign contributions (Delaware has an appointed judiciary). "What do judges maximize?" is an enduring question. There is the satisfaction of getting things right, but what defines "right" for a given judge? Other motivations, such as the desire to increase their prestige, to win promotion to a higher court or office, to become more attractive as lawyers should they leave the bench, also provide some incentive to act, yet without (necessarily) providing an incentive to make the law more efficient. The debate about whether the common law is efficient, or could be so through "invisible hand" processes, is no less germane here.[9]

OPPORTUNISM

Once they are ensconced, and have raised the capital the firm needs, managers may elect to behave opportunistically—to main-

8. Jonathan Macey and Geoffrey Miller have argued that Delaware's organized bar has influenced the development of Delaware's corporation law. "Toward an Interest-Group Theory of Delaware Corporation Law," 65 *Tex. L. Rev.* 469 (1987). We doubt that the bar receives substantial rents—after all, lawyers can represent Delaware corporations no matter where they reside, and out-of-state lawyers can practice in or move to Delaware. Entry into the legal profession is slow; movement from state to state can be much faster. Still, the organized bar has proven to be an effective interest group for many kinds of legislation, such as the retention of the diversity jurisdiction in federal courts.

9. See the survey by Robert D. Cooter and Daniel L. Rubinfeld, "Economic Analysis of Legal Disputes and Their Resolution," 27 *J. Econ. Lit.* 1067, 1091–94 (1989).

tain themselves in office or raise their compensation at the expense of investors. Of course there is an opportunity cost. Funds not raised, or funds used internally when the market rate is greater, produce losses for the firm. Eventually it must be ground under, and the managers will pay the price in the labor market if they do not pay immediately when the price of their shares drops (see Chapter 4). Yet to any firm, and to any manager, there comes a last period. The firm may be in trouble and not anticipate indefinite survival. The senior managers may be near retirement and think that the short-term gains exceed the loses in the (now-short, for them) long term.

Entrepreneurs who want to raise funds for new ventures bear the loss if they decide to incorporate in a state with an inferior corporation law because investors will pay less for shares. Entrepreneurs can avoid this loss, however, if the firm goes public in a state with a superior corporation law and in its (or its managers) last period pressures the state to adopt inferior corporate law provisions or switches its state of incorporation.

Considerations of this kind have led Winter to temper his original belief that there is a "race for the top."[10] Competition is a good mechanism but need not be perfect. Delaware can win the race for revenues by being "best" without being "optimal"—and given the impossibility of optimality, satisficing rather than optimizing is likely. The race will not be for the bottom; the long-run pressures will favor investors over managers; but the movement toward long-run equilibriums may be erratic. States no less than managers fish for successful combinations, not knowing what the market really wants; survival is the best sign of success. As we shall see later in this chapter, the combination of opportunism and the receptivity of state legislators to campaign contributions and implicit payments (such as political support) provides the most plausible explanation for the proliferation of state antitakeover statutes.

Antitakeover Statutes and the Incorporation Debate

The proposition that the competition among states for corporate charters is beneficial to investors has been challenged by the proliferation of state antitakeover statutes. These statutes take a variety

10. Ralph K. Winter, Jr., "The 'Race for the Top' Revisited," 89 *Colum. L. Rev.* 1526, 1528–29 (1989).

of forms. The first generation imposed delay and gave state officials veto power over offers. These statutes also frequently governed offers made to firms incorporated in other states. In *Edgar v. MITE Corp.*[11] the Supreme Court held that this type of statute is unconstitutional because of its extra-territorial effects.

A new wave of statutes appeared. Second-generation statutes took a variety of forms ranging from "control share statutes," which require a vote of "disinterested" shares before an offer can be consummated, to "fair price statutes," which prevent an acquiring firm from effectuating a two-tiered acquisition. These statutes typically did not give governmental officials veto power and did not apply to firms incorporated in other states. In *CTS Corp. v. Dynamics Corp.*[12] the Supreme Court upheld a second-generation control share statute against a constitutional challenge and also concluded that it is not preempted by federal law.

There then developed yet a third generation of takeover statutes. These, generally known as "business combination statutes," allow the transfer of shares to proceed unimpeded but regulate transactions such as mergers, after a bidder has gained control, unless the firm's former managers gave their assent before the shares changed hands. Delaware has enacted a statute of this type.[13] Third-generation statutes differ in severity. Wisconsin's forbids any merger or sale of assets for three years, without exception, and so effectively precludes transactions, opposed by management, designed to alter corporate structure.[14] Delaware's, at the other extreme, allows firms to opt out by provisions in their articles and provides that if the bidder obtains 85 percent of the stock that is not held by managers and their allies, the bidder may do as it pleases. A law of this kind raises the costs of offers, but only to the extent necessary to acquire the bulk of the stock.

Why Do States Hamper Tender Offers?

Approximately forty states have enacted one or another flavor of antitakeover statute.[15] The implications of this proliferation of anti-

11. 457 U.S. 624 (1982).
12. 481 U.S. 69 (1987).
13. 8 Del. Code §203.
14. Wis. Stat. §180.726.
15. Gilbert Manning Warren III, "Developments in State Takeover Regulation: *MITE* and Its Aftermath," 40 *Bus. Law.* 671, 671 nn.2 & 3 (1985), gives a list of the

takeover statutes for the incorporation debate requires an under-standing of the rationale for the statutes and their effect. Consider four explanations for this development.

First, the statutes may protect shareholders from the effects of "coercive" tender offers—tender offers compelling reticent investors to tender despite the fact that they believe the shares worth (in the long run) more than the price offered. This explanation supposes that offers ought to be blocked. Second, the statutes may provide the target firm's management with more bargaining power. Individual shareholders will tender to any price over market, which allows bidders to keep the gains. Statutes giving managers a blocking position allow investors to coordinate their response, to hold out for a larger portion of the benefits of the transaction. This understanding supposes that acquisitions should proceed, but at better prices than bidders offer initially. Third, the laws might facilitate managers' entrenchment, a version of Cary's hypothesis (with our last-period problem modification). Fourth, the statutes may prevent firms from quitting the state. Transfers of control frequently result in a change of management. The new team may move the firm, close plants, fire workers. To prevent the takeover is to prevent the movement, on this approach.

Politics depends on what people *believe,* not necessarily on what is true. Roberta Romano studied the politics behind state anti-takeover statutes and has concluded that the laws are passed in response to lobbying by large firms within the state that may be takeover targets.[16] Other groups such as labor, community organizations, and the organized bar (with the exception of Delaware) play little role. Professor Romano's study was not exhaustive—it considered the passage of antitakeover laws in only a few states and focused intensively on only one (Connecticut). Nevertheless, the source of political support for the laws is inconsistent with the fourth explanation. It is consistent with the other three.

If we address the "merits" rather than the politics, it is easy to discard the first possibility, the prevention of coercive, value-reducing offers. Chapter 7 explains why, in excessive detail; we will

thirty-seven state antitakeover statutes enacted prior to *MITE*. Since then other states, including Delaware, have enacted takeover statutes.

16. Roberta Romano, "The Political Economy of Takeover Statutes," 73 *Va. L. Rev.* 111, 145–180 (1987).

not review the bidding. It is also possible, though less easy, to discard the fourth explanation. All available data show that acquired firms are no more likely to close plants and pull up stakes than are others—although there are many fewer studies. (See footnote 23 to Chapter 7.) The second and third explanations (coordination and entrenchment) are hard to separate, for managers may coordinate only by saying no, at least some of the time. Sellers at an auction pull the item off the block if the bids are too low. Yet even managers determined to stand their ground may be overwhelmed. So both the second and third explanations imply that state statutes will lead to fewer bids but higher premiums when offers succeed—which is exactly what the studies find.

At the level of theory, the second explanation (coordination) also poses problems. It is another version of the auctioneering approach discussed at length in Chapter 7. Although we argued there that auctions are good for investors in targets *ex post,* they are bad for investors in targets *ex ante* and bad for investors in both bidders and bystanders *ex post* and *ex ante.* Thoughtful scholars do not agree with us. Incomplete *a priori* analysis drives even lawyers to facts. And the dominant fact is that stock prices fall when states enact antitakeover laws, or when managers adopt devices (such as poison pills) that give them the ability simultaneously to defeat bids or coordinate auctions, at managers' option. The second explanation flunks the test of reality. Which leaves the third, embarrassing though that is for the fundamental thesis of this book.

Maybe we could rescue the position by trimming a little. Perhaps there is a *fifth* explanation: antitakeover statutes help states where targets are located exploit states where bidders are located. The absence of bidders in a state appears to be one of the main determinants of whether it adopts an antitakeover statute.[17] This will not get us far, though, for firms designate collections of investors and others scattered through the nation. Delaware does not "own" the investors in "its" firms; they do not live in Delaware. Anyway, an exploitation hypothesis implies that the price of stock in local firms rises when states adopt these statutes. Prices go down, not up.

We learn, then, that competition does not eliminate the opportu-

---

17. Romano, supra note 16 at 142–145. This result is surprising, however, for bidders in any particular state (except perhaps Delaware) typically are interested in acquiring corporations incorporated in other states.

nistic behavior by corporate managers. The typical statute is enacted hurriedly with little or no debate. Managers fearing takeover
benefit; their relatively small number goads them to mobilize in
support of the law. The (greater) losses imposed by law are borne
by dispersed shareholders and future entrepreneurs who want to
raise capital for firms incorporated in the state. If the state is clever,
it allows these entrepreneurs to opt out of the statute, making
credible commitments to serve investors faithfully by exposing
themselves to ouster. Established managers get protection even
while future capital raising is unhindered.

Still, investors, having seen the cycle once, will be chary of
repetition. If fewer firms incorporate in the state as a result of the
law, revenues from incorporations will decline. But this loss will be
felt by citizens of the state in the future. It may be felt outside the
state, too. Investors come to realize that any state can pass such a
law by the time the firm becomes a plausible candidate for acquisition. There is no haven; therefore no investment is safe and the
states having antitakeover laws today do not suffer so much in
competition as they might. From the perspective of individual legislators who may receive contributions and other support in the
present if the law is enacted, it may be quite rational to support
passage.

COMPETITION AND STATE LAW REVISITED

Does the "race for the top" survive the adoption of antitakeover
statutes? The answer depends on how the thesis is characterized. If
the claim is that the competition among states for incorporations
always produces the optimal result, it stands refuted. But if the
thesis is that competition creates a powerful tendency for states to
enact laws that operate to the benefit of investors (the opposite of
the Cary view), it is alive and well. Competition among states does
not eliminate the possibility of opportunistic behavior but imposes
a constraint.

It is indicative, we think, that Delaware has been among the least
willing to enact an antitakeover statute. For twenty years after the
first antitakeover statute was enacted, Delaware had none. What
Delaware did adopt is a relatively innocuous third-generation type.
The Delaware statute prohibits an acquirer of more than 15 percent
of the voting stock of a target firm from engaging in transactions
such as squeezeout mergers with the target for three years. But the

law does not prohibit (or even regulate) the initial acquisition of shares; moreover, it does not apply to liquidations, dissolutions, sales of assets, or business combinations with unaffiliated third parties. Finally, the statute governs second-step transactions only if an acquiring firm obtains less than 85 percent of the target's independently held shares in the same transaction where the 15 percent threshold is crossed. Managers cannot activate the statute by holding 20 percent; their shares are carved out. So the law is some impediment, but not much of one. It is no impediment at all for the future; new firms can exempt themselves by so specifying in the articles.

Delaware's antitakeover statute is milder than earlier statutes that imposed long delays before an offer could proceed or gave state officials veto power over whether an offer could be consummated. Nevertheless, we believe the Delaware statute is inimical to shareholders' welfare, though less so than other statutes. For this reason, Delaware's decision to adopt an antitakeover statute will create opportunities for other states. It is no coincidence that California, which has both the largest number of incorporations and by far the largest number of new firms going public, has never had an antitakeover statute.

Finally, it must be remembered that state antitakeover statutes are a recent phenomenon. When the Williams Act was enacted in 1968, just one state (Virginia) had such a statute, and even there only for one year. It is too early to know what the long run holds. Perhaps they will vanish. Perhaps the empirical work will be exposed as poorly done and the laws vindicated. No one should be confident that federal regulation would be superior to the current pattern. Competition does not necessarily drive laws to the top, but it drives them up. Federal laws face less competition; it is harder to move to France than to Nevada. Because the current situation is fluid and the consequences of denying to states the power to act uncertain, it is unwise to exchange the power of competition for federal legislation that today looks superior. We consider, however, the possibility that this has occurred already.

ANTITAKEOVER STATUTES AND THE WILLIAMS ACT

The Supreme Court has twice addressed contentions that federal law occupies the field of takeover regulation. In *Edgar v. MITE Corp.* a plurality thought that the first-generation Illinois statute preempted—both because it upset a "balance" Congress struck between bidders and targets and because it injured investors. (A majority held it unconstitutional). In *CTS Corp. v. Dynamics Corp.* a majority found the Indiana second-generation law compatible with the Williams Act, stating that it was neither unbalanced nor detrimental to investors.

The exercise of looking at balance and effects is hard to square with the Securities Exchange Act of 1934, which contains the Williams Act. The 1934 act has a section preserving state regulation.[18] Presumably that means "bad" regulation as well as "good" regulation. The only way to imply a limit on state law is to lean heavily on the portions of the legislative history emphasizing that the Williams Act was "neutral" between bidders and targets, a neutrality state law upsets. Yet *all* state laws upset the balance struck by *some* federal law. Congress always could have done more (or less); the state law necessarily does more (or less), else it has no effect. Upsetting a balance cannot be a basis for knocking states out of the arena.

Anyway, the legislative references to "neutrality" are eyewash. The Williams Act was enacted in reaction to the growing use of hostile tender offers. The act imposed disclosure obligations on bidders, established waiting periods during which offers had to remain open, required the bidders to accept shares tendered pro rata (rather than first come, first served), and provided target shareholders with withdrawal rights. In each of these areas, no comparable federal regulation had existed; in each area the statute regulated bidders *but not targets*. It thereby changed the "balance" between bidders and targets, no matter how many speeches denied that fact. It eliminated quickie takeovers and dramatically strengthened the hands of targets' managers. Before 1968 defense was unthinkable because impossible; now it is routine. The Williams Act, in short, imposes the same kinds of disclose and delay burdens on bidders as state antitakeover statutes do. It is no more "neutral" than state laws are—than any law is. Laws are not "neutral" filters, changing density but not color; they are more like polarizing filters.

---

18. 15 U.S.C. §78bb(a) provides: "Nothing in this title shall affect the jurisdiction of the securities commission . . . of any state over any security or any person insofar as it does not conflict with the provisions of this title or the rules and regulations thereunder."

Laws have bite; why else do they exist? Nonneutrality of state antitakeover statutes therefore cannot be the basis for their invalidity.

It is conceivable that Congress wanted a *particular* balance between the contending factions, which states could not disrupt. Congress did not say so, however, and the 1934 act says the opposite. State securities laws frequently strike a "balance" different from federal law. For example, the federal securities laws (which we discuss in Chapter 11) are disclosure statutes. Many state blue-sky laws are "merit" regulation statutes. Under a merit regulation statute, full disclosure is not enough. The offerer must also satisfy the state securities commissioner of the merit of the securities being sold. State law is preempted only if Congress not only struck its own balance but also precluded the states from striking any other. Congress could do that and maybe it should (though we think not—not yet, anyway). It has not. Courts need not laud state rules to conclude that states are entitled to legislate.[19]

ANTITAKEOVER STATUTES AND THE COMMERCE CLAUSE

Corporate law has long been based on the principle that a firm's internal affairs are governed by the law of its state of incorporation. Corporations of any size have investors throughout the country. It is routine for the laws of a state where a corporation is incorporated to govern transactions between investors in other states. This serves as the foundation for competition among states to design better laws.

Yet this system of corporate governance, where the laws of one state regulate transactions between individuals in others, could be questioned. The Commerce Clause (Art. I, Sec. 8, cl. 3, of the Constitution) grants Congress the power to regulate interstate commerce. For the past hundred years, the clause has been taken to prohibit attempts by states to discriminate against interstate commerce. This is the "dormant Commerce Clause." Do state antitakeover statutes violate the dormant Commerce Clause by discriminating against interstate commerce?

19. A point Justice Scalia made. 481 U.S. at 96 (concurring). See also *Amanda Acquisition Corp. v. Universal Foods Corp.*, 877 F.2d 496 (7th Cir. 1989).

226 The Economic Structure of Corporate Law

Suppose state *A* wants to attract a particular industry located in state *B* and state *B* passes a law preventing the move. In the short run, state *B* may be able to impose costs on state *A*. In the long run, however, the harm to state *A* will be dissipated by entry and the development of substitutes. The incidence of the law will shift to state *B*, as the barrier to exit causes firms to be less willing to locate there in the first instance. A barrier to exit imposes a cost sometime in the future. This cost has a present value, depending on the side of the eventual penalty and how far in the future it lies. The present value is equivalent to a tax on entry into the state.

There is, however, a difference between laws that affect capital markets and those that affect product, labor, and other markets. Because of the mobility of capital, the "long-run" adjustment may occur quickly—at least it will if investors believe that the exit-blocking laws will endure until the time comes for exit. It is much easier to move investment dollars than to relocate a factory or a work force. For this reason, there is less need for legal intervention to protect nonresidents in their capacity as investors. Perhaps this explains why state corporation laws are rarely thought to be in tension with the dormant Commerce Clause. No state can export the costs to nonresidents.[20]

What then is different about state antitakeover statutes? A state antitakeover statute applied to firms incorporated in other states makes it easier for a state to export costs, for investors cannot simply take their capital elsewhere. So it makes sense to cut down under the Commerce Clause an extra-territorial law, even though laws regulating only domestic firms may survive. This is precisely what has occurred. The statute struck down in *MITE* applied to firms incorporated in other states, while the law upheld in *CTS* applied to domestic corporations.

One could say, of course, that all takeover laws are special cases because they gum up a national market in corporate control. Yet that approach paves the road to exclusively federal corporate law. Suppose a state adopted a law that investors would have one vote apiece, rather than one per share, or that only shares held for a year could be voted, or that mergers had to be approved by unanimous consent, or that members of the board serve for twenty years and

---

20. See generally Frank H. Easterbrook, "Antitrust and the Economics of Federalism," 26 *J. L. & Econ.* 23 (1983).

may not be recalled. Each of these laws would have a far greater effect on the market for corporate control than would any of the existing antitakeover statutes. Each would be just as much an interference with the national market for corporate control. Each is unwise, but none is unconstitutional.

Competition among the states, not constitutional law, prevents such silly statutes from taking hold. Just as the Constitution "does not enact Mr. Herbert Spencer's *Social Statics,*"[21] so it does not enact the efficient capital market hypothesis or turn the latest issue of the *Journal of Financial Economics* into the law of the land. Just as the business judgment rule leaves to capital markets the punishment of errant managers, so the Constitution leaves to markets the discipline of errant states.

21. Lochner v. New York, 198 U.S. 45, 75 (1905) (Holmes, J., dissenting).

9

Close Corporations

So far we have focused on the publicly held corporation and said little about the much more common closely held corporation. This is not because one analysis will cover both. Risk bearing and management are separated in public but not in closely held corporations. The extent of this separation determines the governance mechanisms and legal rules that evolved in the two types of firms.

This chapter discusses the economic structure of closely held corporations. We analyze the contractual monitoring mechanisms designed to minimize agency problems in close corporations and the enforceability of these contractual arrangements. We also catalog the costs and benefits of legal rules designed to assist minority shareholders in closely held corporations and analyze the argument that legal rules for closely held corporations should approximate those for partnerships.

Although we treat public and closely held corporations as distinct, we recognize that the line is blurry. Managers in publicly held corporations typically own a significant amount of their firm's shares and thus bear some risk. At the same time, many "close" firms are financed by debt and venture capital, separating management from risk bearing. We employ a dichotomous treatment to illustrate the different kinds of incentives and structures in play, not to suggest that all firms were cast in one of these two molds.

The Economic Structure of Closely Held Corporations

Closely held corporations have many characteristics in common. Most important, they tend to have relatively few managers, who are the largest residual claimants. Because the firm's principal investors also manage, it is often necessary to restrict the investors' ability to alienate their shares. Such restrictions increase the probability that those who manage will be compatible. When the firm begins as a family venture, the restrictions also ensure that control remains in the family, which may aid in reducing opportunistic conduct. Both the restrictions on alienation and the apportionment of jobs become more important when, as often happens, the firm decides to distribute its profits as salary; salaries are (usually) deductible to the firm and thus reduce the taxes the firm must pay. Once the distribution of profits is divorced from formal ownership of shares, it is essential to use contractual devices to keep people in a position to receive the return on their investment.

When the same people both manage and bear the risk of investment, the firm loses the benefits of specialization. Because those who manage must also put up capital and bear risk, the pool of qualified managers is smaller. Similarly, investors in closely held corporations have large percentages of their wealth tied up in one firm and lack access to capital markets. Thus they are less efficient risk bearers than investors in publicly held corporations, who may diversify a larger portion of their portfolios. Nevertheless, when projects are sufficiently small that they do not require many managers with specialized expertise or large pools of capital, closely held corporations may have a comparative advantage.

The primary disadvantage of the closely held corporation—lack of specialization—is also its primary advantage. Because the few participants both manage and bear the cost of their actions, each is more likely to find that what is good for him is also good for the firm (and for the other participants). All else equal, managers who own a large percentage of the outstanding shares of a firm will work harder and engage in less self-dealing than managers who own a smaller percentage. Moreover, the relatively small number of residual claimants in closely held corporations facilitates contracting and monitoring to reduce agency problems.

Participants in closely held corporations frequently have familial or other personal relations in addition to their business dealings. The continuous and nonpecuniary nature of these relationships reduces agency problems. The bond between parents and children, for example, constrains conflicts of interest. It is thus no accident that some of the famous cases dealing with closely held corporations involve situations where these informal bonds have broken down as a result of death, divorce, or retirement of the patriarch.[1]

But investors in closely held corporations lack a public market for claims. (We refer to claims as shares or equity, but the debt in close corporations also may be a residual claim, as it is in LBOs and MBOs.) The absence of a liquid market has profound implications. Many assume that it yields a unique risk of exploitation. Because minority shareholders cannot dispose of their shares, the argument runs, a majority can "oppress" them by diverting a disproportionate share of the firm's income to itself, eventually forcing the minority to sell their shares at a distress price. But this argument really has little to do with the absence of a market. Consider the extreme case in which a majority shareholder appropriates 100 percent of the firm's income. Even if a minority stockholder had an unrestricted ability to sell his shares, nobody would buy. Illiquidity is not the problem.

There are, however, at least four ways in which the lack of an active market for shares can injure investors in closely held corporations. First, the absence of a secondary market makes valuation of residual claims highly uncertain. Because there is no market price for shares, and because contracts limit the number of buyers, even permitted transfers of shares will be made more difficult by high transaction costs. The investor in a closely held corporation who wants to disinvest faces costly haggling that may frustrate the sale. The alternative is a formula price, which may prevent transactions altogether when, as is inevitable, the formula yields a price other than the value of the stock.

Second, the lack of an active market in shares creates conflicts over dividend policy and other distributions. For example, an investor in a closely held corporation who needs a large amount of cash at a particular time might be prejudiced if the firm retained a large percentage of its earnings. If lenders are unwilling to accept the stock of the firm as collateral, the investor might be forced to sell his shares to the corporation (the other shareholders) at a discount. The shareholder in a publicly held corporation with the same needs would be less concerned about the firm's dividend policy.

---

1. For example Galler v. Galler, 32 Ill. 2d 16, 203 N.E.2d 577 (1964); In re Radom & Neidorff, Inc., 307 N.Y. 1, 119 N.E.2d 563 (1954). See also Mortell v. Mortell Corp., 887 F.2d 1322 (7th Cir. 1989).

Investors can turn future profits into today's cash by selling stock, a form of homemade dividends.

Third, the absence of an active market in shares precludes reliance on public monitoring. Recall from Chapter 7 that both takeovers and the monitoring by would-be bidders (whether or not a bid occurs) not only constrain manager's conduct but also transfer assets to higher valued uses. Monitoring by persons who are not investors thus helps align managers' interests with those of investors in publicly held corporations. In closely held corporations, where the ability of outsiders to acquire shares is restricted, the market for corporate control is less important. (Outsiders always could make bids too generous to refuse, but this describes the merger market rather than the takeover market.) Publicly held corporations also can and do devise compensation packages that link managers' compensation to changes in share prices, automatically rewarding good results and penalizing bad ones; closely held firms cannot readily do so.

Fourth, the lack of a liquid market for shares deprives uninformed investors of the protection of purchasing at market price. Many buyers and sellers compete to acquire information about public corporations; the competition and ensuing trading cause the price of securities to reflect reasonably well the available information about their value. This is not true in closely held corporations, for there is no market price.

Still, it is a mistake to conclude that shareholders in closely held corporations face unique risks of oppression, just as it is wrong to argue that shareholders in publicly held corporations face unique risks of exploitation because of the separation of ownership and control. Each organizational form presents its own problems, for which people have designed different mechanisms of control. At the margin the problems must be equally severe, the mechanisms equally effective—were it otherwise, investors would transfer their money from one form to the other until the marginal equality condition was satisfied. Because the world contains so many different investment vehicles, none will offer distinctively better chances of return when people can select and shift among them.

Most people can work for either public or closely held firms, and public firms pay in cash or tradable shares. A closely held firm that insists on joint management and investment must offer a better deal to attract capital. Even if there are some skills for which there is no market in publicly held firms, there are tens of thousands of closely held firms, which must compete against each other for talent and capital. This competition requires firms to make believable (meaning enforceable) promises of an equal or greater anticipated return in order to attract capital. Closely held firms may generate some special returns; if family-owned ventures reduce the agency costs of management, there will be gains for all to share. The most the controlling parties of any closely held firm can do is to deny outside investors these extra gains, which economists call "rents." The parties who possess the scarce resource, the elusive ability to create these gains, will get the rents. The firms, however, must promise to outsiders, and on average deliver, at least the competitive risk-adjusted rate of return available from other sorts of ventures. Scholars can contribute by exploring the different agency problems in the two types of firms and the different mechanisms that have developed to control them. Nothing useful can come of efforts to say that one is better or worse than another.

Governance in Closely Held Corporations

Investors in any venture are concerned about the possibility that the actions of others will reduce their return. Those who attempt to attract other people's money have incentives to adopt governance mechanisms that respond to potential investors' concerns, a point we established in the first chapter. Closely held corporations have different governance mechanisms because of their different economic structures.

THE RELATION BETWEEN MANAGEMENT AND RISK BEARING

Publicly held corporations employ many mechanisms to align managers' interests with those of investors: independent directors, accountants, investment bankers, and analysts typically monitor managers' conduct. Residual claims are freely traded and carry voting rights. This facilitates efficient risk bearing, accumulation of large blocks of shares, and transfers of control while ensuring that management teams have incentives to maximize the value of the firm. Compensation agreements link changes in managers' wealth to the performance of the firm, which reduces though it cannot eliminate the divergence of interest implied by the separation of management and risk bearing.

Because closely held corporations do not separate management from risk bearing, monitoring is less costly. There is less need for outsiders to monitor managers. (The smaller size of closely held corporations also makes it less worthwhile for the participants to incur the extra costs of independent monitors.) But the lack of separation calls forth other types of governance mechanisms. We have mentioned that firms restrict the alienability of shares to ensure that those who are investors are also compatible as managers. The restrictions also preserve an agreed-on division of profits. A manager who retires or dies no longer receives the salary component of the return on investment. Any time an active manager leaves a job, it may be necessary to transfer the shares as well. Buyout agreements, which require the firm to pay dividends or acquire the stock if the corporate treasury is in funds, may serve the same function.

Another common concern for minority investors in closely held corporations is that those in control will prefer themselves when distributing earnings. Any system that distributes profits in part through salary presents this danger. There can be no presumption that those who have invested equal amounts are entitled to equal salaries as managers. Thus those in control, undisciplined by outside monitors, may award disproportionately high salaries to themselves. Potential investors who recognize this possibility will be reluctant to become residual claimants. Again contractual mechanisms have evolved to handle the problem. These include high voting and quorum requirements as well as employment and compensation agreements that make it hard for managers to act without the consent of minority shareholders. Agreements to keep people in office enable those not in control to get some return on their investment.

The more power minority shareholders have, the more likely is deadlock. Deadlock also looms where the number of shareholders is small and shares are distributed so that votes can be evenly split. When deadlock may be a problem, parties frequently create a way out: arbitration, voting trusts, third parties who have the right to vote only to break deadlocks. None of these is costless—not only because of the costs of error in any dispute-resolution mechanism but also because the easier it is to escape deadlock, the more deadlocks there will be. Deadlocks often arise from rent-seeking

234 The Economic Structure of Corporate Law

(each party demands a larger slice of the pie), and mechanisms that make deadlock very costly to escape may be rational responses to the costs of rent-seeking. We return to this when discussing dissolution.

THE RELATION BETWEEN LEGAL RULES AND GOVERNANCE MECHANISMS

Judges once viewed unusual contractual mechanisms in close corporations with suspicion. Today courts enforce whatever the participants invent. The evolution of corporate statutes from prescriptive rules into enabling laws has provided participants in both public and close ventures with considerable flexibility in structuring the firm. Some states also have special close corporation statutes, standard-form contracts designed for particular needs. These statutes are even more explicitly contractarian than are the enabling laws used for public corporations, authorizing the adoption of any contractual arrangements that do not injure third parties.[2]

With some lag, common law courts have followed legislatures in deferring to contractual arrangements. Many an early decision was hostile to private arrangements such as restraints on alienation, voting trusts, and agreements limiting the discretion of directors.[3] Judges did not know or care what the parties were trying to accomplish; they mechanically transferred to private firms the approaches

2. See 8 Del. Code §§341–356; Ill. Rev. Stat. ch. 32 ¶¶1201–16; 15 Pa. Stat. §§1371–1386. For an example of a specialized statute allowing participants in closely held corporations maximum flexibility, see the ABA's *Model Statutory Close Corporation Supplement,* adopted in 1982 and amended in 1984. The text and commentary appear in 4 *Model Business Corporation Act Annotated* 1803–1880 (3d ed. 1989). Even Professor Eisenberg, a resolute opponent of the contractual model of the public corporation, believes that participants in closely held ventures should be allowed to adopt any governance structure they please. Melvin Aron Eisenberg, *The Structure of the Corporation* 9 (1976).

3. Early cases sometimes viewed shares as property governed by the rule against restraints on alienation and ignored the mutual interests of the participants in restricting alienation. For a discussion of the property-contract debate, see William H. Painter, "Stock Transfer Restrictions: Continuing Uncertainties and a Legislative Proposal," 6 *Vill. L. Rev.* 48 (1960). On voting agreements see Bostwick v. Chapman (Sepaug Voting Trust Cases), 60 Conn. 553, 24 A. 32 (1890); Warren v. Pim, 66 N.J. Eq. 353, 59 A. 773 (1904). On agreements limiting directors' discretion see McQuade v. Stoneham, 263 N.Y. 323, 189 N.E. 234 (1934); Manson v. Curtis, 223 N.Y. 313, 119 N.E. 559 (1918).

used for different structures. In the famous *McQuade v. Stoneham*,[4] for example, the court refused to enforce an arrangement between a majority shareholder and two minority shareholders entered into at the time McQuade, one of the two, bought the shares. The parties agreed to use their "best efforts" to continue each other as directors and officers. The contract appointed McQuade treasurer at a salary of $7,500. It further provided that without unanimous consent there could be no change in salaries or other action that might "endanger or interfere with the rights of minority shareholders." As part of the transaction, McQuade paid Stoneham, the controlling shareholder, $50,338.10 for his shares. Some time later McQuade was sacked, and he tried to enforce the agreement. The court refused, saying that "a contract is illegal and void so far as it precludes the board of directors, at the risk of incurring legal liability, from changing officers, salaries, or policies or retaining individuals in office, except by consent of the contracting parties."[5]

The court never considered why the parties agreed in the first place. McQuade was willing to invest $50,000 but wanted to minimize the possibility that the controlling shareholder could deny him a return on his investment. To induce McQuade to invest, Stoneham guaranteed McQuade a minimum return (the $7,500 salary) and also gave McQuade a veto over any material changes to the initial agreement. Without these inducements, McQuade would have been less likely to invest, would have paid less for his shares, or would have demanded a severance payment. Any of these could have been worse for all concerned. By invalidating the agreement, the court allowed Stoneham to welsh on the guarantees that induced McQuade to invest. It is difficult to see what "public policy" this could serve.[6]

McQuade is a fossil. Today courts enforce voluntary agreements of all sorts in close corporations. *Clark v. Dodge*,[7] for example, a decision from the court that decided *McQuade*, enforced an agree-

---

4. 263 N.Y. 323, 189 N.E. 234 (1934).

5. 263 N.Y. at 330, 189 N.E. at 237.

6. See Kaplan v. Block, 183 Va. 327, 31 S.E.2d 893 (1944) (unanimity agreements offend public policy because they create the possibility of deadlocks). *Kaplan* ignored the trade-off faced by investors in closely held corporations. The parties may well have concluded that the protections of a unanimity rule outweighed the potential costs.

7. 269 N.Y. 410, 199 N.E. 641 (1936).

ment specifying that a minority shareholder be continued in office and receive one-fourth of net income as salary or dividends.[8] In *Galler v. Galler*,[9] the Supreme Court of Illinois upheld a shareholders' agreement providing for salary and dividend payments to the shareholders themselves as well as to their immediate families despite the death of an original signatory. Other courts have allowed participants to agree to use arbitrators or other third parties to break deadlocks and restraints on alienation.[10] Many statutes codify this willingness to enforce whatever suits the investors.[11]

The Role of Corporate Law in the Absence of Shareholders' Agreement

DOES THE RULE OF LAW MATTER?

We have argued throughout that corporate law, both statutory and judicial, acts as a set of standard terms that lowers the cost of contracting. Because of the differences between the two types of

8. See also Zion v. Kurtz, 50 N.Y.2d 92, 405 N.E.2d 681, 428 N.Y.S. 199 (1980) (agreement requiring unanimous consent in conduct of business activities held valid as between the parties to it notwithstanding failure to comply with notice provisions in statute); Jones v. Williams, 139 No. 1, 39 S.W. 486 (1897) (a surprisingly astute decision enforcing an agreement to keep an investor in office). But see Long Park, Inc. v. Trenton–New Brunswick Theatres Co., 297 N.Y. 174, 77 N.E.2d 633 (1948) (unanimous shareholders' agreement invalid because it deprived the board of directors of the power to select management and operate the business).

9. 32 Ill. 2d 16, 203 N.E.2d 577 (1964).

10. On deadlocks see, for example, Lehrman v. Cohen, 43 Del. Ch. 222, 222 A.2d 800 (1966); In re Vogel, 25 A.D.2d 212, 268 N.Y.S.2d 237 (1966), affirmed, 19 N.Y.2d 589, 224 N.E.2d 738, 278 N.Y.S.2d 236 (1967). On restraints on alienation see Colbert v. Hennessey, 351 Mass. 131, 217 N.E.2d 914 (1966); Allen v. Biltmore Tissue Corp., 2 N.Y.2d 534, 141 N.E.2d 812, 161 N.Y.S.2d 418 (1957). But see Rafe v. Hindin, 29 A.D.2d 481, 288 N.Y.S.2d 662 (1968) (contractual restriction on transferability void because certificates of stock are "property" and thus not subject to unreasonable restraints on alienation).

11. *Model Statutory Close Corporation Supplement* §20(a) ("All the shareholders of a statutory close corporation may agree in writing to regulate the exercise of corporate powers and the management of the business and affairs of the corporation or the relationship among the shareholders of the corporation"); ibid. at §§20(b) and 21 (agreements eliminating the board of directors or restricting their power are valid); 8 Del. Code §350 (shareholder agreements in a closely held corporation are not invalid "on the ground that it so relates to the conduct of the business and affairs of the corporation as to restrict or interfere with the discretion or powers of the board of directors").

corporations, different standard terms are apt to be best. Thus many states supply automatic rules for involuntary dissolution in closely held but not publicly held corporations. Development of special close corporation statutes reflects the utility of a set of presumptive rules tailored to closely held corporations. One should avoid exaggerating the importance of these laws, though. The statutes largely track the terms people have been negotiating for years, statute or no. As long as the statutory terms may be adopted or rejected by contract, the primary contribution of special close corporation statutes is a savings, probably a minor one, in the costs of transacting to the preferred solution.

Sometimes the rule of law plays a more important role. The most obvious is dealing with third parties, where voluntary contracting is not feasible. Limited liability to tort creditors is an example. Rules of law also matter when they cannot be varied by agreement. Immutable rules are rare, but there are a few.[12] Rules bite most frequently, though, when parties are ignorant of them until a dispute arises; then they are bound by whatever the standard term happens to be. Many commentators believe that such ignorance is widespread and that the law of closely held corporations is defective because it fails to protect investors who neglect to protect themselves. The extent to which minority shareholders are ignorant of problems they might face is impossible to tell. Close corporations often transact around rules (for example by abrogating their own limited liability), suggesting that real contracts are possible.

Participants in closely held corporations are better informed about their legal rights and obligations than participants in either partnerships or public corporations. Investors in close corporations often put a great deal of their wealth at stake, and the lack of diversification (compared with investors in publicly held firms) induces them to take care. Partnerships can arise by operation of law without any express agreement between the parties; closely held corporations exist only as a result of formal documents and (typically) the assistance of an attorney. The attorney is a specialist provider of information; questions that never occur to the parties have been addressed and solved long ago by others, and attorneys transmit this accumulated expertise. This process of learning (through counsel) from the mistakes of others works reasonably

12. See Md. Corps. & Ass'ns Code §§4–504, 4–601 (prohibiting mergers or transfers of assets of closely held corporations absent unanimous consent).

well in assuring intelligently specialized contractual terms for closely held corporations. The ignorance theory predicts that investors in closely held corporations would fail to provide for restraints on alienation, but they do.

When the organizing documents of a firm fail to provide, say, for dissolution at the will of any investor, while providing for restraints on alienation, this implies that the parties desired the latter type of provision but not the former. We know they got over the cost-of-contracting hurdle and reached agreement. Still, there is residual ambiguity. A missing term likely means that the parties did not want it, but it *could* mean that they were ignorant or that the costs of negotiating a particular term were too high for reasons that are not apparent at scholarly remove. Unfortunately the frequency of a given device will not resolve doubt. If 90 percent of all close firms explicitly provide that dissolution is unavailable, this may mean that the other 10 percent forgot this beneficial provision or that the other 10 percent have an organizational difference that makes this provision unwise.

Drafters of the organizing documents of a closely held corporation cannot avoid a trade-off. On the one hand, they must provide some protection to minority investors to ensure that they receive an adequate return on the minority shareholder's investment if the venture succeeds. On the other hand, they cannot give the minority too many rights, for the minority might exercise their rights in an opportunistic fashion to divert returns. The drafters also must worry about the chance that judges will err in construing the minority's entitlements. Dissolution at will and strict fiduciary duties—the two entitlements whose omission is most commonly chalked up to ignorance—create precisely these problems. In light of the costs of these provisions, it is conceivable, nay certain, that all parties often decide that they are better off without. This makes it inappropriate to imply such terms as a rule. Moreover, the costs of certain contractual terms designed to protect the minority make it far from obvious that such terms should be implied by law, even if many or all of the parties were ignorant at the time of initial investment.

UNCONDITIONAL BUYOUT RIGHTS

Corporations have perpetual life. Because minority shareholders may be locked in while they receive little or no return on their investment, corporate law has long permitted minority share-holders to obtain relief in the form of dissolution in a few situations, including deadlock. Involuntary dissolution requires a valuation of the business (either by a court or by sale of the entire business to a third party) and a distribution of the proceeds to the complaining shareholder. Alternatively, one or more of the parties can buy out the others.

Courts grant involuntary dissolution sparingly. Statutes typically require either a deadlock that makes operation of the business impossible or serious misconduct by those in control. The Model Act, for example, authorizes involuntary dissolution if deadlock causes "irreparable injury" or if those in control "have acted, are acting, or will act in a manner that is illegal, oppressive, fraudulent, or unfairly prejudicial" to the complaining shareholders.[13] Most statutes contain similar provisions.[14]

Even where the relevant statutory criteria arguably have been met, courts have been reluctant to grant involuntary dissolution. In *In re Radom & Neidorff, Inc.,*[15] to take one well-known example, the court declined to dissolve a profitable firm at the request of one of two equal shareholders, even though the other refused to sign salary checks and did not contribute to the running of the business. Other courts have been similarly reluctant despite allegations that those in control have acted wrongfully.[16] These decisions appear odd at first blush. Why should investors be locked forever in mortal combat, dragging down profitable businesses?

The answer is closely related to the reason why people do not put dissolution provisions in their contracts to start with. If it is easy to dissolve a firm there will be more deadlocks, more claims of op-pression. The threat to create a deadlock (or claim oppression) may

13. *Model Statutory Close Corporation Supplement* §40(a)(2), (1), establishing grounds for judicial action, together with §43 (identifying dissolution as a remedy).

14. Ill. Rev. Stat. ch. 32 ¶157.86; N.Y. Bus. Corp. Law §§1104-a, 1118. Robert B. Thompson, "Corporate Dissolution and Shareholders' Reasonable Expecta-tions," 66 *Wash. U. L. Q.* 193 (1988), collects many of the statutes and the deci-sions interpreting them. Although Professor Thompson is the editor of F. Hodge O'Neal and Robert B. Thompson, *O'Neal's Oppression of Minority Shareholders* (2d ed. 1985), the title of that treatise rather overstates the extent to which O'Neal and Thompson think close corporations cast minorities into a pit of ordure.

15. 307 N.Y. 1, 119 N.E.2d 563 (1964).

16. Polikoff v. Dole & Clark Bldg. Corp., 37 Ill. App. 2d 29, 184 N.E.2d 792 (1962); see also Baker v. Commercial Body Builders, Inc., 264 Or. 614, 507 P.2d 387 (1973).

be used to induce the other party to hand over more of the firm's profits. The anticipation of opportunistic behavior of this sort will make the entire business transaction less attractive at the outset. And when dissolution is readily available, trying to settle differences after a threat to create a deadlock (or cry foul) is very touchy. Ordinarily, if the number of contracting parties is small enough, and property rights are well specified, the parties will dicker to the optimal solution no matter what the legal rule may be. (The Coase Theorem again.) The right to call on a judge may undermine the specificity of the property right, because the parties must predict how a judge will decide. The more open-ended the standard, the more trouble they have predicting; the more trouble they have predicting, the less likely they are to resolve their differences short of litigation, even when there are only two parties. In short, the parties may want to make deadlock costly (so there will be less of it) and keep the courts out when deadlock occurs (so they can settle their own disputes).

Restrictive legal rules concerning involuntary dissolution also create incentives for the parties to establish less expensive methods of adjusting conflicts. They may do this when they start the firm, for example by including buyout provisions or voting agreements with some procedure for resolving deadlocks. Although negotiations in the absence of a prior agreement may be difficult because of problems of bilateral monopoly, the parties nonetheless have strong incentives to resolve their differences in one way or another to obtain the benefits of a profitable business.[17]

Doubtless a minority shareholder who has not bargained for protection will be in a weak bargaining position in the event of oppression. Private settlement is likely to produce a sale by the minority to the corporation or other shareholders on unattractive terms. Those who sympathize with the plight of investors who turn out to be powerless *ex post* have advocated relaxing the standards for involuntary dissolution and allowing a minority shareholder to obtain dissolution whenever his "reasonable expectations" have been frustrated. One judge has adopted this view.[18] John Hetherington

17. See Richard A. Posner, *Economic Analysis of Law* 14.13 (3d ed. 1986).

18. Topper v. Park Sheraton Pharmacy, Inc., 107 Misc. 2d 25, 433 N.Y.S.2d 359 (Sup. Ct. 1980) (discharge of shareholder from employment constituted "oppressive" conduct within meaning of New York statute whether or not discharge was for cause). *Topper* transforms a fault-based statute into a strict liability statute.

and Michael Dooley have gone further and argued that shareholders in closely held corporations should have the right to force the corporation or other shareholders to purchase their shares at an agreed on price or, failing agreement, at a price fixed by the court.[19] Only a nonwaivable right to "put" one's shares to the firm, Hetherington and Dooley argue, solves the "unique" problems of illiquidity and exploitation faced by minority shareholders in closely held corporations.

These proposals, particularly an option to be cashed out on demand, depend on the suppressed assumptions that existing law does not adequately constrain those in control from taking actions to the detriment of the minority and that allowing shareholders to force dissolution of the firm is costless. Neither is accurate. The restrictive rule of involuntary dissolution based on fault does not leave the minority shareholder without any remedy but rather limits involuntary dissolution to egregious cases. Other remedies, such as damages for breach of fiduciary duty (discussed below) or the appointment of a custodian or provisional director, are available. If these are insufficient in a particular case, investors have the option of bargaining for more protection. They don't, which ought to tell us something.

Options and puts are costly to provide and worth something to those who have them. The benefits do not seem to match the costs. Few firms other than open-end mutual funds hold the liquid financial assets that permit withdrawal of investments on demand. When the firm holds illiquid assets, the right to withdraw capital may imply a need to borrow—which for a close corporation is difficult because lenders, too, are outsiders. A firm might be willing to cash out its investors if it could either attract new investment or borrow money from a bank, but the terms of the new capital will not be favorable if anyone else can generate the problem anew. When investors double as managers, access to capital from third parties changes the nature of the firm even when it is readily available, making it unlikely that the venturers meant to require cashouts.

A right to withdraw capital from a firm that has no liquid assets

19. John A. C. Hetherington and Michael P. Dooley, "Illiquidity and Exploitation: A Proposed Statutory Solution to the Remaining Close Corporation Problem," 63 *Va. L. Rev.* 1 (1977); see also F. Hodge O'Neal, "Close Corporations: Existing Legislation and Proposed Reform," 33 *Bus. Law.* 873, 883 (1977).

and that does not have an active secondary market in shares also creates difficult (costly) problems of valuation. Any method of valuation is inexact (recall the difficulties of determining "fair value" in an appraisal, covered in Chapter 6); different estimators will reach radically different conclusions regarding the value of the firm and a particular shareholder's proportionate interest. Demands for cash in exchange for stock may reflect the error of the process more than anything else: when the investor thinks the appraiser will make a mistake, he puts his stock, and otherwise he keeps it. That bias makes having outsider investors more costly to the firm and so makes it harder to raise capital. All of the uncertainties also compound the problem of negotiating.

Each effect of a right to put stock to the firm—the possibility of having to sell illiquid assets at distress prices (or borrow at high-risk rates) and the uncertainties in valuation—encourages opportunistic behavior by minorities. The automatic buyout right, in other words, gives minority shareholders who have a relatively smaller stake in the venture the ability to impose costs on other investors that is absent under a fault standard for involuntary dissolution. Minorities can use this to extract a disproportionate share of benefits from other investors. The majority might be able to avoid the problem by selling the firm as a unit to a third party and paying off the minority; a threat to sell also might work. But in close firms, much of the value comes from the specialized services of the entrepreneur-managers; a change in the management and ownership structure may greatly reduce the value of the firm. A sale of the firm as a unit would destroy value unless the original managers bought the firm once again. The venturers will wish to avoid the costs of this complex transaction.

An unconditional right to withdraw capital from the firm also may be prejudicial to creditors. Under the rule of limited liability, creditors look only to the assets in the corporate treasury for satisfaction. If any shareholder can withdraw assets from the corporate treasury for any reason, the likelihood that a particular extension of credit will not be repaid increases. Creditors will demand compensation for the new risk. Controlling shareholders will make their own adjustments, such as selling debt rather than equity to potential dissidents or charging more for shares. Given competition in capital markets, this would not work to the "detriment" of either majority or minority, but it would make the close corporation a less satisfactory vehicle and squander some of its comparative advantage in controlling agency costs.

Ex ante, therefore, it is unlikely that an unconditional right to withdraw capital from the firm is desirable even from the perspective of minority shareholders. Although a right to bail out would deter the majority from committing "oppressive" acts, it would also deter the majority from committing profitable acts that might lead the minority to use (or threaten to use) its entitlement to withdraw as a lever to get a larger share. It would give a minority greater protection against opportunistic behavior *ex post,* but at the cost of greater transaction costs as deadlocks multiply, an increase in the price of equity and debt capital, and perhaps the denial of any opportunity to invest. We therefore think it useful to observe what people actually do when they negotiate buyout rights. Typically, shareholders do not have extensive rights to withdraw capital from the firm. They may do so only on certain events such as termination of employment, retirement, or death.

The failure of the parties themselves to provide routinely for a right to withdraw capital from the firm has important implications. It suggests, for example, that it would be inefficient to impose this provision on shareholders in closely held corporations and not allow them to opt out. It also suggests that courts should not readily infer a right to withdraw capital from the firm on behalf of minority shareholders. It vindicates the current corporate law, which (here's our refrain again) follows the contractual path of wealth maximization despite the cries of "unfairness."

STRICT STANDARDS OF FIDUCIARY DUTY

Courts rarely interfere with the decisions of managers of publicly held firms (see Chapter 4). Some say that judges should treat the acts of managers of close corporations with suspicion, however, because of the absence of the disciplinary effects of the capital market and other market mechanisms. One rationale for the business judgment rule is that managers who make errors (and even those who engage in self-dealing) are penalized by market forces while judges who make errors are not. Managers have better incentives to make correct business decisions than do judges. If neither managers nor courts are disciplined by markets, this justification has less force. Still, the smaller number of participants in closely held corporations ensures that managers bear more of the costs of their actions and facilitates contractual arrangements between the parties to reduce the likelihood of self-dealing. The differences between publicly and closely held corporations, in other words, do not suggest unambiguously that the level of scrutiny should vary or, if it does, in which direction.

Now courts might use the same standard of review for the two types of corporations but apply it differently based on the structural differences in corporate organization. *Michaels v. Michaels*[20] provides a good illustration. The question in *Michaels* was whether two shareholders had a duty to disclose the possibility of the sale of the company to a third, who had agreed to sell his shares after a falling out but had not yet sold them. Although publicly traded firms may not tell material fibs about negotiations, they are under no duty to disclose spontaneously.[21] The Seventh Circuit stated that close corporations would be governed by the same formal rule but that its application could lead to a different result in the two contexts. The court held that the manager should disclose the negotiations for two reasons: a minority shareholder in a closely held corporation, faced with a choice of selling out at a given price or continuing in a minority position after a falling out with no prospect of return on investment, would undoubtedly consider the possibility of the sale of the entire company important information; too, disclosure of preliminary merger discussions would present none of the problems it does for public firms.

This approach has implications beyond the duty to disclose. For example, managers of publicly held corporations may not engage in self-interested transactions unless they convince a court or disinterested decision makers within the firm that the transaction is beneficial. The same fiduciary rule could be applied in closely held corporations, but its application would vary because of differences between the two types of firms. For example, the decision to terminate an employee in a publicly held corporation is a classic example of the exercise of business judgment that a court would not second-guess. In a closely held corporation, by contrast, termination of an

20. 767 F.2d 1185 (7th Cir. 1985). See also Jordan v. Duff & Phelps, Inc., 815 F.2d 429, 434–439 (7th Cir. 1987).

21. Basic, Inc. v. Levinson, 485 U.S. 224, 239–240 & n.17 (1988); Flamm v. Eberstadt, 814 F.2d 1169, 1174–79 (7th Cir. 1987).

employee can be a way to appropriate a disproportionate share of the firm's earnings. It makes sense, therefore, to have greater judicial review of terminations of managerial (or investing) employees in closely held corporations than would be consistent with the business judgment rule. The same approach could be used with salary, dividend, and employment decisions in closely held corporations where the risks of conflicts of interest are greater.[22]

Many courts, however, apply a unitary business judgment rule in reviewing employment, salary, and dividend decisions in closely held corporations.[23] One defense of this result is again to observe that a hard-nosed judicial attitude creates incentives for parties to protect themselves by contract or otherwise (for example, by arbitration).[24] Although application of the deferential business judgment rule no doubt is harsh in some cases, it does have the advantage of limiting the judicial role to enforcing, rather than writing, contracts between the parties. It is one thing for a court to require disclosure, as in *Michaels;* it is quite another to invent substantive terms as it must when asked to decide whether a particular dividend, compensation, or employment decision is appropriate.

If a court is unavoidably entwined in a dispute, it must decide what the parties would have agreed to had they written a contract resolving all contingencies. The difficulties that result when a court misses this point are illustrated by the much applauded case of *Donahue v. Rodd Electrotype Co.*[25] The closely held corporation purchased the shares of its long-time manager, who had been with the firm for thirty-five years but was seventy-seven years old and in

22. See O'Donnell v. Maring Repair Serv., 530 F. Supp. 1199 (S.D.N.Y. 1982); Exadaktilos v. Cinnaminson Realty Co., 167 N.J. Super. 141, 400 A.2d 554 (Law Div. 1979), affirmed, 173 N.J. Super. 559, 414 A.2d 994 (App. Div. 1980); Meiselman v. Meiselman, 309 N.C. 279, 307 S.E.2d 551 (1983).

23. See Gay v. Gay's Supermarkets, 343 A.2d 577 (Me. 1975); Gottfried v. Gottfried, 73 N.Y.S.2d 692 (Sup. Ct. 1947); Ziddell v. Diddell, Inc., 277 Or. 413, 560 P.2d 1086 (1977). Some courts seem to apply both a stricter standard and the business judgment rule in the same case. See, for instance, Alaska Plastics, Inc. v. Coppock, 621 P.2d 270 (Alaska 1980); Romanik v. Lurie Home Supply Center, Inc., 105 Ill. App. 3d 1118, 435 N.E.2d 712 (1982); Miller v. Magline, Inc., 76 Mich. App. 284, 256 N.W.2d 761 (1977); Masinter v. WEBCO Co., 262 S.E.2d 433 (W. Va. 1980).

24. See Jordan v. Duff & Phelps, Inc., 815 F.2d 429, 445–450 (7th Cir. 1987) (Posner, J., dissenting), for an especially strong statement of this position.

25. 367 Mass. 578, 328 N.E.2d 505 (1975).

poor health. He no longer owned a controlling interest. The dominant shareholders (the founder's sons) wanted him to retire and authorized the purchase of some of his shares. The remaining investor (the only one unrelated to the controlling family) demanded that the corporation purchase her shares on the same terms. The corporation refused, stating that it did not possess adequate funds. The ensuing suit alleged that the controlling shareholders breached a fiduciary duty by causing the corporation to purchase some shares while refusing to extend the same benefit to other investors.

The trial court found that the price was less than either the liquidating or book value, that the purchase did not alter control or prejudice plaintiff or creditors in any way, and that the directors acted in good faith in approving the purchase. Nonetheless, the Supreme Judicial Court of Massachusetts held the transaction unlawful. Shareholders in closely held corporations, the court wrote, owe each other the utmost duty of good faith and loyalty, a higher duty than their counterparts in publicly held corporations. This higher duty requires controlling shareholders who use their positions to confer benefits on themselves to do the same for all investors. Thus the controlling group's purchase of shares breached its fiduciary duty. As a remedy, the court ordered the firm either to rescind the purchase or to offer to purchase plaintiff's stock at a price per share equal to that paid to the long-time manager.

Grave reflections on the plight of minority investors in closely held corporations and stirring proclamations of fiduciary duty fill the opinion. Completely overlooked in all of this rhetoric was the basic question—which outcome would the parties have selected had they contracted in anticipation of this contingency? Although no one can answer such a question with certainty (precisely because the parties did not), it is most unlikely that they would have selected a rule requiring an equal opportunity for all. Buyouts facilitate the retirement of a manager who, by virtue of advancing and age and poor health, no longer contributes. Stock transactions on death or retirement are common in closely held corporations, mandatory in many. Buy-sell agreements provide some liquidity and ensure that the identity of the managers and the investors remains the same, reducing agency problems. At the same time, the limited scope of the obligation reduces the cost of cash payouts or profitable patterns of investment. No comparable commonly used agreement requires a firm to purchase all shares if it buys any. Firms often undertake to buy the shares of all who retire, and the court might have made something of this. The plaintiff was the widow of a long-time employee whose shares were not purchased when he died. Among the firms that have written explicit contracts concerning the repurchase of shares, some allow selective repurchases from departing employees and some make repurchase mandatory. It would have been difficult to determine into which category a firm such as Rodd Electrotype fit. The court did not pursue this line, however, and it did not suggest that anything turned on the employment history of the current owners of the shares.

Not surprisingly, courts have found the equal opportunity rule of *Donahue* impossible to administer. It is hard to imagine, for example, how closely held corporations could function under a requirement that all shareholders have an "equal opportunity" to receive salary increases and continue in office regardless of their conduct. Yet this is the logical implication of *Donahue,* which holds that the business justifications for unequal treatment are irrelevant. In light of this threat to the day-to-day functioning of closely held corporations, it was predictable that judges would either refuse to follow *Donahue* or limit its scope.[26] In *Wilkes v. Springside Nursing Homes, Inc.,*[27] for example, the court that decided *Donahue* stated that an employee and shareholder of a closely held corporation may be fired or denied a salary increase when there is a legitimate business purpose for the action that could not be furthered without disadvantaging the minority. *Wilkes* inquired into the business purpose of the conduct at issue, precisely what it had disdained in *Donahue.* Thus the court effectively repudiated the equal opportunity rule and adopted instead a standard similar to the one used to review conflict of interest transactions in publicly held corporations. This standard, which gives some but not absolute protection to the minority, is in all likelihood closer to the bargain the parties would have reached themselves if transactions costs were zero.

Understanding fiduciary duties as implied terms in contractual

---

26. See Commolli v. Commolli, 241 Ga. 471, 246 S.E.2d 278 (1978); Toner v. Baltimore Envelope Co., 304 Nd. 256, 498 A.2d 642 (1985); Wilkes v. Springside Nursing Home, Inc., 370 Mass. 842, 353 N.E.2d 657 (1976); Ziddell, 277 Or. at 423, 560 P.2d at 1091; Masinter v. WEBCO, Inc., 262 S.E.2d 433 (W. Va. 1980).

27. 370 Mass. 842, 353 N.E.2d 657 (1976).

agreements also sheds light on the question whether minority shareholders owe fiduciary duties to the majority. Unanimity agreements, which exist in many closely held corporations, create a risk of deadlock. A minority shareholder may refuse to consent to corporate acts, paralyzing the firm. Although this right helps minority shareholders protect themselves against opportunistic behavior by the majority, it creates incentives for the minority to behave opportunistically toward the majority to extract disproportionate concessions.

Would fiduciary duties running from minority to majority diminish the costs created by the minority's ability to exercise veto power? Several courts have said that fiduciary duties have net benefits.[28] The issue is difficult because any constraint on the minority's veto power increases the probability that the majority will be able to exploit the minority notwithstanding the minority's bargained-for protection. One guide is whether the decision at issue might have a disproportionate effect on the minority. A minority shareholder in a closely held corporation with a supermajority voting or quorum requirement would be justified in failing to attend a meeting and blocking the election of a new director who might act adversely toward him but might not be justified in failing to attend a meeting to authorize the purchase of a machine in an arm's-length transaction. The veto in the former situation is consistent with the function of the protection, while the same action in the latter situation is likely to be opportunistic.[29]

28. See Smith v. Atlantic Properties, Inc., 12 Mass. App. 201, 422 N.E.2d 798 (1981) (minority shareholder's use of veto power unreasonable). But cf. Neuman v. Pike, 591 F.2d 191 (2d Cir. 1979) (no implied covenant that minority shareholders vote reasonably). The need of a legal rule to protect the majority against the minority is questionable given the majority's ability to dissolve the firm or take other action to eliminate a minority shareholder. See Matteson v. Ziebarth, 40 Wash. 2d 286, 242 P.2d 1025 (1952).

29. The problem of distinguishing legitimate exercise of contract rights from opportunistic behavior is pervasive in the law of contracts. See Varouj Aivazian, Michael J. Trebilcock, and Michael Penny, "The Law of Contract Modifications: The Uncertain Quest for a Benchmark of Enforceability," 22 *Osgoode Hall L. J.* 173 (1984); Benjamin Klein, Robert G. Crawford, and Armen A. Alchian, "Vertical Integration, Appropriable Rents, and the Competitive Contracting Process," 21 *J. L. & Econ.* 297 (1978); Timothy J. Muris, "Opportunistic Behavior and the Law of Contracts," 65 *Minn. L. Rev.* 521 (1981); Oliver E. Williamson, "Credible Commitments: Using Hostages to Support Exchange," 73 *Am. Econ. Rev.* 519 (1983).

THE PARTNERSHIP ANALOGY

That closely held corporations are really "incorporated partnerships" is a common refrain.[30] The participants in the venture view each other as partners; therefore, the argument runs, they should be governed by the law of partnerships. Equal sharing rules, automatic buyout rights, and strict fiduciary duties are fundamental principles of partnership law and so, sponsors of the analogy contend, also should be fundamental principles of the law of closely held corporations.

There is something to the analogy. Participants in smaller firms who are unable to reduce risk by diversifying their investments are more likely to contract for equal sharing rules and to opt for other principles that constrain managers' discretion. Still, there are problems with pushing the analogy too far. First, at least with respect to automatic buyout rights, the analogy is based on a misstatement of partnership law.[31] Although partnership law allows any partner (unless all agree otherwise in advance) to disinvest at any time and dissolve the firm,[32] the withdrawing partner may be liable in damages for "wrongful" termination[33] and may be able to disinvest only on disadvantageous terms.[34] A withdrawing partner gets only the current value of the partnership, not a claim on future cash flows; equity securities, by contrast, represent the present value of future

30. See Hetherington and Dooley, supra note 19, at 2 (close corporation is the "functional equivalent" of a partnership); Carlos D. Israels, "The Close Corporation and the Law," 33 *Cornell L. Q.* 488, 488 (1948) ("the participants in a close corporation consider themselves 'partners' and seek to conduct the corporate affairs to a greater or lesser extent in the manner of a partnership"); F. Hodge O'Neal, "Preventive Law: Tailoring the Corporate Form of Business to Ensure Fair Treatment of All," 49 *Miss. L. J.* 529, 533 (1978) ("Businessmen forming a close corporation frequently consider themselves partners; they incorporate only to obtain limited liability or other corporate advantages").

31. A point forcefully made in Robert M. Hillman, "The Dissatisfied Participant in the Solvent Business Venture: A Consideration of the Relative Permanence of Partnerships and Close Corporations," 67 *Minn. L. Rev.* 1 (1982).

32. See *Uniform Partnership Act* §31(1)(b), (2) (1914) (dissolution of partnership may be caused by express will of partner).

33. Ibid. at §38(2) (partner who acts wrongfully in dissolving the firm is liable in damages).

34. Ibid. at §38(2)(c) (dissolving partner not entitled to proportionate share of goodwill if remaining partners continue in the business).

profits. For both reasons the Hetherington and Dooley proposal for automatic buyout rights in closely held corporations goes well beyond existing doctrine.

Second, the assumption that participants in closely held corporations want to be governed by partnership law is questionable. The participants incorporated for a reason. Perhaps the reason was limited liability or favorable tax treatment, and in all other respects they wanted to be treated like partners. But this is not the only possibility. Corporate law is different from partnership law in many ways, and the venturers may desire to preserve these differences. Partners, for example, are entitled to share equally in the profits and management of the partnership,[35] are agents for each other, have the right to veto any decisions made by the majority on matters outside the ordinary course of business,[36] and may dissolve the partnership at any time if they are willing to bear the consequences. Corporate law treats each of these differently. Proponents of the partnership analogy assume that participants in closely held corporations are knowledgeable enough to incorporate to obtain the benefits of favorable tax treatment but ignorant of all other differences between corporate and partnership law. There is no support for this assumption once you recognize that people have to jump through a lot of formal hoops (assisted by counsel) to incorporate but can become partners by accident.

The right inquiry is always what the parties would have contracted for had transactions costs been nil, not whether closely held corporations are more similar to partnerships than to publicly held corporations. Failure to recognize the limited role of analogical reasoning can have significant consequences. The court that decided *Donahue* was apparently so concerned about establishing the similarities between closely held corporations and partnerships that it never considered the possibility that its rule of equal opportunity might be inconsistent with the observed behavior of participants in both partnerships and closely held corporations. Both types of firms must provide some mechanism for dealing with retirements or terminations in situations where the firm will continue to exist. Most firms could not survive if the purchase of the interest of a retiring member required that everyone else be given the opportu-

35. Ibid. at §18(a), (c).
36. Ibid. at §18(g), (h).

nity to sell out at the same price. Because the court never asked what the parties would have found in their joint interest, it missed the boat.

Participants in business ventures are free to reflect their wishes explicitly in a written contract. Both partnership and corporate law enforce private decisions. When the parties do not or cannot contract explicitly, it is often difficult to discern what they would have done if contracting were costless. This subtle inquiry is not made any simpler by asking whether closely held corporations are really partnerships. This latter focus simply puts everyone off the scent; indeed, it may be perverse because it directs attention away from the questions why people formed the corporation and why, having done so, they did not adopt partnership-like rules by contract. Even if the parties did not consciously decide to opt out of the partnership rule, all this means is that they were asleep. What reason have we to think that if they had been awake they would have selected the partnership rule?

One reason might be tax. Sometimes people pick the corporate form solely because of its tax consequences. This is not, however, a problem of somnambulation. Whether investors select the corporate form for tax reasons or for any others, they want to operate under the rules that maximize the expected return from the business venture. Investors who are aware of the tax consequences of the form they select are likely to be aware of other consequences; they commonly hire expert advice. A claim that people alert to the tax effects of incorporation were unaware of other effects is hard to take seriously, and when such people do not contract for the use of partnership-like rules, it is appropriate to apply corporate rules.

A second reason might be the anticipated triviality of the rule. It is costly to dicker for the application of a rule other than the standard term supplied by law. Parties (or their experts) must identify the problem and then transact in sufficient detail to solve it; the accumulation of cases under the existing legal standard supplies a level of detail that is costly to duplicate through private bargaining. As we suggested at the end of Chapter 1, some "contractual" terms for infrequently occurring problems may be public goods.

If the gains from private bargaining are small—perhaps because the legal rule is only slightly inferior to some alternative, perhaps because it is sufficiently unlikely that events will bring a given legal rule into play, perhaps because the parties cannot appropriate all benefits of a new and better solution—people will not incur the costs of striking a bargain. If the costs of bargaining are high enough, we may be left with terminal ambiguity. We suspect, although we cannot prove, that this is not a frequent problem. Once the lawyers identify a problem, new lawyers can reuse the solution the first lawyers develop. Different lawyers solve different infrequent cases.

Close corporations differ in size, and the larger ones will find it worthwhile to incur greater costs of transacting. (A 1 percent chance of encountering a problem is worth more to a $10 million firm than to a $100,000 firm.) Larger firms routinely have detailed provisions for handling deadlocks or buying out the shares of retiring employees, even though smaller firms may leave these issues unaddressed. Courts should observe how the larger firms tackle a given problem. These firms are the most likely to surmount any transaction cost hurdle and to spend the most time dealing with the problem once they have elected to do so. The solutions these larger firms offer may be copied and applied to other close corporations, unless there is some reason to think that the proper solution is a function of the firm's size. If larger firms elect not to address a subject through contract, then it is best to conclude that the presumptive rule does not need tinkering.

10

Trading on Inside Information

Our focus in this chapter is the relation between insiders' trading and fiduciary duties. Whether investors would want managers to trade on particular information depends on the effect trading has on shareholders' wealth. This in turn depends on whether a firm's managers or its investors value more the property right in information. We discuss this and the related issue whether firms can allocate the property right in valuable information by contract. We then look at the state and federal rules regulating inside trading. Your authors have written separately about this topic and have reached conclusions that differ in emphasis about its likely effects.[1] We offer here not resolution but assessment. Before addressing substantive issues, however, we define "inside trading."

The Meaning of Inside Information

One definition is trading by parties who are better informed than their opposite numbers. No market could exist with such a broad definition of prohibited trading. If each trader has the same information as every other, there is little incentive to trade. More important, the incentive to acquire information in the first place goes down if the opportunity to profit by virtue of superior information

1. Dennis W. Carlton and Daniel R. Fischel, "The Regulation of Insider Trading," 35 *Stan. L. Rev.* 857 (1983); Fischel, "Insider Trading and Investment Analysts: An Economic Analysis of Dirks v. Securities and Exchange Commission," 13 *Hofstra L. Rev.* 127 (1984); Frank H. Easterbrook, "Insider Trading as an Agency Problem," in *Principals and Agents: The Structure of Business* 81 (J. Pratt and R. Zeckhauser eds. 1985); Easterbrook, "Insider Trading, Secret Agents, Evidentiary Privileges, and the Production of Information," 1981 *Sup. Ct. Rev.* 309, 314–339. This chapter is a lot shorter than these four articles, to which readers should repair if intrigued.

is eliminated. And if there is no incentive to acquire information, markets lose their function of providing price signals to diverse participants in the economy.

An alternative definition is trading by those with unequal access to information. Managers are said to have "unequal access" and so are forbidden to trade when the news is "material." The difficulty with this definition is timing. Unequal when—before the information comes into being or after? An analyst has valuable information. Does everyone have "equal access" because anyone could have hired the analyst or become one himself? The same can be said in the case of corporate managers. Corporate managers have access to information, which is valuable in the market. If one who is an "outsider" today could have become a manager by devoting the same time and skill as today's "insider" did, is access to information equal or unequal? There is no principled answer to such questions.

Better, then, to identify property rights in information. Trading by managers (or others) in possession of valuable information is appropriate if the insiders own that information. They may get the right by dint of hard work (as stock analysts do when evaluating obscure clues about a firm's performance), or generate it themselves (as tender offer bidders create the news about their own future acts) or buy it from the firm (as managers may do expressly or implicitly). Or traders may steal news from others who create or own the information. Such an approach replaces the unanswerable "what is inside information?" question with tractable matters of contract. We may ask whether certain persons do (or should) own the right to use information. Still, difficult problems abound. Perhaps the most difficult is whether, in the absence of explicit contracts, managers should be deemed to own valuable information obtained during their tenure.

Before we turn to this, a warning. Much of the lore about inside trading treats it as a unitary phenomenon, typified by the corporate manager who learns that the firm has struck a mother lode and then buys stock before the news escapes, depriving unsuspecting public investors of their profit without having done anything to make gains more common.[2] Those who decry inside trading as "unfair" con-

---

2. The paradigm is SEC v. Texas Gulf Sulphur Co., 401 F.2d 833 (2d Cir. 1968) (in banc), where exactly this happened.

centrate on such episodes. Rhetoric being what it is, the name—freighted with this nasty connotation—is applied to quite different activities that the speaker wishes to condemn. None of the Supreme Court's "inside trading" cases deals with the manager who trades ahead of public release of corporate news. Vincent Chiarella, a printer, decoded the name of a tender offer target and bought its stock before the bid could be announced. Ray Dirks, a stock analyst, nosed out a fraud at a widely held firm and alerted his clients to sell. R. Foster Winans, a writer for the *Wall Street Journal,* told friends to buy the stocks to be touted in forthcoming columns. Charles Lazzaro, a broker, duped his clients into buying stock by leading them to think that they were receiving tips about corporate secrets.[3]

These are vastly different problems. Chiarella broke his promise to his employer's customer, effectively stealing information—but it was information the client had every right to use for his own benefit without telling investors. Dirks nosed out a scam, and the right to reveal the news to his own clients compensated him for his efforts, which leads to more digging by other analysts. Winans broke his contract and in so doing dragged down the reputation of the *Journal* for honest reporting. Lazzaro committed a classic fraud, injuring his clients. All of these cases may be resolved without reference to the inside trading paradigm, just as all may be resolved by using the property rights approach we discuss.

Other cases tagged "inside trading" present still other kinds of problems. "Warehousers" who line up stock in advance of a tender offer on the bidder's tip have consensual access to the information they use; the legal status of their conduct depends on whether their stock counts as part of a group for purposes of the prebid limits in the Williams Act. This is independent of any more conventional approach to inside trading. Investment bankers who use information obtained from clients to sabotage their clients' plans—by

3. See Chiarella v. United States, 445 U.S. 222 (1980) (the printer's case); Dirks v. SEC, 463 U.S. 646 (1983) (the analyst's case); Carpenter v. United States, 484 U.S. 19 (1987) (the reporter's case, in which the Court affirmed a conviction for defrauding the newspaper by using the mails and divided 4–4 on the securities law question); Bateman Eichler, Hill Richards, Inc. v. Berner, 472 U.S. 299 (1985) (the bogus inside information case, resolved by holding that the broker could not use the *in pari delicto* defense to escape liability on the theory that his clients should have known that they were forbidden to trade on material inside information).

leaking the news to rivals, by taking the opposite side in trades, and so on—not only break their contracts but also are knaves whose deeds reduce the efficiency of markets. Again their acts may be condemned without asking complex questions about inside trading. We put such matters to one side for now in order to concentrate on the paradigm.

Why Firms Might Allocate to Managers Property Rights in Information

Trading by insiders (for this purpose, managers and those who receive the news from managers) may provide firms with a valuable mechanism for communicating information to market participants. Allowing insiders to trade also may create incentives to maximize the value of the firm to the benefit of insiders and outside shareholders alike.

TRADING AND THE TRANSMISSION OF INFORMATION

We discussed in Chapter 7 the efficiency of capital markets, and we take up in the next chapter the effects of mandatory disclosure rules. A brief recap and preview will be useful here. The better stock prices reflect information, the more useful they are as a guide to capital investment. From the perspective of any one firm, however, efficient capital markets are a public good. Why, then, does a firm disclose information about itself?

One reason is that disclosure can reduce wasteful expenditures on search and reduce investors' uncertainty about the firm. A second is that disclosure of information by the firm also may enable the firm's current investors to sell their shares to outsiders at a higher price, on average. If the firm discloses no information, outsiders may assume the worst and discount the price they are willing to pay for shares by a factor that reflects their uncertainty. Finally, accurately priced securities give firms information about whether their managers are successful. Markets for managerial services and for corporate control then function more effectively. Better managers signal their quality by willingness to tie a higher proportion of their compensation to stock performance. Accurate prices then enable these managers to receive the rewards for their superior performance.

Complete disclosure, however, would not make sense. Disclosure is costly, and at some point the costs exceed the benefits of increased disclosure. Moreover, disclosure might destroy the information's value. It would not be in investors' interest to disclose, for example, that a confidential study revealed the presence of valuable ore on land the firm seeks to purchase. Information about plans for future products or acquisitions also is less valuable if released.[4]

Investors would like the price of the stock to reflect the value of this information, without the information itself coming out. The combination of desires is hard to achieve, but trading by insiders may help. If managers trade, the price of stock moves closer to what it would have been had the information been disclosed. The effect may be powerful when trading joins with partial or vague disclosures ("We have good news but can't say just what"), for outsiders who see insiders put their money where their mouths are will be more likely to credit the firm's statements. The same effect occurs when insiders' trades imply the truth of more concrete disclosures.[5]

Whether trading without disclosure can move the price close to the one reflecting full information depends on the amount of "noise" surrounding the trade. The greater the ability of market participants to identify inside trading and deduce its cause, the more information such trading conveys.[6] At the extreme, trading by insiders is as revealing as disclosure. But as insiders limit the size of their positions because of risk aversion and camouflage their trading to some degree, they convey less information by trading than by (credible) disclosure.

Inside Trading as a Compensation Device

Firms try to deal with the agency costs of management by writing contracts that align managers' interests with those of investors. Paying a worker a piece rate rather than a salary creates correct

4. See Flamm v. Eberstadt, 814 F.2d 1169, 1176–78 (7th Cir. 1987).

5. Mark Hirschey and Janis K. Zaima, "Insider Trading, Ownership Structure, and the Market Assessment of Corporate Sell-Offs," 44 *J. Fin.* 971 (1989).

6. See Charles R. Plott and Shyam Sunder, "Efficiency of Experimental Security Markets with Insider Information: An Application of Rational-Expectations Models," 90 *J. Pol. Econ.* 663 (1982) (demonstration using simulation techniques that markets adjust very rapidly to inside information).

incentives if the employer can observe output more easily than effort—so too with bonuses to managers if the firm succeeds—but such arrangements do not work automatically. The principal may have difficulty in observing output, especially the product of managers. Even if output can be observed, it typically depends on factors other than one person's performance, including the efforts of other managers and random events such as developments in the industry or the economy as a whole.

Contracts that provide for periodic adjustments based on (imperfectly) observed effort and output are superior to contracts that fix compensation in advance of either effort or results. Adjustment by renegotiation is hard given the difficulty of monitoring the effort and measuring the output of individual managers. To reduce the costs of contracting, firms seek to minimize the number of renegotiations by choosing "incentive-compatible" arrangements, which link managers' and investors' fates automatically.

Inside trading allows a manager to alter his compensation package in light of new knowledge, avoiding continual renegotiation. The manager "renegotiates" each time he trades. This in turn increases the manager's incentive to acquire and develop valuable information in the first place (as well as to invest in firm-specific human capital). A manager who observes an investment for the firm—such as a potential value-increasing merger or a new technology—will be more inclined to pursue this opportunity if rewarded on success. Profits in the market are such a reward. The alternative is to tell others of the opportunity, explain that it can be realized with extra effort, and hope to be compensated by some form of *ex post* settlement. Insiders' trades reduce the uncertainty and cost of renegotiation and thus prod managers to produce valuable information. Moreover, because managers determine the frequency of trades, they can tailor their compensation scheme to their attitudes toward risk.

Inside trading also provides firms with valuable information concerning prospective managers. It is difficult for firms to identify those prospective managers who will work hard and not be overly risk-averse in their choice of projects for the firm. Basing compensation in part on trading is one method for distinguishing superior from inferior managers. Because trading rewards managers who create valuable information and are willing to take risks, managers who most prefer such compensation schemes may be those who are the least risk-averse and the most capable. Self-selection reduces the costs of screening potential managers, the monitoring costs created by risk-averse managers, and the opportunity costs from suboptimal investment decisions.

Why Firms Might Restrict Trading on Inside Information

We have offered a number of reasons why shareholders' wealth may be greater if managers who possess valuable information are allowed to trade. But it does not follow that investors always benefit if anyone in possession of valuable information may trade. Here are some reasons why firms might restrict the use of their information.

PREVENTING THEFT

Trading on information can be a form of theft. Firms regularly forbid lawyers, accountants, printers, and others to trade on news about the firm. Those who trade notwithstanding promises to abstain are stealing assets of the firm as surely as if they reach into the till for cash exceeding their salaries. Contractual bans on trading were customary long before federal law entered the picture. Persons who are responsible neither for creating the information nor for selecting the business projects that generated it (a category that includes lawyers, investment bankers, and many others) promise not to use it. These contracts are the best evidence of the efficient allocation of property rights. Even employees who create information—such as inventors and salesmen compiling customer lists—frequently assign it to the firm by contract.

Consider Vincent Chiarella, a printer who received information about imminent takeover bids. Potential acquirers have powerful reasons to maintain secrecy until they announce their bid, and the bidders encoded the information provided to their printer. Chiarella deciphered the code and bought shares of the targets, which he resold at a profit as soon as the announcements of the bids drove up the price. Although the Supreme Court held that Chiarella did not violate Rule 10b-5 because he did not owe a fiduciary duty to the shareholders of the targets (the prosecutor's only theory), Chiarella appropriated value from the bidders. The extent of the harm to them depends on the extent to which Chiarella's trading increased the cost of the acquisition or, by alerting the target, reduced the probability of success. Appropriation of information from another reduces the incentive to create information and thus indirectly the efficiency of capital markets; and it is harmful (and should be forbidden) for the same reasons theft is harmful.

PERVERSE INCENTIVES

Inside trading may create a moral hazard. Instead of aligning managers' interests with investors' it may separate them. For example, the opportunity to gain from trading may induce managers to increase the volatility of the firm's stock prices so they will have more opportunities to make profitable trades. They may do this by choosing risky investment projects. The greater the volatility of prices, the greater the opportunity for trading profits even if the projects have lower mean returns than other options.

   Prospects of trading also could induce insiders to create bad news. Advance knowledge allows profitable trading whether the news is good or bad, and bad news is easier to create. At the extreme, if bad information yields private profit, managers may be indifferent between working to make the firm prosperous and working to make it bankrupt. A variant is that inside trading creates incentives for insiders to disseminate false information about the firm so that they can profit by buying and selling mispriced securities.

ATTITUDES TOWARD RISK

Shareholders who have the ability to hold diversified portfolios are efficient risk bearers. Managers, by contrast, hold much of their wealth in human capital, which, together with much of their financial capital, is committed to a single firm. Managers thus want to reduce risk that shows up in the volatility of their compensation. Most would prefer the certainty of $100,000 salary to a salary of $50,000 and a 10 percent chance of a bonus of $500,000, even though the two have the same expected value. Inside trading, then, may be an inefficient compensation scheme. It amounts to paying managers in lottery tickets. The package costs the shareholders the actuarial value of the payoff, but risk-averse managers value the ticket at less than that. The managers receive less than the firm gives up. To the extent this is an important phenomenon, both shareholders and managers gain by curtailing inside trading.

UNFAIRNESS

Public debate, and much of the legal literature, pays little attention to the problems with inside trading we have identified. "Fairness" is the refrain. Managers' trading is said to be "unfair" because managers receive the gains in lieu of the shareholders, who "deserve" them. Information "intended for a corporate purpose" should not be put to private use.[7] To the argument that managers pay in advance, through lower salaries, for the opportunity to reap these gains, throngs respond, "No they don't; they get the salary and the profits too."

Assertions of this stripe beg the question whether information is "intended for a corporate purpose." Information does not "intend" things; people intend things, and they intend to maximize wealth. If the information is more valuable to the firm, then managers will be forbidden to trade; if the right is more valuable when held by managers, they will exercise it. Investors seek to maximize expected returns rather than the payoffs in each case. When unequal divisions contribute to higher expected returns, investors prefer inequality (see Chapter 5). So if some risk of not receiving a gain today (because insiders buy the shares) goes hand in glove with higher average returns over all firms (because the opportunity to trade is useful in inducing managers to create more gains), investors prefer the risk and the higher return. It is not "unfair" to investors to use a device that makes them wealthier!

Most of those who think inside trading unfair assume that investors want managers to be treated "just like me." Why would a sane investor wish this? Managers must be paid for their effort; shareholders do not receive salaries or bonuses or stock options. Is this unfair or other evidence of skulduggery? If managers receive salaries, the value of the firm is greater than if managers work for love. An argument that inside trading is inconsistent with fiduciary duties, therefore, requires an explanation why managers are al-

---

7. The catchphrase is from In re Cady, Roberts & Co., 40 S.E.C. 907 (1961), the SEC's leading decision denouncing managers' trading. The Supreme Court picked up the phrase in *Dirks*, 463 U.S. at 653–654.

lowed to receive a salary—why top managers may set their own salary—but not to trade when in possession of valuable information. Such arguments exist (we have just given three of them), but they have nothing to do with "fairness."

If we suppose that managers can exploit their position to extract unearned returns, then we must worry about inside trading as a form of exploitation—but we must worry equally about salaries, bonuses, and other forms of compensation (including perquisites). Managers with the power to pay themselves can take their profits once only. They can't take it in salary, and a second time in options, and a third time in trading profits, and a fourth time in perks. Grant that managers can wring so much from investors; then they will take it, and the division between trading profits and skyboxes to football games matters only if the form of compensation has efficiency properties. Thus our fundamental question: what *are* the consequences of trading for investors' wealth? That is unrelated to fairness and beliefs about managers' preferred position.

To the extent "fairness" arguments suppose that managers snap up profits that otherwise would go to deserving, long-term, investors, there are two further problems. First, the only investors who lose out to insiders are those who have already decided to sell. A buy order from a manager does not force anyone to sell. Second, if managers are knocked out of the market, investors are not the winners. Readers of the *Wall Street Journal,* however early in the morning they call their brokers, come too late. Next in line behind managers are market professionals—analysts, arbitrageurs, investment advisers. These pros act on information in advance of the average investor. To disqualify managers from trading is to pass the informational advantage to brokers, investment banks, and others on the Street. This may account for the political support the professional investment community offers for restrictions on managers' trading.[8]

Inside Trading and the Coase Theorem

Trading by insiders or others in possession of nonpublic information will not be uniformly beneficial or detrimental. Whether such

8. Credit for this insight belongs to David D. Haddock and Jonathan R. Macey, "Regulation on Demand: A Private Interest Model, with an Application to Insider Trading Regulation," 30 *J. L. & Econ.* 311 (1987).

trading is beneficial varies from firm to firm, industry to industry. Even within firms, the effects of trading depend on the context and positions of the employees involved. Firms that allow top managers to trade may want to preclude the general counsel from trading in advance of a takeover bid, or engineers from trading in advance of a patent.

That no uniform rule is optimal implies that the subject is best left to negotiations between insiders (and others) and the firm. Courts would enforce actual contracts, just as they regularly do concerning salary and access to trade secrets. The Coase Theorem implies that firms and insiders have strong incentives to allocate the property right in valuable information to the highest valuing user. If, as many say, shareholders' wealth plummets when insiders trade on non-public information, both insiders and shareholders will gain from prohibiting the practice. Such contracts are negotiated routinely with investment banks, lawyers, scientists, and salesmen. If shareholders' wealth is increased by trading in some situations but not in others, this can be (and is) handled by contract too.

Perhaps the difficulty of enforcing such contracts makes it impossible for firms to achieve optimal allocations of the rights. Insiders' trades are notoriously hard to detect, for a trader can disguise his identity by using a street name. If firms seeking to curtail inside trading by contract cannot enforce their choices, then the benefits are lost. Firms that gain from the restrictions cannot distinguish themselves (in investors' eyes) because other firms will disingenuously claim to be similarly restrictive. Firms might attempt to overcome this by requiring insiders to report their trades and auditing their tax returns. Yet such devices are imperfect, for insiders can provide valuable information to family members or others and avoid detection. Although firms may try to detect trades by entering into agreements with stock exchanges that have computer surveillance of trading patterns, the difficulty of tracing sources of information necessarily means that enforcement will be spotty.

If the probability of detecting improper trades is low, public enforcement may be best. When detection is rare, the penalty must be increased to create deterrence. When detection is highly unlikely, the optimal fine can exceed the net wealth of the offender. Thus public enforcement, which can lead to imprisonment and other penalties firms cannot adopt for themselves, may be efficient.

Two caveats. First, public enforcement creates costs of its own (including the possibility of overdeterrence) that must be compared with the costs of imperfect private enforcement. Second, even if public enforcement is superior, this does not justify prohibition of trading itself unless enforcement is so weak that firms desiring to enforce no-trading rules cannot do so in a market of mixed trading and abstinence. Whether there should be public enforcement of a private prohibition is distinct from whether there should be a ban in the first place. Superiority of public enforcement sheds no light on this latter question, which turns on the effect of trading on shareholders' wealth. Public enforcement of antitheft laws does not imply that consensual transfers of property ought to be forbidden; just so with inside trading rules.

Legal Rules Restricting Inside Trading

We turn to the rules governing inside trading. Although conclusions must be tentative because theoretical arguments on the economic effects of inside trading are inconclusive, economic analysis provides insights.

COMMON LAW

At common law, managers and other insiders may trade the stock of public corporations on the basis of their inside information unless obliged by contract not to.[9] Insiders need not disclose what they know. When federal securities laws do not apply (for example, when the transaction does not take place in interstate commerce), this is contemporary law.

This rule has exceptions. Some jurisdictions, following the lead of the Supreme Court in a case decided under federal common law,

9. Goodwin v. Agassiz, 283 Mass. 358, 186 N.E. 659 (1933), is one example. See Robert Charles Clark, *Corporate Law* 311–312 (1986); Comment, "Insider Trading at Common Law," 51 *U. Chi. L. Rev.* 838 (1984). One well-known case holds that the corporation has a claim against insiders for trading on nonpublic information. Diamond v. Oreamuno, 24 N.Y.2d 494, 248 N.E.2d 910, 301 N.Y.S.2d 78 (1969). *Diamond* departs from the common law rule and has not been followed by other courts. See Freeman v. Decio, 584 F.2d 186 (7th Cir. 1978); Schein v. Chasen, 519 F.2d 453 (2d Cir. 1975). Moreover, *Diamond* may have involved trading for which contractual consent could not have been implied—the insiders traded in advance of a negative earning announcement.

condemn trading if the plaintiff proves "special facts"—that his trade was induced by express or implied misrepresentations concerning the value of the securities or the identity of the purchaser.[10] Corporations also have been allowed to recover under the corporate-opportunity doctrine from insiders who take advantage of their knowledge in ways that harm the firms' business. For example, an employee who, upon learning of an impending land purchase or corporate repurchase plan, rushes out and purchases the land or shares in order to resell to the firm at a high price would be held to have usurped a corporate opportunity,[11] a proposition consistent with our treatment of that doctrine in Chapter 5.

Knowing of the rule, firms rarely attempted to prohibit trading by managers in possession of nonpublic information. Inferences are not straightforward, though. Maybe firms failed to contract around the common law rule because detection was so difficult (until computer stock watch programs were devised) that it was not worth the candle to try to devise and enforce efficient rules.

The "special facts" rule is easier to understand. If the insider (or someone acting on his behalf) makes misrepresentations about the value of the firm or his identity in convincing an uninformed outsider to sell, any informational benefits of the trade are lost. Indeed the trade, like other types of fraud, moves prices away from, rather than toward, the "correct" price, particularly if the trade is a face-to-face transaction as opposed to an impersonal one. Moreover, the incentive created by allowing such trades is to distort information as opposed to producing new information. The "special facts" rule, therefore, grows out of recognition that trading by insiders is not always efficient. Permitting trades in public corporations and prohibiting them in close corporations shows a close correspondence between the common law and economic analysis.

The rationale for applying the corporate opportunity doctrine to inside trading also is clear. Actions based on inside information that harm the firm are prohibited—if not by contract, then by implication in the absence of a writing. In the land case, the firm must

10. Strong v. Repide, 213 U.S. 419 (1909), is the leading case. See also Jordan v. Duff & Phelps, Inc., 815 F.2d 429, 434–439 (7th Cir. 1987). These cases typically did not involve publicly traded corporations and thus do not qualify the common law rule allowing trades on anonymous exchanges.

11. Guth v. Loft, Inc., 23 Del. Ch. 255, 5 A.2d 503 (1939).

negotiate with the employee instead of buying in a competitive market. Transaction costs and prices have risen. Similarly, the purchase of a target's shares in advance of a takeover probably usurps the bidder's opportunity. The action may drive up the price of the target firm's shares or tip the bidder's hand, making the acquisition less likely to succeed.[12]

SECTION 10(B) AND RULE 10B-5

Courts have interpreted §10(b) of the Securities Exchange Act of 1934 and the SEC's Rule 10b-5 to require corporate insiders and their tippees either to disclose material information or to abstain from trading.[13] We discuss several aspects of the disclose-or-abstain rule.

Disclose or Abstain from Trading

Section 10(b) and Rule 10b-5 do not prohibit insiders from trading; they proscribe fraud. Their application to inside trading depends on an equation between "fraud" and the omission to state a material fact—for trading after full disclosure is never "fraud." Insiders therefore may either disclose the nonpublic information and then trade, or keep silent and refraining from trading. Despite this formulation of the rule in the alternative, however, the rule effectively prohibits trading (provided other elements such as materiality and scienter are present). In many cases, the insider may not be able to

12. Similar problems arise outside the takeover arena. In Brophy v. Cities Serv. Co., 31 Del. Ch. 241, 70 A.2d 5 (1949), an employee's purchase of his firm's shares in advance of an impending corporate repurchase program was held a breach of fiduciary duty. The insider's purchase of shares may have made the firm's contemplated action more expensive.

13. Willis W. Hagen II, "Insider Trading under Rule 10b-5: The Theoretical Bases for Liability," 44 *Bus. Law.* 13 (1988), provides a good overview of the law and the ambiguities in the contemporary rules. Two recent statutes, the Insider Trading Sanctions Act of 1984 and the Insider Trading and Securities Fraud Enforcement Act of 1988, codified as §21A of the Securities Exchange Act of 1934, 15 U.S.C. §78uA, provide that traders who violate §10(b) and Rule 10b-5 must make restitution and pay up to treble damages. (Chapter 12 discusses how damages are computed.) The 1988 act also provides that employers that have deficient systems of controls may be fined up to $1,000,000. The new statutes prescribe penalties while leaving the definition of the offense to the common law process under Rule 10b-5.

disclose the information. For example, the information might be valuable to competitors. It is in precisely such situations that inside trading may provide firms with a valuable method of transmitting information to the market by price without revealing the details. Compulsory disclosure removes firms' ability to use inside trading when it is most needed. The upshot is neither trading nor disclosure.

When disclosure is possible and not harmful to the firm, the release of news to an efficient capital market eliminates gains from trading. This is undesirable to the extent that the lure of profits from trading gives managers an incentive to maximize the value of the firm. The disclose-or-abstain rule weakens this incentive. Effects extend beyond managers. Investment analysts deemed "insiders" when they acquire news may be discouraged from searching. Prospective tender offerers also search less if they cannot use information about their own plans to increase the chance their bid will succeed.[14] Problems would be fewer if courts and regulators would distinguish between consensual and nonconsensual uses of information. Ray Dirks exposed one of the largest securities frauds in recent years, at the price of telling his clients what was afoot; the SEC should have given him a medal even while condemning forms of inside trading that injure investors.

"Material" Inside Information

The effect of Rule 10b-5 should not be exaggerated. The disclose-or-abstain rule applies only if a defendant trades on the basis of "material" inside information. That means *big* news, such as knowledge of an oil field, an impending merger, or a major change in earnings. Trades motivated by knowledge of "bombshell" events

---

14. Acquirers may purchase large amounts of a target's stock before they need to disclose their position. Section 13(d) of the Securities and Exchange Act of 1934, 15 U.S.C. §78m(d), requires a potential acquirer to make a public filing within ten days of acquiring 5 percent of a target's shares. The ten-day window allows a potential acquirer to purchase more than 5 percent of a target's stock before disclosing its position. This enables shares to be purchased at lower prices and thus facilitates value-increasing acquisitions. The SEC has forbidden would-be bidders, who could themselves lawfully purchase without public disclosure, to share information with arbitrageurs (Rule 14e-3). This effectively prevents (presumptively) beneficial transfers of information between bidders and their agents. The effect is to raise the cost of takeover activity to the detriment of investors.

are the substance of lawsuits but the aberration in practice. Most news is less dramatic; insiders remain free to trade on their knowledge. They do so and earn rates of return that are on average slightly in excess of the market as a whole.[15] These trades, though based on "inside" information in an economic sense (that is, information not yet reflected in stock prices), are not subject to legal attack because the materiality requirement is not satisfied. Knowledge that one of the firm's top managers is dispirited because of family problems, for example, may be very valuable but is almost surely not legally material. As long as insiders own and trade shares, therefore, Rule 10b-5 is likely to have slight effect on insiders' ability to outperform the market.

There is more. Because of their superior access to information, insiders will outperform the market without trading. They can earn superior returns through careful selection of their initial purchases. Their knowledge may tell them *not* to sell at times the less well informed would sell. Knowledge about the industry may be the basis of trading in other firms' stock—trades on the basis of "material" information, surely, but not "inside." They may also earn superior returns through careful timing of initial purchases.

The materiality requirement tends to limit the operation of Rule 10b-5 to inefficient inside trading. Lawyers, accountants, brokers, printers, football coaches, and public officials receive valuable information after it has been produced and are not responsible for (and incur none of the costs of) the risky decisions that led to its

15. Managers outperform the market when trading in their firms' stock, after all appropriate adjustments for risk. See J. B. Baesel and B. R. Stein, "The Value of Information: Inferences from the Profitability of Insider Trading," 14 *J. Fin. & Quantitative Analysis* 553 (1979); J. E. Finnerty, "Insiders and Market Efficiency," 31 *J. Fin.* 1141 (1976); Jeffrey F. Jaffee, "The Effect of Regulation Changes on Insider Trading," 5 *Bell J. Econ. & Management Sci.* 93 (1974); Jaffee, "Special Information and Insider Trading," 47 *J. Bus.* 410 (1974); Arthur J. Keown and John M. Pinkerton, "Merger Announcements and Insider Trading Activity: An Empirical Investigation," 36 *J. Fin.* 855 (1981); James H. Lorie and Victor Neiderhoffer, "Predictive and Statistical Properties of Insider Trading," 11 *J. L. & Econ.* 35 (1968); Stephen H. Penman, "Insider Trading and the Dissemination of Firms' Forecast Information," 55 *J. Bus.* 479 (1982); H. Nejat Seyhun, "Insiders' Profits, Costs of Trading, and Market Efficiency," 16 *J. Fin. Econ.* 189 (1986). These studies also show that the value of information dissipates quickly. Outsiders who try to mimic the insiders' trades do not make money; by the time the copycats act, prices have adjusted to impound the information.

generation. Because the benefits of allowing them to trade are trivial, the firm may want to ban such trading. Explicit contracts between firms and these outsiders typically require confidentiality and bar trading. Rule 10b-5 puts teeth into these promises. Most of the inside trading cases brought in the last decade involve conduct squarely prohibited by contract. In the rare cases of bombshell events, where the rewards are large and uncertain, the value of the uncertain trading profits to risk-averse managers (and others) will be low compared to the expected value of the event. Here again inside trading might be an inefficient compensation scheme. In both classes of cases, firms might want to ban inside trading, but because the precipitating event is so rare (and perhaps because the enforcement costs are so high) it is not worth the cost of including the prohibition in a contract. If the materiality requirement acts as a filter distinguishing these two classes of cases from the more typical but less dramatic cases where insiders earn positive abnormal returns, the rule may turn out to be beneficial without regard to the damage a general ban could do.

Fiduciary Duty

The Supreme Court has drawn a line between the ability of managers to trade on material inside information and the ability of others, such as printers or government officials, to do so. Because managers are employed by the firm and thus owe a fiduciary duty to investors, the Court has reasoned, they may not trade on the basis of inside information. Outsiders owe no such duty and so may trade without violating §10(b) or Rule 10b-5.

"Fiduciary duties" are a questionable basis on which to distinguish insiders from others. The difficulty with limiting the class of "insiders" to those within the firm is that long-term contracts are often a substitute for horizontal or vertical integration. Outside suppliers or outside counsel may have as much inside information and ability to affect the fortunes of the firm as employees. Under current rules, for example, a supplier to a firm could not be liable for selling the shares of the firm short, but it could be liable if the supplier were vertically integrated into the firm. That's not a useful line.

Fiduciary duties are standard-form contractual terms that govern agency relations, as we explained in Chapter 4. Implied duties allow the parties to avoid excessively lengthy and detailed agreements, reducing the costs of contracting. But such duties should be imposed only as a constraint on conduct if there is very clear evidence that most parties would impose the constraint by contract if bargaining were costless. It is not at all clear that the distinction between "insiders" and "outsiders" matches the class of trades that would be prohibited by contract in a world with no transactions costs. *Actual* contracts, when we observe them, forbid trading by outsiders such as printers and messengers but not insiders, the opposite of the result derived from an emphasis on "fiduciary" duty.

One positive outcome from the emphasis on duty, though, has been the development of the misappropriation theory. People may accept duties by agreement. If by contract a person promises not to trade, the argument goes, he has a "duty" not to trade; the identity of the misappropriating party becomes irrelevant. Consistent application of this approach would go a long way toward bringing the law of inside trading into harmony with the economics—making the legal rules more predictable in the bargain. (Of course, it is important that the corollary of the misappropriation theory also be recognized—that there should be no prohibition where the use of information is allowed by explicit contract.)

The Proper Plaintiff

Federal law creates both private and public enforcement devices. Rule 10b-5 gives shareholders who bought and sold during the time insiders were trading standing to bring private damages suits. The Department of Justice also may bring injunctive and criminal actions on behalf of the United States. Finally, the SEC may file suits to recover restitution and up to three times the trading profits from those who trade illegally.

One of our themes is that the dispute concerning inside trading is really about how managerial and other contracts allocate the property right in valuable information. If this property right is allocated to the managers, neither shareholders nor the government should have a claim—at least, no greater claim than they would have on account of excessive managerial salaries. In cases of nonconsensual trading, the firm should have a claim analogous to damages for breach of contract or recovery of the value of stolen property.

Shareholders could pursue derivative actions in the right of the corporations; if so it should make no difference whether the complaining shareholder traded at the same time as the insider or, for that matter, traded at all.

Because the probability of detection in situations involving nonconsensual trading is less than one, and because the gains from trading are potentially great, public enforcement is appropriate to increase the sanction (if necessary, to send to jail those whose wealth is too small to pay an optimal monetary penalty). Inside trading laws to this extent do not differ from the use of public prosecution to enforce other limitations on the use of intellectual property, such as trade secrets, trademarks, and copyrights.

Takeovers and Trading

In all corporate control transactions the acquiring firm acts through many agents with access to inside information. We have emphasized that theft of this information, as in *Chiarella,* is the core case for liability. Other than clapping the offender in leg irons, though, how does the legal system respond? Suppose Bidder's lawyer uses the information to buy shares of Target. Doubtless Bidder may recover the trader's profits. What if Bidder maintains that Lawyer's trades caused it to pay more for Target and seeks this increment from Lawyer?

A higher price is a consequence of the trading and may create social as well as private loss. (This is an implication of the proposition in Chapters 5 and 7 that gain sharing, here with both Lawyer and Target's shareholders, reduces the number of value-increasing transactions.) Offenders must pay for the social loss they create as well as the private gains they reap, a point we develop in Chapter 12. Yet Bidder will face an uphill fight to demonstrate that it suffered loss. It is unaffected unless Lawyer's trades lead to a higher price for Target's stock before the bid, *and* that higher price forces Bidder to raise its offer.

Anonymous trades do not affect price. Other traders do not infer information from (apparently) random purchases by unheard-of persons. Unless professional investors deduced Lawyer's identity and inferred that something was afoot, the price of Target's stock would not budge. If its price moves, what of it? Run-ups are common before control transactions, often caused by bidders' own purchases and those of persons Bidder deliberately let in on the secret.[16] Acquirers take these into effect when planning their bids. Whether investors tender at a given price depends on their next-best options—whether a bid from someone else, a buy-back, or holding in the hope that the market price will adjust. This next-best option, not the market price the day the bid lands on the table, dominates what Bidder must pay. Any run-up attributable to insiders' purchases does not affect the next-best option and therefore does not affect the price Bidder pays.

Sometimes insiders trade in connection with a recapitalization, as in *FMC Corp. v. Boesky*.[17] FMC recapitalized, giving managers a larger portion of the firm's equity; investors whose stakes were cut down got cash. FMC maintained that Boesky and others misappropriated information about the impending transaction and bought its shares, driving up the price. As a result, FMC believed, it had to pay more in order to compensate the investors for relinquishing their equity positions.

Cases such as this pose starkly the question: What is a corporation? Can a corporation be "injured" by distributing more cash to investors? The recapitalization shifted the relative positions of management and outside investors. The managers got a larger portion of the equity, and the outsiders a larger portion of the cash. Whether or not Boesky's trading led the firm to distribute more cash to the investors is beside the point. The firm—that aggregate of contractual interests—was unaffected.

Section 16

Section 16 of the Securities Exchange Act of 1934 requires directors, officers, and large stockholders (owning over 10 percent of the firm) to report trades in equity securities of their firm on a monthly basis, provides the firm with a right to any profits made from the purchase and sale of securities in a six-month period, and prohibits short selling. Section 16 differs from §10(b) and Rule 10b-5 in sev-

16. See Gregg A. Jarrell and Annette B. Poulson, "Stock Trading before the Announcement of Tender Offers: Insider Trading or Market Anticipation?" 5 *J. L. Econ. & Org.* 225 (1989).

17. 673 F. Supp. 242 (N.D. Ill. 1987), reversed in part, 852 F.2d 981 (7th Cir. 1988), on remand, 1989 U.S. Dist. Lexis 13353 (N.D. Ill.).

eral respects: (1) §16 is not limited to trading on inside information; (2) it applies only to matched purchases and sales within six months; (3) it covers only specified insiders; (4) it allows only the firm to recover.

Reporting Requirements

Reporting of insiders' trades allows investors to make more accurate inferences about insiders' compensation. Moreover, reports provide information to future managers about potential compensation that is available. An additional benefit is that the information effect of the insiders' trades will be strengthened if trades are observable. These benefits may be small, however, because of the difficulty of inferring information from trading profits when portfolio decisions may be governed by many factors, and because those who trade in violation of contracts and substantive rules are unlikely to report their misdeeds. But because the cost of reporting is small, even a slight benefit carries the day.

The Ban on Profit from Short-Swing Trading

Section 16(b), which authorizes the corporation to obtain its insiders' short-swing profits, has the advantage of directing recovery to the corporation. What is less clear, however, is whether the six-month rule serves a useful purpose. If trading is non-consensual, it should not matter whether a matched purchase and sale occur within six months; if the trading is consensual, why should the wash matter?

One reply is that the prohibition of short-swing trading decreases insiders' incentive to manipulate stock prices (that is, to move prices away from their equilibrium value).[18] Suppose insiders know that their purchases cause the price of shares to rise. In this event, insiders could gain by purchasing shares and then immediately selling (or selling short) before the market became aware of the manipulation and settled back to its former level. Prohibiting matched buying and selling within a short time reduces the ability of insiders to play games of this kind.

18. See Henry J. Manne, *Insider Trading and the Stock Market* 30 (1966) (suggesting this argument).

Yet the prohibition may entail substantial costs. Both the incentive and information effects of inside trading are weakened if a substantial set of trades is off-limits. The prohibition of short-swing trading also has the effect of forcing managers who buy their firms' stock to hold nondiversified portfolios for longer periods. This makes purchases less attractive, undercutting firms' efforts to align managers' interests with investors' by inducing them to hold stock. Firms must compensate by raising managers' compensation from other sources. Moreover, the ability of insiders to manipulate stock prices should not be exaggerated. The reason the market price might rise if insiders purchase is that investors believe such purchases are based on (and so imply) valuable information about the firm's prospects. Investors believe this a second time only if the message is borne out by an increase in the firm's earnings. Manipulation is a short-run or one-shot phenomenon. Insiders who mislead investors will find future attempts discounted by the market. And managers will balance any short-run gains against long-run losses resulting from their inability to communicate (truthful) information and, more generally, from a decrease in the value of their human capital.

The Prohibition of Short Sales

The perverse incentives created by the ability to trade are most acute when insiders engage in short selling. Many explicit contracts prohibit short sales; it is appropriate to imply such agreements widely in the absence of evidence that firms desire to permit the practice. (We know of none.) Any corporate manager observed to take large net short positions would be fired. Section 16's prohibition against short selling enforces these enduring patterns.

Short selling, though, is neither universally forbidden nor always harmful. It is only an exaggerated version of selling in advance of a downturn and buying again once the price reflects the bad news, a maneuver outside the scope of §16 (and for the most part outside the scope of Rule 10b-5). Short sales may be a powerful way to communicate information about the firm's prospects. Ability to sell short could induce managers to make superior investment decisions. Insiders are concerned about the value of their human capital. When a project succeeds, the insider's value as a manager is increased. When a project fails, even if the investment was optimal *ex ante,* the manager suffers a loss in the value of his human capital because he may be blamed for the failure (how do outsiders know the real reason for the failure?). Managers reduce the cost of failure by pursuing less-risky projects (fewer failures) even if these projects have lower value *ex ante* to investors. Trading may cushion the fall and so induce managers to take on projects with a high expected return even if they are riskier.

The effect of §16 on shareholders' welfare, therefore, is ambiguous. The reporting requirements, the prohibition against short-swing trading, and the ban on short sales all have a plausible basis but also impose costs. No one knows the relative magnitudes of the costs and benefits, from §16 or from any of the other legal rules about inside trading.

Society knows a good deal more about next year's weather than about the effects of this common commercial transaction. This makes it easy to speculate (no one can refute you) and condemn those who behave as you would not. It is correspondingly important to discipline the inquiry, to discard platitudes and fits of righteous indignation, and to begin a concerted search for telling data.

11

Mandatory Disclosure

We turn to the principal federal component of corporate law: the need to disclose information before selling securities or collecting proxies from investors. Fitting these mandatory rules into the contractual framework poses something of a challenge. Why are the securities laws mandatory rather than enabling? Why do they govern disclosure rather than the price or contents of securities? Why are they federal? On the normative side, do the securities laws offer benefits for investors? This chapter takes up the general questions, and the next looks at some more specific topics in the selection of remedies for violations.

The securities laws have had, since their enactment in 1933 and 1934, two basic components: a prohibition against fraud, and requirements of disclosure when securities are issued and periodically thereafter. The notorious complexities of securities practice arise from defining the details of disclosure and ascertaining which transactions are covered by the disclosure requirements. There is very little substantive regulation of investments. To be sure, the SEC occasionally uses the rubric of disclosure to affect substance, as when it demands that insiders not trade without making "disclosures" that would make trading pointless, when it insists that a going private deal "disclose" that the price is "fair," and when the price of accelerated registration of a prospectus is "disclosure" that directors will not be indemnified for certain wrongs. Although several of these and other refinements are important—we dealt in earlier chapters with the regulation of inside trading and tender offers, subjects added to federal law after 1934—the dominant principle of securities regulation still is that anyone willing to disclose the right

276

things can sell or buy whatever he wants at whatever price the market will sustain.[1]

Why have the laws survived when other regulatory schemes of that vintage have been transformed or eliminated? Those who enacted these statutes asserted that they were necessary to eliminate fraud from the market and ensure that investors would receive the returns they expected; otherwise, the argument ran, people would withdraw their capital and the economy would stagnate. This explanation seemed especially pressing in 1933, for there had been frauds preceding the Depression and much disinvestment during it.[2] On this public interest story, the interests served by the laws are the same now as they were then, and so the laws have the same beneficial structure.

No one should be comfortable with this simple tale. Fraud was unlawful in every state in 1933, and every state except Nevada then had an administrative apparatus for investigating and preventing securities fraud. Fraud in the sale of houses and education is more important to most people of moderate means (the supposed beneficiaries of the securities acts) than fraud in the sale of securities; these people have a much greater portion of their wealth invested in real estate and human capital than in the stock market. Yet there are no federal laws addressing these other assets. There were many securities frauds before 1933, and there have been many since. The Investors Overseas Services, National Student Marketing, Equity Funding, and OPM Leasing frauds of the last generation are every bit as spectacular as the frauds of the 1920s.

The recognition that much legislation is the outcome of the interplay of pressure groups—and that only by accident will interest group laws serve the broader public interest—suggests another hy-

1. A principle with such force that a court of appeals held that the SEC exceeded its statutory authority in promulgating Rule 19c-4, 17 C.F.R. §240.19c-4. which restricted stock exchanges' ability to trade classes of common stock with different voting rights. Business Roundtable v. SEC, 905 F.2d 406 (D.C. Cir. 1990). Rule 19c-4, the court concluded, offended against the principle that firms may use any corporate structures or issue any instruments that they have adequately disclosed to investors.

2. For a recounting of the public statements of those who lobbied for and enacted the laws, and of the events they cited as establishing the need for legislation, see Joel F. Seligman, *The Transformation of Wall Street* (1982).

pothesis.[3] The securities laws may be designed to protect special interests at the expense of investors. They possess many of the characteristics of interest-group legislation. Existing rules give larger issuers an edge, because many of the costs of disclosure are the same regardless of the size of the firm or the offering. Thus larger or older firms face lower flotation costs per dollar than do small issuers.[4] The rules also help existing investment banks and auditing firms obtain an advantage because they acquire expertise and because rivals cannot compete by offering differentiated products.[5] The securities laws' routinization of disclosure reduces the number of paths to the market and insists that all firms give investors "the best," stifling lower cost alternatives with higher risks.

Some parts of the securities laws had obvious interest-group support. The foremost of these is the regulation of the exchanges, which until 1975 permitted the SEC to shore up a price-fixing cartel of brokers. We do not discuss these parts here, although it is conceivable that the regulation of the securities business is related to the regulation of investments in the sense that SEC enforcement of the cartel was the political price of obtaining regulation of investments.[6] It is harder to find private interests behind the principal features of regulation, though. Lawyers specialize in corporate and securities work, and other market professionals depend on the in-

3. The general statements of the interest group approach are Gary S. Becker, "A Theory of Competition among Pressure Groups for Political Influence," 98 *Q. J. Econ.* 371 (1983); Sam Peltzman, "Toward a More General Theory of Regulation," 19 *J. L. & Econ.* 211 (1976); Richard A. Posner, "Taxation by Regulation," 2 *Bell J. Econ. & Mgt. Sci.* 22 (1971); and George J. Stigler, "The Theory of Economic Regulation," 2 *Bell J. Econ. & Mgt. Sci.* 3 (1971), revised and reprinted in his *The Citizen and the State* (1975).

4. See Jay R. Ritter, "The Costs of Going Public," 19 *J. Fin. Econ.* 269 (1987).

5. Henry Manne emphasizes both of these points in a comprehensive and thoughtful legal critique of the securities laws from an economic perspective. Henry G. Manne, "Economic Aspects of Required Disclosure under Federal Securities Laws," in *Wall Street in Transition* 23, 31–40 (Manne and Solomon eds. 1974). See also Homer Kripke, *The SEC and Corporate Disclosure: Regulation in Search of a Purpose* (1979); Nicholas Wolfson, "A Critique of the Securities and Exchange Commission," 30 *Emory L. J.* 119 (1981).

6. See Gregg A. Jarrell, "Change at the Exchange: The Causes and Effects of Deregulation," 27 *J. L. & Econ.* (1984), for a careful exposition of the evidence on the price fixing at the exchanges.

tricacies of the law for much revenue. These favored groups (larger issuers, investment banks, the securities bar) have too many members to permit monopoly prices.[7] Delaware's bar has thousands of corporate lawyers, with lawyers in other states practicing its law too; the securities bar is much larger; in both cases, competition prevents monopoly returns. Yet these lawyers, investment bankers, and others have human capital at stake. Thus they have every reason to oppose the abolition of the regulatory system. And if the losses from existing laws are spread across a large number of people (individual investors), each of whom would benefit only slightly from abolition, regulation could survive even if it reduces social welfare.

Unfortunately, no one knows why some pieces of legislation are enacted and survive while others do not. The interest-group explanation that might account for securities litigation also could explain airline and trucking regulation, yet these systems have been almost obliterated. The survival of securities regulation could be attributed to "stronger interest-group support," but this smacks of tautology. Perhaps the laws endured because they are not predominantly interest-group legislation. We think it appropriate, therefore, to search for the "public interest" justifications of the securities laws.

The Federal Prohibition of Fraud

Securities are claims to the future income of firms. The problem in selling securities is that this income is subject to many risks, and no entrepreneur can make a binding promise about the amount of income the firm will yield in all possible circumstances. The entre-

---

7. We are therefore skeptical of recent efforts to explain corporate or securities law on the ground that particular rules benefit practitioners. See Jonathan R. Macey and Geoffrey P. Miller, "Toward an Interest-Group Theory of Delaware Corporate Law," 65 *Tex. L. Rev.* 469 (1987). Roberta Romano's efforts to understand some rules by emphasizing the interests of established firms, which have assets that cannot readily be moved from state to state, are more promising. See the following articles by her: "The Future of Hostile Takeovers: Legislation and Public Opinion," 57 *U. Cin. L. Rev.* 457 (1988); "The Political Economy of Takeover Statutes," 73 *Va. L. Rev.* 111 (1987); and "The State Competition Debate in Corporate Law," 8 *Cardozo L. Rev.* 709 (1987). Mechanisms of the sort she emphasizes do not explain federal legislation, however.

preneur or managerial team, however, has better information than the prospective investor about both the nature of these contingencies and how the firm will fare under them. Some business prospects have higher expected returns than others; some managers will produce more than others out of any given business prospect. The market is inefficient unless it matches projects, managers, and funds until, at the margin, the returns are equal. The better prospect-manager combinations should attract more funds until this equality condition is satisfied.

THE MARKET WITHOUT LEGAL INTERVENTION

How does an investor recognize the better combinations? Unless people who offer the "better securities" (representing claims in the superior combinations) can distinguish them from others, investors will view all securities as average. Higher quality securities will sell at prices lower than they would if information were available costlessly, and there will be too little investment in good ventures. Meanwhile low-quality securities will attract too much money. It is cheap to offer a low-quality security; such offerings will be overcompensated. "Lemons" will dominate the market as the quality of investments offered deteriorates. No firm could recover the costs of offering high-quality securities. Investors and society both lose. This is roughly the picture painted by many proponents of the securities laws.

One cannot leap from the difficulties of a market with asymmetric information to the conclusion that there is need for regulation—even such mild regulation as a prohibition of fraud. Sellers of high-quality securities can identify themselves no matter the legal rule. One is to disclose the information demonstrating quality. Some of the information can be verified by the buyer; this will lend credence to the rest. Verification will not work perfectly, though. Sometimes a firm must withhold information in order to avoid giving commercially valuable secrets to rivals. A firm thus will be hard-pressed to convince buyers of the value of some secret production process or new but unreleased product. The other problem is that low-quality sellers can mimic the disclosure of ascertainable facts while making false statements about things buyers cannot verify. The low-quality firms erode the informational content of the disclosures of other firms, and again consumers cannot identify the high-quality investments.[8]

Indeed, in securities markets only a limited amount of information can be verified at all. Investors cannot "inspect" a business venture in a way that enables them to deduce future profits and risks. Investors do not even want to inspect; they seek to be passive recipients of an income stream, not to be private investigators. When investors spend time and resources inspecting, each one's effort will duplicate what another has done. The whole system of inspection by buyers forfeits much of the benefit of the division of labor.

Even after the business has been in operation for some time, it is hard to tell whether a good or bad outcome was attributable to changed conditions or luck rather than to an inaccurate description of the prospects. True, information about how a whole industry is doing will provide a basis for comparison so that some claims of a member of the industry can be checked. Some of the firms' managers and promoters are repeat players and thus will seek to preserve their reputations by telling the truth. Even so, however, it is possible that the promoters may find the gains from deception greater than the reputational loss. This is especially likely if the public contains a pool of persons who cannot evaluate information and therefore cannot tell good projects from bad. Call them suckers. If there are enough suckers, sellers may make a living dealing exclusively with them, abandoning all prospect of sales to the informed. It follows that some firms will find fraud to be the project with the highest net present value.

---

8. This problem is more serious for securities than for most physical goods because of the difficulty of verification. A seller of a house must expect many buyers to verify statements about square footage, termites, and structural flaws. A seller of charcoal does not expect the buyer to test on the spot whether the charcoal will ignite without lighter fluid, but any misstatement will affect the probability of repeat purchases, and so the seller has little incentive to misrepresent. Many sellers have competitors eager to expose misstatements. All of these are effective in controlling the release of information no matter what the law does about fraud. See Richard A. Posner, *The Regulation of Advertising by the FTC* (1973); Phillip Nelson, "Advertising as Information," 82 *J. Pol. Econ.* 729 (1974); Michael R. Darby and Edi Karni, "Free Competition and the Optimal Amount of Fraud," 16 *J. L. & Econ.* 67 (1973). But because each security is an interest in a unique project, neither competitors' statements nor the prospect of repeat purchases will impose constraints, and it is very hard for a buyer to verify statements before the sale.

High-quality firms must take additional steps to convince investors of their quality. One traditional step is to allow outsiders to review the books and records and to have these outsiders certify the accuracy of the firms' representations. The accountant who certifies the books of many firms has a reputational interest—and thus a possible loss—much larger than the gains to be made from slipshod or false certification of a particular firm. Similarly, firms may sell their securities through investment bankers who inspect the firm's prospects, put their money on the line in buying the stock for resale, and put their reputations on the line in making representations to customers. The larger the auditor or investment banker relative to the size of an issuer, the more effective these methods of verification are. (This suggests why investment banks form syndicates to distribute securities even though any one could have handled them alone. Syndication increases the amount of reputational capital put behind the offering.)

Firms may take actions and make commitments that render their disclosures more believable. One is to ensure that their managers hold substantial quantities of their stock. This can be accomplished by stock options or by "cheap stock" when the firm goes public, as well as by inducing managers to buy in the market. If the firm does poorly, the managers lose with the other investors. The higher the quality of the stock, the more of it managers will be willing to hold in undiversified portfolios; the more managers hold, the more willing other investors will be to believe the firm's statements. Another action open to the firm is to issue debt, which (a) forces the managers to pay out the profits, and (b) if there are no profits, forces the firm into bankruptcy. Compulsory payouts ensure that the managers return to the capital market for funds, and investors then may check up on their performance before recommitting funds. Bankruptcy (the other option) does great damage to managers' careers, and of course causes huge losses if they own their firm's stock in quantity. Debt therefore enables managers with the best prospects to identify themselves to investors. Of course, managers could warrant their statements in the traditional way: make a legally enforceable promise (perhaps backed up by an insurer) to pay the investors if the firm does worse than promised (perhaps, say, in a comparison against a market index). The person vouching for the payment obligation would look very carefully at the firm's claims, so that only high-quality firms could find a solvent guarantor, and the investors would be protected.

Even in a market without a rule against fraud, these methods of verification would offer investors substantial protection and make it possible for high-quality firms to raise money. Investors, after all, need not donate cash to new firms. They can put their money in government securities or bank accounts with no risk; they can invest in regulated public utilities that have very little risk; they can purchase land or other productive assets. New or less known firms can obtain money only if they offer packages more attractive than those already existing.

THE EFFECTS OF A RULE AGAINST FRAUD

For the reasons we have spelled out, a rule against fraud is not an essential or even necessarily an important ingredient of securities markets. Each of these certification methods is costly, however. Auditing, investment banking, and underwriting firms are expensive to establish and operate; payments via debt and dividends entail transaction and tax costs; managers must be paid extra to induce them to hold undiversified portfolios, and their risky position may lead them to make inferior investment decisions later on; verification of claims by thousands of buyers may be the most expensive of all.

A rule against fraud can reduce these costs, especially for new firms. The penalty for fraud makes it more costly for low-quality firms to mimic high-quality ones by making false disclosures. An antifraud rule imposes low or no costs on the honest, high-quality firm. Thus it makes it possible for high-quality firms to offer warranties at lower cost. The informational warranty, if enforced, makes it unnecessary for buyers to verify information or for sellers to undertake expensive certification.[9] The expenses of offering high-quality securities go down, while the expenses of passing off low-quality securities rise.

The rule against fraud will not drive the costs of the high-quality firms to zero, however, because the rule may be underenforced. Firms still will use some additional certification devices. Moreover,

9. See Sanford J. Grossman, "The Informational Role of Warranties and Private Disclosure about Product Quality," 24 *J. L. & Econ.* 461 (1981). When legal enforcement is expensive, or suckers numerous, this method breaks down. Paul Milgrom and John Roberts, "Relying on the Information of Interested Parties," 17 *Rand J. Econ.* 18 (1986).

a fraud rule does not have much effect when a firm is silent. The silence of a firm whose securities are trading in secondary markets could mean no news, bad news, or good news that cannot be disclosed because disclosure would benefit rivals. Investors have incentives to investigate to find the meaning of the silence, and firms will incur costs either to preserve secrecy or to communicate the tenor of the news without saying too much. The fraud rule and other verification methods are complements in some respects, substitutes in others.

Antifraud rules impose costs of their own. Enforcement (investigation, prosecution, and judges and their staffs) is expensive. The costs of overenforcement or inaccurate enforcement are harder to see but no less real. Start with an extreme case of inaccurate enforcement. Suppose the probability of being prosecuted for any given statement is .55 if the statement is false, .45 if the statement is true. This could come about if, for example, the prosecutors and courts adopted a theory of "strict liability" and penalized all firms whose projections of profit turned out poorly. Because market conditions cause many plans, even those well laid and truthfully described, to fail, while firms that tell lies could succeed, prosecutions would be brought against honest firms, and many dishonest ones would escape.

The deterrent force of any rule is the difference between how the rule treats those who obey and how it treats those who disobey. If the difference is small—if, for example, a person driving at 55 miles per hour is only a little less likely to be charged with speeding than a person driving at 85—then the rule does not deter. If there are gains from violating the rule, one may as well violate it. The world of inaccurate enforcement is similar to the world of no enforcement. Statements are no longer trustworthy unless the firm undertakes the costly certification and verification methods described in the previous section, and even truth-tellers will say as little as possible in order to avoid paying the penalty for lying. The higher the penalty for the offense, the more discriminating the enforcement must be in order to prevent both deterring appropriate behavior and stimulating undesired behavior.

Overenforcement is similar to undiscriminating enforcement. For any offense, there is an optimal level of enforcement at which the costs of expending an additional enforcement dollar just equal the gains from reducing the incidence of the offense. The optimal level of enforcement allows some violations to occur, because the costs of stamping out these violations exceed the costs of the violations themselves. Excessive penalties for fraud—especially if these penalties are available in actions brought by private plaintiffs—can lead both to overenforcement and to excessive deterrence of truthful statements.

The rule against fraud, then, is most beneficial when enforcement costs are low and when it is possible to separate untruths from statements that, although true, do not accurately predict the future. Enforcement costs are least, and the chance of error lowest, when prosecutions are concentrated on verifiable statements of historical fact rather than on predictions. The SEC's administration of the securities laws has emphasized the making of accurate historical statements rather than projections, which are not required. Most projections and other "soft" assessments are left to outsiders, with little regulatory oversight; projections that firms choose to make are sheltered from prosecution by the "safe harbor" of Rule 175.[10] This approach is consistent with one in which fraud rules are used where they yield maximum net benefits.

WHY IS THE RULE AGAINST FRAUD NATIONAL?

In 1933 every state had a rule against fraud. What, then, was the point of the many new rules contained in the 1933 and 1934 acts? Supporters of the acts usually say that the national rule was necessary because the state rules were "ineffective" (witness the discovery of frauds), but this is not a good explanation. The existence or even increase of reported frauds is no more proof that the state laws against fraud were "ineffective" than the existence of murder shows that state criminal law is "ineffective" and should be replaced with a national murder statute enforced by a Federal Homicide Commission.

The justification of federal legislation lies, rather, in the efficiency of enforcing in one case all claims that arise out of a single transaction. Many new issues of securities are sold to purchasers in several states; even issues initially sold within a single state ultimately find their way into the hands of out-of-state owners, if only because the owners move. Thus almost all substantial firms' securities sell

10. See Wielgos v. Commonwealth Edison Co., 892 F.2d 509 (7th Cir. 1989).

in interstate markets—and firms whose securities trade only in one state are exempted from most federal regulation. If claims arising out of securities in multistate enterprises were litigated where each investor resided, there would be multiple cases for every security, with the possibility of inconsistent decisions and inconsistent legal standards. Claims of fraud usually involve written documents, and there is no good reason to have the identical claim litigated in multiple forums.

The securities laws create nationwide service of process and have a liberal venue rule that permits litigation to consolidate all defendants and all claims in a single forum. Class actions make it easy to bring all plaintiffs together. We discuss below some of the reasons why a single rule of law about what must and cannot be disclosed is beneficial. For now it is enough to note that the federal prohibition of fraud would be beneficial even if the single federal suit enforced multiple rules based on state law.

Mandatory Disclosure

In a world with an antifraud rule but no mandatory disclosure, firms could remain silent with impunity. Firms that disclosed could do so in any way they wished, provided they did not lie. They could attempt to sell securities with ads in glossy magazines and on television featuring sexy models or herds of bulls, as sellers of other products (including brokerage services) do.

A mandatory disclosure system substantially limits firms' ability to remain silent. Just as important, it controls the time, place, and manner of disclosure. Firms must wait until a registration statement is filed before saying anything that may be construed as touting (the "gun jumping" rule); they must wait until the registration statement is effective and a prospectus has been delivered before putting anything in writing (the "free writing" rule); they must mail prospectuses and proxy statements at designated times but may not resort to ads on television.

DISCLOSURE AND THE PUBLIC GOODS ASPECT OF INFORMATION

What does a mandatory disclosure system add to the prohibition of fraud? The implicit public interest justification for disclosure rules is that markets produce "too little" information about securities when the only rule is one against fraud. One often hears the assertion that information is a "public good," meaning that it can be used without being "used up" and that the producer of information cannot exclude others from receiving the benefits. If the producer of information cannot obtain all of its value, too little will be produced. It seems to follow that there are gains in a rule requiring production of all information that would be forthcoming were gains fully appropriable.

This rationale gets us only so far. For one thing, it proves too much. No one can fully appropriate the value of information about toothpaste, but there is no federal rule about disclosing the efficacy of toothpaste in preventing cavities. Why are securities different? We leave other products to competitive markets because we believe that people who make or use a product (or test it, as Consumers' Union does) will obtain enough of the gains from information to make the markets reasonably efficient.

Similarly, those who learn about a security may profit from their information. They cannot obtain all of the benefits, because others in the market will infer the news, and the price of the securities will adjust. The new price will "contain" the news, preventing the person who first learned it from taking further gains. This also means, however, that the value of news decays quickly in securities markets; the information *is* "used up," and other people then have their own incentives to go out and find more information. Information is far from free even when given away *for* free. Those who receive the information must spend time digesting it, and this time is lost to other uses. Investors' time is costly. So it is inaccurate to treat information as enduring, cheap to disseminate, and cheap to use.

The more sophisticated version of the public goods explanation is that although investors produce information, they produce both too much and too little of it. They produce too little because the benefits are imperfectly appropriable. If information is worth $100 to investors as a group, but no one can capture more than $10 of gains, then no one will obtain more than $10 worth of information. Investors produce too much information, though, if several create the same $10 bit of information (redundant production). Mandatory disclosure will prevent redundant production of information, the argument concludes.

The other source of excessive production is the gain available from forecasting the future. Some information, such as the quarterly earnings of a firm, offers opportunities for trading gains; the person who learns the news first can make great profits. In one important sense, though, the information is worthless. Trading on news that is bound to come out anyway does not change the future or lead to better investment in new securities. The price will ultimately change to reflect the true earnings. That it changes a day or so quicker is not of much moment for allocative efficiency. The lure of trading profits may induce people to spend a lot of effort and other resources "beating the market"; this is wasteful because the profit opportunity is much larger than the efficiency gains from expediting the transition of prices. The argument concludes by observing that the prompt disclosure of information by the affected firm will extinguish the trading opportunity. When everyone knows the truth, no one can speculate on it. Investors as a group would pay to have these trading gains (and the costly search for information) eliminated. What better way to do this than disclosure by the firm that knows the truth?

These arguments share a problem, because they leap from the benefit of disclosure to the benefit of *mandatory* disclosure. If disclosure is worthwhile to investors, the firm can profit by providing it. The firm is in privity with its investors, and they should be able to strike a mutually beneficial bargain. A decision by the firm effectively "coordinates" the acts of many investors who could not bargain directly. As we have emphasized from the beginning, managers who omit cost-justified steps for the protection of investors will receive less money for the securities the firm issues; the entrepreneurs and managers, not the investors, pay the price.

Take a firm that wants to issue new securities. It has a project (say, the manufacture of a new computer) that it expects to be profitable. If the firm simply asked for money without disclosing the project and managers involved, however, it would get nothing. Investors would assume the worst because, they would reason, if the firm had anything good to say for itself it would do so. Silence is bad news. A firm with a good project, seeking to distinguish itself from a firm with a mediocre project (or no project at all), would disclose more and more as long as the cost of disclosure (both direct costs of dissemination and indirect costs of giving information to rivals) was worthwhile to its investors. It might even disclose *too much* from society's perspective, because it would know that time investors devoted to studying its disclosures would be unavailable to study its rivals'.[11] Self-induced disclosure occurs in the secondary market too. The firm's investors want to be able to sell their stock in the aftermarket for the highest price. Their ability to do so depends on a flow of believable information (otherwise potential buyers reduce their offers), which firms must supply if they hope to obtain the best price for their stock on issuance.

The process works for bad news as well as good. Once the firm starts disclosing it cannot stop short of making any critical revelation, because investors assume the worst. It must disclose the bad with the good, else investors will assume that the bad is even worse than it is. And the firm's word is not sufficient. Mere disclosure would be enough if the rule against fraud were perfectly enforced, but it is not. Thus the firm uses the many verification and certification devices we have described. Given these devices, a rule compelling disclosure seems redundant. If the fraud penalty and verification devices do not work, a rule compelling disclosure is not apt to be enforceable either.

Firms have been disclosing important facts about themselves—and certifying these facts through third parties—as long as there have been firms. It is possible to trace the use of auditors back to the beginning of the corporation. By 1934, when Congress first required annual disclosure by some companies, every firm traded on the national markets made voluminous public disclosures certified by independent auditors.[12] Between 1934 and 1964, annual disclosure was required only of those firms traded on national exchanges. (In 1964 the statute was amended to cover all firms with more than a specified number of investors.) Firms could avoid disclosure by de-listing or not listing initially. Nonetheless, firms eagerly listed themselves on exchanges and disclosed; firms that were not listed also disclosed substantial amounts of data, following the pattern set by those covered by the statute. Even today,

11. This intriguing possibility was first raised by Michael J. Fishman and Kathleen M. Hagerty, "Disclosure Decisions by Firms and the Competition for Price Efficiency," Department of Finance, Kellogg Graduate School of Management, Northwestern University, working paper no. 50 (Apr. 1988).

12. See Ross L. Watts and Jerold L. Zimmerman, "Agency Problems, Auditing, and the Theory of the Firm: Some Evidence," 26 *J. L. & Econ.* 613 (1983); George Benston, "Required Disclosure and the Stock Market: An Evaluation of the Securities Exchange Act of 1934," 63 *Am. Econ. Rev.* 132 (1973).

although the securities of state and local governments are exempt from the mandatory disclosure rules, these issuers routinely supply extensive information to purchasers.

Disclosure for the purpose of stilling investors' doubts also reduces investors' incentives to search too much for trading information. The problem, as we have mentioned, is that knowing the future creates profit opportunities without making investors as a group better off. Because searching out such information is costly, investors as a group gain if firms disclose so as to minimize the opportunities for these gains and thus the incentives to search. The net return on a security is its gross return (dividends plus any liquidating distribution) less the costs of information and transactions in holding the security. A firm can increase this net return as easily by reducing the cost of holding the stock as by increasing its business profits. Firms that promise to make disclosures for this purpose will prosper relative to others, because their investors incur relatively lower costs and can be more passive with safety. The more convincing the promise, the more investors will pay for the stock.

LIMITATIONS ON THE SELF-INTEREST MODEL OF DISCLOSURE

Although the self-interest of firms' managers leads them to supply roughly the amount of information investors as a group desire, "roughly" is an important qualifier. Certification and verification costs intrude. If disclosure rules, like fraud rules, could reduce them, then firms' disclosure would be improved. There is one other reason why firms' disclosures may not be optimal: third-party effects.

The information produced by one firm for its investors may be valuable to investors of other firms. Firm A's statements may reveal something about the industry in which firm A operates—if only the size of firm A's anticipated production—that other participants in the industry can use in planning their operations. There may be other collateral benefits to investors in rival firms. Yet firm A cannot charge the investors in these other firms for the benefits, although they would be willing to pay for them. Because they cannot be charged, the information will be underproduced.

The firms and investors, acting as a group, would want the firms to disclose information with both firm and industry specific components. Each firm acting individually will not do so, in part because the others would get a free ride and in part because some of the information (such as that pertaining to new products) may give a competitive advantage to rivals. Each firm would be willing to disclose, but only if all others were required to do likewise. Then the costs and any business risks would be distributed more evenly. In the absence of some requirement or strong inducement to disclose, each firm will want to be a holdout.

There is a similar free-rider problem in the disclosure of information that facilitates comparisons among firms. Firm *C* may know something that makes it attractive relative to *D*. It cannot convey this information effectively, however, without conveying information about *D*'s plans and prospects. The information about *D* will redound partly to the benefit of present or prospective investors in *D*, and firm *C* cannot obtain compensation. (Firm *C* could appropriate part of the gain by buying or selling *D*'s stock, but this is a costly transaction, and firm *C* could not appropriate the full gain without owning *D, E, F, G*, and so on, outright. An increase in the size of firms to allow greater internalization of information has other costs, including monopoly and a reduction in investors' ability to diversify their holdings.)

Firm *C* also encounters difficulty in appropriating the value of information affecting risk-return characteristics. The lesser the degree of difference among firms, the more spillover the disclosures of one firm will have, and the poorer this firm's incentives to disclose. Many firms will have similar risk-return characteristics. Some form of collective action (whether or not through the government) could be beneficial in principle here. Which method of tackling the collective action problem has the lowest net costs is an empirical problem.

Or suppose there is an optimal format for communicating information to investors. Some disclosures are easier to understand and verify than others, while some disclosures tend to hide more than to reveal information. If contracts among all investors in society could be written costlessly, the investors would require all firms to identify and use the optimal format of disclosure. The costs may be too high, though, for one firm acting on its own. The optimal form of disclosure may entail use of some specialized language (one can think of accounting principles, with their detailed definitions, as a specialized disclosure language), yet no one firm can obtain a large share of the benefits of inventing and employing this language; others will be able to use the format without charge. Sometimes, too, the ease of using a given method of disclosure will depend on other firms adopting the same format, facilitating comparisons. The other firms may not be eager to cooperate in this way; they may want to impose costs on persons considering investing in their rivals.

These problems are similar to those involved in bringing new products of all sorts to market. Color television was not feasible until manufacturers and broadcasters agreed on a standard method of transmission. Compact disk players are greatly aided in competing against tapes and records by the standards promulgated by Phillips, the holder of an important patent. Sometimes standards may be devised by trade associations, as they are in much of the electronics industry and, in part, in the accounting industry. Standardization could occur through mandatory disclosure rules promulgated by a governmental agency, too.

PRIVATE OR COMPETITIVE METHODS OF CREATING OPTIMAL DISCLOSURE

We have assumed so far that firms act independently in creating and communicating information to investors. Sometimes firms will not disclose because the costs of this self-help exceed the value of the information. Sometimes they will not disclose because the information would decrease rather than increase the firms' value, even though investors would gain from having the knowledge; information about a new product or a new technology may be in this category. Because of these "good" reasons for nondisclosure, investors cannot infer unambiguously that no news is bad news, the power of the self-interest model of disclosure is reduced, and high-quality firms will have trouble distinguishing their offerings from those of low-quality firms.

Informational Intermediaries

Informational intermediaries are a partial solution to these difficulties. Consider the case of a firm that wants to raise money to take advantage of a technological breakthrough, the details of which it cannot disclose. This firm may disclose the information to an underwriter, which will price the securities appropriately. Investors realize that underwriters may have information that is not relayed to the public and that they have reputational interests in not deceiving customers. Investors pay more for these securities than they would for those of similar firms that had not made such breakthroughs.[13] Firms also can spread the news indirectly—although not as well, because of the weaker reputational interests of the intermediaries—by disclosing portions to investment analysts or other intermediaries, who communicate to the public by making recommendations rather than by spelling out details.

Accountants also serve as intermediaries, putting their reputations behind the accuracy of a firm's disclosures. Moreover, to the extent accountants agree on a common language, they standardize (reducing the costs of) any amount of disclosure. Accountants spread over all firms the costs of creating and maintaining the language. Of course accountants may face pressures from individual firms to misuse their language, or they may be unable to agree on a language; governmental intervention may reduce these costs of agreement and enforcement.

Informational intermediaries obviously cannot ensure accuracy or completeness of information. Their employees may be incompetent or deceived; they review events periodically rather than continuously, so things may change between the time they inspect the situation and the time any investor acts in response to their findings. But any other disclosure device has these problems as well. The essential point is that the informational intermediaries increase the amount of accurate information about firms that can be conveyed to investors.

Informed Traders

Some traders know more than others. Insiders and those who receive information from insiders, brokers, those who search out

13. The articles in Symposium, Investment Banking and the Capital Acquisition Process, 15 *J. Fin. Econ.* 1–281 (1986), present evidence about the effects of investment banks and underwriters in the sale of securities and cover the underlying economic theory. James R. Booth and Richard L. Smith II, "Capital Raising, Underwriting, and the Certification Hypothesis," 15 *J. Fin. Econ.* 261 (1986), is particularly appropriate for current purposes.

tidbits and draw inferences, and those who purchase information from the better informed (such as analysts and money managers), are informed traders. People become informed to "beat the market" and earn superior returns. Their ability to earn these returns is limited, though, by the fact that other investors follow the same strategy and trade on what they learn. Other traders become informed, and the act of trading—moving the price of the stock toward the one the informed traders think is "right"—causes the price of the stock to impound the value of the information these traders possess. When the price reaches a level at which informed traders are indifferent between being buyers and being sellers, the price conveys the information about the firm more effectively (and cheaper) than direct disclosure. Trading will never be completely revealing; uninformed traders may not be able to tell whether particular trades are motivated by new information or by portfolio adjustments. Nonetheless, trading and not trading by informed parties will supply other investors with a great deal of information.

Stock Exchanges

Organized exchanges reduce the costs of transacting. By making it easier for parties with different beliefs about the future to transact, organized exchanges increase liquidity and reduce the unnecessary risk of investing. The greater the liquidity of the secondary market, the more successful the exchange. Because the success of an exchange depends on the amount of trading, exchanges have incentives to adopt rules governing trade that operate to the benefits of investors. Such rules attract more trades, reducing the costs (and increasing the profits) of those who run the exchanges.

Exchanges gain, for example, by adopting rules that minimize the amount of deceit committed by listed firms, because investors who are misled are less likely to be repeat players. For the same reason, exchanges have an incentive to adopt rules that require listed firms to disclose the amount and type of information that investors demand. Competition among organized exchanges for both the listing of firms and the business of investors, as well as competition between exchanges and other methods of investing, increases the incentives of the exchanges to adopt beneficial rules.

Firms, in turn, have incentives to list their securities on exchanges with rules that maximize investors' wealth. To see this, assume for the moment that firms acting by themselves would disclose less (or different) information than that demanded by investors, and that the social loss from this inappropriate level of disclosure is less than the costs to these individual firms of contracting to produce the right amount of information. This might occur, for example, because of the third-party effects discussed above. Organized exchanges offer the firms a way to cope with the collective action problem. The firms can agree to be bound by the rules set by the exchange, and these rules can come closer to requiring optimal disclosure because they will "internalize" many of the third-party effects. Firms that bind themselves to follow the exchange's rules will have a competitive advantage in attracting capital. We see a process of this sort at work in the rivalry among exchanges, with the New York Stock Exchange, which sets rules governing disclosure of information and the issuance of new stock by listed firms, attracting business at the expense of other methods of trading. Before the federal legislation, the New York Stock Exchange had an especially elaborate program requiring detailed disclosure at the time stock was issued and annually whether or not the firm sold new securities.[14]

States

Competition among states for corporate charters, like competition among exchanges for business, ameliorates the collective action problem. This competition is never more powerful than in the market for corporate charters. Because investors have the ability to shift their investments almost at will among firms chartered in different states, and because firms have the ability to select and move the place of incorporation at low cost, the jurisdictions that select the rules that are beneficial to investors will attract and hold the most capital. Aspects of corporate law that survive across jurisdictions and over time are likely to benefit investors. It means that the states that have attracted the largest sums of investment are most likely to have adopted efficient rules. If compulsory disclosure of certain matters is optimal, we would expect to see state law require

14. See Adolf A. Berle and Gardiner C. Means, *The Modern Corporation and Private Property* 64 (1932); Benston, supra note 12.

it, because the requirement would make the state more attractive to investors (and thus to firms).

SOME POORLY SUPPORTED RATIONALES OF MANDATORY DISCLOSURE

The existence of self-induced disclosure by firms, in addition to the variety of competitive mechanisms external to firms for acquiring, disseminating, and requiring the disclosure of, information, will get much knowledge to investors directly or indirectly. Is this "enough" knowledge? One market may suffer "market failure," but at least five markets extract information from corporations. If there is to be a good argument for the national government's compelling disclosure, it must establish why all of the other mechanisms fail. Several of the arguments offered in favor of mandatory disclosure conspicuously fall short when measured by that standard.

Increasing Public Confidence in the Markets

The justification most commonly offered for mandatory disclosure rules is that they are necessary to "preserve confidence" in the capital markets. It is said that investors, especially small and unsophisticated ones, withdraw their capital to the detriment of the markets and the economy as a whole when they fear that they may be exploited by firms or better-informed traders. Disclosure rules both deter fraud and equalize "access" to information, restoring the necessary confidence.

This argument is not surprising; between 1929 and 1934 the securities markets suffered great outflows of capital, which could be attributed to "lack of confidence" among many other sources, whereas during the next fifty years investors appear to have had "confidence." Unless we are satisfied that *post hoc, ergo propter hoc*, however, we cannot stop here. There were extended periods of "confidence" before 1934. A greater percentage of the public invested in equities in the 1920s than at any time since (although indirect investments through mutual funds and pension trusts make investment more widespread now). Why would federal disclosure rules breed confidence otherwise missing?

The explanation cannot be that fraud reigns supreme in the absence of mandatory disclosure. We have shown above that it does not, and the proponents of mandatory disclosure have not established that there is a lesser incidence of fraud with disclosure rules than with antifraud legislation alone. To show one, ten, or hundreds of frauds in the 1920s does not fulfill the obligation; we can point to an equal number of contemporary frauds. To make the confidence argument based on fraud, one would need to show that any reduction in fraud attributable to the disclosure rules was more valuable than the costs of administering them. No regulation can be satisfactorily justified without such analysis: arguing that disclosure reduces fraud without toting up the cost makes as much sense as arguing for the reduction of auto fatalities by requiring all automobiles to be built with five-inch steel plate. After fifty years, the proponents of regulation have no scientifically acceptable evidence of net benefits for any disclosure rule that rests on reducing fraud or increasing confidence.

Protecting Unsophisticated Investors

The companion to the fraud argument is that unsophisticated investors need especial protection. Some say that uninformed investors are exploited investors; whoever knows less will get a raw deal. Others maintain that fear of such exploitation erodes confidence whether or not these investors lose out. Disclosure rules equalizing access (and simplifying the presentation of information, so all can understand it) overcome the problem, whichever way it is put.

This argument is as uninformed as the traders it is supposed to protect. It disregards the role of markets in impounding information in prices. As long as informed traders engage in a sufficient amount of searching for information and bargains, market prices will reflect all publicly available information. The actions of informed traders influence the price until these traders are satisfied with it (on the basis of information); the price cannot be "improved" until new information comes along. The uninformed traders can take a free ride on the information impounded by the market: they get the same price received by the professional traders without having to do any of the work of learning information. These traders are simply made worse off if information is foisted on them: they have to read it or throw it away, yet it does them no good because it is all old hat to professional traders and so cannot influence prices. Informed traders also get rewarded for their news by being slightly ahead of the rest of the market. Such rewards do not come "at the expense of" the less informed; they are compensation for effort that benefits all traders. No matter what the disclosure laws say, the "average investor" who gets disclosure statements through the mail will always be too late to take advantage of any bargains available to those who use information first.

Markets do not impound information until trading starts. Perhaps, then, the suckers get took when they buy stock direct from the issuers, or from brokers who make and control the only markets. (Markets must be two-sided to capture information.) Tales of boiler rooms preying on widows and orphans add verisimilitude. Admirers of P. T. Barnum have nothing to fear from mandatory disclosure rules, however. Boiler rooms make money the old-fashioned way: they defraud people out of it. Enforcement of the rule against fraud takes care of this brand of misconduct, and as we are here interested in mandatory disclosure we press on.

If unsophisticated investors are not exploited by failure to disclose (as opposed to fraud), they do not logically fear exploitation and so do not lack confidence. True, one can say that investors irrationally lack confidence, so that mandatory disclosure is necessary, but this comes close to being a tautology. How could it be proved or refuted? We are willing to concede that some investors always suspect that informed traders are getting secret advantages, but where does this lead? Paranoid traders can protect themselves at minimal cost. They can, for example, put their money in the hands of professional advisers or managers of mutual funds, getting for themselves whatever advantage accrues to the insiders. The existence of informational inequalities—real or imagined—is therefore an inadequate basis for mandatory disclosure.

Increasing the Supply of Truthful Information

A third common justification for mandatory disclosure is the need to provide the most sophisticated investors with the copious information they need to make astute decisions. Under this justification, it is unimportant whether the average investor has or can understand the information. The focus is on getting the information out, with little concern about who gets it first. This argument, in other words, assumes that prices will reflect information efficiently; it justifies disclosure on account of its beneficial effect on the accuracy of prices.

There may well be gains to be had from additional disclosure to the market. We have discussed the reasons why private incentives to disclose, even in connection with competition among markets and states, will not produce all information and may not produce the right amount. If federal disclosure laws reduce the costs of investors' becoming informed, they will increase investors' net returns, and capital markets will be able to allocate funds to higher valuing users.

One must be careful to avoid the fallacy that if some information is good, more must be better. It is not enough to show—although it is unquestionably true—that disclosure rules have led corporations to disclose more information now than they did before 1933. Information is costly to compile and disseminate and to digest, and the costs are borne in large part by investors. Whether investors benefit by more information depends on whether the marginal benefits of increments of knowledge exceed the marginal costs. No one would argue that investors would gain on net if Chrysler "disclosed" the contents of its corporate files, down to the purchase price of each conveyor belt and the details of its bargaining strategy for the next round of negotiations with employees. Thus the observation that more information is released now than fifty-seven years ago may show that there is excessive disclosure now and the right amount fifty-seven years ago. Or it may show only that conditions have changed over time, and that markets now demand more information. If this is true, the amount of disclosure would have increased with or without a statute.

There is some irony in the argument that disclosure rules bring valuable information to market. Many of the "disclosure" rules prohibit the transmission of information at certain times and in certain forms. "Gun jumping" and "touting" rules restrict predistribution statements. The information most important to the market concerns the future; what's past is reflected in prices. Yet for more than forty-five years the SEC discouraged firms from making any projections of profits or other forward-looking disclosures, on the ground that this information was inherently misleading. Rule 175, issued in 1979 after long study, permits the disclosure of projections and forecasts, provided they are adequately supported (that is, tied to yesterday's facts). To understand the disclosure rules as they are or were, one must explain these restrictions and omissions of information along with the mandatory disclosures.

Disclosure Rules as a Response to Third-Party Effects, Legal Error, and Rent Seeking

Although the rationales usually advanced for the disclosure provisions of the securities acts are unconvincing, there is a more plausible line of argument.

THE OBJECTIVES OF DISCLOSURE REQUIREMENTS

Controlling Third-Party Effects

We discussed three reasons why the self-interest model of disclosure might not lead to optimal release of information: (1) some data would concern the industry as well as the firm, and firms would underproduce this data both because they could not charge for benefits conferred on others and because they would want to learn the plans of others without disclosing their own; (2) comparative data would be underproduced because of the inability to charge for it; (3) no firm would have the appropriate incentives to create the least-cost formula for disclosure. We discussed private and state methods by which these may be addressed, but these solutions are incomplete. Private organizations cannot compel adherence, so there will be holdout problems. Competition among the states cannot produce all benefits because of the interstate nature of some of these effects; if being a holdout is in the interest of some firms, it could pay states to be havens to the holdouts.

Controlling Interstate Exploitation

This difficulty with coordinating disclosure through competition among the states reflects the fact that such jurisdictional competition is most effective when the consequences of a decision will be experienced in one jurisdiction. Because only one state's law governs the "internal affairs" of a corporation, competition can be effective. Disclosure rules for a firm chartered in state D, in contrast, affect many firms incorporated elsewhere. Indeed, the multistate nature of securities markets creates opportunities for states to attempt to exploit investors who live elsewhere.

Consider the problem of a firm incorporated in state D, which prescribes disclosure of facts X, Y, and Z. Suppose for the moment that this amount of disclosure is optimal; additional disclosures would cost more than the benefits bestowed on investors. The investors reside throughout the nation. A group of investors living in state N might bring litigation there, contending that under the law of N, the firm should have disclosed Q. It may well be in state N's interest to sustain this claim and order the firm to pay damages to N's residents, even if state N's officials know that the disclosure of Q is counterproductive. This is so because most of the investors live outside state N and will not receive damages. The money to pay to state N's residents will come from residents of other states. State N may seize the occasion to "exploit" the residents of other states, once the firm is underway. State N's residents gain more from the award of damages than they lose from future "inefficiently large" disclosures, since the costs of these disclosures will be borne in the other forty-nine states. State N's residents end up with 100 percent of the benefits of this transfer payment, while they pay a smaller percentage of the costs of excessive future disclosure.

If state N attempts such exploitation, other actors in the markets will adjust. The firms may sell less stock in state N, but they cannot prevent it from migrating there. Firms may start to disclose fact Q, but this is by hypothesis not optimal, and the disclosure of Q will not prevent state N from insisting on some new disclosure tomorrow. Finally, other states may retaliate: they may penalize firms incorporated in state N if these firms do not disclose fact Q in their dealings with residents of other states. A retaliatory equilibrium could develop in which states systematically called for too much disclosure by firms incorporated in other states.

Everyone will be better off if the states desist from such attempts to exploit one another's residents, but it may be costly to control this exploitation. Nations use tariffs as methods of protecting their nationals at the expense of others', and it proves very hard to counteract these efforts. The Commerce, Privileges and Immunities, and Interstate Duty Clauses of our Constitution owe their existence, at least in part, to the recognition that similar problems can occur among the states. But the constitutional provisions (and the judicial holdings applying the Commerce Clause to prevent one state's raw favoritism of its residents) have not prevented all forms of exploitation. One can understand much of modern state tax and products liability law and current doctrines of conflicts of law as efforts to favor domestic residents at the expense of out-of-state persons. Only federal regulation may be able to prevent states from engaging in exploitation in securities transactions.

Controlling the Costs of the Common Law Process

The state law of fraud that existed in 1933 had the elasticity customarily found in the common law. States prohibited not only outright falsehoods but also statements that misled the reader by selective revelation and omission or by crafty language. The calculated ambiguity of the common law has substantial costs, however.

One is risk. A party cannot know, until long after the fact, whether he will be found in violation of the law. Firms that disclose what they think appropriate for investors may be surprised to learn, a few years later, that they did not disclose enough things or the right things. This is a needless risk, and greater risk increases the firm's cost of capital. Investors would be better off if the risk could be reduced without any corresponding reduction in the prospects of the firm. Investors would pay for certainty, and they could be better off even if the price of certainty included the cost of disclosure that would be "excessive" if risk were of no concern. Litigation also is expensive. Litigants spend more, because settlements are harder to strike, when there is more risk. Securities issues often are quite large, and the stakes of fraud litigation are correspondingly large. Thus resources invested in litigation could be immense. Everyone might gain if firms and investors could find some way to reduce the amount of litigation. If, for example, it were possible to create an administrative mechanism to determine in advance whether some disclosure is adequate, the total costs of disclosure could fall. Again investors might be made better off, even if the cost of the administrative system included disclosure that would be excessive in a world of no-cost litigation.

THE CONTOURS OF EFFICIENT MANDATORY DISCLOSURE

So there are, after all, some potential benefits of mandatory disclosure. Whether these are realized in fact is an empirical question.

We have no desire to commit the Nirvana Fallacy of asserting that if markets are "imperfect," then regulation must be better. Detecting the "imperfections" of markets may be no more helpful than observing that all good things have irreducible costs, much as paying for steel is a cost of building a car rather than an "imperfection in the automobile market." Regulation is more failure-prone than markets, because there are few automatic forces that correct regulation gone awry. The regulatory system lacks a competitor, and the very fact of regulation often suppresses the information necessary to detect regulatory failure.

The initial inquiry is whether the federal regulatory system's features track those that we would expect to see if the disclosure rules were reasonably well designed to achieve the objectives we have surveyed. The features implied by our discussion are: (1) standard, routinized disclosure; (2) disclosure by all interstate firms but no intrastate firms; (3) an emphasis on historical facts; (4) a corresponding ban on written disclosure of other facts or of oral "variances" from what is written; (5) prior review of disclosures and other risk-reduction devices; (6) sparing use of a "material omissions" test to find fraud in written disclosure documents. The securities laws embody all of these elements. In the last section of this chapter, we spell out why the elements are appropriate responses to the costs of disclosure and how the securities laws provide them.

THE PATTERN OF MANDATORY DISCLOSURE REQUIREMENTS

Standard, Routinized Disclosure

Standardization of disclosure goes straight to the source of third-party effects. Imposition of a standard format and time of disclosure facilitates comparative use of what is disclosed and helps to create an efficient disclosure language. If every firm must disclose the same things, there will be reciprocal benefits to each firm's investors even though the firm will be compelled to disclose information of advantage to rivals.

The securities laws standardize disclosure by creating "schedules" to be completed by each firm at designated times and by giving the SEC power to promulgate and define accounting terms. The SEC has used its regulatory power to create many forms of disclosure appropriate to the size of the firms and the industries in which they operate. There is, for example, a special form for mineral extraction corporations. Larger firms disclose less than others (Schedule S-3, for the largest firms, is quite streamlined in recognition of the fact that markets generate great quantities of information about such firms). The great specificity of these regulatory schedules both reduces the costs of making the disclosure and increases the comparative value of what is disclosed.

The SEC has not, however, significantly regulated the accounting profession. Our argument in favor of a common disclosure language may seem to imply substantial regulation of accounting. The difficulty here is that no one knows the optimal amount of standardization. Attempts by the SEC to prescribe accounting conventions may interfere with the development of better conventions. It may be that the most effective regulation is to allow the accounting profession to establish the language by common usage and then to prevent significant and misleading deviations from that usage.

Disclosure by All Interstate Firms but No Intrastate Firms

The requirement of universal disclosure responds to the third-party problems discussed above by prohibiting "holdouts" of any substantial players. All gain from the disclosures of others; all must pay by making their own disclosures. The distinction between firms with investors in many states and those with investors in one state also responds directly to the problem of interstate exploitation. Only when holdings are dispersed among many states, so that each state thinks it can "export" damages awards and the costs of excessive disclosure, is there a risk of exploitation. When the majority of a firm's investors live in one jurisdiction, however, exportation becomes difficult, and competition among jurisdictions is more likely to lead to optimal rules.

The statutes implement this approach by restricting initial disclosure (at the time stock is issued) to securities in interstate commerce. Section 3(a)(11) of the 1933 act exempts intrastate sales, and the SEC's Rule 147 offers still broader exemptions for transactions that are primarily within a state. Subsequent disclosure (annual reports and 10K forms, proxy materials, and so on) is restricted to firms traded on national exchanges or having more than a certain number of investors. This effectively exempts all small or closely held corporations from the rules.

Many people find the exemption of these small firms and intra-state deals mysterious, because they believe that such small trans-actions (with less sophisticated investors) are those in which fraud is most likely and in which stock markets and professional invest-ment analysis offer the least protection. They find the exemptions justified, if at all, only by a need to reduce the costs of making relatively small placements. Our approach, by contrast, does not need to excuse the statutes' inattention to the small offerings. The structure of the acts follows logically from the ability of state rules to offer optimal structures in single-state but not multistate transac-tions.

This leaves open the question why the securities laws reduce interstate exploitation. The statutes do not expressly ban damages judgments by state courts; indeed the statutes have savings clauses. Nonetheless, very few awards by state courts could be character-ized as exploitative. Some of this may be attributable to the prior review and safe harbor features of the federal statutes; some may be attributable to the threat that the Supreme Court would interpret the federal statutes to ban exploitation, notwithstanding the savings clauses, as a burden on interstate commerce. We need not offer a complete explanation; something in the structure of the federal law has in fact stopped securities cases from following the pattern of failure-to-warn products liability cases.

An Emphasis on Historical Facts

A recitation of specified objective facts is the least-cost method of disclosure. Historical facts also are the easiest to compare across firms. Verification is cheapest, and the fraud rule works best, when applied to statements of issuer-specific historical fact. Our ap-proach therefore predicts that the securities rules would emphasize such objective disclosures, leaving to market forces any additional (future-oriented) disclosures or information about the industry or economy as a whole.

The laws and regulations have indeed promoted backward-looking statements, despite much academic criticism pointing out that the market puts more weight on future performance and profits. The SEC's schedules emphasize disclosure of profits, cost of assets, and so on, with little more than a passing nod to "plans" and similar information about prospects. Until the promulgation of Rule 175 in 1979, an issuer acted at its great hazard in saying anything about anticipated profits or new products. Today there is a "safe harbor" for projections, sheltering them from being grounds for liability in most cases. This effectively leaves projections to the market: they are neither required nor penalized.

A Ban on Written Disclosure of Other Information or Oral Variances

A set of disclosure rules designed to facilitate use of a common language and comparison among firms must root out novel methods of disclosure; the novelty of one firm's disclosures may erode the utility of the disclosures in comparison. A firm could deny to investors in other firms the reciprocal advantages of disclosure by choosing to disclose things that were sufficiently unusual that the ordinary standards of comparison could not be employed.

Any effort to reduce the costs of litigation, moreover, must ensure that the written disclosures on file with the SEC are the operative disclosures. If one set of disclosures applies to all investors, it is possible to litigate securities cases as class actions, with consequent reductions in cost per investor (and an increase in the likelihood of recovery in at least some amount). The disclosure will be the nucleus of the claim, and difficulties that often arise in tort or contract cases ("The contract says X, but the salesman said Y") can be avoided.

When all investors have a common claim, moreover, the aggregation of these claims in a single suit will present the class with the right incentives. Solitary investors will disregard the precedential value of the suit for others and thus will tend to underinvest. The lawyers in a class suit, by contrast, will tend to consider the interests of all investors in deciding the appropriate sums to spend in investigating claims and pursuing the litigation. Because all of the interested parties are before the court, there are no significant third-party effects. Undoubtedly even if "the class" has the right incentives, the attorneys for the class will not, but this is a separate problem. No matter what the incentives of the attorneys, those who represent a class have better incentives than those who represent isolated parties.

The securities laws follow a path consistent with this approach. The emphasis is on written disclosure. Section 5 of the 1933 act prohibits oral or written statements that precede or differ from the prescribed disclosures. Although firms with securities trading in the aftermarket may and do make oral disclosures—which are necessary to reveal many firm-specific facts—courts decline to entertain claims that these oral statements differ from the written ones.[15] This ensures that writings control. Except in the case of small deals or individual transactions with brokers, oral statements prove largely irrelevant.

Prior Review and Safe Harbors

Prior administrative review may be much cheaper than subsequent (and risky) judicial decision making. Parties would be willing to "overdisclose" to reduce risk. Securities law follows the approach of prior review and risk reduction in a variety of ways. For a long time the SEC's staff reviewed every registration statement and prospectus with care before allowing it to become effective. Although the process of review created no formal legal immunity, it did so as a practical matter because the administrative process ensured compliance with all formalities and created precautionary overdisclosure. (This regularity of practice and review also contributed to the routinization of disclosure, and within the last fifteen years the SEC has been able to rely on the accumulated expertise of the bar to keep up the forms without such detailed review.)

15. See Zobrist v. Coal-X, Inc., 708 F.2d 1511 (10th Cir. 1983) (dismissing a suit because the party relying on the supposed oral statement could not show reliance; in other words, the court declined to allow the oral statements to contradict the written ones); Teamsters Local 282 Pension Trust Fund v. Angelos, 762 F.2d 522 (7th Cir. 1985); Acme Propane, Inc. v. Tenexco, Inc., 844 F.2d 1317 (7th Cir. 1988). The same result would be achieved by a rigorous application of the parol evidence rule. The considerations advanced in Blue Chip Stamps v. Manor Drug Stores, 421 U.S. 723 (1975), which discussed the difficulties that arise when a person can litigate on the basis of personal statements about how disclosures influenced inaction, tend to a similar result. One recent counterexample is Bruschi v. Brown, 876 F.2d 1526 (11th Cir. 1989), which allowed the plaintiff to argue that a variety of factors, including his own ignorance, excused failure to read the written disclosure documents and allowed him to attack the veracity and completeness of oral statements. The court did not appear to see the reasons that have led securities law in a different direction.

The matters not covered by prior review are covered by statutory or regulatory "safe harbors"—provisions taking advantage of §19(a) of the 1933 act and §23(a)(1) of the 1934 act. These statutes say that nothing done in good faith in reliance on rules of the SEC shall be the basis of liability under the acts. These safe harbor regulations often require a firm to take a complicated series of steps to obtain their shelter; hence the attraction and challenge of securities practice for lawyers. From the investors' point of view, however, the regulations offer a way to reduce their exposure, often in exchange for little disclosure.

The upshot of the procedures available under the acts is that while firms face large and unpredictable liabilities concerning the products they make, they face small expected liabilities concerning the securities they issue—even though the performance of the products is more predictable than the prices of the securities. One must look long and hard to find cases imposing liability on the basis of disclosure documents prepared in the ordinary course and filed with the SEC. There are lots of cases imposing liability, but almost all involve the sales of small businesses or some other unusual, person-specific transactions. The incidence of liability proves our basic point: the broad disclosure rules are effective in reducing risk in exchange for minor alterations of firms' disclosures.

The Sparing Use of the Material Omission Test

All of the methods for formulaic disclosure and the production of certainty that we have discussed could be undone by a broad definition of fraudulent nondisclosure. The statutes and rules prohibit the omission of material information that is necessary to make that which was disclosed not misleading. Terms such as "material" and "misleading" are vague. The SEC and courts could read them as requiring unbounded and uncertain disclosures, undermining every other device we have discussed. Again the analogy to torts is instructive. Courts have been imposing stupendous liabilities for "failure to warn" of certain dangers, the tort equivalent of the materially misleading omission.

In securities cases, though, use of the "material omission" standard has been limited. The Supreme Court has concluded that an omission is material only if "there is a substantial likelihood that a reasonable investor would consider it important in deciding how to vote."[16] In the case containing that definition, the Court held not material an omission to state that a package of securities, valued in an initial disclosure at one price, was worth as much as 20 percent less. The Court reasoned that so much other information was disclosed that the change in price could reasonably have been inferred, and that in any event the nondisclosure was so limited in relation to what was disclosed that it need not be the basis of liability.

Under this standard of materiality, the ample disclosures required by the SEC's forms and schedules offer insulation from subsequent efforts to show material omissions. The standardization and risk-reduction functions can be achieved. True, many cases in the lower courts find certain omissions in formal disclosure documents "material"; we cannot deny that some of these holdings involve omissions that were trivial and unimportant from most perspectives. But with few exceptions,[17] these cases do not award damages. Most litigation concerns subsequent transactions. (Perhaps the difference is that once stock has been issued, firms are no longer free to give the cautious assessments that accompany new issues. Undue gloom might be portrayed as manipulative.) State courts, acting under state law, have used a much broader definition of materiality, giving credence to the interstate exploitation hypothesis.[18] Nevertheless, the existence of five or ten "material omission" holdings every year in federal injunction cases does not undermine the more important observation: damages are rarely available on account of omissions in formal papers filed with the SEC.

Evidence on Costs and Benefits

Assertions about the effects of the securities laws cry out for testing. After fifty-seven years, though, we know very little. Neither the costs nor the benefits permit ready measurement.

16. TSC Indus., Inc. v. Northway, 426 U.S. 438, 449 (1976). This formula applies to purchases and sales of stock as well as to votes. Basic, Inc. v. Levinson, 485 U.S. 224, 232, 239–240 (1988).

17. For example, Feit v. Leasco Data Processing Equipment Corp., 332 F. Supp. 544 (S.D.N.Y. 1971); Escott v. Bar-Chris Construction Corp., 283 F. Supp. 643 (S.D.N.Y. 1968).

18. Lynch v. Vickers Energy Corp., 429 A.2d 497 (Del. 1981), overruled in part by Weinberger v. UOP, Inc., 457 A.2d 701 (Del. 1983).

Direct Costs

The direct costs of securities regulation are those of compiling, disseminating, regulating, and litigating about information. These include the opportunity costs of the time of all who participate in the disclosure process (corporate executives, lawyers, staff), plus expenses of printing and mailing disclosure documents and rules about disclosure. Susan Phillips and Richard Zecher conclude that out-of-pocket costs exceeded $1 billion for 1980—not including the opportunity cost of the time of the issuers' employees.[19] Firms voluntarily incur larger costs to make disclosures. Mailing the firms' certified statements and annual reports to investors, which the statutes do not require, costs more than $2 billion annually. These mailings do not produce new information: everything in an annual report is old hat by the time it is mailed, and the dissemination of the report itself does not assist in making better decisions about investments.

This suggests a substantial problem in all efforts to determine the cost of required disclosure: we do not know what things firms would disclose, and to whom, in the absence of the securities laws. Much of the $1 billion figure covers costs that would be incurred in the absence of the statutes—recall that voluntary disclosure was extensive in 1933—and the marginal direct cost of mandatory disclosure may be small. If the uncertain benefits of mailing the annual statements lead firms to spend $2 billion voluntarily, it would not take much on the benefit side to justify the SEC's incremental requirements.

Indirect Costs

Indirect costs are potentially more substantial and harder to measure. One cost is that disclosure may lead firms to change or abandon profitable projects that they otherwise would have pursued. A new product might be profitable if built in secrecy, stealing a march on rivals; if the rules require advance disclosure, rivals' responses make the project less attractive. Proponents of disclosing information on subjects such as foreign payments and pollution frequently argue that disclosure is beneficial precisely because it leads firms to change what they do. Such disclosures do not pro-

19. Susan E. Phillips and J. Richard Zecher, *The SEC and the Public Interest* 27–51 (1981). The voluntary costs (mentioned in the text below) appear at 50 (table 3.3).

duce benefits *for investors,* no matter the net social effects. The alteration of profitable behavior—whether the profit comes from new products or from not paying the full social costs of emitting pollutants—is a cost from investors' perspective.

It may be that few projects are abandoned because of disclosure; the backward-looking, formulaic, and reciprocal nature of required disclosure makes it unlikely that disclosure will give away valuable and uncompensated information. Reciprocal disclosure of pollution may even turn out to be beneficial to investors as a group, although each firm would profit from being a holdout and staying silent while others disclose. The costs (and potential benefits) of the disclosure-induced changes in firms' behavior are unknown.

Disclosure systems have other potential indirect costs. One is noise. If the law forces firms to disclose more information than they otherwise would, investors then must spend extra time combing through the disclosures to find what really matters. Another is substitution. Firms may cease disclosing some category of useful information and switch to some obfuscatory (but complying) information. Firms may become more cautious and leaden on paper, making their important disclosures in discussions or other oral exchanges that will be less precise and less widely disseminated. Poorly understood or "coded" disclosures will be decoded imperfectly (and at some cost). In the extreme, a mandatory disclosure system's specification of what to reveal may stop firms from conveying categories of information altogether.

BENEFITS

The principal benefit asserted for mandatory disclosure is that investors will make more money. They will suffer fewer losses from deceit; even if the level of fraud is unaffected, they will invest more wisely when they know more. Society gains with investors, because wise investment means efficient matching of funds with projects. Unfortunately—both for investors and for those who would like to identify benefits—competition makes it hard to obtain benefits or measure those that occur.

Profits for Investors?

There have been three detailed studies of returns to investors before and after the 1933 act; none found evidence of substantial benefits.[20] George Stigler (1964) and Gregg Jarrell (1981) found no benefits at all, concluding that investors before and after the federal law earned the normal rate of return on their investments in both stock issued by firms going public ("IPOs") and new sales of stock by firms already traded ("seasoned" securities). Investors in both IPOs and seasoned issues received the same risk-adjusted rate of return they could have had from investing in other vehicles, such as stock trading in the aftermarket. Carol Simon (1989) verified these findings, with an interesting exception: investors in IPOs that were not traded on the New York Stock Exchange did better after the act. This implies that the statutory disclosures furnish something of value that a combination of the New York Stock Exchange's rules and the scrutiny of professional investors had supplied to investors before 1933. Stigler, Jarrell, and Simon agree that the 1933 act had a further effect: it reduced the variance of outcomes among firms that went public. The losses in unsuccessful firms were not so large after 1933, but the gains from the "hits" were smaller too. Lower volatility is a benefit (most investors dislike risk).

What do we learn from these findings? That investors in new issues do (about) as well as investors in other instruments should not be surprising, no matter what the extent of disclosure. These are, after all, the same investors, and every investor has access to new and old issues as well as to bonds, precious metals, commodities, and other investments. Markets in equilibrium would produce similar risk-adjusted profits in all of these. Even if information is scarce and investors stupid, we would not expect them to be more stupid when buying new issues.

There was a good deal of disclosure before 1933, and professional traders acquired by hook or by crook important information that firms declined to reveal. If the 1933 act simply codified firms' "good practice," slightly reducing the amount of search by the professionals, it would leave little trace in the data. Suppose, however, that before 1933 some issuers did not produce "enough" information, that the 1933 act forced them to produce the "right" infor-

20. George J. Stigler, "Public Regulation of the Securities Market," 37 *J. Bus.* 117 (1964), revised and reprinted in Stigler, supra note 3, at 78; Gregg A. Jarrell, "The Economic Effects of Federal Regulation of the Market for New Security Issues," 24 *J. L. & Econ.* 613 (1981); Carol J. Simon, "The Effect of the 1933 Securities Act on Investor Information and the Performance of New Issues," 79 *Am. Econ. Rev.* 295 (1989).

mation, and that this was beneficial to investors. We probably still would not see profits unless some issues (perhaps IPOs outside the New York Stock Exchange) had been targeted to suckers. If the new securities are more attractive with information attached, they will sell for more too; the promoters and underwriters will see to that, and the price adjustment will disguise the gains from the regulation.

Another problem: the Securities Exchange Act of 1934 changed the benchmark against which the profits of investors in new issues are measured. A demonstration that investors in new issues in (say) 1940 did as well as investors in the aftermarket would not show a gain if changes in the aftermarket had boosted the accuracy of both kinds of investment. Although this introduces a bias against finding effects, there is a bias the other way. Informational intermediaries have become more common since 1933, and improvements might be attributable to them rather than to the statutes. A study immediately before and after 1933 might show gains, but the presence of gains in a world with fewer informational intermediaries would not support the inference that the 1933 act continues to produce today any improvements we can measure.

The finding that the 1933 act reduces the variability of returns also is ambiguous on benefits versus losses. If lower variability comes from more accurate information, implying better matching of funds to projects, there is an unambiguous gain; if instead it comes from deferring the sale of stock—keeping firms in the hands of venture capitalists for a longer time before public sale, while information accumulates—the gain may be offset by the delay in firms' access to capital markets, which may or may not be costly. As long as the venture capital market is large and reasonably efficient (which it is today), private placements will raise all of the necessary funds, at optimal rates, from the pros who deal in new ventures.

Profits and Losses to Intermediaries and Firms

If the data on comparative returns among types of issue or over time are ambiguous, we may do better with data on instantaneous price changes. It is possible to inquire what happened to the prices of stock when the statutes were enacted. If the new disclosure requirements were beneficial, the argument goes, investors would value stock more highly. Prices should rise smartly to reflect the gains to investors.

George Benston (1973) studied the reaction of the market to the passage of the 1934 act.[21] Because every firm traded on the principal exchanges in 1934 conducted and revealed the results of an annual independent audit, Benston analyzed the effects of the statute by looking for differences in the stock performance of those that previously had disclosed their sales (62 percent) and those that had not. He found no significant difference in the performance of firms in the different groups between February 1934 (when the first hearings on the act were held) and June 1935 (by which time every firm had disclosed its sales). Benston inferred from this that the new disclosure rules were of no benefit to investors.

It is hard to know what to make of this. Perhaps "sales" were not the critical bit of information investors desired (although there is evidence that disclosure of this fact often affected the price of stock). Perhaps there were no significant differences in the performance because the market inferred the sales of the nondisclosers from the sales of disclosers in the same industry. Then we would treat the nondisclosers as free riders, trying to take advantage of other firms. This interpretation is consistent with Benston's further finding that during the period 1929–1934, the stock price of firms that did not disclose their sales rose slightly compared with firms that did. Benston suggests that this shows that required disclosure of sales damaged investors; we could say as easily that the nondisclosers' extra profits came from their status as free riders, holdouts attempting to get information from disclosures of other firms without tipping their own hands.

We do not want to sound too critical. Studies of the effects of legislation are hard to carry off, because even inefficient markets impound a great deal of information. The more information about disclosure and legal rules is reflected in prices in advance, the harder it is to discern the effects of new legal rules. It is fair to say that there is no good evidence that the disclosure rules are beneficial for seasoned issues; there is some evidence of benefits for IPOs of stock traded outside the New York Stock Exchange. There is also no good evidence that the rules are harmful or very costly. We are left, for the moment at least, with arguments rather than proof. And the arguments are themselves inconclusive.

---

21. Benston, supra note 12, 63 *Am. Econ. Rev.* at 141–152.

12

Optimal Damages

Remedies in securities cases offer a good test of our proposition that economic rationality is implicit in corporate law. At first the law of remedies seems chaotic. The principal statutes articulate a number of different principles, ranging from rescission to profits to damages.[1] The cases contain a mélange of rules. Some courts emphasize the plaintiff's out-of-pocket loss; some emphasize the defendant's profits; some award rescission and some restitution; often a court gives up and announces that the judge has discretion to fashion "a remedy to suit the particular case"—as if there were no need for legal rules to evaluate the significance and effects of the facts of "the particular case."[2] The academic literature is little

1. Section 12 of the Securities Act of 1933 allows those who purchased unregistered securities (or securities from sellers who made material misrepresentations) to recover the price paid "less the amount of any income received thereon, upon the tender of such security, or . . . damages if he no longer owns the security." Section 11(d) of the 1933 act provides for the award of price paid less value at the time of suit or sale, when there was a misrepresentation in the registration statement, but it creates a defense that the difference is not recoverable if it "represents other than the depreciation in value of such security" resulting from the event creating the liability. Section 9(e) of the Securities Exchange Act of 1934 establishes "damages sustained" as the standard in certain manipulative practices cases, and §18(a) covers "damages caused" by misstatements in documents filed with the SEC. The Insider Trading Penalties Act, amending §21(d)(2) of the 1934 act, allows a court to award to the SEC up to three times the defendants' "profits" from inside trading; private plaintiffs may receive the profits without a multiplier, §20A(b)(1). There are variations on each theme.

2. Hackbart v. Holmes, 675 F.2d 1114, 1121 (10th Cir. 1982), is the source of the quotation. For compendiums of the approaches of different courts, see Thomas Lee Hazen, *The Law of Securities Regulation* §§7.5.3, 13.7 (2d ed. 1990); Arnold S. Jacobs, "The Measure of Damages in Rule 10b-5 Cases," 65 *Geo. L. J.* 1093 (1977); Robert B. Thompson, "The Measure of Recovery under Rule 10b-5: A Restitution Alternative to Tort Damages," 37 *Vand. L. Rev.* 349 (1984).

better. Scholars frequently observe that the rules are poorly articulated and inconsistent. But recognizing this does not lead to a neat solution. The American Law Institute's Federal Securities Code, designed to serve as a model for legislation and interpretation, contains all of the competing rules and then states that these rules "may be varied on a showing that a different definition of rescission or measure of damages would be plainly more appropriate on consideration of such factors as the plaintiff's loss, the defendant's profit, and the deterrent effect of the particular type of liability."[3]

Our thesis, as usual, is that things appear to be more chaotic than they are. Some fairly simple principles lead to intelligible rules of damages. These rules are not only elegant in theory but also applied in practice. We use here the economics of sanctions. The objective of a legal rule is to deter certain undesirable behavior without simultaneously deterring (too much) beneficial behavior. Rules should minimize the sum of the losses from (a) undesirable behavior that the rules permit, (b) desirable behavior that the laws deter, and (c) the costs of enforcement. The legal system balances these competing objectives through the choice of sanctions as well as through the choice of substantive doctrines. Indeed, a thoughtful selection of the sanction may promote desirable outcomes even though the substantive rule is necessarily incomplete or overbroad.

The Economics of Optimal Sanctions in Securities Markets

Securities are specialized contracts, as we have emphasized. Investors agree to contribute capital and bear the risk of the enterprise; in exchange they get promises of a role in running the business and a share of the returns. A "securities fraud" is a form of breach of contract. One party fails to furnish another with information required in the regular course of dealing, or he furnishes information but defaults in his duties, making the information inaccurate. We should expect a close relation between damages in securities cases and damages in other contract cases.

Damages in most of contract law mediate among the costs of extreme positions. At one extreme, the legal rule could ensure that parties keep all their contracts. Draconian damages rules would do

3. Federal Securities Code §1723(e) (1980). The commentary announces that perhaps "there is no law of damages under Rule 10b-5." Ibid., comment 1.

this. At the other extreme, the legal rule could permit breach whenever convenient to the breaching party. A rule of zero damages would have this effect. Courts do not adopt either extreme. Plaintiffs in contract cases commonly recover the lost value of the contract (the "expectation" measure of damages). A person who contracted for a ton of peas, at $1 per pound, to be delivered on July 1 in New York, is entitled on breach to the difference between $1 and the market price of peas on July 1 in New York—the price at which he can "cover" the contract. The aggrieved party cannot get "lost profits" or "consequential damages" recoveries unless the contract applies to a unique good.

The measure of damages in contract cases permits parties to a contract to commit "efficient breaches." The seller of the peas may have them on hand in California. Suppose the price of peas rises to $1.10 per pound in California. The best disposition of these peas is to make them available in California (where buyers value them more highly) rather than to ship them to New York, where the current price may be only $1.05. The damages rule induces the seller to divert the peas to California; the buyer may secure peas for $1.05 in New York, and the seller will pay the buyer 5 cents per pound. The rule permits the parties to take account of the costs of performance of their contract and of changing relative values. It acts as if the parties had the foresight to negotiate about such contingencies. Damages rules may approximate the results of contracts that provide for all contingencies.

It is easy to see that there may be an "optimal level of breach" in ordinary contracts. It is not so obvious that this is so with securities contracts. Nevertheless, the same principles apply. "Truth," like all good things, is costly to produce. Chapter 11 covers many of these costs. Whole industries—accounting, investment banking, much of the bar, much of the financial press—are the embodiments of the costs of investigation and certification of information about firms and their securities. Economizing on these costs is everyone's objective.

EFFICIENT LIABILITY RULES AND EFFICIENT DAMAGES RULES

Because there are benefits in less than total candor—ranging from a reduction in paperwork to the ability to hide vital facts from one's business rivals—legal principles must recognize the value of non-disclosure. There are two ways to do this, just as with other contracts. For ordinary contracts the methods are elaborate specification of excuses and other contingencies in the contract (or implied in law), and the selection of the measure of damages. For securities contracts the two methods are elaborate specification of the substantive law (such as careful attention to "materiality" and other substantive doctrines), and the selection of the measure of damages.

Either freedom from liability or low damages in the event of liability will lead firms to conserve resources and not disclose. Yet the two approaches—substance and re.nedies—are not always equivalent. They have different implications for the treatment of uncertainty. Suppose investors would agree that it is not worthwhile for managers to investigate and discuss every remote business contingency; the investors agree that it is better to take the chance that a remote (but undisclosed) bad event will come to pass than to incur the certain costs of investigating many remote possibilities. The legal system can permit this to occur either by defining a particular contingency as "not material" (and hence nondisclosure is not a violation) or by saying that the nondisclosure is a violation but the damages nil.

The "materiality" approach requires courts to investigate just how likely an unlikely event may have been. Because the stakes of the case are apt to be high, the parties will invest heavily in litigation. But it will prove hard to reconstruct after the fact the probability of poorly investigated events, and so litigation of this sort is apt to be chancy as well as costly. The damages solution could reduce the importance of the answer to this difficult question. If damages are set correctly, the seller will investigate and disclose up to the point where an additional dollar spent on this activity produces just one more dollar for investors. The person with the best access to information will make the decision on the spot, saving the resources that could be spent on *ex post* inquests years later in court. In many cases it will be much more efficient to establish a damages rule to induce the seller to make the decision than to have a judicial inquiry into the optimal level of disclosure.

Sellers of securities may investigate thoroughly and disclose all possibilities; they may hire experts (who may be more or less skilled); they may rely on financial intermediaries such as investment bankers to do the investigation and replace "complete" disclosure with the assurance of their reputations; they may choose not to disclose certain things at all because they fear that disclosure could tip off rivals to ongoing developments; they may choose to leave certain investigating to the investors. Each of these options has associated costs and benefits. Well-chosen damages rules can induce sellers to select the strategy with the greatest net benefits. This is what "efficient offenses" mean in practice. The legal system may call some nondisclosure an offense not for the purpose of extirpating all conduct of that class, but for the purpose of bringing home to the decision maker the costs of his conduct. The rules in securities cases may have the same function as the rules in contract cases (which are not designed to abolish breach) or tort cases (which are not designed to abolish risk-taking behavior). In contract and tort, like securities, rules may serve the purpose of inducing the most knowledgeable party to compare the costs and benefits of its acts.

Often, though, it is better to find no liability than to fine-tune damages rules. The assumption that liability rules are beneficial in securities laws rests on answers to a series of difficult factual inquiries. Damages actions create costs as well as benefits. Though information is the basis of all contracts, many contracts are enforced best through self-help remedies rather than actions at law.[4] Private actions for damages in securities cases create significant costs. Investors routinely sue managers whenever the price of stock falls dramatically, and it is very hard for a court to determine whether the decline was caused by some extrinsic event or by something known to managers, but not disclosed, at an earlier time. If courts equate bad outcomes with bad actions, the ensuing damages will do more to discourage the conduct of business enterprises than to encourage the revelation of important facts. But in this chapter we do not question further the scope of the rules. We assume that the existing allocation among liability rules, damages rules, and freedom from liability is roughly correct.

4. See Benjamin Klein and Keith B. Leffler, "The Role of Market Forces in Assuring Contractual Performance," 89 *J. Pol. Econ.* 615 (1981); Charles R. Knoeber, "An Alternative Mechanism to Assure Contractual Reliability," 12 *J. Legal Studies* 333 (1983); Lester G. Telser, "A Theory of Self-Enforcing Agreements," 53 *J. Bus.* 27 (1980); Oliver E. Williamson, "Credible Commitments: Using Hostages to Support Exchange," 73 *Am. Econ. Rev.* 519 (1983).

THE NATURE OF OPTIMAL SANCTIONS IN SECURITIES TRANSACTIONS

Damages as a Measure of Net Harm

When particular activity may have both costs and benefits, the optimal sanction is the net harm that activity imposes on other people, divided by the probability that the activity will be detected and prosecuted successfully.[5] Suppose, for example, that a failure to investigate and disclose some contingency saves $100 in the costs of investigation and has different effects on two classes of investors: one class loses $200 if the contingency comes to pass, and another class gains $50. We postpone for the moment whether money losses sustained by investors are the same as real economic harm. We also assume that investors want firms to maximize their expected value, which is equivalent to assuming that investors are risk-neutral. Chapters 4 and 5 elaborated on this.

If the nondisclosure is sure to be detected and prosecuted, then the appropriate award is $150, the net harm. The firm, observing that it must pay $150 in damages to save $100, will conduct the investigation. If the savings from not conducting the investigation is $175, by contrast, the firm will save the costs of investigating and pay the damages. Investors will be $25 better off as a result, because the investors ultimately are the beneficiaries of "the firm's" savings. If the probability of successful prosecution is one in two, the damages should be doubled. Then over a run of, say, ten similar cases, the firm would expect $175 in savings per case (total of $1,750) and would expect to pay $300 in each of five cases (total $1,500) and would again save the resources. The firm (which is to say, all of the venturers, as we explained in Chapter 1) would conserve the costs of investigation whenever the costs exceeded $150, just as it should.

Other Considerations of Optimality

Although the "net harm" rule creates the right incentives for people deciding how much to investigate and disclose, it does not neces-

5. Gary S. Becker, "Crime and Punishment: An Economic Approach," 76 *J. Pol. Econ.* 169 (1968), is the seminal treatment; it is reprinted in his *Economic Approach to Human Behavior* 39 (1976).

sarily send the appropriate signals to the other actors. It may be essential to adjust the damages to avoid some collateral problems.

Investors do not respond to net harm directly. In the example we gave above, the nondisclosure of a fact helped some investors and harmed others. The investors who stood to lose $200 might attempt to protect their own interests. They could hire agents (such as investment advisers) to do investigation on their behalf. Yet they ought not to have such an incentive; by hypothesis the optimal investment in information is either zero or an amount less than $150 to be spent by the firm. In general, expenses by investors on investigation are a substitute for effective private incentives or legal rules that induce optimal disclosures. It would be nice to arrange a damages measure that removes the incentive for private investigation. Yet in the example we have given, only a certain award of $200 to the "losing" investors would remove their incentive to investigate. This is too large an award from the perspective of the firm. If it must pay $200 to the "losing" investors, it will spend up to that amount on investigation itself, and again (by hypothesis) that is too much.

This example illustrates two things. First, it is important that the rule of damages compensate investors to at least some extent for their private losses, and not just for social or net loss. Too little compensation leads to too much private investigation. If the victim of a trespass could not obtain compensation for private harms, potential victims would spend money erecting unnecessary barricades; the award of damages prevents this. Second, a rule providing compensation for private injuries may lead firms to invest too much in investigation and disclosure. As a result, there may be no one "best" remedy. It is necessary to choose some system of sanctions that mediates these conflicting objectives.

It is important to give people the right incentives to enforce the rules and thus compel people to pay the damages that induce them to take correct decisions. The structure of rewards should induce enforcers to expend resources finding and prosecuting violations until, at the margin, the last dollar of resources spent on enforcement reduces the social costs of nondisclosure by just one dollar. This is almost impossible to achieve, for at least three reasons.

First, only by accident will the damages in a particular case, the standard against which the enforcer will compare its expenditures, equal the social loss from future, similar decisions about disclosure. Second, the rule that damages be increased in response to a lower probability of successful prosecution implies an inverse relation between the multiplier and the probability of prosecution. But this cannot easily be achieved in a system of private enforcement. The higher the multiplier, the higher the payoff from suit; the higher the payoff, the more people will spend investigating and bringing suits. This may lead both to excessive net penalties and to excessive enforcement.

Third, if the victims of nondisclosure or fraud own enforcement rights in proportion to their injuries, each will spend too little investigating and prosecuting the offense because each can obtain redress only for his own loss. Each person's activities in investigation and prosecution produces a gain for former and future victims, a gain that cannot be appropriated. One way around this is to assign the enforcement right to a single "entity"—usually the "class" in a class action. It turns out, however, that this just changes the locus of the problem. Now the question becomes: who speaks for the class? Each of the class's agents (attorneys and experts) faces the problem of unappropriable gains. It is possible to devise elegant mechanisms through which would-be enforcers could purchase enforcement rights for lump-sum payments; quite a number of such mechanisms would in theory overcome the problems in question. These are not available in our legal system, however, and will not work if enforcers are risk-averse (as most are, even plaintiffs' lawyers with portfolios of claims that help them hedge risk).

The net harm rule for damages applies only when there are efficient offenses. The net harm rule induces the firm to spend the right amount in investigation and dissemination of information. Many kinds of conduct have no associated savings. Take, for example, deliberate lying about the firm's assets. A firm puts out a prospectus saying that it has 10,000 tons of tobacco in inventory, when all of the firm's officers know that the actual amount is 1,000 tons. The lie does not enable the firm to save the costs of investigation; to the contrary, it is usually more costly to fabricate a lie and cover up the traces than to tell the truth, and lies create incentives for others to investigate to pierce the disguise. Here the legal rule should be designed to deter unconditionally—not to force the firm to compare costs and benefits, but to channel its conduct into approved forms. The very stiff penalties for armed robbery channel behavior into the more accepted form of negotiation; the robber can negotiate with merchants, and the rule induces him to do so rather than resort to force. One can safely ignore a claim of "efficient robbery," and so too with many kinds of fraud. If we are certain enough that some kinds of conduct are always inappropriate, then no penalty is too high. (This is a big "if." When the legal system makes mistakes, whether in choosing which conduct to proscribe or in concluding that the defendant committed the proscribed behavior, severe penalties deter desirable conduct.)

Not quite "no" penalty. It is necessary to preserve deterrence on the margin. If the expected penalty for telling a small lie is the dissembler's entire wealth, then no one will stop with a small lie. If you're going to tell a lie, you might as well tell a whopper. Any system of penalties must graduate the anticipated sanction with the seriousness of the offense in order to avoid driving offenders to the high end of the seriousness scale.

The upshot of this discussion is that the net harm rule, though a useful starting point for assessing the incentive to make appropriate disclosures, is not a satisfactory rule for all cases. It must be modified to preserve incentives to enforce the rules and to prevent excessive precautions by investors. It may be abandoned when the kind of statement or omission in question cannot be thought efficient. A few other modifications are appropriate when the firm in question is closely held. We return to these issues. Now, though, we specify what a net harm rule would use as a starting point.

Finding the Net Harm

There are at least four components of the net harm in securities transactions. First, and usually largest, is the net transfer to the offender. When A steals $100 from B and keeps the money, the transfer of wealth is part of the harm. If A is Robin Hood and gives $90 to C, then the net transfer to the offender is only $10. To see why the net transfer rather than the gross transfer is the right measure, consider a variation of the example we presented above. Suppose the managers of a firm decide to skimp on investigating a contingency that affects the relative rights of two classes of investors. If the contingency comes to pass, class 1 loses $200, class 2 gains $40, and the managers gain $10 personally. The net harm is $150, the $200 loss less the $50 gain ($40 + $10). The parties as a group would like "the firm" to conduct the investigation and disseminate the information only if the costs of doing that are less than

$150. If the legal rule levies a judgment totaling $150 (against the firm and the managers in any combination), the managers will take steps to avoid that result whenever they can do so for less than $150. A higher penalty leads to excessive investment in information; a rule that lets those in charge of the decision keep personal profit also warps the judgment. So one can think of the first component of the net harm rule this way: the harm is the gross loss minus any benefit created by the transaction (whether the benefit is a transfer to investors or the saving of resources in investigation).

The second source of harm from fraud and nondisclosure is the total cost of carrying out the offense, unmasking the offense, taking precautions against similar offenses, and litigating about offenses. The cost of hefty locks and burglar alarm systems is part of the cost of theft; the cost of extra resources spent investigating the truth of statements about securities is part of the social cost of securities offenses. These costs include the costs that "truthful" firms must spend to distinguish themselves from slipshod and untruthful firms. (Firms bear the costs of carrying out frauds "automatically," however; these are "costs of doing business." We need not include them a second time in the penalty for the offense.)

The final sources of harm are related reductions in the allocative efficiency of the economy. One is that incomplete or inaccurate disclosure about investments leads people to invest in the wrong projects. They will spend "too much" in resources to produce goods and services. The other is that incomplete or inaccurate disclosure can send the wrong signals about risk, and this distorts the choice between investment and consumption. To see these effects, consider three cases. In each case people invest in a firm that promises to make widgets. They have the option of purchasing riskless securities (such as T-Bills) and will invest in a risky venture only if the firm yields enough of an increase in productivity to pay for the risk premium.

In the first case the manufacture of widgets is riskless. At a cost of $1 per widget, anyone can make as many widgets as he wants. When there is no risk in the underlying technology, a securities offense would take the form of promising to build more widgets than the firm actually does. The firm might collect $10 and build only 9 widgets. Here there is no reduction in the efficiency with which goods are produced: the firm spends $9 to build 9 widgets, and the promoters keep $1. The only injury is the creation of uncompensated risk. People fearing that this sort of thing could occur will demand a small amount of additional compensation for bearing risk, and this shifts a little investment out of risky endeavors. The net harm in a case such as this is the $1 transfer plus the (small) increment to risk plus the costs of making, defending against, and unmasking frauds of this sort.

In the second case the manufacture of widgets is risky, and the promoters misrepresent the risk of the technology. Perhaps they represent that there is no risk, when in fact there is a .5 chance that an investment of $10 would produce 8 widgets and a .5 chance that it would produce 12 widgets. Once more the only injury to the efficient conduct of the economy is the creation of uncompensated risk. The net harm is the (small) increment to risk plus the costs of making, defending against, and unmasking such misrepresentations. If the costs of making accurate representations about the risk of building widgets exceed this small sum, then this case is an "efficient offense." Setting damages equal to the net harm induces the promoters to incur the expense of investigation or pay the damages, whichever is less.

In the third case the manufacture of widgets is risky, and the promoters misrepresent the productivity of the technology. Perhaps they represent that an investment of $10 in their new technology will on average produce 11 widgets, but in fact it will produce only a .5 chance of 8 widgets and a .5 chance of 10 widgets. Here, too, there is uncompensated risk. This also creates a loss of efficiency as society spends $10 to produce (on average) only 9 widgets; had the promoters told the truth, the investors would have insisted on using the risk-free technology guaranteed to produce 10 widgets for $10. The net harm in this case is the $1 reduction in productive efficiency plus the (small) increment to risk plus the costs of making, defending against, and unmasking fraud. If the promoters spent less than $10 to build the widgets, there is also a transfer that must be extracted as part of the net harm. Finally, this case also creates a loss in allocative efficiency. The consumer who would have valued the tenth widget at more than $1 loses the value of that widget. The new elements of loss in this third case are the hatched areas in Figure 1. The shaded triangle is the allocative loss, the reduction in consumers' surplus; the shaded trapezoid is the reduction in productive efficiency.

We cannot say how often securities offenses fall into these dif-

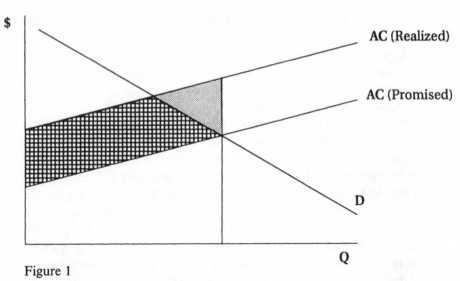

Figure 1

ferent categories. Moreover, neither we nor anyone else has a good way to determine the level of the costs involved. As a rule the cost of increased risk is small, and for many offenses the transfer of wealth will be far and away the largest element of the net harm. Some multiple of the net transfer payment therefore would be a useful starting point, with a further increase in cases that involve identifiable reductions in allocative and productive efficiency.

The Role of Liquid Markets

Prices observable in markets supply much of the information needed to make this approach work. Suppose the question is the amount of harm inflicted by a firm's decision not to release information about the risks of new medical imaging equipment. The technology may not work, or it may be subject to adverse regulations, or it may be displaced by newer technologies. Assessing and revealing these risks may be costly and chancy, so that a strategy of saying little may (or may not) be optimal. Ultimately something goes wrong (maybe new regulations limit to one per city the number of the costly machines), and the investors claim that the lack of disclosure was wrongful. It is possible to establish an upper limit on the net transfer by observing the change of price of the stock when the bad news is released.

Suppose everything happens in an instant. The firm decides to save the costs of investigation and issues stock for a price that reflects (undue) optimism. Moments later the bad news comes out. The price of stock would fall to the one fully informed investors found appropriate in light of the news. The drop in price would be what courts often call the "out-of-pocket loss"—the difference between the price paid and the price that would have been paid had all the information that should have been released been released. This drop in price is a ceiling on the net harm. It is a ceiling because the losses here may be offset by other investors' gains, and because not all of the loss shows up in a reduction in society's wealth or in profits to the decision makers. Recall from the preceding discussion that the "overpayment" for stock commonly is greater than the net harm. Much of the overpayment will be a transfer to people not responsible for the nondisclosure, and such transfers are not part of the net harm. As a rule, it is safe to assume that the net harm approaches but does not exceed the total loss.

Things do not happen in an instant, however, so we cannot know the exact overpayment for the stock. The problem is that during the time between the sale of the security and the release of the pertinent information, many other things happen. Events in the economy, and the fortunes of the firm in the interim, confound efforts to use price differences to find out the value of the missing information.

The solution is a technology that permits us to "take out the market," breaking the change in the price of a traded firm's stock into two components. We introduced this method in Chapter 7, where we used it to evaluate the costs and benefits of tender offers. Recall that movements in the price of any one firm's stock depend in part on the economy as a whole (which the market and the industry reflect), and the rest on firm-specific changes. It is possible to measure the relation between changes in the price of a firm's stock and changes in some larger basket of stocks (whether the market as a whole, an industry group, or some weighted mix). This relation takes the form:

$$r_i = \alpha_i + \beta R_m + \gamma R_x + \varepsilon$$

where r_i is the change in the price of a firm's stock, α_i is a firm-specific constant (zero, as things turn out), βR_m is the market-firm relation (β) times the market's movement in the interval (R_m), γR_x is the industry-firm relation (γ) times the industry group's movement in the interval (R_x), and ε, the "residual," is the unexplained portion of the change in price. This portion we attribute to firm-specific information. With this relation in hand, and knowing how the market or other reference group behaved during a particular interval, we may determine the expected change in price of the firm's stock if nothing peculiar to the firm took place. If the firm's stock does not behave according to the prediction, we chalk up the difference to some firm-specific news.

This method obviously is not a perfect substitute for the ideal "instantaneous" price change. Intervening events may be hard to disentangle. The method works much better for actively traded securities than for thinly traded stocks; it does not work at all for stock in closely held firms. The method will perform badly if there is a change in the coefficients relating this stock to others during the interval under examination. It does not reveal the effects a disclosure would have had if made at a different time. And even an "instantaneous" price change would not tell us one very important fact: whether managers knew or could have known the firm-specific information in order to disclose it at any particular time.

This method also relies on the assumption that the price accurately reflects public information, but this is not a "limitation," for it is also the fundamental assumption of securities law. The securities acts stand for the proposition that disclosure of information is the basis of an efficient securities market, and that whatever price the traffic will bear once the information is out is "right." Recall that we have introduced this method of getting information from the market in order to approximate the ideal, instantaneous measure of price change—which itself embodies the principle that "the price is right."

We therefore think it appropriate to use the market method to pare away extraneous events and effects. The "residual" in the market model is a reasonable reflection of the effects of the firm-specific information. If the firm's stock sinks faster than other similarly volatile firms in the market, this reflects bad news; if it rises more slowly than they, this also reflects bad news. It is therefore quite sensible to say that a plaintiff may allege that nondisclosure harmed investors because the stock did not rise fast enough. The existence of liquid markets for many stocks has other consequences to which we also turn below. These consequences include the possibility of "cover" to stop the accumulation of damages and the elimination of "bargains" (and hence benefit-of-bargain damages).

The Legal Rules and the Economic Approach

We are now in a position to put the economics of sanctions together with the law of remedies. We start by discussing why some remedies are rarely used in securities cases. We look at the difference between sanctions that start from the plaintiff's "loss" and those that start from the defendant's "profit." Then we examine fraud in the issuance of stock, fraud and omissions in the aftermarket, inside trading, and brokers' deceit.

THE MISSING REMEDIES

Although courts apply a welter of remedies in securities cases, some commonly used in other parts of the law are missing. With exceptions so rare as to be practically unimportant, courts do not award benefit-of-bargain damages, consequential damages, or punitive damages in securities cases. These omissions from the arsenal fit the theory of optimal sanctions.

Benefit-of-Bargain Damages

Suppose a firm offers securities to the public for $30 per share, representing that they are "worth" $40 in light of the nature and prospects of the business. Someone buys the stock in reliance on that representation. Or suppose a firm announces, while its stock is trading for $30, that it has concluded that the stock is "undervalued" by the market and is "worth" at least $40 per share. Again someone buys stock in reliance on the representation. A while later, each investor finds that the stock is trading for $30—that the supposed elements of extra value are not worth very much (or never existed)—and brings suit. Unless the investor can show that the stock was worth less than $30 on the day of the purchase, the investor will lose. Even if he wins, the investor will get only the difference between the $30 purchase price and the "value" of the stock on the day of the purchase.[6] Why do courts not award investors the benefit of the bargain they suppose they are getting?

The principal answer is that there are no bargains in liquid securities markets. People continually search for "bargains," but the process of search ensures that bargains quickly vanish as prices adjust. If stock is trading for $30 when the firm's management believes it should trade for $40, the most likely explanation is that sophisticated investors think the managers unduly optimistic. Things are not quite so easy when the stock is the initial issue of a new firm. Here, however, there is a different reason to think that the price is not a bargain. The promoters of a firm have no particular reason to give stock away for less than it is worth. An investor is not deeply harmed when he learns that the sellers' claim to be giving things away is not true. The buyer suffers no lost opportunity. Had he invested in another firm, he would not have had a bargain there either.

There is another definition of a bargain: the existence of consumers' surplus. If Perkins values a particular house at $50,000 because it is uniquely suited to his tastes, and no one else would pay more than $40,000 for the house, Perkins can purchase it for $40,001 and enjoy a "bargain" of $9,999. Benefit-of-bargain damages in contract cases often are designed to compensate people for a loss of consumers' surplus. A breach of contract that prevents Perkins from occupying this house destroys the consumers' surplus, which is a real economic loss. But there is no similar consumers' surplus in securities markets. Money is fungible even if particular securities are not. The price an investor is willing to pay for securities in one firm depends on the rate of return available from some other investment. Professional investors move funds from one security to another until, at the margin, each produces the same anticipated return (adjusted for risk). The activities of these professionals set the price everyone receives. Because one share of a given firm's stock is the same as another, the marginal return from a stock is the same as the average return. This implies that every

6. Compare Astor Chauffeured Limousine Co. v. Runnfeldt Investment Corp., 910 F.2d 1540 (7th Cir. 1990), and Levine v. Seilon, 439 F.2d 328 (2d Cir. 1971) (Friendly, J.) (no benefit-of-bargain damages in securities cases), with Osofsky v. Zipf, 645 F.2d 107 (2d Cir. 1981) (damages available to ensure that a seller of securities gets the consideration for which he contracted).

share of stock is a marginal one, and there can be no capital market equivalent of consumers' surplus in other markets. (One small qualification: some stocks may have special value in diversifying a portfolio. There are also transaction costs in trading stock that decline with the size of the trade. An investor thus will not be indifferent to a choice between one thousand shares of one firm and one share each of one thousand firms. These are not large effects, however, and it is therefore safe to compute damages on the assumption that there is no surplus value from inframarginal shares.)

There may be consumers' surplus in close corporations, however. The holder of stock in such a corporation often does not want to diversify fully, so that marginal and average values may differ. The absence of a liquid market means that the price of stock may not reflect all information. Sometimes the price at which stock in a closely held firm is offered is designed to create a surplus; perhaps the stock is meant as a "bargain" in order to apportion returns among investors unequally. (Other investors may take their returns through higher salaries or perquisites in their roles as managers.) Thus it may be appropriate to use a benefit-of-bargain measure to implement the contractual arrangement designed for a particular close corporation. As it turns out, this is the only time such damages are awarded in securities cases.

Another sense of bargain in securities laws is the discount common in initial public offerings of stock. Such shares appreciate on average after issue, making their acquisition a "bargain." Some economists have asked whether investment bankers are taking advantage of the issuers to funnel gains to favored customers. It may be, though, that the apparent bargain is nothing other than a substitute for additional expenses on investigating and promoting the firm; it is a trade of (undisclosed) risk for extra expected return, and hence no bargain. We need not resolve the characterization of this new-issue discount, however. It is no more than a few percentage points on average, and no one believes that investors are entitled to this kind of bargain under the securities laws. The absence of a new-issue discount cannot be traced to any "wrongful" behavior, and hence it is not a problem in the design of optimal sanctions.

Consequential Damages

In contract cases courts sometimes award consequential damages. Perkins contracts to sell a specialized machine to Smith. Smith plans to use the machine on an assembly line producing widgets. Perkins defaults, and Smith's assembly line lies idle for months while Smith obtains a replacement. Smith commonly can recover consequential damages such as the profits lost during the idling of the plant. These are parts of the net harm from the breach, because they represent the productive value of the equipment that was forced to remain idle. In tort law consequential damages are the norm. Those who suffer business losses may recover profits lost in consequence.

In securities law, by contrast, there are no consequential damages. If Perkins claims that a decline in the price of stock (attributable to Smith's fraud) caused Perkins to miss out on some other profitable opportunity, Perkins will collect only guffaws for his trouble. The theory of optimal sanctions requires that Perkins lose, because changes in the price of securities do not themselves create economic injury. Unlike the missing part, which can leave a plant useless, a change in prices does not affect the employment of real assets.

If Perkins owns a plant that needs a part, he could sell securities to obtain the price for that part. He may claim that the decline in price prevented him from raising needed funds. But if Perkins's plant produces goods worth the cost of keeping the plant in operation, Perkins also can borrow the funds needed to pay for the part. There is no link between the use to which funds are put (here, buying parts) and the source of those funds. A claim of consequential damages in securities litigation almost always supposes that there is some link between sources and uses of funds, and such claims properly fail.

Punitive Damages

Punitive damages are unavailable in securities law.[7] This is puzzling at first glance, because punitive damages, which give the plaintiff more than his actual loss, are one way of increasing the damages as

---

7. Byrnes v. Faulkner, Dawkins & Sullivan, 550 F.2d 1303, 1313 (2d Cir. 1977); Gould v. American-Hawaiian Steamship Co., 535 F.2d 761, 781 (3d Cir. 1976). Both the Racketeer Influenced and Corrupt Organizations Act (RICO) and state tort law offer some investors the opportunity to obtain damages multipliers (RICO) or punitive damages (state law). We disregard these possibilities as too tangential for current purposes.

the formula for optimal sanctions implies. The rule "net harm divided by the probability of successful prosecution" implies a multiplier, because prosecution is never certain. Most securities offenses are concealable. Fraud is concealment; omissions may not come to light; fraud and omissions that do not produce actual loss (or just temper the rate of gain) are not apt to be prosecuted.

The absence of punitive damages is anomalous. It may be defensible, though. We show below that many measures of damages—especially rescission and awards based on the plaintiff's out-of-pocket loss—have multipliers built in. Because these awards exceed the net harm, often by substantial amounts, it is inappropriate to make further adjustments through punitive damages. The absence of punitive damages is no more than a second-best solution; it would be preferable to establish optimal damages for trading in the aftermarket and then allow a multiplier to take account of concealment.

The Choice between Plaintiff's Loss and Defendant's Gain

"Injury" and "restitution" are the competing paradigms of damages in securities law. The injury measure, often called "out-of-pocket damages," looks at the plaintiff's loss. The court asks whether the investor got a security that was "worth" what he paid (or got what the security was worth, if he was a seller). If not, the defendant must make up the difference. There are quite a few ways to produce a damages remedy based on injury, including rescission, which forces the defendant to bear the entire risk of the transaction, but the differences among them are not important for current purposes. The restitution measure, by contrast, looks at the profit the defendant obtained from the transaction. The court requires the defendant to disgorge the profit, which may be greater or less than the other party's loss.

Courts have great difficulty deciding when to set damages based on injury and when to set damages based on restitution. They wander back and forth with little explanation, and there is even authority for the rule that damages should be set as either plaintiff's loss or defendant's gain, whichever is larger.[8]

8. Affiliated Ute Citizens v. United States, 406 U.S. 128, 155 (1971); Siebel v.

As an economic matter, much of the dispute is of little moment. Losses and benefits often match one another. If *A* defrauds *B* about the value of stock and so induces *B* to pay too much for the stock, *B*'s loss will equal *A*'s profit. If the promoters of a corporation (or the general partner of a limited partnership) tell fibs and so collect too much for the investment interests they sell, loss again equals profit. And profit is a pretty good starting point in the theory of optimal sanctions. The offender's profit is usually a transfer from the victim and thus part of the net harm, often the largest part of the net harm.

Profit-based remedies run into difficulty, though, because a simple rule requiring the offender to pay all his profit from the transaction would make the economic gains from the transaction part of the sanction. If the firm's promoter saved resources by not investigating some contingency, a rule that counted these savings as part of the "profit" would fail. The damages rule would no longer induce the promoter to compare the savings from reducing the scope of inquiry against the harms imposed on other people. It is therefore necessary to exclude from the definition of "profit" any savings that result from the transaction in question or other productive efforts of the defendant. This is indeed the legal rule.[9] If the filtering is done imperfectly (as it will be), this should not be cause for great concern, because profit-based remedies themselves are too low when detection and prosecution are not certain.

The hard question is why we should ever see loss-based remedies. Although some multiple of the defendant's gain is apt to be a good proxy for the net harm of a violation, the investor's loss in some kinds of cases could be wildly off the mark. Consider a manager who fecklessly announces that the firm has made a fabulous invention that will be worth billions. The price of the firm's stock soars. Two days later the manager sheepishly announces that it was all a false alarm, and the price returns to the original level. Everyone who bought stock during these two days suffers a sub-

---

Scott, 725 F.2d 995, 1001–1002 (5th Cir. 1984); Pidcock v. Sunnyland America, Inc., 854 F.2d 443 (11th Cir. 1988); Bruschi v. Brown, 876 F.2d 1526 (11th Cir. 1989).

9. Siebel v. Scott, 725 F.2d 995, 1002 (5th Cir. 1984); Janigan v. Taylor, 344 F.2d 781, 787 (1st Cir.), cert. denied, 382 U.S. 879 (1965).

stantial loss; neither the manager nor the firm gets any gain. Those who violated the rule get no profit. There is, of course, a match between profit and loss; the buyers' loss is exactly offset by gains realized by those who sold stock during the two days. These gainers have not violated any rule, however, and cannot plausibly be called on to pay their gains to the losers. A rule that required the firm to compensate the buyers for their full loss would impose damages far in excess of the net harm. Cases such as this one have some net harm—such episodes lead investors to do some investigating on their own, and they increase by a little the amount of uncompensated risk in the economy—but the harm is small. We therefore should expect to see a variety of devices by which even damages that are stated as loss-based are converted into recoveries tied to defendants' gains. We return to these limiting devices; we concentrate first on the most prominent of the subjects for which loss-based measures are used, the fraudulent issuance of stock.

FRAUD IN THE ISSUANCE OF SECURITIES

The doctrines that apply to fraud in the issuance of securities can produce quite spectacular recoveries. If securities are not properly registered, or the selling documents contain lies or material omissions, the ordinary remedy under §12 of the 1933 act is the purchase price less the value of the security at the time of trial or sale. This "rescissionary" remedy not only compensates the investor for out-of-pocket loss but also may compensate the investor for an intervening drop in the market. It throws onto the defendant the entire risk of the market while the investor holds the security. If the firm fails or the market declines, the investor may recover; if the firm succeeds or the market rises, the investor will keep the security and the profit. It is a no-lose situation.

If the problem lies in the registration document rather than the selling documents—or if the investor seeks a remedy from someone other than the issuer or seller—the rule is a modification of rescission. Under §11 of the 1933 act any defendant may claim that the decline in the value of securities was caused by something other than the fraud or omission; this permits use of the market model to correct the award, to filter out changes in the market as a whole. No underwriter may be held liable for more than the amount it received; this liability is divided among members of the under-writing syndicate.

What accounts for the severity of these rules and for the fact that the sellers, which are liable under §12, face higher penalties than other participants, such as accounts and law firms that are liable only under §11? To a substantial extent the rules rest on the distinction between unconditional and conditional deterrence. There is no good reason for not registering stock required to be registered or for telling lies in the issuance of stock. By throwing all the risk on the defendants under §12, the statute channels activity toward more appropriate routes.

The circumstances are ripe for unconditional deterrence in the issuance of stock. The SEC has an administrative process offering guidance to issuers before stock is sold, and a firm believing that it is appropriate to withhold certain information (or not to register the security) can ascertain whether its view is correct. The allocative efficiency loss from fraud or omission is greatest in the process of issuing stock—this is where resources may be diverted into businesses that are less efficient than the best available production process, which creates real loss. It is exceptionally difficult to measure this loss, which again suggests the utility of a rule that throws on the defendant the burden of uncertainty.

There are no third-party gainers in the issuance of securities. The net harm is therefore likely to be the gross harm, unlike the situation of the aftermarket, to which we turn below. There is also a substantial congruence between loss and profit. Suppose the promoters of a firm represent that they have put $1,000 in inventory into the firm, when in fact they have put only $200 there. They sell the stock for $1,000. The investors' loss of $800 exactly matches the promoters' gain. We have discussed above the reason for thinking it a good idea to start with a gain-based measure of net loss, and the statutory remedy apparently does this.

There are two potential objections to this line of analysis. First, suits often are brought against the underwriters rather than the promoters, and the underwriters do not get the profits; second, the statute permits the recovery of $1,000 in the event the market falls, not just the $800 the promoters extract as profit. The observation that defendants may be people other than the promoters is accurate but not terribly important. The defendants will be in privity with the promoters and can arrange for indemnification, require the promoters to post a bond, or take the precautions necessary to ensure that they will not be liable. The potential defendants can apportion duties and liabilities to achieve compliance at the least total cost; this is yet another implication of the Coase Theorem. The observation that the recovery can exceed the profit is true only in part— many of the players, such as the accountants and law firms, can be liable only under §11, which allows an adjustment for changes in the market. More to the point, even those who must stand by to compensate investors for a drop in the market can hedge against that risk. An underwriter that sells a new issue of stock can deal with the risk of a falling market by selling a market index future short. The promoter, too, can hedge against the risk of a falling market and a consequent increase in his exposure. The existence of liquid public markets makes this hedging possible, so that ultimately there is not much (systematic) difference between the §11 remedy, which allows an adjustment for movement in the market, and the §12 rescission remedy, which apparently does not.

It is nonetheless interesting that §11(b) gives the issuer's assistants (such as accountants) defenses unavailable to the issuer. This difference will be reflected in the terms of trade on which these specialists offer their services. Courts have been receptive to arguments through which these specialists substantially reduce their exposure in cases of material omissions (as opposed to fraud). Here the argument for unconditional deterrence is at its weakest. There may be benefits in reduced investigation and presentation of information. Accountants and other specialists perform valuable services, and a rule that imposed the equivalent of no-fault liability on these specialists would simply reduce the amount of specialists' services offered at the time a firm issues securities. Thus the courts' creativity in reducing the awards against these specialists. One court found the use of a rescission standard in a suit against accountants "unjust insofar as it compensates an investor for the nonspecific risks which he assumes by entering the market" and therefore ordered a reduction in the award to take account of changes in the market.[10] Another court held that an accountant may not be required to compensate investors for any element of loss attributable to business problems of the issuer (as opposed to the

10. Huddleston v. Herman & McLean, 640 F.2d 534, 555 (5th Cir. 1981), reversed in part on other grounds, 459 U.S. 375 (1983).

actual consequences of the misstatements).[11] Adjustments such as these, ad hoc from one perspective, make more sense from the perspective of the economics of sanctions. So too does the Supreme Court's holding that an investor's tax benefits may not be used to reduce the damages otherwise due;[12] tax benefits are not elements of real wealth attributable to the offense and are unrelated to the defendant's profits, so the economics of optimal sanctions requires their disregard.

We have treated the issuance of securities as if the firms were either closely held or going public. In such cases there is a close match between the profit received by the promoter and any excessive payment extracted from the investors. What of public corporations that issue new stock? Here the match breaks down. The "beneficiaries" of any wrongdoing will be the prior investors in the firm. These investors may sell their stock after the new issue hits the market, and they will realize the gains of any falsification. When the issuer pays damages in a suit by the new investors, much of the compensation will come from other new investors—those who bought the first series of stock while its price was inflated by the misrepresentations made to the second wave of investors. The investors who bought the first series of securities in the aftermarket lose twice—their stock falls (just like that of the purchasers of the second series of securities) when the truth comes out, and it falls further because the firm must pay out assets preferentially to the purchasers of the second series.

This brings us back to the nagging problem of matched gains and losses. Some investors gain, others lose, and the gains and losses are approximately equal. The net harm may be small. In a case such as this, it is only the reduction in allocative efficiency caused by an increase in risk, the reduction in productive efficiency if the new sales are used to install an inferior productive technology, and the usual costs of making, defending against, and prosecuting fraud. It also turns out, however, that the real damages awarded in cases of sales by public corporations are small. The purchasers of the first issue in the aftermarket could bring their own suit against the issuer, because (by hypothesis) the issuer's misdeeds inflated the price they paid just as it inflated the price the purchasers of the

11. Sharp v. Coopers & Lybrand, 649 F.2d 175, 190–191 (3d Cir. 1981).
12. Randall v. Loftsgaarden, 478 U.S. 647 (1986).

new issue paid. If the issuer pays damages to almost all its investors at once, it is the next best thing to paying very little in damages; it becomes the equivalent of a dividend or partial liquidation. (If the defendant in these cases is an accountant or other specialist rather than the issuer, then the problem is fundamentally the same as with the firm going public. Damages computed with all market movements filtered out will give these specialists incentives to take the appropriate degree of precautions.)

FRAUD AND NONDISCLOSURE IN THE AFTERMARKET

When the offense in question concerns only trading in the aftermarket, it is impossible to get away from the problem of matched gains and losses. Recall the example of the manager who announces good news for the firm and two days later takes it all back. Here the investors who sold during the two days gained; those who bought during the two days lost what the sellers gained; those who neither bought nor sold were unaffected; and there was almost no net harm. Because the sellers are no longer investors in this firm, and because there are bystander-investors, a payment of damages by the firm would not be a wash. Damages computed on the basis of the loss of the investors who purchased in the two days would greatly exceed the optimal sanction.

We cannot justify this by saying, as we did above, that the excessive remedy promotes desirable unconditional deterrence. A firm issuing securities can delay while investigating, or it can make pessimistic statements without risking liability. A damages rule that "unconditionally" deters certain conduct is not likely to cut off valuable opportunities for long. But a firm that discloses information in the aftermarket as it goes along inevitably takes the risk of excessive optimism and excessive pessimism. A rule penalizing excesses in either direction would lead to silence, not (necessarily) to an increase in the portion of truth. Investors would not want a rule that promoted silence whenever possible. As we demonstrated in Chapter 11, the firm generally is the best supplier of information about itself. If the firm is reticent, then other actors (investment bankers and advisers, brokers, and so on) will produce information. They have more difficulty getting access to the information, so this news will be more expensive and less accurate than that produced by the firm itself. It is therefore essential to have a rule that induces the firm to balance the costs of producing more (or more accurate) news against the net harms inflicted by error.

It is not possible to escape from this difficult problem by fixing the liability on the managers rather than "the firm." Liability that is assigned to one actor will not stay there. It can be moved by contract. If the law prevents its explicit movement (prohibiting indemnification of managers), there will be a change in relative prices. Managers will demand higher salaries in light of their increased risks, and they can use the new income to purchase insurance. The trick is to set the optimal level of damages, so that those who then transact against the background of the damages rule will be led to take the right amount of care.

There is another reason to be skeptical of proposals that fasten liability on managers. One common justification of damages rules is that they move losses to those best able to spread risks. Moving risks to those who are less risk-averse (or more able to transfer the risk to a risk-neutral insurer) produces real economic gains. The structure of securities markets suggests, though, that differences in degrees of risk aversion do not support damages awards against managers. The public corporation as an institution is designed to move risk away from managers and toward investors. The equity investors are purchasing risk; in exchange they obtain the residual returns of the venture. They have a comparative advantage as risk bearers because they can hold stock in many different firms at once. Diversified investors act substantially as if risk-neutral. Well they should. An investor with a diversified portfolio will be the hidden gainer in a transaction like the example in this section as often as he will be a loser. Every losing buyer during the two-day period is matched with a gaining seller. Over the long run, any reasonably diversified investor will be a buyer half the time and a seller half the time. Such an investor perceives little good in a legal rule that forces his winning self to compensate his losing self over and over.

A manager is undiversified and acts as if risk-averse. Much of his human capital and a substantial portion of his other wealth are tied up in a single firm. Lack of diversification induces the manager to work in the investors' interests; it ties his fortunes to those of the firm. It also makes the manager a singularly poor recipient of additional risk. The more of the inevitable risks of the venture the manager bears personally, the more cautiously he behaves. Yet the effectively risk-neutral investors do not want overcautious managers.

This is not to say that the optimal damages in aftermarket cases are zero just because most gains and losses net out. Net harms include the costs of guarding against and litigating about the wrong, and there will be an allocative efficiency loss if transactions of a particular sort create uncompensated risk. The larger the transfer among investors, the more they will spend guarding against the problem. Even a diversified investor would like to be on the winning side of every transaction. The large size of the securities information industry suggests that the costs of guarding against transfers are not small. The availability of compensation will lead to a reduction in these expenditures. But the optimal award is surely a good deal smaller than the gross transfer of wealth. There should be a presumption in favor of netting out gains before computing the award. That translates to a rule of the wrongdoer's profits, plus some measure of the costs of carrying out and thwarting these affairs and a measure of the costs of risk. The best rule might be a mechanical one—say, 1 percent of the gross movement in the price of the firm's stock attributable to the wrong. This avoids the need to compute the real, yet utterly unquantifiable, loss. Such a mechanical rule could be established only by statute, though, and we do not consider it further.

The question remains whether courts should use a profit-based approach. Certainly so in cases involving close corporations. There the wrongdoer's profits almost always equal the other investors' losses, so that profit and loss measures collapse. Things are less clear for traded corporations. For many years courts articulated a rule under which all investors who traded while the price of stock was affected by the firm's misstatements were entitled to the difference between the price they paid (or got) and the "true value" of the stock. That loss-based measure remains a verbal point of departure in the cases. Yet recent cases also express dissatisfaction with this measure.

For example, a firm gave some material and adverse corporate information to outsiders, who traded before the firm released the information generally. (This is nominally an inside trading case, the subject of later discussion. But because it was brought against the firm, and the gravamen of the claim was that the firm permitted its other investors to trade while inadequately informed, we treat it as a case of ordinary material omission in the aftermarket.) Those who bought in the market between the privileged release of information and the ultimate release sought to recover their losses from the firm. The district court used the loss-based measure of damages, but the Second Circuit reversed.[13] It ordered a remedy based on the profits the traders realized by getting out before the market dropped. The court worried that a full recovery of losses would be excessive (though on unarticulated grounds), and it also doubted that there was a causal connection between the withholding and the losses. People would have traded (and some would have suffered loss) whether some investors got tips or not, and the truth would have led to loss anyway. This is just another way of stating the point that gains and losses net out when the revelation of the truth is delayed.

It is difficult to know whether such profit-based measures are displacing loss-based measures because there are so few cases involving the firm's violations in relation to trading in the aftermarket. Cases arising out of such circumstances are routinely settled before trial, sometimes for nuisance value and sometimes for substantial sums, but always without resolution of the question whether the court would have used loss or profit as the starting point for computing damages.

Litigators usually assume that the courts will continue to use loss-based measures; instances of this remedy persist. In one recent case investors sued the firm for disseminating annual reports that were "too favorable." Investors who bought during the three years affected by the reports claimed that they paid too much for the stock, and they recovered the difference between what they paid and the "true value" of the stock at the time of each purchase.[14] The court used a market adjustment to set a cap on the amount of loss. Observing that when the truth came out, the price of the stock fell 11 percent, the court used that as the measure of recovery.[15] The use of price data from the market at least gives an

---

13. Elkind v. Liggett & Myers, Inc., 635 F.2d 156 (2d Cir. 1980).

14. Sirota v. Solitron Devices, Inc., 673 F.2d 566 (2d Cir. 1982).

15. 673 F.2d at 577. It reversed a valuation by the jury, which concluded that the stock was 52 percent overpriced before the truth was revealed. The court did not use the complete model, though, because it did not account for the movement of the market during the period Solitron fell 11 percent. (Apparently no one asked it to.) The court also used the jury's valuations for earlier years, concluding that the ulti-

accurate picture of loss; the use of market movements to exclude market effects, leaving only firm-specific effects, is better still. But it is nonetheless an inappropriate starting point.

Maybe it is possible to justify loss-based remedies on a combination of grounds. First, they redress people's incentives to take too much precaution, an incentive they would have if private losses were not compensable. Second, they serve as very rough multipliers of the real net harm, increasing the anticipated penalty to take account of the fact that most wrongful omissions (and even most falsehoods) are not caught and prosecuted. Third, over the run of cases, the "excess" of a loss-based measure is reduced by the fact that courts do not award damages for failure of people to gain. Suppose a material omission by a firm holds the price of that firm's stock constant while the market (or industry group) is rising. In our terminology, this is a real loss to investors; the failure to rise is no different from an actual decline. Yet few investors litigate in such cases, and we have not found an award of damages based on a claim that the firm's misconduct caused the investors not to participate in a profitable advance. We have not found a use of the market model to increase damages in any fashion, although as a logical matter it should have this effect frequently.

All of these are excuses rather than explanations, however. A fourth ground may be more substantial. The private damages action based on Rule 10b-5 has a "scienter" requirement. Willful misconduct is a condition of liability; negligence is insufficient. The willfulness requirement is designed to filter out many cases in which there was wrongful conduct, but the plaintiff cannot adequately establish state of mind. The more cases are filtered out, the more appropriate it is to use a multiplier in the cases of remaining liability. If liability is confined to truly egregious acts, we no longer have as much worry about optimal deterrence. The interaction of the scienter requirement with the damages rule should get rid of

---

mate price adjustment did not reveal how the overstatements had affected price in the early years. The court's distinction was roughly accurate. Doubtless information reached the market no matter what the annual reports said. As a result the extent to which a firm's misstatements could keep the price artificially high would decline steadily as information leaked out. The first purchasers' overpayments would exceed the overpayments of the last purchasers—who, as the court observed, could not have lost more than the 11 percent adjustment.

excessive (or, what is the same thing, inaccurate) enforcement. With employment of the substantive rules to handle marginal cases, it is more appropriate to move in the direction of unconditional deterrence for the rest. But if the scienter rule does not filter out dubious cases—if it turns out always to be possible to find some culpable omission when things go bad—then loss-based damages are far too high, and it is necessary to put a more modest remedy in their place.

Fraud on the Market and Truth on the Market

One part of the law of remedies follows the economic analysis explicitly. An investor is entitled to recover damages when a lie adversely affects the price of the stock, even though the investor in question never heard the incorrect statement or acted in reliance on it. If the lie affected the price of the stock, then price impounds the news (true or false), injuring the investor whether or not he knew of it. This "fraud on the market" doctrine, once controversial, was adopted by the Supreme Court in *Basic, Inc. v. Levinson*.[16] The rule depends on the methodology we have been using throughout this chapter.

Fraud on the market has several corollaries. One could be dubbed "truth on the market." The baldest lie does not support damages if the market knew the truth.[17] So a firm loudly pro-

16. 485 U.S. 224, 241–247 (1988). See also Daniel R. Fischel, "Efficient Capital Markets, the Crash, and the Fraud on the Market Theory," 74 *Cornell L. Rev.* 907, 917–922 (1989). Whether *Basic* understood either the basis or significance of what it was adopting is open to question, because the economic rationale supporting the doctrine implied no liability in the first place in *Basic* itself, and the Court also may have confused causation with "reliance." See Jonathan R. Macey and Geoffrey P. Miller, "Good Finance, Bad Economics: An Analysis of the Fraud-on-the-Market Theory," 42 *Stan. L. Rev.* 1059 (1990). Fraud may cause price to change; phrasing this effect as "reliance" by an investor leads to nothing but confusion. (It would be best to eliminate "reliance" as a distinct inquiry when stock is widely traded.) *Basic* fudged all questions concerning *how* efficient the Court assumed the market to be. Details in the implementation are vital in litigation but unimportant for current purposes.

17. No court has adopted the truth on the market doctrine explicitly, but it was the subject of favorable comment in Flamm v. Eberstadt, 814 F.2d 1169, 1179–80 (7th Cir. 1987), and In re Apple Computer Securities Litigation, 886 F.2d 1109, 1115–16 (9th Cir. 1989).

claiming that it is environmentally safe does not injure its investors if it does not mention (while the professionals whose trading sets the price of the stock know) that it is facing large judgments for environmental damage and expensive retrofitting of its plants. Claims of truth on the market may pose difficult evidentiary questions. Even if the stock's $\varepsilon = 0$ on the date the truth is revealed explicitly, implying "no news" in the announcement (and therefore prior knowledge of the truth), we do not know *when* the truth became known. If news gradually leaked to the market between the initial lie and the ultimate revelation, there may have been injury to investors that will be hard to detect and quantify using the market model. Still, the principle is straightforward.

A second corollary is that inaccurate disclosures slowing a rise in the nominal price of stock may be injurious and actionable. As we have been at pains to point out, the investors' loss must be measured net of market movements. Not doing as well as expected (given changes in the market) is an opportunity cost, as much a loss as a fall in the stock's price. Once courts adopt the market model (as the fraud on the market doctrine does), remedies for losses relative to expectations follow even though there is no out-of-pocket loss.[18]

INSIDE TRADING

Inside trading, which we discussed at length in Chapter 10, is usually characterized as a form of misconduct in the aftermarket. The firm delays release of information, while insiders or recipients of tips trade in advance of the price change that will occur when the news comes out. If the principal complaint is delay in the release of material information, then the analysis of the preceding section applies. Most delays are not actionable at all,[19] and for actionable delays, gains and losses should be offset. If the principal complaint is the trading rather than the fact of delay, it is necessary to look farther.

Suppose the parties agree that the firm released all necessary information to the public on schedule, and some people traded

18. See Goldberg v. Household Bank, f.s.b., 890 F.2d 965 (7th Cir. 1989).
19. Provided the firm keeps silent during the delay. Basic, Inc. v. Levinson, 485 U.S. 224, 239 n.17 (1988).

before the release. It is hard to identify any harm in such a case. The insider's trading partners are not injured by the transaction; they were buying (or selling) anyway, and the insider's trading activity did not induce others to trade. In liquid markets, the insider's orders are matched against the orders of others preexisting the insider's. Even if the insider's activity had an effect on the price of the stock, that would not induce others to trade. A stock does not become less appropriate as part of an investor's portfolio just because its price moves a little. A movement in price might attract close followers of a firm because the new price appears to be inappropriate in light of all the public information about the firm. But these professional investors could as easily decide to investigate or wait as to buy or sell. The effect of the insider's activity therefore appears to be the same as the effect of the firm's decision to withhold release of the information.

This is not quite right, however. The insider's activities may lead the price to move in the direction implied by the undisclosed information, making the price a better indicator of value. The insider's trading also may compensate the insider for producing the information, which may be of value to the firm. For these and other reasons inside trading may be valuable to investors, in which event it should not be penalized at all. Yet the opportunity to trade may induce managers to take inappropriate risks (in order to increase the volatility of the stock's price) or to delay the release of information, and the lure of trading may lead insiders to release the news (if only by accident) or permit others to infer the news at a time when the firm's best interest lies in secrecy. In that event the trading creates net harms—not losses incurred by investors trading in the market while the secret is still secret, but losses perceived by all investors in the firm. Each finds that stock sells for a little less because of the increased volatility (a form of risk) and because of the chance that insiders will appropriate gains or spill the beans without offering something of equal value to the firm.

If inside trading is harmful at all, then, the compensation should flow to all investors. As a practical matter this means to the firm itself. Again the net harm is the transfer in the wrongdoer's favor plus reductions in efficiency, all divided by the probability of successful prosecution. The law of inside trading has moved steadily in this direction. The remedy is now based squarely on the insider's "profit," not on any "loss" sustained by other traders, and the

Insider Trading Penalties Act permits a court to increase the damages up to threefold to take account of the substantial likelihood that a secret trader will not be caught.[20]

This leaves some interesting questions about what "profit" might mean. The statute defines profit as "the difference between the purchase or sale price of the security and the value of the security as measured by the trading price of the security a reasonable period after public dissemination of the nonpublic information."[21] The cases have used similar formulations. This approach is an application of the market model, because it defines the profit (the value of the information) as the difference between the market price of stock with information and the market price without. The use of a "reasonable period" after the release of information picks up the fact that the price of thinly traded stocks will not adjust as quickly or as accurately as the price of stocks such as IBM. It is therefore necessary to give the court discretion to ascertain how responsive the price of a given stock is to new information. If there is a problem in this formulation, it is the lack of reference to an adjustment for the movement of the market in the interim. The statute implicitly assumes that the market and industry group remain constant. The longer the delay between the trade and the release of the information, the less accurate this assumption. The statute does not preclude an adjustment to remove market movements—an adjustment as likely to enhance the award as to reduce it. The adjustment is appropriate as an economic matter, and it can be implied in the statute as part of the computation of the purchase or sale price of the security.

Judge Coffin has argued for a different definition of "profit." He maintains that the trader's profit is the difference between the price he pays and the actual price he realizes when he sells, even if the sale comes long after the release of information.[22] An insider buys stock for $10; after the information comes out the price rises to $12; a year later the insider sells the stock for $20. Judge Coffin would have computed the profit as $10 rather than $2. In some cases such

20. 15 U.S.C. §78u(d); SEC v. MacDonald, 699 F.2d 47 (1st Cir. 1983) (in banc), after remand, 725 F.2d 9 (1984); Elkind v. Liggett & Myers, Inc., 635 F.2d 156 (2d Cir. 1980).

21. Section 21(d)(2)(C), 15 U.S.C. §78u(d)(2)(C).

22. SEC v. MacDonald, 699 F.2d 47, 55–58 (1st Cir. 1983) (in banc) (dissenting in part).

a computation increases the damages in a rough offset for the fact that detection is unlikely. This is the only possible justification for what is otherwise an inaccurate computation. The insider's gain from his knowledge is $2; after the news is out the insider is free to buy as much stock as he wants, and the remaining $8 is a return to the insider's activity as a risk bearer.[23] There is no reason to treat the reward to risk bearing in this stock as a "profit" of the "inside information"; the insider's function here is no different from his role as investor in any other firm of which he had no knowledge. The stock might as easily have gone to $4, or the insider might have sold at $12, bought the stock again, and held. The gain from the prohibited conduct is $2 in any of these cases. The insider's risk bearing, once the news is out, is a socially productive activity that should not be penalized through damages.

BROKERS' MISCONDUCT

We conclude with a brief look at misconduct by brokers in dealing with their customers, a subject that is related only incidentally to the principal purposes of the securities laws. Brokers often exercise discretion over trading in customers' accounts. When the value of an account falls, the customer may charge the broker with violation of duties. He may say that the broker "churned" the account to generate higher commissions, selected stocks not "suitable" for the customer's income and age, or induced the customer to buy stocks he would not have bought if left to his own devices. These complaints have nothing to do with the securities themselves and everything to do with the broker's breach of the promise to be an honest agent, but they raise a few issues of valuation.

For some years, the courts awarded damages based on the customer's gross losses. If the broker induced the customer to purchase stock in firm Q, perhaps withholding the information that the broker made a market in Q's stock, and Q later fell in price, the

23. This is a mirror image of the situation as the other investors see things. Those who sold to the insider at $10 were free to reassess the wisdom of their sale and to buy new stock, once the news came out, if the price of $12 appeared to be attractive. They did not "lose" more than $2. The possibility of cover in the stock market—like cover in a contract for the sale of beans—cuts off the damages on the day when the violation becomes clear and the parties can secure in the market whatever quantities of the commodity they desire.

court would award the difference between the price paid and the price realized.[24] This is a rescissionary measure of damages, putting on the broker the entire risk of the firm's success and the entire risk of the stock market as a whole. Yet this is not a subject on which deterrence should be absolute. Questions like how much disclosure to make to a customer of a given level of sophistication and how much trading to do in a discretionary account are judgment calls. There may be savings in revealing less, and the selection of a damages rule may induce brokers to reveal the right amount to customers. A rule giving the customer the benefit of any increase in the security's value while calling on the broker to make up a deficit would not send appropriate signals. The customer's losses match someone else's gains. They are not part of the net harm.

Today courts almost never compute damages on the basis of the customer's trading losses. They instead assume that markets are reasonably efficient in pricing stock and that the customer therefore gets what he pays for, even if it is not what he wanted to buy. The risks of investment belong to the customer, who assumed them intentionally even if he would have preferred a different stock. One stock is as likely *(ex ante)* to rise or fall as another, and therefore the decline in the value of the portfolio is not part of the damages. Nevertheless, any commissions generated by excessive trading must be returned to the customer.[25] This tracks the line of optimal damages. The commissions are the bulk of the net harm in brokers' misconduct cases. The commissions are transfers away from the victims without offsetting benefit (except to the wrongdoer); that would be reason enough to require their surrender. The reason is reinforced by the fact that excessive trading consumes real resources—the time of brokers, exchanges, and transfer agents. (There is no need to assess this loss as a separate item of damages; the broker suffers these items as "automatic" costs because he must pay for them out of the commissions.)

Courts sometimes take a slightly different approach. They say that the broker must compensate the customer for the reduction in

24. Chasins v. Smith, Barney & Co., 438 F.2d 1167 (2d Cir. 1971); Perlstein v. Scudder & German, 429 F.2d 1136 (2d Cir. 1970) (over the dissent of Judge Friendly).

25. Costello v. Oppenheimer & Co., 711 F.2d 1361 (7th Cir. 1983); Arrington v. Merrill Lynch, Pierce, Fenner & Smith, Inc., 651 F.2d 615 (9th Cir. 1981).

the value of the portfolio but that they will "take out the market." Thus if the portfolio drops 10 percent and the market (or some other index) drops 10 percent during the same period, the broker is free of liability. The damages cover only the extent to which the portfolio falls faster than the market.[26] At first glance, it looks as if this is the same as a rule under which brokers simply return the commissions. On average, the clients' portfolios will do as well as the market. But of course not all clients will bring suit. Only those whose portfolios do worse than average sue, and brokers cannot recoup the shortfall from the other clients whose portfolios beat the market. Thus this measure of damages forces brokers to bear some of the risk of investment, even though the courts set out to relieve them of that risk.

The courts that adjust for the market's movement in brokers' misconduct cases proceed by asking how the client's portfolio did when compared with a larger portfolio of similar stocks. Suppose the broker bought some very risky stocks for the client, say stocks with β coefficients of 2. A stock with a β coefficient of 2 rises (and falls) roughly twice as fast as the market. To make things simple, suppose the broker put the client's entire assets in one such stock, and the market promptly fell 10 percent. This stock would be expected to fall 20 percent. Assume it fell 25 percent. The court making the adjustment might proceed: a portfolio of similar stocks would have fallen 20 percent, so subtract 20 percent from the purchase price of this stock, find the difference between that "adjusted purchase price" and the price realized from selling the stock, and award the difference to the client. This is fine if the client wanted a risky stock, one that would rise and fall faster than the market, even if the client did not want this particular stock. What if the client wanted a safe portfolio, one that would rise and fall with the market, or even more slowly than the market? Often the real problem in a brokers' misconduct case is that the broker exposed the client to more risk than the client contemplated. If risk is the harm, then an adjustment like the one we have described leaves the client without compensation for the broker's default. Instead of comparing the client's portfolio against a similarly risky portfolio, the court should compare the client's portfolio against how the target risk classification would have done. In the example we gave,

26. See Rolf v. Blythe, Eastman Dillon & Co., 637 F.2d 77 (2d Cir. 1980).

the adjusted purchase price should be only 10 percent less than the actual one, and the damages would be about 15 percent of the value of the initial investment.[27]

Rolf illustrates another, though smaller, misfire. The court tried to make rough adjustments using stock indices, which are efforts to measure the average performance of a group of stocks. Indexes have some notorious quirks, and they do not accurately represent either the market as a whole or the relation between a particular stock and the market. It is significantly more accurate to make adjustments of this sort using the market model than to do it in this seat-of-the-pants fashion.

This illustration suggests a better measure of net harm in brokers' misconduct cases: the excess risk produced by the brokers' choices. The court could compute the extent to which the portfolio the broker put together was riskier than the kind the client wanted. People must be paid to bear risk. That suggests as a measure of damages the amount the client would have demanded to bear the excess risk. The award should be based on excess risk viewed *ex ante,* not on how things turned out. The problem, perhaps an insoluble one, is determining both the risk the client "really wanted" (*ex post,* the client will say "none") and the compensation necessary to induce a person in the client's position to bear that risk. Because the risky portfolio brings the returns the market as a whole provides for risk, some of this compensation is built in; the difference may be impossible to determine.

The client's object in giving a broker discretion over a securities account is to enable the broker to assemble a desirable portfolio. Portfolio management is a skill, and the client seeks to hire the broker's expertise. If the broker assembles a portfolio containing

27. *Rolf,* supra note 26, shows how the court can miss this point. The broker put the client into an exceptionally high-risk group of stocks (mostly startup companies not traded on major exchanges). During the time covered by this misconduct the Standard & Poor's Industrial Index rose some 9.79 percent; the Standard & Poor's Low-Priced Index fell 7.5 percent. (Negative correlation of these indexes is a rare but possible occurrence. The more volatile a group of stocks, the more likely something like this can happen.) The court concluded that the basket of stocks purchased by the broker was "like" the low-priced index and so deflated the adjusted purchase price by 7.5 percent. It would have been more appropriate to assume that the client wanted a safe portfolio. Had the broker given him such a portfolio, it would have appreciated rather than depreciated.

excess risk, when the risk could have been hedged by diversification or reduced by selecting different stocks, the broker has harmed the client. Almost as bad, if the client fears that the broker will not put together a well-designed portfolio, the client will try to supervise the broker more carefully. Because the purpose of the venture was to use the broker's comparative advantage, the client's supervision is another economic cost of the agency relation. Compensation based on excess risk is a substitute for excessive monitoring by clients, and it measures the real economic harm of poorly designed portfolios.

Acknowledgments

Our view of corporations is in a tradition beginning with R. H. Coase, "The Nature of the Firm," 4 *Economica* (*n.s.*) 386 (1937), reprinted in Coase, *The Firm, the Market, and the Law* 33–55 (1988). Coase first asked the question why firms differ from markets, and what determines when one stops and the other begins. See also Coase's elaboration on his work in the new introduction to *The Firm, the Market, and the Law* 3–31, and three lectures delivered as part of a *festchrift*. Coase, "The Nature of the Firm: Origin, Meaning, Influence," 4 *J. L. Econ. & Org.* 3–47 (1988).

The particular form of our elaboration on Coase's insights owes much to Michael C. Jensen and William H. Meckling, "Theory of the Firm: Managerial Behavior, Agency Costs, and Ownership Structure," 3 *J. Fin. Econ.* 305 (1976). Other important contributions include Armen A. Alchian and Harold Demsetz, "Production, Information Costs, and Economic Organization," 62 *Am. Econ. Rev.* 777 (1972); Eugene F. Fama and Michael C. Jensen, "Separation of Ownership and Control," 26 *J. L. & Econ.* 301 (1983), and "Agency Problems and Residual Claims," ibid. at 327; Sanford J Grossman and Oliver D. Hart, "The Costs and Benefits of Ownership: A Theory of Vertical and Lateral Integration," 94 *J. Pol. Econ.* 691 (1986); Henry Manne, "Mergers and the Market for Corporate Control," 73 *J. Pol. Econ.* 110 (1965); Ralph K. Winter, Jr., "State Law, Shareholder Protection, and the Theory of the Corporation," 6 *J. Legal Studies* 251 (1977); Oliver E. Williamson, *The Economic Institutions of Capitalism: Firms, Markets, Relational Contracting* (1985). See also John W. Pratt and Richard J. Zeckhauser, eds., *Principals and Agents: The Structure of Business* (1985); Nicholas Wolfson, *The Modern Corporation: Free Markets vs. Regulation* (1984); Steven N. S. Cheung, "The Contractual Nature of the Firm," 26 *J. L. Econ.* 1 (1983); Benjamin Klein, Robert

G. Crawford, and Armen A. Alchian, "Vertical Integration, Appropriable Rents, and the Competitive Contracting Process," 21 *J. L. Econ.* 297 (1978); Henry B. Hansmann, "Ownership of the Firm," 4 *J. L. Econ. & Org.* 267 (1988).

Our treatment also has much in common with Richard R. Nelson and Sidney G. Winter, *An Evolutionary Theory of Economic Change* (1982), even though it is an application of neoclassical analysis that Nelson and Winter challenge. The more sophisticated and rapid the process of natural selection, the more informative the survival of a practice or institution. Firms are a paradigm for evolutionary pressure in economic organization.

Objections have been leveled against this tradition, sometimes on economic grounds: see Lucian Arye Bebchuk, "Limiting Contractual Freedom in Corporate Law: The Desirable Constraints on Charter Amendments," 102 *Harv. L. Rev.* 1820 (1989); Jeffrey N. Gordon, "The Mandatory Structure of Corporate Law," 89 *Colum. L. Rev.* 1549 (1989); more often on the basis of arguments drawn from outside economics: for example, Robert Charles Clark, "Agency Costs versus Fiduciary Duties," in *Principals and Agents: The Structure of Business* 55–79; and occasionally on the basis of mixed arguments: see Melvin Aron Eisenberg, "The Structure of Corporate Law," 89 *Colum. L. Rev.* 1461 (1989). We have addressed these objections generally throughout this book rather than attempting to deal sequentially with particular styles of counterargument.

Portions of this book have been presented at workshops at the law or business schools (sometimes both) of the University of California at Los Angeles, University of Chicago, Columbia University, Cornell University, Georgetown University, Harvard University, University of Michigan, New York University, Northwestern University, University of Pennsylvania, University of Southern California, Stanford University, Swarthmore College, University of Toronto, University of Virginia, and Yale University. We thank the participants at these workshops for their substantial contributions. We have also received comments from hundreds of persons, too many to mention, and although we thank all we extend special gratitude to Douglas G. Baird, Walter J. Blum, Dennis W. Carlton, William M. Landes, Henry G. Manne, Bernard D. Meltzer, Richard A. Posner, Kenneth E. Scott, Steven Shavell, and George J. Stigler.

Portions of this book derive from articles we have published previously. Chapter 2 is based on "Limited Liability and the Corporation," 52 *U. Chi. L. Rev.* 89 (1985), © 1985 by the University of Chicago Law Review. Chapter 3 is based on "Voting in Corporate Law," 26 *J. L. & Econ.* 395 (1983), and is © 1983 by the University of Chicago. Chapter 5 and some of Chapter 1 are based on "Corporate Control Transactions," and are used by permission of the Yale Law Journal Company and Fred B. Rothman & Company from *The Yale Law Journal,* vol. 91, pp. 698–737. Chapter 9 is based on "Close Corporations and Agency Costs," 38 *Stan L. Rev.* 271 (1986), © 1986 by the Board of Trustees of the Leland Stanford Junior University. Chapter 11 is based on "Mandatory Disclosure and the Protection of Investors," 70 *Va. L. Rev.* 669 (1984), © 1984 by the Virginia Law Review Association. Chapter 12 is based on "Optimal Damages in Securities Cases," 52 *U. Chi. L. Rev.* 611 (1985), © 1985 by the University of Chicago Law Review. We thank the copyright holders for permission to use this material.

Case Index

Author Index

General Index

Agency costs, 9–11, 14–15, 69; and managers, 38, 217–218; and voting, 73–74, 74–76, 87–88; and fundamental corporate changes, 79–80; and fiduciary duties, 91–93; and control transactions, 112, 113–117; and corporate opportunities, 141; and tender offers, 171–173

Amendments. *See* Voting

Antitakeover laws: effect of, 197–198; first generation, 219; second generation, 219; third generation, 219; and Wisconsin, 219; and Delaware, 219, 222–223; motivations for having, 219–222; and the Commerce Clause, 225–227

Appraisal, 139, 241–242; and Delaware law, 139, 145n, 150n, 152, 153–158; functions of, 145–147; and stock market exception, 149–152; exclusivity of, 157–160; and injunctions, 158–159; and damages, 158–159; and fraud, 159–160

Articles of incorporation, 6, 16

Auctions, 27–28, 187–190, 194–195, 204–205, 221

Audits, 282, 283, 289–290

Background terms, 14–15, 22, 34, 36

Bankruptcy, 48–49, 69

Board of directors, 2, 3, 64; classified boards, 72. *See also* Directors

Business judgment rule, 2, 93–100, 163–164; and fraud, 98; and risk, 99–100; and informed decisions, 107–108; in Delaware, 107–108; and close corporations, 243–245

Capital asset pricing model, 191–193, 327–329

Charter amendments, 33. *See also* Voting

Class action lawsuits, 306

Classified board of directors. *See* Board of directors

Close corporation, 13, 55–56, 228–230, 237–238; and piercing the corporate veil, 55–56; and risk, 229, 232–233; and specialization, 229; and agency costs, 229–230, 233–234; and lack of a share market, 230–231; and rent-seeking, 234; and contractual arrangements, 234–236; and default rules, 236–238, 251–252; and dissolution, 238–243; and fiduciary duties, 238, 243–248, 249; and buyout rights, 241–243, 249; and business judgment rule, 243–245; and optimal damages, 331

Coase Theorem, 51, 141, 240, 337. *See also* Third-party effects

Commerce Clause, 301–302; and antitakeover laws, 225–227

Common law fraud. *See* Fraud

Conflict of interest. *See* Duty of loyalty

Conglomerates, 177

Control blocs, sale of, 126–129

Control structure, changes in, 131–132

Control transactions, 109, 111, 112–117; and agency costs, 112, 113–117; costs of, 115–116; and unequal division of gains, 117–124

Corporate contract, 15–22, 35; evolution of, 6–7, 31–32; protecting contracting parties, 22–25; difficulty in enforcing, 26–27; and investor mistakes, 30–32; and regulation, 167–168; and fiduciary principles, 168

Corporate opportunities, 115, 140–142

Corporate opportunity doctrine, 17, 265

Inside trading *(cont.)*
　Theorem, 262–263; and public
　enforcement, 263–264; under
　common law, 264–266; and the
　corporate opportunity doctrine, 265;
　and Rule 10b-5, 266–272, 274; and
　optimal damages, 345–348
Insurance for corporate officers, 105
Interest group legislation, 216–217,
　277–279
Interstate Duty Clause, 301–302
Intrinsic value. *See* Value

Last-period problems, 169–170
Latecomer terms, 32–34, 161
Lawsuits. *See* Class action suits;
　Derivitive suits
Lemon markets, 280–283
Leverage, effect of, 175–177
Leveraged buyout, 114, 139, 202–203
Limited liability, 11; of non-equity
　holders, 40–41, 44–47; benefits of,
　41–44; and insurance, 47–49, 53–54;
　and voluntary creditors, 50–52, 59;
　and involuntary creditors, 52–54, 59
Liquidity problems, 241
Lock-up options, 165
Looting, 129–131, 207–208. *See also*
　Theft

Management buyout, 114, 138–139,
　202–203
Managers: and compensation, 5,
　141–142, 257–259; and agency costs,
　38, 217–218; liability of, 61–62,
　340–341; and incentives, 68, 69; and
　tender offers, 173–174; and inside
　trading, 257–259
Mandatory disclosure, 25–26, 286,
　288–290; and information
　production, 298–300; and
　standardization, 303–304; and
　interstate firms, 304–305; and
　intrastate firms, 304–305; and
　historical facts, 304–306; and
　nonstandard disclosure, 306–307;
　and prior review, 307; and safe
　harbors, 308; and material
　omissions, 308–309; costs and

benefits, 310–314. *See also*
　Disclosure
Mandatory insurance, 60–61
Mandatory terms, 25
Market price method. *See* Valuation
Mergers, 67, 118. *See also* Leveraged
　buyout; Management buyout;
　Takeovers; Tender offers
Miller and Modigliani Theory, 176
Minimum-capitalization requirements,
　60
Monitoring, 9, 10, 11, 45–46, 69,
　79–80, 84, 91–92, 114, 171–173,
　188–189
Moral hazard, 49, 50, 58, 59, 61; and
　inside trading, 260

Nexus-of-contracts theory of
　corporations, 8–11, 12, 14, 90–91,
　163

Optimal damages, 316–317, 320–323;
　net harm rule, 320, 322–326; and
　liquid markets, 326–329;
　benefit-of-bargain damages,
　329–331; and consumers' surplus,
　330–331; and close corporations,
　331; and consequential damages,
　331–332; and punitive damages,
　332–333; and plaintiff's loss,
　333–335, 341–343; and defendant's
　gain, 333–335, 341–343; for fraud in
　the issuance of securities, 335–339;
　and close corporations, 338–341;
　and traded corporations, 338,
　341–342; for fraud in the after
　market, 339–344; manager liability,
　340–341; for fraud on the market,
　344–345; for inside trading, 345–348;
　for brokers' misconduct, 348–352.
　See also Damages

Pareto optimality, 126, 145
Partnerships, 143; and close
　corporations, 249–252
Piercing the corporate veil, 54–55; and
　Delaware law, 54n; and close
　corporations, 55–56; subsidiaries,

Harvard University Press is a member of Green Press Initiative
(greenpressinitiative.org), a nonprofit organization working to
help publishers and printers increase their use of recycled paper
and decrease their use of fiber derived from endangered forests.
This book was printed on 100% recycled paper containing
50% post-consumer waste and processed chlorine free.

CPSIA information can be obtained
at www.ICGtesting.com
Printed in the USA
BVHW041711160622
639817BV00002B/105

9 780674 235397